Rationalizing Culture

Rationalizing Culture

IRCAM, Boulez, and the
Institutionalization of the
Musical Avant-Garde

Georgina Born

UNIVERSITY OF CALIFORNIA PRESS
Berkeley · Los Angeles · London

University of California Press
Berkeley and Los Angeles, California

University of California Press, Ltd.
London, England

© 1995 by
The Regents of the University of California

Born, Georgina, 1955–
    Rationalizing culture : IRCAM, Boulez, and the
Institutionalization of the Musical Avant-Garde /
Georgina Born.
        p.   cm.
    Includes bibliographical references and index.
    ISBN 0-520-08507-8 (alk. paper)
    IRCAM (Research institute : France) 2. Avant-
garde (Music) — Social aspects. 3. Research
institutes — France — Anthropological aspects.
4. Boulez, Pierre, 1925– — Influence. I. Title.
ML32.F82I745 1994
306.4'84 — dc20   93-39386
                                                    CIP
                                                    MN

Printed in the United States of America
9   8   7   6   5   4   3   2   1

The paper used in this publication meets the
minimum requirements of American National
Standard for Information Sciences — Permanence of
Paper for Printed Library Materials, ANSI
Z39.48-1984. ♾

For my parents, Andrew, and Irma

Modern art as an art of tyrannizing — A coarse and strongly defined logic of delineation; motifs simplified to the point of formulas; the formula tyrannizes. Within the delineations a wild multiplicity, an overwhelming mass, before which the senses become confused; brutality in color, material, desires.

Friedrich Nietzsche, The Will to Power *(1887)*

Contents

Illustrations

Acknowledgments

This study began as a Ph.D. thesis for the Department of Anthropology, University College London. The initial ideas were stimulated by the teaching of Mike Gilsenan, and later supervision was provided by Steve Nugent and, above all, Mike Rowlands. I consider the basis of my intellectual formation to be my first degree there, and no one could ask for a richer environment. I am grateful, and I hope that this work repays some of my debt. The Economic and Social Research Council supported the study for three years. The thesis was examined by Rosemary Harris and the late John Blacking, whose comments were both provocative and affirming. Like many others, I miss his presence enormously.

Throughout the research I have been immensely fortunate in having the informal guidance and friendship of Simon Frith. It was Simon who encouraged my inclination to return to my roots and think critically about contemporary music. My thinking on music and cultural politics remains deeply marked by the following people and groups with whom I have worked: Henry Cow, the Feminist Improvising Group, Lindsay Cooper, Mike Westbrook, and the London Musicians' Collective.

Several people gave feedback on the ideas and text, or helped with specific areas of expertise. Without meaning to implicate them in the result they include: from musicology, Simon Emmerson, Richard Middleton, and Bayan Northcott; on computing and electronic music, Alan Bundy, Hugh Davies, and Pat Hall. The following friends and colleagues read part or all of the text in progress and offered valuable thoughts and editing suggestions: Peter Dews, Ken Hirschkop, Howard Morphy, Peter

Osborne, Gareth Stanton, and most of all, Gregory Elliott and Ann Scott. More recently, my editors at California — Doris Kretschmer, Erika Büky, and Bud Bynack — have been efficient, encouraging, and a pleasure to work with.

A large number of people made the ethnographic fieldwork possible, and I want to convey my gratitude to all of them here. Many individuals gave me insight into themselves and their world, and some were especially open and made the research a fascinating voyage of learning and attempted understanding. In order to protect their confidence, it is inappropriate to name most of them here. However a few stand out as having supported the study to an extent beyond any reasonable expectation, and I am profoundly grateful to these people for their efforts and warmth and for their commitment to a dialogue with someone whose beliefs were, in different degrees and ways, at odds with their own: Tod Machover, who made the study possible and has been a frank and generous friend; Jean-Baptiste Barrière, for his friendship, help, thoughtfulness, and loyalty during the entire research; Adrian Freed, George Lewis, Stephen McAdams, Alejandro Viñao, and David Wessel, for many hours of serious talk, insight, and fun; and Gerard Asseyag, Laurent Bayle, Gerald Bennett, Denis Lorrain, Yves Potard, Mark Seiden and Marco Stroppa as well. I hope that the book will be of interest to some of those who made it possible.

For practical and moral support when engaged on fieldwork, I thank Carolyn, Stuart, Hannah Rose and Ben Douglas, and Corine Leonet. While I was in Paris, Kaija Saariaho and Panda Vamos Smith became girlfriends with whom, to combat periodic feelings of loneliness and alienation, I shared good music, bad movies, and psychoanalytic talk. For being my closest soulmate in the sociology/anthropology of music, and for sharing his complete collection of Bach Cantatas with me, I thank Antoine Hennion. For putting me up many times, I am grateful to Antoine, Christine Chapuis, and family.

It remains to share my deepest sense of gratitude. For her enduring support throughout the research, and for training me in the sympathetic perception of underlying forms of thought, I warmly thank Irma Brenman Pick. For her friendship, stimulation and understanding, I am grateful to Ann Scott. More than can be acknowledged here, my parents contributed to the research effort, not least by their intelligent questioning of, and yet belief in, what I was doing: I thank Ann and George Mully, Gustav and Faith Born. In the course of the work, my partner Andrew Barry provided constant moral and practical help, at times having to see me through much turmoil and physical tiredness. His intellectual receptivity and imaginative openness, by challenging and complementing me, have made his (deferred) voice a significant one in this book. Our small son Theo came along in the process of writing. Thanks to Tom and Jean Barry for being there in times of need to help with him, and thanks too for the loving and vivacious help of Elli Antoniou and Conni Buerkle as my sometime substitutes — without which, no book.

Camden Town, London
June 1993

Introduction

The creator's intuition alone is powerless to provide a comprehensive
translation of musical invention. It is thus necessary for him to col-
laborate with the scientific research worker in order to envision
the distant future, to imagine less personal, and thus broader, solutions. . . . The musician must assimilate a certain scientific knowledge, making it an integral part of his creative imagination. . . . At
educational meetings scientists and musicians will become familiar
with one another's point of view and approach. In this way, we hope
to forge a kind of common language that scarcely exists at present.

Technology and the composer: collaboration between scientists
and musicians . . . is, therefore, a necessity. . . . Our grand design
today . . . is to prepare the way for their integration and, through an
increasingly pertinent dialogue, to reach a common language. . . .
The effort will either be collective or it will not be at all. No individual, however gifted, could produce a solution to all the problems
posed by the present evolution of musical expression.

Research/invention, individual/collective, the multiple resources
of this double dialectic are capable of engendering infinite possibilities. That invention is marked more particularly by the imprint of an
individual, goes without saying; we must still prevent this involving
us in humdrum, particular solutions which somehow remain the
composer's personal property. What is absolutely necessary is that
we should move towards global, generalizable solutions.

*(Pierre Boulez, from IRCAM publicity 1976 and
from Boulez (1977) quoted in publicity ca. 1981)*

This book centers on an ethnographic study of IRCAM (Institut de Recherche et de Coordination Acoustique/Musique). IRCAM is a large
computer music research and production institute in Paris, which opened
in 1977, and which is handsomely funded by the French state. IRCAM
was founded, and until 1992 was directed, by the renowned conductor
and avant-garde composer Pierre Boulez.

IRCAM embodies Boulez's ambitious vision for advancing the future of music, as sketched in the quotes above. According to Boulez, the basic aims of IRCAM are to bring music, science, and technology into a new kind of collaborative dialogue in order to produce research and technologies that will aid the progress of musical composition. The institute is best known as a center that hosts visiting commissioned composers, who come to produce a piece using IRCAM research and technologies, aided by IRCAM assistants. In addition, the institute offers major concert seasons and educational programs, so that it incorporates both cultural production and reproduction. Boulez's vaunted rhetoric — with mention of global solutions, infinite possibilities — reveals his sense of IRCAM's historic mission. And indeed, IRCAM has an international reputation and a leading position in the fields of serious contemporary and computer music. It is the largest such dedicated music center in the world, and in the attempt to institutionalize creativity itself it represents a new departure in the institutionalization of music.

The book develops an ethnography of IRCAM as part of a detailed and critical examination of the social and cultural character of one important area of the contemporary musical avant-garde. The ethnography is also combined with history — specifically, with discursive characterizations of modernism and postmodernism in music, the historical traditions that underlie IRCAM's aesthetic. The aim of the book is therefore simultaneously to give insight into IRCAM, and to provide a historical analysis of musical modernism and postmodernism.

The study is addressed primarily to readers from the anthropology and sociology of culture and from cultural studies, but also to musicologists and to those with a general interest in contemporary music. I write from the perspective of social and cultural theory, and in touching on issues that have hitherto been the province of musicology and music criticism I hope to indicate the insights gained by a widening of theoretical scope.

I want to outline in this introduction two motives for the study. One concerns the state of contemporary serious music and composition, and the other that of cultural anthropology. Both areas touch on problems and debates associated with the rubric of postmodernism.

The first motive has been to pursue research that might provide insight into the sense of crisis in late-twentieth-century composition, and in particular into the crisis of musical modernism. Boulez has a key place here since he became, arguably, the leading figure in the promulgation of a renewed aesthetic modernism from the 1950s on. Central to this was the extension of serialist techniques[1] and their interdependence with a growing resort to electronic media and scientistic theory. Serialism and its elaborations became the centerpiece of postwar musical modernism, with the ambition to remake completely the foundations of the western musical "language," to provide a universal basic system for composition, as tonality had once been. This was the epitome of a high modernism, founded on a belief in the possibility of a total, deep-structural, and scientistic renewal of the grounds of musical progress.

Whatever the subtle trajectories of Boulez's thought, his writings, teachings, and polemics have stood as a beacon of certainty — (even a certainty about uncertainty in his ideas about aleatoric or nondetermined musical processes) — amid a wider climate of intensifying doubt about the legacy of serialist modernism. In recent decades, and with increased vigor since the early 1970s, there has been a split within the world of serious composition between, loosely, the advocates of scientistic postserialism and its critics and dissenters, the latter the proponents of various forms of postmodernist aesthetic and composition.

To leave it at this, however, would not convey the chronic sense of impasse, the profound doubt and loss of confidence, that have accompanied this split, especially for those many composers who have experienced a disenchantment with the high-modernist project and with the perceived failures of serialism. The sense of a threat to the continued existence of western art music has, despite certain differences, been widespread in both Europe and the United States.

The wave of critique of serialism occurred earlier in the United States, just as various postmodernist alternatives developed more fully there. The character of the split between the extremes of the pro-serialist, modernist and anti-serialist, postmodernist camps can be grasped by comparing two notorious articles by American composers who have been seen as prime representatives of the two sides: Milton Babbitt and George Rochberg. Babbitt's 1958 article, "The composer as specialist" (originally entitled "Who cares if you listen?") argued that contemporary music had become such a complex area of theoretical enquiry that it was necessarily unintelligible to the layman. To secure the future evolution of music, it must therefore withdraw from the public and find support and protection, like the sciences, within the universities. By contrast, Rochberg, who engaged with serialism before renouncing it dramatically in favor of a return to a classical or romantic style, gave a speech in 1971 called "Music: science vs. humanism" (Rochberg 1984) in which he rejected absolutely the "rational madness" of the serialists. For Rochberg, the conversion of music into a "new form of applied science" (1984, 537) and the misapplication of dehumanized theories and technologies would surely lead to the demise of music as we have known it. Both positions, then, employed a "rhetoric of survival" (McClary 1989, 62) which implied that the continuity of western art music was at stake.

Ironically, during the '50s and '60s, the very period in which this rhetoric was being produced, and especially in the United States, serialist composition did secure a home within the universities, as Babbitt proposed. Thus, the musical avant-garde gradually became legitimized by the academy and gained increasing financial subsidy. It became, in other words, established. The same process occurred in relation to the modernist avant-garde in the visual arts. But beyond this, the visual and musical avant-gardes have fared very differently. The visual avant-garde has also spawned a growing commercial market, while modernist visual techniques have become influential in certain areas of design and popular culture; so that modernism in the visual arts has, in various ways, been absorbed into wider cultural practices and public consciousness. By contrast, the modernist musical avant-garde has failed to find success with a broad public or to achieve wider cultural currency: it remains an elite form of high culture.[2] The musical avant-garde thus inhabits several contradictions. On the one hand, being no longer marginal and critical of the dominant order as in the earlier period of modernism, but itself established, it has not only undermined its initial raison d'être but it must also continually legitimize its present position of official subsidy in the absence of a large audience. On the other hand, it continues to promote an avant-garde view of history in which the present state of things is denigrated in promise of greater things to come, of advancing the future of music.

A central interest of this study is how these contradictions are expressed in IRCAM culture, and the aim is to gain insight into the processes by which they are negotiated. The case of IRCAM illuminates these questions well since IRCAM represents an extreme of legitimacy and subsidy in the contemporary music world: it is a uniquely authoritative and well-funded institution. Yet rather than an aberrant development, IRCAM is the outcome of certain converging, if distinct, historical processes and can be seen to epitomize contemporary musical modernism. The investigation of how IRCAM continually legitimizes itself in order to reproduce its current dominant position, in the absence of great public or industrial success and while at the same time enunciating avant-garde ideology, is thus at the heart of the book.

The critical issues for contemporary composers are not only aesthetic, but ontological and sociological. In relation to modernism, a key issue, both ontological and aesthetic, has been the relation between music and science. To what extent should music be considered a science? How far is it appropriate to use scientific analogies in composition? Sociologically, questions arise from the crises in both the production and reception of avant-garde music. How should serious composition be supported? By the market (in which case it would barely continue to exist)? By the universities? By the sphere of subsidized cultural life? How should composers respond to the very small public for avant-garde music and the extreme alienation of most audiences from modernist music? These issues might justifiably appear to be linked, in that the crisis in production cannot easily be divorced from that in reception. However, it is the question of their linkage that forms the crux of the division between certain composers and critics.

In the past decade, critical views of modernism such as Rochberg's have become increasingly prominent in the United States. There has been a concerted attempt by many to argue that postmodern pluralism has become the equal of, if not surpassed, postserialism as the dominant trend in American serious composition. Of course, the case for such a shift must be made not only ideologically but by the evidence of institutional legitimacy, support, and funding, and it is unclear to what extent this has become a reality. What is unmistakable is the common espousal of various postmodernist rhetorics by the younger generation of American composers, and one senses that the certainty with which they are propounded must be proportional to the doubts and fragmentation they are attempting to transcend. Postmodernism is, then, the rising ideology; and it is supported by a new generation of music critics who in the past few years have begun to attack the Boulezian worldview for its perceived failings and for its ideological closure against other kinds of music.[3]

In Europe, the situation remains more openly tortured, and composers seem to find the question of the failures of modernism a less resolved affair. An article by the leading German composer Karlheinz Stockhausen, for example, portrays contemporary art music as under threat of extinction and the general state of music today as worse than in "the entire history of music" (Stockhausen 1985, 39). The reasons are sociological: a lack of sufficient support from both performers and the state for the production and diffusion of new music. More complex are the views of the British composer Alexander Goehr. Goehr (1988), in his BBC Reith Lectures, appeared to want to integrate aesthetic questions with sociological ones, arguing against the simple subordination of artistic imperatives to social ideals, and vice versa, and for a retention of the symphony orchestra as at once a sociomusical institution and as the basis of a living musical form. Despite his cogent comments on the limitations of the Boulezian avant-garde, Goehr posed no clear solutions. More generally, the European music press contains repeated ambivalent and soul-searching reflections by critics and composers on the problem of composers finding a livelihood, and on the lack of a substantial audience for their work.

The point is that for many composers the crisis is both aesthetic and sociological. For some — for example Stockhausen and, as we will see, Boulez — these are distinct, and the primary problem is not so much aesthetic (since that is amenable to their own innovations) but sociological: that is, how to ameliorate the conditions of the production and reception of avant-garde music such that more people can be helped to understand it. But for other composers the two dimensions cannot be separated in this way, and it is their separation — in the idea of the composer being answerable only to himself, or to an ideology of compositional progress, and so to an indecipherable future — that was responsible for the current malaise, and that must be resisted. From this perspective, the evidence of profound public antipathy to serialist music cannot be ignored and must be translated into a transformed compositional practice or risk a music that cannot communicate, because no one will listen.[4]

This cursory review indicates the general climate surrounding late-twentieth-century composition: the sense of western art music having reached an impasse, a state of chronic doubt. It is against this background that Boulez's recent interventions, IRCAM central among them, must be seen; and it is from this context that the driven imperative to continue, and to renovate, a discourse[5] founded on modernist concepts of progress, scientificity, and universality emerges. The place of IRCAM in these historical developments is particularly significant. The institute is often depicted as the latest and most megalomaniac embodiment of Boulez's personal vision. It is also widely held to be a progressive experiment, both aesthetic and sociological, in the transformation of contemporary composition and one that might provide a path out of the historical impasse. Despite these gigantic ambitions, IRCAM is shrouded in mystery. Little is known, beyond publicity and polemics, about the internal dynamics of the organization. My study aims to remedy this.

A different take on these issues comes from my personal history as a musician. As a middle-class child of central European descent, I was brought up in the early 1960s on classical music. Along with many, I stumbled across popular music in my adolescence, which led to me playing all kinds of music, including that of composer friends. I began a professional training at a conservatory in the early '70s, but I left after a while because of a strong sense of the conformist and repressive character of this scene — its parochial closure — in broader cultural and social terms. Instead, I began to play professionally in various areas of experimental jazz, rock, and improvised music. When I came upon IRCAM years later, on tour playing music for a dance show at the Centre Georges Pompidou, and having trained meanwhile as an anthropologist, I was drawn by the idea of making a study of such a high-profile and "progressive" contemporary music institution and of trying to work out whether my earlier intuitions about the institutions of serious music were accurate, and if so, why.

The second and most encompassing aim of my project has been to address a new kind of anthropological object. I was sure I had found a fascinating object in IRCAM, and as I worked I became convinced that the study of IRCAM culture would vindicate ethnographic method as surely as that of any other complex sociocultural body. I believe it does more, and indicates that ethnographic method may have unique capacities to elucidate the workings of dominant western institutions and their cultural systems. Because these phenomena have the capacity to absorb and conceal contradiction, it takes a method such as ethnography to uncover the gaps between external claims and internal realities, public rhetoric and private thought, ideology and practice.

The aim to expand the framework of anthropology to include the critical analysis of dominant elements of western culture and of modernity resonates with certain recent reworkings of the field (Marcus and Fischer 1986, Rabinow 1986, 1989). It is my view that such a direction will reinvigorate anthropology in a more productive way than some of what has passed under the name of reflexive postmodern anthropology.[6] In short, it seems to me less apposite to engage at this time in abstract autocritique of anthropology as a discipline, and particularly of its textual forms, than to turn its techniques of analysis and criticism toward new objects: forms of power, forms of society and culture that have not yet been thus analyzed. Only such a reorientation will provide the tools for a truly reflexive anthropology, one that can analyze the interrelations between dominant forms of knowledge and their institutional and sociohistorical contexts — whether reflexively, with regard to anthropology, or more generally, after Foucault, in developing an increasingly astute social theory of culture, knowledge, and power.[7]

To these ends, as well as due to the nature of its object — a complex institutional culture subsuming music, science, and high technology — this book is interdisciplinary. It therefore also indicates how anthropology can be effectively brought together with and renewed by broader areas of social and cultural theory than are usually associated with the discipline. The recourse to ideas ranging from ethnomusicology to sociology of culture to art history to semiotics to psychoanalysis has, at each point, been necessary to account for the particularities of the phenomena to be understood. For such a pragmatic use of theory I am unapologetic. Rather, I attempt to show the productivity of engaging what are often considered — unnecessarily, in my opinion — discrete and incommensurable domains.

The ethnographic fieldwork on which the book is based was mainly conducted at IRCAM between January and November 1984. Since then I have continued to make return visits, to interview informants, and to attend conferences and concerts related to IRCAM. I began fieldwork by taking IRCAM's introductory course for visiting composers, the *stage*. Over the course of my stay I spent time with several different subcultures and occupational groups within the institute, and I was fortunate in having access to all meetings but those of the highest executives. Participant observation was augmented by a substantial body of taped interviews which, although they did not aspire to scientific sampling, did attempt to reach each significant group within the institute. With certain groups and individuals in whom I was particularly interested — composers, programmers, researchers — I maintained an intensive dialogue and carried out serial interviews that provided continuing commentary on developments within IRCAM and on its history. The main limitation to my fieldwork was my lack of computer programming skills, which meant that although I was able to use very basic programs and to observe and question programmers with increasing insight, I was unable to enter fully the culture of music software research and development that is a major and fascinating area of IRCAM's work.

I was known at IRCAM primarily as a graduate anthropologist come to study IRCAM's "primitive tribe": a conceit that seemed to amuse my intellectual informants. Most interesting to me, in terms of its implications for future ethnographic studies of intellectuals, was my intuition that despite their knowledge of anthropology and despite my explaining the purpose of my study as far as I then understood it, even my intellectual informants had difficulty at times conceiving what I might be doing or bearing in mind the "double" nature of my presence. As one informant and friend said, "I never know when we're talking if we're simply talking, or whether you're going back home to write it up as notes"; to which I could only reply, "both." This touches on the inherently reflexive character of the ethnographic encounter — a reality that makes it no less problematic for intellectual informants or ethnographer.

Some people also knew me as a musician, although of dubious lineage, since the music that I play professionally did not command great respect in the dominant musical ideology of IRCAM. For others my musicianship was a positive asset, and at times I was invited to take part in music research and events.

I have always been the beneficiary of good relations with IRCAM, both officially and informally in terms of friendships made and sustained. However I decided at the outset of the study not to speak directly to Boulez, for several reasons. First, and pragmatically, because when I began I considered it wise not to draw attention to myself from the highest in command. I was fortunate to gain entry through the mediation of a dynamic young IRCAM director who gained permission for my visit from the higher executives on my behalf. Boulez was thus aware of my presence and of the study, and greeted me on occasion during my stay. Second, and a central principle of ethnographic fieldwork, I thought it unwise to be seen within the institute as in some way allied to, or the client of, as powerful a presence as Boulez. This would have made it extremely difficult for me to go about my business unobtrusively, and virtually impossible to be perceived by ordinary workers as on their level or to speak to them as an equal. It would also have imbued me with certain ideological perspectives that might have blocked informants' open discussion of their own, different views. Third, I consider the study to be about a social and cultural formation, IRCAM, and whatever the enormous influence exerted on this formation by Boulez — which I attempt to analyze through secondary sources and through its mediated expression within IRCAM in later chapters — this formation cannot be reduced to Boulez. Finally, it has seemed to me far more to the point to report the representation of Boulez, and the sense of his impact, through informants' testimony and my own observations rather than to invite being overwhelmed by his own authoritative, and better-known, account of things.

It may be apt here to discuss briefly the status of my own discourse. I conceive of this study as an exercise in critical hermeneutics, one that focuses on interrogating power in relation to cultural forms and their social and institutional bases. By calling it hermeneutic I stress above all the historicity and the socioculturally sited character of my own interpretations. But this does not amount to a surrender of any claims to approaching objectivity or imply that the status of my discourse is no different from that of the subjects whom I have studied. By moving "beyond" their discourse in order to trace its embeddedness in certain historical and contemporary social and cultural formations, and by moving "behind" and "across" their discourse in order to elucidate its gaps and contradictions, I have attempted to analyze forces that are not readily perceivable by those subjects. Given that the subjects at issue are themselves in many cases formidable intellectuals with their own complex grasp of the problems being discussed in this study, there is the potential for a profound tension between my interpretation and those of my informants. Given also that the cultural and historical problems being addressed are long-term and intractable ones, it would be naive to think this tension could be resolved in any short-term manner or through some kind of immediate "feedback" into the institutional workings of IRCAM. I can only hope that the tension proves productive in a less direct way and that the study will provide insights that may gradually be "worked through" and so inform changed cultural practices in the future.

If in the course of this book I make a critical analysis of IRCAM as a high-cultural institution and of its cultural forms, this is not with the intention of initiating a relativizing exercise. The existence of other cultural orders of value and complexity I take for granted, as will be clear from aspects of the analysis. Nor should the study be read as a masked critique of all forms of subsidized culture; nor, finally, does it have a hidden agenda of vindicating postmodernism or the neoliberal promotion of market forces in culture. My intention is to assert the necessity of cultural critique that is not simply relativizing or engaging with culture only at the level of ideology, form, or aesthetic value. Instead, I sketch a theoretical basis from which to engage in critique of cultural forms as at once social, theoretical, technological, and aesthetic: as complex totalities operating at all of these levels, all of which must be addressed if we are to attempt to develop new possibilities both for contemporary music and for cultural production in general. It seems to me probable, and very necessary, that some kind of cultural sphere defined not by the market but by judgments of legitimacy fueling cultural policy and subsidy will continue to exist. The question then becomes: what kinds of legitimacy, judged how and by whom, how instituted, how productively, and with what status vis à vis other cultural orders?

The book opens with three chapters that lay out the theoretical framework (chapter 1) and various dimensions of historical and contextual analysis (chapters 2 and 3) that underpin the study as a whole. Chapters 4 to 10 constitute the ethnography of IRCAM, for which the "ethnographic present" is 1984, the main period of my fieldwork. I have generally used the past tense in these chapters to combat any illusion that the state of affairs being described is current. Chapter 11, the conclusions, updates the study to the early 90's following Boulez's retirement in 1992 as IRCAM's active Director and traces developments in the intervening period. The bulk of the ethnography thus derives from a study ten years old, and this of a field — computer music — renowned for its rapid evolution. There are two complementary justifications for publishing such a study. First, because despite its specificity, 1984 was a significant transitional period at IRCAM, and the insights remain instructive. Second, because even given this specificity, many of the themes of the analysis are not temporally specific and continue to be relevant in the present, as I argue in the conclusions.

Publishing an ethnographic study of a well-known institution is a sensitive business, especially given the responsibility to respect informants' confidences. In order to protect their identities as far as possible, I have either generalized events and statements when this does not adversely affect the analysis[8] or I have identified certain key informants by coded initials. These acronyms, and the roles of these informants, are listed for reference in the appendix.

CHAPTER I

Themes and Debates

Although the basic analytic approach and ethnographic method of this study are drawn from anthropology, its object is unusual for anthropology, which has been little concerned with studying the powerful intellectual groups or specialist institutions of western culture.[1] In general, there is an absence of empirical social research on contemporary high culture and cultural institutions,[2] on cultural production,[3] and, specifically, on these in regard to serious music.[4] The empirical focus of this book is unusual, then, for the sociology and anthropology of culture, art, and music.

There are five main areas of theoretical debate with which I am concerned, which I discuss in this and the following chapter. The first is that of developing a sociocultural analysis of music. To this end I sketch a social semiotics of music that may inform both ethnographic and historical work. The second is that of the sociology of high culture and of artistic and cultural institutions, particularly those involved in cultural production. Of the few writers who have engaged with these issues, I draw on the productive work of Pierre Bourdieu and Raymond Williams.

The third is the question of the character of modernism and postmodernism and the relationship between them, in general and particularly in music. Later chapters provide a critical portrait of the contemporary face of musical modernism and postmodernism as expressed by IRCAM and its milieu and place this within a historical perspective. The aim is to locate music within the wider debates about modernism and postmodernism in culture and the arts and around the concept of the avant-garde.

This raises the fourth area: that of bringing contemporary cultural analysis together with history in order to theorize the reproduction and transformation of modernism and postmodernism as long-term cultural systems. I develop ideas from Marshall Sahlins, and in particular, Michel Foucault, and I sketch the issues raised by analyzing the aesthetic as a discursive formation and attempting a genealogy of the avant-garde.

The final area of theoretical debate involves authorship and cultural production. I examine authorship in relation not only to musical composition at IRCAM but also to computer technologies, and insights are generated into each. At one level these concern the different kinds of collaborative labor and the social relations of each area of cultural production,[5] illuminating issues such as the pleasures and tensions of collaborative cultural production and related questions of intellectual property.

But I go further than this. While for some decades it has been an article of poststructuralist faith to interrogate the "author" as construct, this has not been supported by much empirical or historical research.[6] Here I examine the construction of authorship at many levels: not only the strategies by which individuals become invested with the extraordinary charisma of the creative artist, the motivations, contestations and contradictions of the process, and how the discourse of authorship is used in strategies of individual and institutional legitimation, but also the ways in which the process is subjectively internalized, the ambivalence to which this gives rise, and the internal violence that may be involved in overcoming this ambivalence.

Central among the questions raised by the crisis of musical modernism is to what extent composers are aware of the relation between their aesthetic and the likely fate of their music in terms of public reception and economic subsidy. Or does this relation, and the way that it might feed back into composers' aesthetic choices, remain largely an involuntary and/or unconscious one? This touches on the heart of romantic conceptions of the artist, in which the artist is simply an involuntary vessel through which inspiration flows. The aesthetic is seen here as an essential extension of the self, almost beyond conscious reach, and integrity is gauged by the artist's determined commitment to this aesthetic. In questioning this view, a different conception of the artist as subject and of the artistic oeuvre may be required (Foucault 1984c). Both are pursued in the later part of the book. Poststructuralist critiques of authorship are therefore metonymic of the wider questioning of classic humanist notions of a unified, sovereign, and rational subject. I employ psychoanalytic theory to sketch an alternative conception of the composer-subject.

Two less prominent themes also deserve mention. One, raised in my preface, is the question of music's relation to science, a recurrent controversy throughout the history of western music. IRCAM culture is the historical culmination of attempts to integrate musical composition with advanced scientific developments. I analyze these attempts through their existence within IRCAM culture, and in this chapter I outline a theoretical scheme that provides the necessary basis from which to do so.

Another is the relation between aesthetics and technology. In theorizing this, I reject what I will call instrumentalist and evolutionist perspectives. Both of these conceive of technologies as independent of, or preceding, their cultural and aesthetic uses. Technologies are thus "found objects" brought into a particular aesthetic practice, and they are seen as instrumental in, and central to, generating aesthetic innovation. In the more extended evolutionist view, technological evolution is conceived as an independent variable driving music-historical change.[7] Both perspectives fail to examine the actual uses of the technologies, which are often depicted in idealized, unproblematic, and normative ways.

By contrast, I examine critically here a culture that itself holds to the evolutionist perspective, and that is itself involved in the development of high music technologies. I argue that in this culture not only the recourse to technology, but also the injunction to research and produce new technologies as a means of promoting musical innovation, are overdetermined by an aesthetic and philosophical discourse, that of modernism. This is to question the "autonomous" motor of technological development at least in relation to this particular discourse. In later chapters I look behind the discourse to de-idealize the various claims made on behalf of the technologies, scrutinizing the role of technological research and development in musical "progress" and tracing the actual social and cultural character of the technological practices and research process, thereby giving a sense of the problems inherent in the lived experience of a high technological culture. The approach taken here complements recent work on the cultural effects of new audio technologies[8] and sociological studies of new technology.[9] In particular, I offer insight into the materiality and the research culture of advanced computer software, a medium that is overdue for empirically-grounded sociocultural analysis (see Poster 1990, 149).

To elucidate this range of issues, I discuss in the remainder of the chapter four domains that constitute my theoretical framework: sociocultural studies of music, the sociology of high culture, questions of history, temporality, and of the aesthetic as a long-term cultural system, and psychoanalytic theory. No hierarchy is implied by the order of exposition, nor is the intention to convey a seamless web of theory. Rather, held together as a composite they enable a grasp of different dimensions of the object — from the macrosociological and historical to the microsociological and intrasubjective.

TOWARD A SOCIAL SEMIOTICS OF MUSIC

There is at present no concerted theoretical basis for the study of music as a sociocultural form. The broad field of music studies has been fragmented,[10] and some of the most interesting areas of recent cultural theory have bypassed research on music (Goodwin 1986).

In outlining a new approach it is useful, for my purposes, to start with what might be called the critical semiotics of music.[11] This has involved analyses of musical systems, or of music and lyrics, as encoding the dominant social order (Weber 1958; Shepherd et al. 1977; Shepherd 1982) or as conveying ideological messages (Tagg 1979, 1982; Bradby and Torode 1984). The latter studies are particularly productive in uncovering contradictions between various levels of meaning. They suggest that the operation of meaning cannot be ascribed simply to the musical sound or system alone. Sometimes it works through tensions between different levels of meaning: for example an implicit musical association subtly subverting an overt lyrical meaning (Tagg 1979, 60; Bradby and Torode 1984, 197–201). This makes the analysis of meaning and ideology problematic and suggests the need for a more complex analysis of musical meaning as conveyed through the ensemble of mediations surrounding the sound.

Recent studies by Durant (1984), Laing (1985), Attali (1985), Leppert and McClary (1987), Norris (1989) and McClary (1991) broaden the scope beyond a narrow formalism. With the exception of Laing, they are also the first since Adorno's mid-century work to attempt the sociocultural analysis of art music as well as popular music.[12] Laing's study of punk music, with its close reading of the intricate mediations and associations of punk, exemplifies the broader approach. Laing expands the semiotics of music in three ways: by extending the semiotic frame to the practices, social and institutional forms, and political economy of punk; by relating its internal signification to wider historical forces; and by analyzing the place of intertextual bricolage in the process of signification. In doing so his approach invokes two semiotic concepts: multitextuality — the analysis of meaning as operating through many simultaneous, juxtaposed, and interrelating symbolic forms or mediations; and intertextuality—the idea that meaning is created by signs referencing other cultural realms through connotation. Laing therefore moves from a formal to a social semiotics and outlines a theory to which ethnographic and historical research can productively be allied.

Similarly, Attali's speculative account of the forms of power embodied in the institutions, ideologies, and practices of musics in different eras and Durant's work on historical changes in the social, cultural, and technological conditions of music demonstrate the fertility of a broader sociocultural approach. The influence of Foucault is palpable here in the analysis of power in relation to dominant discourses around music and their institutional and social forms.

The direction taken by these writers converges with that proposed by ethnomusicologists such as Feld (1982, 1984a, 1984b) and Roseman (1984, 1991). Even though studying relatively egalitarian nonwestern groups, both find it necessary to examine the forms of power inherent in their musical cultures. Feld derives from his work a general comparative framework for the sociocultural analysis of music (1984a, 385–88), which is useful in emphasizing, like Laing, different levels of mediation—material environment, theories, practices, performance rituals—as well as paying attention to power and mystification around music.

In different ways these writers explore the various social, cultural, and technological forms that together constitute the complex whole through which music is experienced and has meaning. There are two implications. First, their work presages a social semiotics of music, one that stresses the multitextuality of music as culture and the need to analyze its various mediations—aural, visual-textual, technological, social—both in themselves and as an ensemble.[13] Second, they imply that it is only by critically analyzing each level of mediation in this way that it is possible to identify the specific forms of ideology, stratification, and power that inhere in each musical culture.[14]

One reason for attention to multitextuality is to foreground the social character of music, whether the immediate social relations of musical performance or the macrosociological dimensions addressed by institutional and political-economic analysis. This is necessary not only to analyze the different social mediations of various musics, but also to grasp certain kinds of cultural politics and change, since a concern to innovate in or to critique the social relations of music has characterized not only some popular music but several movements in twentieth-century composition.

Another reason for this approach is to develop a critical perspective on the technological mediation of music. It becomes possible to relativize both the nostalgia for a pre-electronically mediated music and concomitant idealization of ambient music found in classical music discourse[15] and the technological fetishism associated with the discourses of popular music, electronic music, and computer music, all of which tend to the evolutionist perspective outlined above. We will see evidence of both positions within IRCAM. It also becomes possible to interrogate the practices and social relations that inhere in the development and use of particular music technologies, their materiality and sociality.

A third reason for interrogating the multitextuality of musical culture is that only with such an analysis of simultaneous levels of mediation is it possible to trace either cumulative effects, or more interestingly, contradictions, operating between the levels of the ensemble. This is the kind of insight provided by Tagg, Bradby and Torode, Laing, and Roseman. In these studies, the contradictions uncovered provide clues to ideology but also to spaces of social and discursive struggle. A good illustration is Roseman's analysis (1984; 1991, 123, 126–28), for the Temiar people of Malaysia, of contradictions between the gender differentiation characteristic of the dominant social order and its inversion in the social relations of musical performance. It is no accident that Roseman's is an ethnographic study, since ethnography provides rich opportunities for tracing disjunctures between different levels of mediation: here, between different orders of social relations, more commonly, between words and actions, ideology and practice.[16]

A fourth motive for attending to multitextuality is that doing so engenders an awareness of the separation between the musical sound itself, its notation or representation as a visual text (the score), and its theorization and elaboration in spoken or written language. This is to dislocate any taken-for-granted synonymy between the "music itself" and the representations produced around it: whether the visual texts that are often taken as transparent and self-effacing reflections of the musical sound, or those critical, theoretical, and analytical discourses that rationalize and interpret the music post hoc, or, more crucially, those that claim to construct and prescribe it in composition. Instead, by separating them from the musical sound object, we can focus on the intertextual character of the visual representations and linguistic practices themselves,[17] as I attempt for IRCAM in chapters 6, 7, and 8. The issues may be clarified at this point by sketching a general analysis of musical signification.

The core of music as culture is organized and meaningful sound. Its character can best be grasped by contrast with other media and their forms of signification. Musical sound is alogogenic, unrelated to language,[18] nonartifact, having no physical existence, and nonrepresentational. It is a self-referential, aural abstraction.[19] This bare core must be the start of any sociocultural understanding of music, since only then can one build up an analysis of its social and cultural mediation. And it is this nonrepresentational core that makes musical sound especially resistant to decoding as ideology. We can amplify by comparing aspects of Barthes's theory of signification (1972a, 1977a) with music. In terms of denotation, and by contrast with representational media, music denotes nothing other than its musical expressivity as part of a specific musical genre. It calls to mind only its difference from other possible expressions within that aesthetic.[20] This peculiar degree of self-referentiality is why musical sound may be considered a (relatively) empty sign.

It is at the level of connotation that music is particularly subject to extramusical meanings through its extraordinary evocative power. The signifieds that music connotes are of many kinds: visual, sensual, emotional, and intellectual — such as theories, domains of knowledge. All are metaphors[21] that can combine into fields of discourse surrounding music. While metaphor implies a set of singular mappings of analogy, discourse suggests that metaphors may cluster into constellations of perceived likeness, systematic fields of experience, knowledge, or theory. The concept of discourse also invokes issues of power — the power of definition, classification, of the sustenance of a belief system and exclusion of alternatives — and of ideology: metaphors may be motivated, distorted, yet naturalized or organized into a pseudocoherence for purposes of irrefutability.

The essential point, however, is that the relation of these extramusical connotations to music as signifier is cultural and historical. Yet they are experienced as "immanent in" the music by a process of projection of the connotations into the musical sound object. It is this process of projection that achieves the "naturalizing" effect — the connotations appear natural and universal when they are conventional — and that makes it apt to describe them as ideology.[22] It is, then, the forms of talk, text, and theory that surround music — the metaphors, representations, and rhetoric explaining and constructing it — that may be liable to analysis as ideological.

Barthes sees denotation as providing a value-free "alibi" for the implicit operations of ideology (Barthes 1977a, 51). Paradoxically, in music the lack of a denotative alibi does not undermine naturalization but effects the opposite: connotation becomes even more transparently attached to the music. This can be illustrated by two phenomena. First, music has been particularly susceptible to a kind of theoretical predetermination, as shown by Allen's (1962) survey of music historiography and by early sociology of music.[23] Second, music has throughout history been subject to two main forms of theorizing: in relation to the emotions, and to mathematics and science.[24] Both kinds of theory tend to provide universalizing explanations of music and to read these properties as immanent in music. Because of music's transparency as a form of signification, it offers little resistance to discursive invasion and universalizing ideology. This analysis points, then, to the omnipresence and centrality of metaphor and discourse as mediations of music-as-sound, and the need for attention to their arbitrary and specific cultural character, their role in strategies of authority, legitimation, and power, as well as for analysis of their intertextual connections with other, nonmusical realms of discourse, other areas of knowledge and practice.

This framework provides the basis for analyzing the prevalence within IRCAM of scientific and technological discourses around music in order to question their "naturalness," to interrogate their relations with other domains beyond IRCAM, and to trace their particular strategies of authority and legitimation.[25] It is not necessary to reject these theories in order to analyze their universalizing and naturalized character, their attempt to construct bases for music that transcend any particular historical aesthetic or compositional form. We will see that IRCAM's various scientific and technological discourses on music tend constantly toward the transcendent and universalizing.

Since each mediation produces meaning, each has the potential for (implicit or explicit) positive intertextual reference: for example, technologically, in the use of pop technological formats by some experimental art music (Philip Glass, Steve Reich), or industrially, in the emulation of rock music marketing by classical performers. Similarly, each mediation has the potential to produce meaning through the play of sonic, discursive, technological, or social differences from coexisting or prior musics. Extending this reading of differentiation makes it possible to trace how, within art music, postmodernism has been constructed in opposition to modernism and, more generally, art musics in opposition to popular musics, and vice versa. The semiotic stress on differentiation may be harnessed, then, to an analysis of musical discursive formations distinguished aesthetically, socially, technologically, and so on. This is what I sketch historically in the next chapter, which in turn underlies the analysis in the rest of the book.

However, it is not enough to read off each level of mediative association or difference in isolation: they must then be rejoined, to trace the cumulative and contradictory effects produced across the musical culture as a whole. By "totalizing" in this way it becomes possible, despite internal contradictions, to assess the final status of the multitextual whole and the relative priority of the different mediations — an issue evaded so far. Without this, not only may one mediation, a partial fragment of a musical culture, be taken to stand for the whole — a common fault in postmodern cultural theory — but one dimension (the sonic, technological, performative) may be taken as superordinate to levels of mediation equally definitive, such as the music's institutional or socioeconomic character.

The point can be exemplified by certain postmodern developments in rock and art music. I refer, in rock, to the avant-garde experimentation with atonality, electronic noise, and complex meter found in some groups from the early 1970s, which led into one kind of punk. In art music, I refer to minimalist or systems composers such as Glass, Reich, and Michael Nyman who assert the influence of rock and pop musics. In both cases the strategy is to "cross over" by referencing taboo aesthetic devices from the "other" side of contemporary music, and to create a provocative tension by remaining firmly grounded in their respective institutional bases (commercial popular music, subsidized high culture). Thus, two crucial levels of mediation — the musical and the institutional — are set up in contradiction. But whatever the sound, the point is that overall, the music as culture remains defined by its primary socioeconomic circuit. Avant-garde rock remains rock; pop-influenced art music remains art music.

We can take this further by discussing strategies of avant-garde cultural production in general. However much an avant-garde attempts to produce work that is unclassifiable, shockingly different, it is a truism that in order to be meaningful it must, by definition, ultimately be classifiable as "art" by an audience; or, it may be understood as the negation of art — the reaction that the avant-garde typically sets out to provoke in the "Philistine" audience. The latter "against art" classification appears, historically, to be particularly permeable, so that by the intervention of critics, "against art" comes eventually to be understood as "part of art." There remains some avant-garde art that is unacceptable to all but a small and "knowing" audience. But as long as "anti-" or avant-garde art is recognized as legitimately "part of art" by the dominant institutional apparatuses, it is granted the status of art and becomes a negational statement within the field of art: a powerful argument for the ontological priority of the institutional over the aesthetic. As we will see, these distinctions are crucial for some writers on the avant-garde who emphasize the difference between those movements limited purely to aesthetic negation and those showing political engagement with the socioeconomic and institutional forms of culture.

This approach contrasts, finally, with Adorno's cultural theory. At his best Adorno sketches the most ambitious method that we yet have: that of combining sociological and aesthetic critique without reducing one to the other, but without neglecting their interrelations; a method that would trace the ensemble of mediations of musical practice — aesthetic, theoretical, technological, social, economic — as a decentered totality. But while his work on popular music follows this program (Adorno 1978a, 1990), he fails to provide a sociology of "autonomous" music to match his aesthetic theory (Adorno 1973). Curiously, Adorno is also part of the object of this book: Adorno the ambivalent champion of serialism and teacher of the Darmstadt school, training ground for the postwar modernist avant-garde; Adorno as an influence on Boulez's thought, and thus on IRCAM. The key lacuna of Adorno's thought, then, is the social critique of subsidized high culture — the sphere in which he was himself enmeshed.[26]

Mention of the aesthetic raises the attitude taken here towards the "music itself." Despite the ideal of integrating an account of IRCAM music into this study, there are major obstacles to analyzing it. IRCAM music is arguably amongst the most complex music ever produced. In addition to some very complicated and large-scale scores, it exists in computer disk and tape form, unnotated, and therefore liable to the severe problems of analysis of all unnotated musics. Moreover, some of the key innovations being attempted in IRCAM music focus on musical qualities — timbral transformations, microtonality, multiphonic and inharmonic sounds — that pose great difficulties for the extant techniques and concepts of music analysis.[27] It would thus be pragmatically difficult and naive to attempt music analysis in this book.

On the other hand, it is axiomatic to the theoretical framework I am proposing that the "music itself" is never outside discourse but is just one of the many simultaneous mediations, or forms of existence, of music as culture as it is produced in discourse (Hennion 1991, 1993). There is thus a simultaneity to the discursive construction of the mediations of music. The point is that, since meaning inheres in the social, theoretical, technological, and visual mediations of music as well as in the musical sound, and since these all play a part in the construction of the musical sound, we should consider the musical object as subsuming these mediations. From this perspective, the social, theoretical, and so on are all constitutive of the object, and the "music itself" no longer stands as the final or only arbiter of meaning. While such an approach rejects the transcendent autonomy of the aesthetic, it also avoids the sociological reductionism of reading the aesthetic purely as an effect of determining social relations (for example, Bourdieu 1979).

This framework is especially suited to the music at issue here: it is bequeathed by the history of the object, musical modernism (Born 1991). I suggested earlier that many musics are subject to prior and post hoc theoretical exegesis. Different musics have different degrees of theorization; popular musics, for example, have little explicit, formalized music theory. However, musical modernism, to which IRCAM is related, has a particularly intense relation with theory. Indeed few musics can be said to have the same degree of prior theoretical determination, so that characterizing the forms of theory prescribing IRCAM composition can to some extent obviate music analysis.

Given these caveats, there is a brief discussion in the penultimate chapter of specifically musical differences in relation to musics both within IRCAM and beyond as part of the analysis distinguishing between modernism and postmodernism in music. This involves not detailed analysis, but basic musical distinctions.

THE CHARACTER OF HIGH CULTURE: BOURDIEU'S SOCIOLOGY AND ITS LIMITS

The preceding discussion outlines a framework for critical interpretation of the internal character of musical cultures, the differentiation between them, and how this interpretation informs the analysis of IRCAM in this study. However, it gives no basis for addressing the broader institutional sphere within which IRCAM is located, subsidized high culture. For this, we must turn to the sociology of culture.

In recent years, several major writers on the sociology of culture and in cultural studies (Wolff 1981, 1983; Williams 1981; Bennett 1990b, 1992) have called for attention to and empirical research on the institutions and practices of cultural production and reproduction, particularly those of high culture. Those who have raised these issues have produced abstract theoretical arguments that, despite their insights, as yet lack engagement with the empirical complexities of contemporary culture.

The desire to address these absences is linked to two important theoretical developments in the sociology of art and culture. First, it is fueled by a recognition that the predominant concern in cultural and media studies with mass media and popular culture has meant ignoring another sphere of cultural power: "official," state-funded or subsidized culture. Second, it can be linked to the increasingly widespread dissatisfaction with the limits of formalist cultural theory, an orientation shared by certain areas of poststructuralism and of cultural studies. For many years, the dominant critical approach to the social analysis of art and culture focused on questions of ideology. Wolff argues convincingly that "ideology-formulations" tend to ignore the social and historical specificity of cultural institutions and practices. Moreover, the art-as-ideology perspective tends to be reductive of the aesthetic dimension. Wolff calls for two new kinds of work: a sociological aesthetics that would escape the universalizing and metaphysical character of traditional aesthetics, and critical research on the institutions, practices, and ideologies of particular areas of cultural production. In a basic sense, this book takes up her challenge.[28]

One way of addressing Wolff's challenge, and one on which she touches, is to turn to Foucault and examine aesthetic theories, artistic practices, and their related social, institutional, and technological forms as constitutive of historical discursive formations: the discourses of the aesthetic. Not only does this avoid reducing art and the aesthetic to their "functions" for "something else" (social reproduction, generalized domination, and so on), but it also invites a close reading of the particular forms of authority, legitimation, and power that inhere in these discourses. This is to take up Foucault's injunction to produce an "*ascending* analysis of power" (1980, 99) that focuses on the day-to-day micropractices and materiality of domination and subjection as they are lived within a particular discursive regime. Ethnography is well suited to providing material for such an approach. In this way a new kind of cultural anthropology — engaged in the ethnographic illumination of western artistic discourses — can contribute to the development of social and cultural theory at large.

It is interesting to clarify in passing the relation of the kind of approach I am advocating here to feminist social and cultural theory. I have myself resisted the deconstructive orientation of recent feminist cultural theory. Rather, this study is implicitly concerned with an older set of feminist themes as they intersect with the work of Foucault: that is, with the politics of microsocial relations, with the lived experience of unequal power relations as they are encountered and endured in everyday life. This, more than any overt reference to women's position or perspectives (although they too are understated concerns),[29] pervades my central ethnographic chapters in their detailed analysis of the social relations, the cultural and technological practices, characteristic of the institution at issue. In sum, for feminism, as for Foucault, it is through these "small," "insignificant" exchanges and moments that the political in its many dimensions is revealed.

From another direction, it is also worth noting the resonance of this approach with one source of cultural theory noted for its emphasis on the politics of cultural production: Brecht and Benjamin. According to this legacy, often eclipsed by the more formalist sociological aesthetics of Adorno, the practices of cultural production must be reflected upon and theorized as a basis for a politicized culture. From this viewpoint, it is not the relation of culture to other historical forces that is at issue, but culture as a formative element within the totality.[30] This, in turn, recalls the Gramscian perspective usually taken as the focus of British cultural studies, in which culture takes a central place in the analysis and contestation of shifting strategies of hegemony.[31] However, the Gramscian approach does not distinguish well between culture as "lived" and culture as professionally produced. Hence the tendency to elide the very different moments of production and of consumption (as "self-production") in some recent work, and to explore consumption while neglecting to theorize the specificities of cultural production.

There are, fortunately, two major exceptions to the general picture of the sociology of culture I have given. Williams (1981) and Bourdieu (1968, 1971a, 1979, 1981) provide analyses of the high-cultural domain, and Bourdieu's are based on a rich body of empirical research on cultural institutions, cultural production, and consumption. Both writers begin by acknowledging the sociological specificity of art and culture. Unlike the majority of scholars working in cultural studies over the past two decades, both are committed to analyzing the cultural field as a totality, to tracking the way that any cultural form must be grasped through its implicit differentiation from coexistent forms. Both add a Weberian dimension to the predominantly Marxist tenor of the sociology of culture. These writers help, then, to construct a framework within which to understand the institutional character of IRCAM. The contributions are at two levels: the macrosocioeconomic and the microsocial processes of "legitimate" culture.

Williams (1981, 206–33) discerns four linked, major tendencies in modern cultural production that span the subsidized and market spheres. First, the development of privileged cultural institutions. Second, the expansion of cultural bureaucracies and the enlarged role of administration. Third, the increased scale of cultural production. Fourth, the development of international cultural flows (the prototype of which he sees as the rise of an international avant-garde early in the century), which lead to uneven cultural dominance and dependence. In this way, he focuses the analysis on the centralization, rationalization, and uneven development of culture, as well as on issues of cultural authority and legitimation. Williams also discusses the relation between market and public/subsidized sectors of culture. The subsidized sector guards cultural legitimacy, "classic" works, the canon, at the same time supporting esoteric avant-garde work that lacks an immediate public. The market sector seeks more direct economic reward and measures success in terms of large sales. The two sectors are rivalrous yet complementary, an interpretation indebted to Bourdieu.

Bourdieu's sociology of culture rests on his analysis of two general forms of power, which he also sees as underlying two fractions of the dominant class: that based directly on economic power (economic capital) and that based on cultural and intellectual authority and power (cultural capital). Bourdieu posits antagonistic but complementary relations between these two general spheres and strategies of accumulation. This mode! informs his analysis of both class-structured cultural consumption (1979) and cultural production.

This is exemplified by a paper on the publishing industry, "The production of belief" (1981), in which Bourdieu also discusses the character of the avant-garde (here within commerce).[32] He traces an opposition within the publishing field between two industrial and institutional forms as they map on to two literary aesthetics. The division of the field consists of the opposition whereby "bourgeois art" is produced by large, integrated firms that seek short-term commercial profits by selling both best-sellers and the dependable classics, while "avant-garde art" is produced by small, personal firms that accept risky, long-term cultural investments with no significant market in the present. The short-term cycle seeks rapid and sure returns, the accumulation of economic capital, while the long-term cycle aims to accumulate cultural capital. Again, the two sectors are seen as antagonistic yet complementary in that the accumulation of cultural capital is predicated on a refusal of economic success. The avant-garde holds to "the 'intellectual' ideal of negation, which . . . tends to establish a negative correlation between success and true artistic value" (1981, 284). The paradox of the avant-garde, then, is that it "risks" eventually obtaining "substantial economic profit from the cultural capital . . . originally accumulated through strategies based on denial of the 'economy'" (ibid, 286). In this ironic quote, Bourdieu implies that the avant-garde cultural strategy is simply a different form of economic calculation, so that long-term cultural investment may reap even greater economic reward than mundane short-term calculation. More often, he argues that economic and cultural capital are incommensurable and antagonistic spheres, embodied, for example, in the very different lifestyles of the two fractions of the dominant class (1979). Certainly, he depicts avant-garde ideology as disdaining material luxury and abjuring economic interest. Overall, he leaves some uncertainty as to whether cultural capital is "really" convertible into the economic, and to what extent avant-garde producers are consciously engaged in a subtle and risky form of economic calculation.

Despite this analysis being based on fractions of the publishing industry, combined with Williams's it suggests a general model of the relation between the two major sectors of cultural production, the commercial and the public/subsidized, with economic capital ascendant in the commercial sphere, cultural capital in the subsidized. We will see that aspects of this analysis become useful in accounting, variously, for Boulez's ideology, the character of IRCAM, and the mentality of IRCAM intellectual workers.

Like Williams, Bourdieu continually stresses how, in the absence of validation through the market, legitimation is the primary concern in the avant-garde and subsidized spheres. Both writers posit a necessary relation between the accumulation of cultural authority and a show of containing minority elements of dissent and opposition (Williams 1981, 225). The relation between subsidized cultural mainstream and margins is therefore, again, one of antagonistic interdependence.

Bourdieu describes high culture as dominated by "a specific logic: competition for cultural legitimacy" (1971a, 163). That competition is also functional complementarity expressed in a system of oppositions between different positions within the field, such as differences of ideology, genre, or style. Yet these oppositions also delineate the implicit boundaries of consensus. "The open conflicts between tendencies and doctrines tend to mask, from the participants themselves, the underlying complicity which they presuppose. . . . This complicity can be expressed as a consensus within the dissensus which constitutes the objective unity of the intellectual field" (ibid, 183). Crucially, Bourdieu goes on to distinguish this kind of opposition within the field from the absolute differences that exist between cultural fields.

These two kinds of difference — internal to a cultural field and between it and external orders — can be generalized as two basic structures of discourse. These are "A to *not A*," (A : -A), a relationship of opposition between two mutually defined antithetical and complementary positions; and "A to B," (A : B), one of absolute difference, nonrelation, with no mutual reference.[33] I use this abstract formulation of the structures of discourse later to analyze both IRCAM culture and the discursive history of musical modernism.

In terms of microsociology, Bourdieu contrasts two kinds of authority in legitimate culture akin to Weber's distinction between the roles of priest and prophet/sorcerer (1971a, 178–79).[34] First, the institutionalized authority of the teacher or curator responsible for pedagogy, devotion to tradition — essentially for reproduction. Second, the authority of the artist or creator with prophetic ambitions, which is personal and rests on flashes of originality. Bourdieu links this with the avant-garde, with youth, asceticism, discontinuity, revolution. The artist becomes equivalent to a charismatic leader. The analysis suggests also the different statuses associated with reproduction and production/creation.

Bourdieu also analyzes the class structuring of cultural consumption (1968, 1979). He delineates two kinds of cultural disposition resting on the acquisition or absence/refusal of cultural and educational capital. For the "cultured" classes, art competence rests on a sophisticated knowledge of the codes of representation, a knowledge that allows them to savor questions of form, genre, school, and so on. The pleasure is highly mediated and readily articulated in exegeses and judgments. For the "uncultured" classes, art perception involves naive sensory and emotional gratification, baser denotative and connotative readings, and so a (relatively) unmediated pleasure that, according to Bourdieu, is mistaken for the "proper" decoding of the work. Bourdieu is unclear to what extent he sees this difference as constitutive of a specific form of domination — in the sphere of culture — which is experienced by the "uncultured" as a lack; or whether he sees it (also) as a knowing, even ironic, resistance — as dissent from dominant cultural values. We will see that the IRCAM material suggests the potential for different positions within the "uncultured," some more actively knowing and dissenting than others.

Bourdieu and Williams thus ground the work that follows in two ways. First, they begin to illuminate the mechanisms of legitimation of high culture and of the avant-garde, issues that echo throughout this study. Second, they attend to the way that relations of difference operate within and across cultural fields, structuring every level: from the dispositions of different classes of cultural consumers, to the aesthetic strategies and ideological conflicts of producers, to the division of roles between producers and reproducers, to the arrangements between legitimate and commercial culture. This last issue is central to recent theories of modernism and postmodernism, which examine the different attitudes of the two traditions toward popular and commercial culture (Crow 1983; Foster 1985a, 1985b; Huyssen 1986). In accord with all of this, a basic analytic tenet of the book, applied in both the ethnography and history, is that IRCAM culture must be understood in relation to the broader cultural field, including not only its close rivals such as electronic music, but also its more distant "others" — commercial music and culture. Thus, the boundaries of IRCAM culture are outlined by tracing not only what is present and what is consciously opposed, but also what is implicitly absent.

I want finally to return to issues mentioned earlier. It will become clear in later chapters that IRCAM is the culmination of an extraordinary degree of centralization and rationalization in the production of art music. Rationalization is evident at many distinct levels: institutionally and administratively; in terms of the "content" of IRCAM's aesthetic, focused on the contribution of science and technology to composition; in IRCAM's extended division of labor and technological production practices;[35] and in the increasing attempts to administer "demand" through marketing and market research.

The last aspect indicates a contradiction between the rationalized character of IRCAM's aesthetic and its rationalized social form. We will see that IRCAM operates primarily according to the discursive "laws" of avant-garde culture: aiming to maximize cultural capital, oriented to the future, and unconcerned with stimulating present demand. Yet we will also see fragmentary signs of a shift in the Institute's terms of legitimation influenced by its bureaucratization, a shift from the avant-garde discourse of the pursuit of future knowledge toward one of legitimation by efficiency or "performativity" (Lyotard 1984, 46) — in which the assessment and manipulation of demand are pivotal.

The phenomenon of IRCAM, and particularly its complex and contradictory rationalization, poses problems for two current theories of culture. First, for sociological accounts that conceive of contemporary culture as a postmodernism driven by a new order of commodification and "dedifferentiation" that spans both high and popular culture (Lash 1990, 1–52, esp. 11). Second, for Habermas's conception of the continuation of the "project of modernity" (1985) through the progressive differentiation of art and the aesthetic.

In obvious socioeconomic ways, IRCAM embodies increased differentiation: the rise of public institutions dedicated to the production of new art music. Yet in this bureaucratization, in the rise of criteria of performativity, it shows common dynamics with other corporate bodies — in other words, dedifferentiation. As for commodification, even with growing pressures of performativity this is not a dominant dynamic. We will see instead other kinds of alliance with powerful corporate capital, for example IRCAM having been "inadvertently" enrolled as a research wing for the French military industrial giant Dassault and for the Japanese Yamaha corporation. This is dedifferentiation or convergence between public and private interests of a no less significant kind.

In IRCAM's aesthetic we find the same contradictory reality. Undeniably, computer music, music research, and so on are increasingly specialized fields of expertise. Yet they exist by virtue of the intertextual importation of scientific and technological discourses into music. They therefore represent the dedifferentiation of music aesthetics from these other highly legitimate discourses — an alliance, and conflation, with which this book is centrally concerned.

It follows that the case of IRCAM weighs against Habermas's vision of modernism's potential to continue the progressive autonomization of art. Rather, we might theorize IRCAM's aesthetic by transposing Habermas's own well-known analysis of the categorial confusion between distinct realms of value — the moral and the scientific-technological — in the ideological scientization of politics (1970a). From this perspective, IRCAM discourse represents a different but no less systematic conflation: here, between art and science-technology in the service of the scientization of art.

IRCAM thus represents both the increased autonomization of art and its opposite: an intensified subsumption — institutional, bureaucratic, scientific, technological — of the aesthetic. This takes us to the limits of a synchronic sociology of culture, since the processes of subsumption and rationalization require historical analysis: they must be understood in the context of long-term aesthetic and cultural-political forces that precede IRCAM.

AESTHETIC DISCOURSE AS A LONG-TERM CULTURAL SYSTEM

I suggested in the introduction that IRCAM exists at the intersection of certain distinct, interrelated, and converging historical processes. Rather than convey the historical background of IRCAM through a single narrative, I describe a constellation of different historical processes and temporal orders that in various ways meet within IRCAM. I argue that IRCAM cannot be understood without reference to such a series of processes and their complex and "haphazard" conjunction.

I divide these processes as follows. In chapter 2, I outline a discursive characterization of modernism and postmodernism in general and in music: the aesthetic systems that underlie IRCAM's work. Later, in chapter 7, I discuss more immediate discursive antecedents to IRCAM: aesthetic, scientific, and technological developments in contemporary and computer music. This updates the analysis of musical modernism and postmodernism and links them to recent highly specialized developments that are central to IRCAM. The primary focus of the analysis is on the recurrent theoretical and aesthetic forms of these discourses, but it touches also on their characteristic practices and technological and institutional forms. It rests on the theoretical ground proposed earlier this chapter, which, having separated these mediations from the "music itself," grants them a new prominence as constitutive of the way that music as culture produces meaning.

In chapter 3, I focus on a series of more local histories with a bearing on IRCAM: aspects of French culture and cultural politics, state music policies, postwar French contemporary music, and IRCAM's relations with the American computer music scene. Finally, I examine Boulez's history, his rise to cultural power, and the development of his ideas for IRCAM.

The type of discursive characterization I attempt in chapter 2 is a departure in relation to music. Although there are many musicological and cultural-historical studies of particular aspects of twentieth century music, as well as works summarizing major compositional developments, there has been little attempt to trace the basic discursive contours

of musical modernism and postmodernism as long-term cultural systems. There are also few studies that look at these in relation to broader
cultural and artistic developments.[36]

Debates about modernism and postmodernism in culture and the arts,
and related discussion of the concept of the avant-garde, have simmered
for nearly two decades since their rise in the 1970s. Although the terms
are beginning to be brought into musicology and music criticism, broadly
speaking these disciplines have not taken up the comparative possibilities
of the debates. This study provides a reason, then, to attempt the initial
outlines of a discursive analysis of modernism and postmodernism in
music, but I frame this within the wider debates in order to contextualize
the specific analysis of music history.

On the other hand, the wider debates around modernism and postmodernism have tended to be abstract, posed in philosophical and aesthetic terms and resorting only occasionally to sociological material.
This can be seen in seminal works by Lyotard (1984), Bürger (1984),
Jameson (1984a) and Foster (1985b). A few writers have been more
sociologically ambitious (for example, Anderson 1984; Harvey 1989;
Lash 1990). But in general, the debates lack empirically based sociological analyses of the cultural domain, particularly of cultural production.
So the case study presented in this book can be seen as contributing to a
more empirically and sociologically informed account of modernism,
postmodernism, and the avant-garde.

The attempt at a discursive characterization of modernism and postmodernism once again invokes Foucault.[37] I mentioned earlier that the
ethnographic material in the book can be seen as a synchronic study of
the micropractices and materiality of the aesthetic institutionalized as a
discursive regime. However my approach to history also echoes his work
in several ways.[38] Above all it is close to Foucault's project of history as
genealogical critique, a history that attempts to demonstrate the complex, multiple, and contingent sources of the dominant discourses of the
present in order to destabilize them, to question their reading of history,
their self-evidence and self-legitimation (Foucault 1984a, 1984b). The
intention, then, is to sketch a genealogy of the avant-garde.

Further, the history in this book has no basis in assumptions of "progress." Rather, it interrogates a discourse founded on notions of progress,
one that espouses a teleological view in which the (white, western, male)
subject posits himself as the key *animateur* or protagonist in artistic
development. Here, this perspective is questioned by dislocating any
taken-for-granted relation between the enunciation of avant-garde rhet-

oric and the longer-term value of the artistic or musical production to which this is attached. Unless we question this, we cannot account for the fact that not all artists who espouse this rhetoric make significant aesthetic contributions. Instead, the aim is to consider avant-garde discourse as itself an object of study and in doing so to question its models of artistic innovation and of history. This suggests two further points. First, that in the analysis of aesthetic change we should deconstruct the avant-garde's dominant motif, the necessity of rupture, change, negation, transgression. Second, that we should theorize the central role of discourse in strategies of legitimation and power in artistic production. The aim is to begin to conceptualize the art-historical process in ways that are loosened from the ideological claims of avant-garde discourse.

To this end, partly out of resistance to the rhetoric of progress and innovation in the culture under consideration in this book, my working hypothesis in the historical analysis posits a basic discursive continuity. But overall, the intention must be to assume neither continuity nor discontinuity and to investigate empirically the degrees, the character, and the mechanisms of discursive continuity and stasis or discontinuity and transformation — here, in relation to musical modernism and postmodernism as long-term aesthetic discourses. This in turn invokes two substantive questions. First, whether modernism itself is a spent force or whether it continues to be reproduced. Despite the common assumption that modernism is dead, it seems essential to examine just how contemporary aesthetic discourses relate to the classic forms of modernism. Second, whether postmodernism represents a radical break with modernism, or to what extent it is a continuation — a modernism subtly transmuted into "post" modernism. Rather than calling for simple periodization (Jameson 1984a, 78), these questions underscore the need for continuing empirical vigilance as to the temporal structures of these aesthetic discourses.

Another writer who, like Foucault, has provided an approach to theorizing cultural systems of the long-term is Marshall Sahlins. His studies of the dialectic of myth and history (Sahlins 1981, 1987) allow for both the continuity and the transformation of long-term cultural systems. For Sahlins, transformation is the result of the interplay of structure and practice, of received cultural orders being enacted in transformed conditions, especially through the conjunction of alien cultural systems and their mutual effects. Above all, Sahlins conveys the power of mythic discourse to construct practice, and the enduring resilience of such discourse, even though mutable and subject to various internal logics of change.

Foucault's substantive historical analyses of discourse and power (1973, 1977, 1981) are similarly concerned with dominant systems of knowledge as they are embodied in practices and technologies, and as they reproduce themselves. Foucault's actual histories can be criticized in two ways. First, despite his intentions to the contrary, for depicting the formations as unfolding continuously (if disjointedly) through history, and so neglecting to theorize their transformation. Second, for lack of attention to the differentiation of discourse, a problem he shares with Sahlins, who does not adequately address the operation of difference within the cultural order.

This book sets out to address these criticisms. In characterizing modernism and postmodernism I trace their regularities but also their "dispersal" — their internal differentiation. This is where it becomes helpful to distinguish opposition within a discourse from the absolute difference between discourses, a structuralism that no doubt violently deforms Foucault. Moreover, as I have said, I aim not to prejudge the issue of the reproduction or transformation of the cultural systems in question. Here Sahlins is most helpful in taking account of both the reproductive momentum of dominant cultural systems, but also their susceptibility to internal change and to transformation conditioned by external circumstances.

The link with Foucault is also apparent in the content of the study: the historical penetration of aesthetic discourse by scientific and technological expertise. This recalls Foucault's theory of power/knowledge. Certain problems are often raised concerning this theory.[39] One is the precise relation between power and knowledge: which "produces" the other, whether the relation is causal or correlative. Another is Foucault's failure to provide an account of "other," subjugated knowledges, without which "power/knowledge" seems all-pervasive. Providing such an account is necessary not only to give life to his own conception of a hierarchy of knowledges[40] but also to delineate a space of potential resistance from which political, ethical, epistemological, and indeed aesthetic questions might be asked of the dominant discourses.

Both criticisms are to some extent met in this study. With regard to power/knowledge, rather than granting "ontological priority to power" (Dews 1987, 175), my analysis suggests that the specific system of knowledge at issue emerged prior to its later association with power: that modernism came increasingly to attract institutionalized cultural power — the classic narrative of the successful avant-garde. But the key point is that the character of this knowledge system was extraordinarily well suited to this augmentation of power, and through its mutations it became increasingly so.

As to the hierarchy of knowledges, in the ethnography we glimpse subjugated knowledges through the guise of the cultural dispositions of lower-status IRCAM workers, some more "insurrectionary" than others. The aim is to look within the social microcosm of IRCAM's own workforce for the hierarchization of cultural knowledges and the illegitimacy that naive knowledges suffer. On another level, popular music and culture surface repeatedly in the book as a space of "other" cultural values, and one subordinate to IRCAM discourse in the hierarchy of legitimate values.

It is also worth considering the relation of the study to the theme of subjectification in Foucault's later work, the production of the subjects of knowledge in discourse (Foucault 1982, 208–16; Gordon 1987, 295–96). Here, aesthetic discourse may be a particularly interesting case, predicated as it is upon a realm of consciousness that we are all, as modern subjects, enjoined to cultivate for our pleasure and edification; but that may in fact prove mystifying and normatively corrective of our untutored cultural tastes. This is the double-sidedness of aesthetic discourse: on the one hand a means of cultural domination infused with a secular ethical program (Bourdieu 1979), on the other, engaged in the production of enlightened and "liberated" subjectivities.

This takes us again to Bourdieu's account of the differentiation of aesthetic dispositions and of the potential for domination in the experience of exclusion from dominant aesthetic codes. We will see how this may produce refusal and resistance, but it may also induce the desire to become subject to this form of consciousness — to "enter" the aesthetic. Aesthetic discourse may thus be more or less effective at generating the subjectivity that it prescribes. Indeed one result of aesthetic subjectification may be to fragment the subject and produce incommensurable aesthetic dispositions: an internal sense of irreconcilable desires, legitimate and illegitimate, explicit and covert. To think about such possibilities I now turn to psychoanalysis.

PSYCHOANALYSIS, ANTHROPOLOGY, AND THE SUBJECT IN CULTURE

I want to suggest some productive links between anthropology, cultural theory, and psychoanalytic theory. This contrasts with the turn toward scientistic psychologies (cognitive psychology, cognitive science) proposed by Sperber (1975, 1985) and Bloch (1991); indeed in this book, cognitive science in music is part of the object of study. Moreover, my ideas bear little relation to the usual themes raised at the juncture of anthropology and psychoanalysis, which in my view read the relation between psychoanalysis and sociocultural theory in a limited way.[41]

The areas closest to my approach are psychoanalytic studies of group relations and Kleinian studies of culture and society.[42] The two meet in the work of Isabel Menzies Lyth (1988a, 1988b) and Robert Hinshelwood (1987), both of whom trace the existence within institutions of unconscious defense mechanisms analogous to those in the individual unconscious. They argue that psychic processes such as projection and introjection, splitting and fragmentation,[43] occur routinely within the group unconscious of institutional cultures rather than due to the aggregate unconscious dynamics of individual members. Thus, while individuals' internal states will have an impact on the institutional culture, the latter cannot be reduced to the former, and unconscious group dynamics will profoundly influence individuals through their introjection of the "social defense system."[44] In this way the psychic mechanisms of the institutional culture mold the subjectivities of its members.[45] This approach focuses on very basic unconscious mechanisms: in Klein's terms, they are primitive defenses.[46]

However, this perspective itself falls short of the intentions of this study. Surprisingly, given the stress on institutional cultures, it lacks an account of wider social and cultural forces operating in the situation and of how these affect both individuals and institutions. While providing insight into particular institutional dynamics, the aim of this work is a therapeutic one: by analyzing destructive forces, to ameliorate the institution's pathological functioning. But this fails to consider whether present dynamics are influenced by historical sociocultural processes that should themselves be part of the analysis, so that it may not be easy to ameliorate the institution's functioning, since this may have tenacious roots. In short, this perspective lacks an adequate theorization of culture and of cultural history beyond the internal, synchronic properties of groups. It has not brought the psychoanalytic insights on group processes together with those deriving from social and cultural theory.[47] However, integrating aspects of the Kleinian scheme with a more developed cultural theory produces an approach that can inform the analysis of classification and the discursive analysis of history.

My recourse to psychoanalytic theory was stimulated by three levels of material: above all, by evidence of fragmentation of the aesthetic subjectivity of some IRCAM individuals. We will see that in different ways these subjects show a dislocation between the legitimate modernist allegiance of their professional IRCAM selves and various "illegitimate" relations with popular musics. Rather than being unified and sovereign, these author-subjects are best conceived as fragmented, their aesthetic dispositions molded by discursive forces. Hence, we see the same psychic configuration replicated at higher levels: in historical evidence of the nearly continuous denigration and disavowal of popular culture by modernist discourse, and by evidence of the same kind of denigration and disavowal in the institution of IRCAM.

The intrasubjective fragmentation derives from subjects' introjection of unconscious defense mechanisms that underlie the aesthetic precepts of modernism as they exist both historically and in the institution of IRCAM. In a Foucauldian vein, I have suggested that the institutional culture of IRCAM is itself overdetermined by modernist discourse. But I want to go further and suggest that in this process, the institution also reproduces unconscious mechanisms characteristic of modernism. My intention, then, is to bring together the historical analysis of this long-term aesthetic discourse with synchronic analysis of an institution, and of the subjectivities inhabiting that institution, that embody the discourse. Psychoanalytic concepts can thus be used in relation not only to present forms of institution and subjectivity, but in relation to the long-term cultural system in which they are embedded.

The first concept to which I will refer is splitting: an unconscious process considered by Melanie Klein to be one of the most primitive defenses against anxiety. Splitting involves a distortion whereby the "object" (of perception) is experienced as split into a "good" and a "bad" object, which are both absolutely separate yet antagonistically bound. The good object is idealized, granted supreme and unquestionable legitimacy, and felt to be a refuge from persecution, while the bad object is denigrated as worthless, but also as a destructive and terrifying persecutor. Extreme splitting is linked with two other mechanisms: denial and omnipotence. Denial involves the omnipotent obliteration of a perception — such as the existence of the bad object — "without reference to actual reality" (Hinshelwood 1987, 266). Thus, splitting, omnipotence, and denial are mutually implicated processes. But splitting can take more or less violent forms: from the less extreme devaluation of the bad object, to the more omnipotent and persecuted "solution" of denial and annihilation in phantasy.[48]

In later chapters the concept of splitting is used to throw light on the binary classifications which structure IRCAM culture. It is the tendency for binary oppositions to be experienced antagonistically and evaluatively — the systematic idealization or advocacy of one pole and denigration of the other — that is captured so well by splitting. This has wider implications and suggests that splitting may provide a crucial link for theorizing the relation between classification and ideology,[49] as well as giving insight into their subjective internalization and power. The concept of denial is used to account for the systematic exclusion of phenomena that might be expected to have some kind of presence: for example, within IRCAM culture, the absence of a politics of high technology, of musical-aesthetic discourse, and the absence in some individuals' IRCAM practices of popular cultural forms that are prominent in other spheres of their lives. To understand these absences fully, they have then to be read for their wider discursive significance.

These concepts can also therefore be used to elucidate the material cited earlier: the denigration and/or disavowal of popular culture by modernism in its manifestation as historical discourse, institution, or subjectivity. This amounts to a splitting of the cultural unconscious in which subjects and the institution of IRCAM identify with an idealized modernism while popular culture is denigrated as completely "other." We will see that this is embodied in a spectrum of positions on popular culture ranging from "neutral" claims of simple difference, through acknowledgment of its existence accompanied by devaluation, to disavowal or denial of its existence. The first may seem a realistic acceptance of difference, yet even this delegitimizes popular culture in that it is not considered by composer-subjects the sphere of "real" or "autonomous" cultural work, while the latter show increasingly persecuting (and persecuted) attitudes. Thus, the entire spectrum shows evidence of splitting through the delegitimation of popular culture.

Such an approach gives insight into two further elements of the discourse: on the one hand, the omnipotence of the modernist avant-garde, which perceives itself as the subject of history with a messianic role of (aesthetic) salvation; on the other, the sense of persecution revealed in my introduction when it is felt that contemporary composition bears the weight of the survival of western art music under the threat of its annihilation (by popular culture).

I want to suggest a term — antidiscourse — to sum up this phenomenon of a discourse (aesthetic modernism) that is produced in the process of simultaneously denying another, coexistent and rival discourse (popular culture). This term contrasts with Halliday's (1978) concept of antilanguage in two ways. First, it refers not simply to linguistic forms but to discourse more broadly conceived. More importantly, Halliday portrays antilanguage as a marginal code that, partly at least consciously, negates aspects of the dominant code in order to express resistance. By anti-discourse I imply a discourse that is engaged in the envious denial[50] or "absenting" (in phantasy) of the existence of a rival discourse. Anti-discursive denial may thus be more characteristic of hegemonic than subordinate cultural systems. It may also be central to the reproduction of dominant cultural systems over time. We will see that in the historical analysis of modernism it is exactly those long-term characteristics — the most rigid and enduring aspects of the discourse — that are susceptible to analysis in terms of splitting and denial.

The omnipotence of hegemonic cultural systems is, then, at the same time a defense (in psychoanalytic terms) against, and a signal of, their impasses vis à vis their "others"[51] — here, the aesthetic impotence of an "autonomous" modernism confronted historically with the aesthetic vibrancy of popular cultural forms. It seems this omnipotence is con-structed at the expense of a drastic denial — or, less extremely, a devalua-tion — of the aesthetic salience of other cultural forms.

Finally, while the introjection of the discursive unconscious may be complete in institutions — which exist, after all, both to reproduce and to "innovate" so as to extend the life of the discourse — the process for indi-viduals is less certain. We will see evidence that while some subjects "nat-urally" adopt the appropriate psychic configuration of the discourse, even in their reading of their own past lives, for others it involves an ambivalent period of adaption, while still others refuse, or continue to go through the motions while dissenting. The process of introjection is labile for subjects; introjection/subjectification may be more or less complete.

CHAPTER II

Prehistory

Modernism, Postmodernism, and Music

I have suggested that IRCAM cannot be understood in isolation from the aesthetic and philosophical traditions that inform it and that in turn it aims to inform. Primary here is musical modernism. But IRCAM culture also evidences, in its internal debates and oppositions, wider historical and contemporary tensions between musical modernism and postmodernism.

In what follows I sketch, first, an analysis of the key discursive features of modernism and postmodernism in general, tracing a set of dominant, recurrent characteristics at the heart of these discourses.[1] The point is to demonstrate that major characteristics of IRCAM culture are prefigured not only by musical modernism, but by significant features of modernist art in general. Thus the evolution of musical modernism must itself be understood within the context of broader cultural-historical forces.

CHARACTERIZING MODERNISM AND POSTMODERNISM

Modernism is a composite term for the new aesthetic movements across the arts that date from the late nineteenth and early twentieth centuries, among them, in the visual and literary arts, symbolism, expressionism, cubism, futurism, constructivism, dada, and surrealism.[2] One defining feature of modernism is its basis in a reaction by artists against the prior aesthetic and philosophical forms of romanticism and classicism. This general feature of modernist art is often referred to as the negative aesthetic or simply negation, since the prime motive is a negation of the principles of the previous tradition: in painting, a rejection of realist representation and the primacy of subject matter in favor of abstraction and an emphasis on formal and perceptual experiment; in music, the destructuring and rejection of the earlier harmonic, melodic, and sonata forms of tonality in favor of the extension of dissonance and ambiguity. In all the modernist arts there thus arose a self-conscious experimentation with form founded on a sense of the necessity of revolutionizing the "language" of art itself.

A second characteristic of modernism, linked to the desire for formal experiment, is a concern and fascination with new media, technology, and science.[3] Modernist scientism arose as early as the 1880s, as shown in the work of Seurat and Cezanne. Both were centrally concerned with changing the basis of art perception and were influenced by its scientific study.[4] The celebration of technology is clearest in early twentieth-century movements such as Soviet constructivism and Italian futurism, both of which advocated new media and drew analogies between industrial production and cultural practice.[5] Technologies affected not only the artistic means of production and reproduction. They were also a new aesthetic stimulus in terms of the subject matter of art, for example in the way that cubist and futurist abstractions recall the forms and movement of machines.

Futurists were especially ardent and iconoclastic proponents of the aesthetics of technology and of science, as in the work of the futurist theorist Severini, who wrote that art should evolve hand in hand with science. His was an eclectic scientism: theorizing the interdependence of perception, psychology, and aesthetics, and also proposing an aesthetics of numbers (Apollonio 1973, 10–11). Futurist visual art was strongly influenced by the new technologies of film and photography. Russolo, the key futurist theorist of music, argued in his 1913 manifesto *The Art of Noises* that "musical evolution is paralleled by the multiplication of machines" (ibid., 75) and called for music to become an "art of noises" embracing the new urban and industrial soundscape. Futurist music theory influenced composers' turn to technology and their search for new sound materials throughout the century, as for example in the French movement *musique concrète*. The futurists' predominantly polemical and aesthetic concerns, however, suggest that this early modernist reference to science and technology was largely symbolic and rhetorical, embedded in a cultish fascination.[6]

A third feature of modernism, implicit in those above, is theoreticism. Modernist art invests an unprecedented power in exegetical texts. Examples are the polemical manifestos and writings that accompany many of the early twentieth-century movements: constructivism and futurism, dada and surrealism. Huxtable writes of modernist architecture: "Nor is it unusual in architecture for theorist and practitioner to be the same person — a notable phenomenon in "'modern' times from Serlio to Le Corbusier" (1983, 31). Art theory and practice were of course linked in earlier periods, but modernist artists attempted to solve the crisis in traditions which they faced by foregrounding theory to construct and determine their practice. This is a profound change of relationship between theoretical text and artistic practice: "The normal point of intersection between the creative process and its recording and analysis has been speeded up and even reversed" (ibid., 29) so that theoretical text precedes creative process. Further, theoretical texts take on the ambiguous role of exegesis and criticism, of proselytizing and publicity, of both expounding and legitimizing practice. Theoreticism, then, has been central to the legitimation of modernist art practices, and closely implicated in the avant-garde's pedagogic and prescriptive mission.

A fourth defining element of modernism concerns its politics and political rhetoric, its vanguard and interventionist aims. Many cultural historians see the politics of the modernist avant-garde as primarily rhetorical and metaphorical, confined to formal critique and terroristic attacks on extant tradition. From one perspective modernist politics was always largely rhetorical, limited to anarchic and libertarian gestures against the structures of official and bourgeois art (Shapiro 1976, Poggioli 1982, Haskell 1983, Williams 1988). Others argue that the avant-garde was gradually depoliticized, and has now become culturally dominant, so that any critical potential that it once had has been irrevocably compromised (Hughes 1980, Guilbaut 1983, Shapiro and Shapiro 1985). Certainly the majority of modernist movements centered on formal experiments designed to subvert and shock the avant-garde's dual enemies: the academic and official art establishment and the bourgeois audience. They sought no broader social engagement or political effect. In their formalism, they thus disdained an involvement with the broader social or political dimensions of culture, preferring critique to be confined within the artwork itself. However, as Haskell suggests, this did not prevent aesthetic experiment from being read as social or political critique, a phenomenon that rests on the close association between mod-

ernism and the avant-garde and on the radical political connotations of
the concept of an avant-garde.

The reasons behind these associations are both historical and discursive. They can be traced through three aspects of the historical context of
the avant-garde. First, the origins of the concept in early French socialism (see chapter 3) and the shifting relations between artistic and political radicalism in nineteenth-century France.[7] Second, the wider political
climate of Europe in the late nineteenth and early twentieth centuries —
as Anderson puts it, the "imaginative proximity of social revolution"
(Anderson 1984, 104) — and its influence on artists; although, as Anderson notes, modernist art was objectively transpolitical, capable of affilia-
tion with both Left and Right.[8] And third, the complete suppression of
modernist art, beginning in the 1930s, in Nazi Germany and Stalinist
Russia, which led after the war to the perception of modernism as inherently antitotalitarian and antifascist.[9]

Several discursive features of the modernist avant-garde fill out its
radical and "critical" connotations. First, in parallel with their interest in
technology and science, modernist artists expounded a rhetoric of progress, constant innovation, and change, and saw their role as leading this
process through a radical intervention in art and culture. Poggioli (1982)
calls this general characteristic "futurism": the notion that the present
must be subordinated to the future. Artists saw themselves as a vanguard
charged with pursuing uncompromising progress, by definition ahead of
current tastes, and so with a pedagogic mission to educate and convert
the unenlightened audience. Haskell (1983) and Poggioli stress that
while such attitudes had existed in earlier times, they became systematic
and intensified to an unprecedented degree with the rise of the concept of
the avant-garde in the late nineteenth century. In addition, modernist experiments in formal negation — expressed in new aesthetics of fragmentation (collage, montage in cubism, dada), abstraction, and the revealing
of underlying structures (cubism, constructivism, futurism) — took on
more than purely formal meanings. They were read as oppositional,
as subversive, as politicized critiques of the extant moral and social
order, so that the language of art criticism became politically metaphorical to an unprecedented degree. Discussions of "continuity" and "tradition" versus "change" and "progress" appeared to be at the same time
aesthetic and political, both metaphoric and "real."

Haskell relates the perception of the avant-garde as "critical" to artists' gradual internalization of an ideology which proposed that art must

attempt to subvert the (aesthetic) status quo, since artistic value depends on being "ahead" of current tastes, which implies that it must necessarily be incomprehensible to the present audience. He traces the institutionalization of the belief, still strong today, that "an instinctive hostility toward contemporary art . . . [is] the necessary breeding ground for true art" (1983, 25).[10] Thus avant-garde artists have sought to alienate the general audience as proof of the value of their work.

However a different, influential reading of the politics of the avant-garde, and of the relations between it and modernism, has been proposed by Bürger (1984). Bürger suggests that although modernism has become hegemonic, a few historical movements — Russian constructivism, Italian futurism, dada, surrealism — did present broader critiques of the social functions and institutional forms of art. He reserves the term "avant-garde" for these politically engaged movements, distinguishing them from formalist or aesthetic modernism, and so retains a political reading of the avant-garde, arguing that it is still a viable concept. With other critics (Clark 1983, 1985a, 1985b; Foster 1985a), he proposes this as the basis for postmodern art: a renewal of the avant-garde's critical potential.

A fifth characteristic of modernism, indicating both the differentiation and the complexity of the discourse, is its oscillation between rationalism and irrationalism, objectivism and subjectivism (Bradbury and McFarlane 1976). Thus the rationalism inherent in the scientistic and technological aspects of constructivism contrasts starkly with the emphasis on intuition, the psychic, and the irrational associated with expressionism, while futurism was both ardently technophilic and irrationalist. In this sense different modernist tendencies took up and intensified two powerful strands of nineteenth-century art: on the one hand a positivistic naturalism and on the other late romanticism. While it is difficult to stabilize this oscillation and to gauge which side exerted the greater force, it is modernist rationalism that was so well allied to the importation of science and technology into art, while modernist theoreticism promoted the fusion between these elements.

Finally, a sixth feature of modernism — a significantly "unconscious" dimension — is its ambivalent relations with popular culture. The development of modernism occurred simultaneously with the rise in the mid-nineteenth century of urban popular culture and the new entertainment industries. The two — modernism and mass culture — coexisted thereafter in discrete domains. The early modernist period was also the height of French and British empire, and witnessed the importation and exhibition of nonwestern art. So modernist artists confronted a variety of popular cultural forms, from the mass culture of the metropolis to "primitive" and "exotic" folk cultures from the colonies. Until recently, the question of the historical relations between high and popular culture had not received much attention in art history. A few writers are now tracing the often obscure congress between modernism and mass culture (Crow 1983, Huyssen 1986, Varnedoe and Gopnik 1990), just as others are beginning to focus on the influence of nonwestern cultural forms on twentieth-century art (Goldwater 1967, Rubin 1984, Hiller 1991).

The decline of overt modernist reference to mass culture and the simultaneous rise of formalist visual abstraction (Crow 1983)[11] — a process paralleled in music, as I will show — discloses as an implicit defining characteristic of modernism the assertion, under the guise of pure, formal autonomy, of its absolute difference from the popular culture with which it coexists. At the same time, stylistic reference to nonwestern forms has remained more acceptable (Coutts-Smith 1991). Thus writers focusing on the relationship between modernism and mass culture argue that the latter should be analyzed as the "other" of modernism (Crow 1983, Huyssen 1986). Modernist assertions of difference from mass culture are expressed variously as simple "uninterest" in that culture, hostility, and also in the occasional surfacing of fascination, envy, and borrowing from the "other."[12] Tellingly, the construction of difference becomes an active antagonism toward and repudiation of mass culture in the writings of major modernist critics such as Clement Greenberg and Theodor Adorno.[13] Popular culture may thus be considered the "other" of modernism, with "authentic" folk and "primitive," "exotic" forms more acceptable and enduring as influences than urban and commercial forms,[14] as, again, I show later in relation to music.

Turning to postmodernism we can examine, from recent debates, how it is held to make a decisive break with modernism. The concept of postmodernism, which arose in literary and architectural criticism (Hassan 1971, Jencks 1977), has been generalized to refer to new cultural forms from the 1960s and '70s on. Like modernism, postmodernism subsumes different tendencies, and its character is still being fought out on the terrain of cultural theory and practice. However postmodernism is unified by common origins in the attempts of artists and intellectuals to supersede the impasses of modernism, and motivated by a common dissatisfaction with modernism.

There are two main senses in which proponents of postmodernism claim that it represents a radical departure from modernism. The first argument itself has two inflections. One is that postmodernism involves an overcoming of the historical division between high and popular culture, a new cultural pluralism and heterogeneity in which those distinctions become obsolete. In this perspective postmodernism reacts against modernism's hostility toward or nonrecognition of popular culture. The other view holds that postmodernism supersedes the modernist negation of the earlier "languages" of art—realism and representation (in visual art), narrative (in literature and film), and tonality (in music). These postmodern works involve a reappropriation of earlier forms: hence neoclassicism, neoromanticism, and so on. In both inflections, however, postmodernism is defined by negation of a modernist negation, thereby reproducing a modernist mechanism and revealing, ironically, an essential kinship with modernism. Unlike many analysts of postmodernism, who stress the discontinuities with modernism, it therefore seems to me imperative that an account of the relation between the two must trace significant discursive continuities as well as divergences—continuities that include negation as well as the embrace of new media and technologies.

Some writers assert that the division between high and mass culture is already superseded (Crane 1987). Others see avant-garde music as having a key role in overcoming the division (Jameson 1984a),[15] while yet others have traced how some popular musics have been influenced by the historical avant-gardes (Frith and Horne 1987, Walker 1987). It is notable that this view of postmodernism was propounded in the editorial of a new contemporary music journal—an issue devoted to "musical thought at IRCAM"—by a British composer who has himself composed at IRCAM (Osborne 1984) The implication of his argument was to link IRCAM with such a form of postmodernism. We will assess how justified this is later.

The second major divergence claimed by some advocates of postmodernism, to some extent linked with the first, also embodies the negation of modernist negation: it is a rejection of the predominantly asocial and formalist, pedagogic and elitist cultural politics of modernism. Foster calls this the "anti-aesthetic" (1985a, xv), by which he means a rejection of modernist belief in the autonomy of the aesthetic. This, and the turn to popular culture and earlier cultural forms, characterize two tendencies within postmodernism that I will call, respectively, the "vanguardist" and the "populist."

The "vanguardist" position, epitomized by Foster (1985b) and Bürger (1984), preserves the modernist notion of a critical avant-garde, now allied to or rooted in the "new social movements" that have developed around race and ethnicity, gender and sexuality. Hence the prominence of feminist postmodern art (Owens 1985). Lyotard depicts postmodernism as the end of the grand modernist narratives (of humanism, Marxism) and as a celebration of heterogeneity, dissent, the proliferation of "*petits récits*" (1984, 60). Foster's view is similar: postmodernism as sensitivity to difference, linked with an interrogation and transformation of the social affiliations and institutional forms of art practice (Foster 1985a).

But rather than this politicized, vanguard postmodernism, it is the populist stream that is more visible. In terms of cultural theory this involves an optimistic pluralism and populism, a celebration of consumption and desire. In cultural practice, it encompasses one of the two strategies outlined earlier: either aesthetic reference to popular culture with the intention to overcome the separation between high and low culture and to appeal to the popular audience, or aesthetic reference, or return, to premodernist cultural forms — realism, narrative, tonality, and so on.

The claims made for postmodernism thus raise questions for the ethnography and history that follow. Does postmodern practice effect an engagement or "rapprochement" with popular culture or with earlier forms? And how politicized or socially engaged is "vanguardist" postmodern culture? This, in particular, demands realistic appraisal given the fact, summarized but not interpreted by Jameson (1984b, 62), of the transpolitical character of postmodern debate — a further continuity with modernism. More specifically, the analysis suggests two important dimensions for empirical enquiry with regard to IRCAM culture that provide clues to its placing in relation to modernism and postmodernism and to the continuing relevance of the concept of the avant-garde: its political character — does it evidence a critique of the social and institutional forms of art?; and its relations with the "other" of mass and popular culture and music. I address these questions below: first in relation to recent music history, including the cultural politics of music in France (chapter 3), and in later chapters in relation to IRCAM.

MODERNISM AND POSTMODERNISM IN MUSIC

In music, the advent of modernism is usually dated from the breakdown of the underlying musical system of tonality that had lasted for over three hundred years, and that formed the basis for baroque, classical, and romantic music.[16] The late romantic composers, such as Wagner and Scriabin, had expanded that system so much that it was under great strain, its basic principles in question, and composers began a search for new organizing principles. First, around the turn of the century, came a period of atonality — the suspension and avoidance of all tonal reference and of thematic form. But in the early 1920s a new compositional technique and philosophy called serialism was developed by Schoenberg and his pupils Webern and Berg (the Second Viennese School). Serialism, a stylistic revolution, became the most powerful development out of the crisis of tonality and was for some decades the organizing force of musical modernism.

Serialism as it was originally conceived focused on the organization of pitch. This approach involves the construction of a twelve-note series or row using all twelve chromatic notes of the scale in a fixed order, each of which must be used once before the series can be started again. To generate material for a piece, four basic structural transformations of the series are produced: the original form, backward (retrograde), upside-down (inversion), and retrograde-inversion. The four transformations can then be transposed to start on each of the twelve chromatic notes, so giving forty-eight permutations that provide the seeds of the composition. Serialism implies the principle of the homogeneity of chromatic space,[17] while by contrast tonality centers on the functional and symbolic hierarchy of the tonic or key note, its dominant and subdominant. In this sense, serialism negates the hierarchical ordering of pitch space in tonality. Compared with the negational character of abstract visual art, serialism — a highly rationalist and structuralist method that aspires to the status of a new musical "language" — can appear a positive and nonnegational development. But serialist principles nonetheless prescribe an aesthetic that is completely antithetical to and so a negation of tonality. We will see that Boulez, like Adorno,[18] conceived of the mid-century serialist aesthetic as negational.

Given that tonal harmony is also one of the aesthetic bases of the history of commercial popular music, the absence of tonal reference is a key marker of the way that musical modernism asserts aesthetic difference from popular musics. Moreover, while the earlier period of atonality involved a "free" avoidance of tonality, serialism went much further than this simple negation by advocating a prescriptive, rationalized, and systematic basis for constructing aesthetic difference from tonality.

Schoenberg was an ambivalent revolutionary, believing his work to lay the basis both for continuing the Germanic tradition, and for an irrevocable break with the past. He felt that he was impelled by a force greater than himself, necessary for the future of music. He wrote in 1910, "I am conscious of having broken through every restriction of a bygone aesthetic. . . . I am obeying an inner compulsion which is stronger than any upbringing" (quoted in Rosen 1976, 14–15). This indicates Schoenberg's self-consciousness about his vanguard mission, which he supported by a number of important teaching texts. In several ways, Schoenberg embodies the antinomies of modernism: advocating both tradition and rupture, instigating the rationalist method of serialism while returning periodically to an expressionist mode in both his music and painting. Adorno later elaborated upon Schoenberg's view of his work, seeing Schoenberg's uncompromising pursuit of the "immanent laws" of aesthetic development as the only progressive direction for modern music. Adorno's remains the most eloquent philosophical defense of the critical potential of modernist aesthetics (Adorno 1973).

But early century musical modernism was highly eclectic, and serialism was not hegemonic in this period. During the 1920s and 1930s it was paralleled by two rival tendencies, tendencies that might almost be considered "proto" postmodern, between which certain composers moved in different periods. One was the neoclassicism associated with composers such as Stravinsky and Hindemith: an attempt to reinvigorate the present by reference to the principles of musics from the eighteenth and nineteenth centuries and earlier. The other main tendency of the interwar period involved a self-conscious appropriation of popular musics, both urban and folk-based, as in the work of the early modernists Debussy, Satie, and Ives. The 1920s saw a turn to jazz as a reference on the part of Poulenc, Milhaud, Krenek, Copland, Antheil, and Gershwin (whose work is perhaps better classified as popular music that sometimes aspired to the condition of "serious" music). At the same time, composers such as Bartók, Kodály, Stravinsky, Falla, and Vaughan Williams drew on the folk musics that were increasingly available to them from archives and field studies and developed distinctly "nationalist" variants of modernism. Both kinds of popular music were used as influences, for their modes, their melodies, their rhythmic or structural forms. Significantly, popular musics were treated by these composers as an "other" to be drawn into their compositional practice or to be played in "other," less serious contexts.[19] By contrast, the serialist tradition in general disdained reference to popular musics altogether. Thus, popular music can be seen as the "other" of musical modernism — in both its serialist and its more eclectic manifestations.

The early-century musical avant-garde also exemplified the phenomena of vanguardism, radical interventionism, and a defensive disdain for immediate audiences. Like the other avant-gardes of the early century, it aroused public scandal and moral outrage. An infamous occasion was the first performance of Berg's Altenberg songs in Vienna in 1913, which provoked such a riot that the police were called out, as did the Parisian premiere of Stravinsky's "Rite of Spring" soon after. This extreme public hostility caused defensive attempts by composers to get their music played. Schoenberg and his circle founded the "Society for the Private Performance of Music" in 1918. Performances were by invitation and unpublicized, and critics and the public were barred. They thus created an elite group by which their music was judged, closed against the ravages of commercialism and of the mass public. These early modernist composers supported themselves mainly by private teaching and occasional conducting jobs. They experienced the usual alternation between marginalization and ostracism, then sudden public acclaim, typical of an avant-garde.

Following the pluralism of the interwar years, the period after World War II saw a renewal and intensification of serialism, so that from the 1950s on it became the main theory and method of composition, eclipsing its earlier rivals. Aided by Schoenberg's pedagogic writings and by the aesthetic teachings of Adorno, as well as those of composers René Leibowitz and Olivier Messiaen, serialism became the ideological rallying point of the new postwar European avant-garde at their meeting place, the Darmstadt summer school. The generation of composers who came to the forefront in this period — led in Europe by Boulez and Stockhausen, in the United States by Babbitt — elected Schoenberg's Second Viennese School, and in particular Webern, as pioneering forefathers. But theirs was no mere reflection of earlier compositional practice. By constructing such a genealogy and making selective readings of the earlier work, the new generation tried effectively to legitimize their own increasingly radical discourse, a heavily theorized extension of serialism. Boulez and Stockhausen at Darmstadt, and Babbitt at Princeton, soon themselves became leading teachers; and through the ramifying influence of these figures and their serialist colleagues, serialism remained for some decades one of the main training techniques for composers.

The serialist composers of the '50s tried in different ways to generalize serialism in order to produce a new, universal method of composition. Following their reading of Webern's late technique, they extended serialism to the rationalist and determinist control not only of pitch but of all other parameters of composition: rhythm or duration, dynamics, and timbre. This became known as "total," "integrated," or "generalized" serialism. It was accompanied by polemical writings against the aesthetic "compromises" of much interwar composition, and, adopting the pedagogic and prescriptive vanguard mission, serialist composers attempted to purify the correct, rigorous direction of the avant-garde — a direction that was posed as absolute and inescapable.

The '50s generation began to add further layers of rationalism to that inherent in earlier forms of serialism. They became involved with science, exploring the acoustics and physics of music. At the same time they began to scientize the conceptual basis of composition, drawing on mathematics, statistics, information theory, logic, and linguistics. Controversies between the serialists in this period illustrate the dominant scientistic discourse through which they conceptualized music. Babbitt, for example, criticized the Europeans for insufficient mathematical rigor in these terms: "Mathematics — or, more correctly, arithmetic — is used, not as a means of characterizing or discovering general systematic, precompositional relationships, but as a compositional device. . . . The alleged 'total organization' is achieved by applying dissimilar, essentially unrelated criteria" (Griffiths 1981, 93). He advocated a more unified and mathematically sound total serialism; whereas Xenakis criticized total serialism for complex incoherence: "[It] destroys itself by its very complexity; what one hears is in reality nothing but a mass of notes" (ibid., 110). Xenakis's "solution" was to improve the mathematical infrastructure by bringing the laws of statistics, probability, and calculus into compositional practice.

In the same period, drawn by the new postwar electronic media, these composers turned to technology for the analysis and generation of sound. Both the scientism and the technological bent were legacies of early modernism in general (as we have seen), and of two specific musical influences. One influence was the sound experiments and philosophy of the Italian futurists, discussed earlier. The other was the work of the French-American composer Edgard Varèse who, from the 1920s on, called for new sound materials, like the futurists, linked the progress of music to the development of new instruments, and pioneered a renewed concern with timbre. His early works explored percussion sounds, and later works the new "liberating medium" of electronics (Middleton 1978, 70). Varèse was perhaps more responsible than any other individual for the importation of scientific terms and rhetoric — "research," "experimentation," "laboratory" — into the theorizing of music. He wrote of music as an "Art-Science" and in 1936 condoned the view, prophetic of IRCAM, that "there should be at least one laboratory in the world where the fundamental facts of music could be investigated" (ibid., 68).[20] Thus Varèse's discourse was an important precursor both of the tenor of the postwar avant-garde and of IRCAM itself.

By the 1950s tape recording technology and electronic wave generators became available to composers with access to radio stations or well-endowed university laboratories, so that access was limited in this period to those affiliated with large institutions, while less-credentialed composers had no such access. The leading Europeans, Boulez and Stockhausen, both worked in radio stations, Babbitt in university labs. Babbitt's combination of electronics with total serialism, extended particularly to rhythm, aimed to produce accurate performances of extremely complex serial scores. His work made use of an early large-scale synthesizer made by RCA and based at the Columbia-Princeton studio.

Stockhausen's work brought together serialism, scientism, and electronics with the aim of total control of timbre, at that time the most elusive and unanalyzable element of music. Stockhausen wanted to create a systematic repertoire of artificially generated timbres, analytically ordered and suited to serial manipulation. He aimed to achieve a combination of perfect sound material (pure sine tones) with a perfect theory (total serialism). But in fact the theoretical, scientific, and technological bases of Stockhausen's electronic music in this period proved reductive and inadequate, and indicate the weaknesses of the rationalism and determinism of the time. It was thought that any timbre could be synthesized simply by setting up a series of oscillators to produce each component partial frequency of the timbral spectrum as a steady-state sine wave. But this produced woefully poor results, since it omitted several other crucial and idiosyncratic elements of timbre, in particular the interrelated evolution of each partial in time and variable degrees of noise, both of which are now known to contribute to the organic quality of interesting timbres. Stockhausen's notion of total serialization of timbre was, then, an extreme expression of the scientistic and technological rationalism of the time. It exemplifies the high point of technological total serialism, while revealing its profound limitations. And it marks the transition to a postserialist discourse, one that, as we will see in the next chapter and in chapter 7, pursues the systematic combination of scientific and technological analysis and generation of sound materials for composition while loosening any necessary commitment to serial organization.

Another characteristic of the leading postwar serialists is their theoreticism. Boulez and Babbitt have been among the foremost theoreti-
cians of contemporary composition, and this is closely related to their
scientism and rationalism, since they have drawn respectively on structuralism, linguistics, set theory, and on mathematics to theorize composition. Both have produced powerful treatises and have been very
influential teachers. These composers followed Schoenberg's example in
uniting theory and practice. The postwar period also saw the consolidation of the new academic music disciplines of musicology, music theory,
and music analysis in the universities, and a proliferation of textual and
theoretical analyses of music. Journals appeared as mouthpieces of the
new theories, led by *Perspectives of New Music* on the American East
Coast and *Die Reihe* in Europe. The theoreticist postwar serialists were
at home in such a context. Babbitt's total serialism became the dominant
school of composition in powerful American East Coast universities
such as Princeton and Yale. Boulez, after stormy earlier relations with
official culture, returned to France in 1970 at President Pompidou's be-
hest to direct the planning of IRCAM, a large institution dedicated to
technological and scientific research around music.

Kerman (1985), describing the bewildering specialization within musicology since the war, says that the new disciplines of music theory
and analysis, as well as studying modernist texts, took a more complicit role in their construction. Music theory became not just descrip-
tive but prescriptive: "Much of the power and prestige of theory derives from its alignment . . . with the actual sources of creativity on
the contemporary musical scene" (ibid., 15). This incestuous union of
theory and composition was cemented by the postwar academiciza-
tion of serialism in the elite American East Coast universities. Kerman
comments:

> Babbitt at Princeton was pointing out that avant-garde music could find its
> niche after all — though only by retreating from one bastion of middle-class
> culture, the concert hall, to another, the university. Like pure science, he
> argued, musical composition has a claim on the university as a protector of
> abstract thought. (The complicity of composition and theory . . . was crucial
> to this argument, the complicity of theory and mathematics extremely help-
> ful). . . . So Princeton . . . set up an academic program for the Ph.D. degree in
> musical composition, for which the final exercise consisted of a musical com-
> position plus a theory dissertation or essay. The marriage of theory and com-
> position was legitimized by graduate councils around the country; the avant-
> garde was house-broken into the academy.
>
> (Kerman 1985, 101)

We can discern, then, in this period a process of growing legitimation of serialism, to which the character of the discourse — rationalist, determinist, theoreticist, formalist, scientistic, concerned with high technology — was particularly well suited, a legitimation that enabled this tradition to become increasingly acceptable to state cultural institutions and to the academy. Central to this process was the fact of composers themselves becoming theorists, providing a metalanguage (science) to rationalize and assess composition — a metalanguage that was itself extremely powerful and legitimate; and the propagation of these ideas through newly established journals. (Kerman writes of *Perspectives* and *Die Reihe*, "Serialism was the main subject and mathematics the main mode of both journals" [1985, 102].) It is, then, the serialists who best exemplify mid-century musical modernism and who became established internationally, beginning in the 1950s, as the dominant tradition of the musical avant-garde. This was a hegemony in which the Europeans and East Coast Americans, despite the apparent conflict arising from their differing positions within the field, were ultimately collusive.[21]

Some argue that the method created by Schoenberg and others in the 1920s should properly be known as the "twelve-tone" or "twelve-note method." In this view the technique was oriented primarily toward pitch in the early period. It was used relatively flexibly for expressive ends, and Schoenberg himself conceived of it not as a revolutionary tool but as a logical extension of historical techniques: it was practice rather than theory that led. From this perspective, it is only the postwar expansion of the approach by Boulez, Babbitt, and others to cover all dimensions of musical expression that deserves the name serialism. In other words, it should be reserved for the period that saw the rise of total serialism. This era was characterized by an intense ideological commitment to serialism as the only direction for composition, by a cult of systematicity, rigor, and purism in which serialism came to be conceived as the basis of the whole compositional frame. As we have seen, even here there were significant differences, with Babbitt the leading proponent of mathematical systematicity, while Boulez's pronouncements rested on a looser, more poetic, less rigorously scientistic relation to serialist theory. But the key point for advocates of this interpretation is that there was nothing immanent in Schoenberg's own work or that of his colleagues, except perhaps for aspects of Webern's work, that led inevitably to the deterministic and scientistic turn taken by serialism after the war, so that the compositional practice of Schoenberg, Berg, and others should not be tainted by association with the "sins" or excesses of the 1950s and after.

However I follow in this study the other common use of "serialism" (for example Rosen 1976; Griffiths 1978, 1986; Neighbour et al. 1983). In this approach, "serialism" is used to designate both the method developed by Schoenberg and others in the 1920s and the postwar expansion of the technique, which may more specifically be termed total serialism. To adopt this usage carries major implications. One is that despite the differences in the two periods, the developments of the '50s can be seen as strongly conditioned by, and in some ways continuous with, those of the '20s. In other words, much of what occurred in the '50s was prefigured by aspects of the thinking of key figures in the earlier period. My argument for this view rests on two observations. First, the "twelve-tone method" was a highly structuralist conception, and structuralist thinking in general, even in this early period, was courting, if ambivalently, scientific status. Second, whatever the subtlety and inconsistency of Schoenberg's own deployment of the method, it was one that was very liable — given its suitability for pedagogic and didactic purposes — to solidify into a rigidly deterministic, heavily theorized system and to be expanded in the scope and range of its applicability. I stress here that such an interpretation in no way condones the ideological gloss overlaid on it by Boulez and others in their writings of the time — that is, that the '50s developments were both inevitable and progressive.

I am suggesting, then, that it was not difficult for the "twelve-tone method" to become a vehicle for a combined and intensified rationalism, determinism, scientism, and theoreticism in the '50s — in line, moreover, with the wider intensifying scientism characteristic of postwar structuralism (Pavel 1989). If these were developments that Schoenberg would have deplored, in my view they are still ones for which he laid the foundations of possibility. There may have been nothing necessary about the later developments, but that they occurred is certainly, after the event, "predictable." As I have continually emphasized, however, the developments of the '50s did not rest on an appropriation of these influences alone. They depended on a discursive bricolage that brought these elements together with additional concerns characteristic of modernism in general: above all, an obsession with science and technology as forces for progress in culture.

Finally, I am using the term "postserialism" to refer to developments beginning in the late '50s and '60s following the demise and fracturing of the total serialist project. Rather than bringing the full range of compositional developments since the '60s under this term, I reserve it for those that continued in the scientistic, deterministic, rationalist, and theoreticist vein of total serialism, to which was increasingly added a prominent technological dimension. In other words, I use postserialism to designate the discourse that followed on from total serialism and that, even if explicitly rejecting serialism at times, attempted to salvage and reinvigorate dominant features of that approach, primarily by reference to science and technology. This was not the only development of the '60s and '70s, although it was a powerful one. As we will see in chapter 3, it is the discourse that Boulez began to enunciate in the late '60s and that became the basis of his manifesto for IRCAM. It is, then, how I will characterize the contemporary discourse of music research and composition within which IRCAM has a leading place.

EXPERIMENTAL MUSIC AS MUSICAL POSTMODERNISM

But serialism, though dominant, was not the only development within the musical avant-garde after the war. In this period also, its fortunes developed in counterpoint with those of rival movements. The main alternative from the 1950s on was the tradition of experimental music that focused on the American composer and guru John Cage and his followers, including composers Morton Feldman, Christian Wolff, Earle Brown, and later La Monte Young and Cornelius Cardew. This is often considered the centerpiece of musical postmodernism. For decades these composers remained less well known, less powerful and less legitimate than the serialists; they were the "unserious" dissidents of the avant-garde.[22]

Cage was subject to a wide range of American and European influences during his formative years in the 1930s. He was taught by Schoenberg and used serialist procedures in some early compositions. But during the mid-1930s he came under the influence of Henry Cowell, a key figure in the burgeoning American avant-garde, and by the late '40s he was developing his own compositional philosophy opposed to the legacy of serialist rationalism. In reaction to serialist determinism and the hypercontrol of all parameters of sound, Cage and his followers wanted to liberate them by introducing aleatory and chance procedures: noncontrol. His watchword was indeterminacy. Nonetheless, experimental composers sought different theoretical determinants for their composition. Cage turned to antirationalist cosmologies — Zen and eastern mysticism — while other experimentalists became involved in alternative belief systems, for example Marxist-Leninist politics. Paradoxically, then, the experimentalists remained theoreticist and determinist while searching for alternative philosophies — nonscientific and more social and spiritual — to legitimize and prescribe compositional practice. The music was still constructed in discursive texts. Cage, like Boulez, was also known as a writer and philosopher.

Against the often unperformed and unperformable complex scores and text-centered composition of the serialists, experimentalists wrote simplistic scores that broke away from traditional music notation: often just a short written description or graphic diagram, aimed at live performance, that was intended to give the performer maximum interpretative play. In opposition to the continuing primacy of pitch logics in serialism, Cage proposed that time should take the central position in music since it was materially central to both sound and silence.[23] Against the serialist view of time as linear, "duration" as mathematically quantifiable, experimental composers viewed time as noncumulative, nondirectional, static, and rhythm as cyclical, repetitive, and processual. Cage called for "non-intention" and (after Satie) "purposeless music," in rebellion against the teleology of classical form. This approach is well expressed in the minimalist, process, or systems music of composers such as Terry Riley, Philip Glass, and Steve Reich, which developed out of the experimental tradition. Influenced by nonwestern musics, for example Javanese gamelan, this music sets up repetitive and cyclic rhythmic structures that permutate as the performance unfolds: a ritual process set in motion. Performances might last for twenty-four hours, and music was stripped to a minimal simplicity.

The mention of nonwestern music and ritual raises two key aspects of the experimental tradition and its postmodern legacy that are significant by their absence from modernist serialism. In other words, they mark the difference between the two avant-gardes.

First, like the eclectic modernists of the early century, experimentalists had an interest in, and made reference to, nonwestern and popular musics. Unlike serialism, with its genealogy centered on the Schoenberg school, experimentalism elected a range of musical ancestors, including Debussy, Satie, Varèse, and the Americans Ives and Cowell, most of whom had drawn in some way on the influence of nonwestern or popular urban musics. Like their forefathers, experimental composers drew on popular musics for their modes, their rhythmic, repetitive, or structural forms, or treated them as pastiche or parody, or created musical montage by overlaying one music upon another (as with Ives). These techniques are now considered central to postmodern aesthetics; yet, as I have shown, they go back to certain early modernists, while they are largely absent from serialist modernism.

Second, influenced by ethnomusicological studies of the ritual and participatory nature of nonwestern musics, the experimentalists were centrally concerned with the social and live, performative aspects of music. Often themselves performer-composers, experimentalists gestured toward effacing the composer's authoritative role and wanted to lessen the hierarchical musical division of labor between composer as creative authority, performer as constrained interpreter, and passive audience.[24] The emphasis was on the performance process, music as an unfolding and participatory ritual event structured by time. But the composer remained the author of these events so that, ironically, the division of labor remained intact.

There was a pervasive two-way influence between experimental music and a series of postwar American visual art movements — abstract expressionism, and then pop art — so that Cage and followers cited the influence of Duchamp, Pollock, Johns, and Calder, and vice versa. Music in its pure abstraction came to be seen as the paradigmatic medium during the heyday of American abstract art.[25] Events were often multimedia, as with Fluxus performances in which the visual and ritual were as important as the sonic/aural, or Cage's long collaborations with the dancer Merce Cunningham and the painter Robert Rauschenberg. Performances were, then, often less than serious events, and a dadaistic iconoclasm linked experimental music to the wider radical art movements of the 1950s and 1960s, including performance and conceptual art.

Beginning in the later 1960s, inspired in part by Marxist-Leninism or Maoism, there emerged out of this a set of experimental composers, including Wolff, Cardew, Frederic Rzewski, and their followers, who were more frankly politicized than those in the postserialist camp. In some cases they attempted to produce political effects through the use of, or by reference to, revolutionary popular musical material or lyrics.[26] Another strategy, developed by some of the same composers but more widely influential, extended the critique of the musical division of labor. Composers such as Cardew, Wolff, and groups such as the Italian-American MEV (*Musica Elletronica Viva*), the British Scratch Orchestra, and AMM, emphasized changes in the social relations of music production and performance in their attempts at a new interactive, collective, and nonhierarchical group practice. The social dimension of music was seen as a crucible for experiments in collective and democratic social relations.[27]

Many politicized experimental groups centered on live, free electronic music improvisation. Free improvisation was both a logical extension of indeterminism, and also in accord with a stress on collective group relations as determining musical output. But while some politicized experimental groups used electronics, not all did. In fact, if we examine the experimental music concern with technology, we can see that while it accommodated some sociopolitical experiment it was also autonomous and important in its own right and bore its own softer political connotations.

Like the serialists and postserialists, and after their common ancestor Varèse, the experimentalists believed strongly in the necessity of technology as a source of new sounds, and, as their name implies, in the need for constant experimentation and "research." But beyond this their relation to technology was polemically opposed to the serialists'. Experimental composers used technology artisanally and pragmatically, in contrast with the scientistic and analytical serialist applications. Experimentalists rejected both the implicit elitism of the serialist adherence to inaccessible and expensive high technologies found only in large and official institutions and the universalizing high rationalism and scientism with which these technologies were deployed. They countered determinism and formalism with technological empiricism and with live, social, improvised, and performance-based use. Above all they countered "high-tech domination" with a practice centered on the celebration of the small and low-tech.

We will see in the next chapter one European manifestation of this technological antagonism: how the opposition between experimental empiricism and postserialist determinism was played out in the major conflict in the 1950s and 1960s within French electro-acoustic music between the pioneers of *musique concrète* — Pierre Schaeffer, Pierre Henry — and Boulez. This began a lasting tension between the *Groupe de Recherches Musicales* (GRM), home of *musique concrète*, and IRCAM, devoted to anti-empiricist technological and scientific research and development.

More typical of American and British experimentalism than this kind of conflict, given that experimental composers were usually unaffiliated with major institutions and so lacked access to high technology, was a commitment to small technologies, either commercial or self-made. This linked to the politics of musical performance. Nyman describes it thus:

Composers began introducing electronics into experimental music in the early sixties, not by taking into concert halls the equipment from the electronic studios which had proliferated in the '50s, but by inventing and adapting a portable electronic technology which was easily accepted into the . . . open world of performance indeterminacy. Live electronics were used in two related ways. First, electronic versions were made of scores whose instrumentation was unspecified . . . which could now draw freely on the new range of sound sources opened up by electronics. Secondly, the way was prepared for pieces which specify a particular electronic system, which may in itself be inherently indeterminate and may or may not include a score.

(Nyman 1974, 75)

Paradoxically, given the principle of indeterminacy, this last development indicates a kind of technological determinism in music, in that the technologies themselves become the composition. Thus, in contrast to the postserialist use of high technologies in the university lab and aimed at the concert hall, experimental composers sought flexible and portable small technologies for live performance, multimedia events and "installations," for use in everyday situations or on the street. Certain composers themselves became electronics bricoleurs, artisanal designers of small technologies tampering with the sources of sounds — a direction initiated by Cage's own instrumental "engineering" in his early works for prepared piano.

The experimental composer as technological bricoleur is exemplified by several Americans, notably Gordon Mumma, David Behrman (members of another live electronics group, the Sonic Arts Union), Richard Teitelbaum (of MEV), and Max Neuhaus, and in Britain by Hugh Davies. All saw their compositional work as centered on technological invention, and designed and built portable electronic instruments and systems for use in live performance. Mumma has said: "My decisions about electronic . . . circuitry and configurations are strongly influenced by the requirements of my profession as a music maker. This is . . . why I consider that my designing and building of circuits is really 'composing'" (Nyman 1974, 77). Writing of Behrman, Rockwell describes his strong commitment to homemade circuitry as a demystification of technology: "Behrman is not a trained engineer. He learned what he needed to know mostly by reading and by corresponding with Mumma" (Rockwell 1983, 139). Neuhaus, like Behrman, began as an autodidact designing his own circuitry and developed a new populist form of environmental electronic sound installation that put space at the center of musical experience. Rockwell notes that the "real revolution in electronic music" for these experimental autodidacts was the access to small and cheap electronic synthesizers that followed the progressive miniaturization of the technology, which in turn followed the broadening of the electronic-instrument market through their use in rock music. It was this small, commercial-technology revolution that allowed Behrman and others to "liberate themselves from deadening institutional associations" (ibid., 135). Such ideological differences over technology between the two avant-gardes fed into continuing debates within computer music over small versus large system development, and over the role or necessity of theory — issues that, we will see, also surface within IRCAM.

MUSICAL POSTMODERNISM AS THE NEGATION OF MUSICAL MODERNISM

The differences outlined above between the experimental and serialist/postserialist traditions define the break between musical postmodernism and modernism. However, it is necessary to scrutinize them and to perceive their limits. First, although a reference to popular and nonwestern musics is largely absent from serialism, the experimentalists' relation to these musics is limited to using them as a source — for quotation, for transformation, for use as an influence. A certain distance is thereby maintained: popular and nonwestern musics retain the status of an "other" — a quality, as we have seen, going right back to their eclectic ancestors, such as Debussy and Ives. Moreover, the popular music drawn on by postmodern composers has mainly been limited to non-commercial forms: to folk, ethnic, and nonwestern musics rather than the commercial stuff of the capitalist music industry and the tastes of the "mass." In this sense, much musical postmodernism has continued to refer to an untainted and idealized notion of a noncommercial, authentic people's music and to disdain the aesthetics and circuits of commercial popular music. Since the late 1970s, as I mentioned in chapter 1, a few experimentalists — Glass, Michael Nyman, Laurie Anderson — have embraced commercial populism, using formats closer to rock and attempting to reach a large popular music audience. However even this work remains aesthetically, ideologically, and institutionally distinct from commercial popular music.[28]

In addition, while the politicization of experimental music has been more developed than in postserialism, it is confined mainly to critiques of the immediate social context and social relations of musical practice, as

62

Prehistory

in the neodada performance events. Only rarely or implicitly does this become a broader cultural politics aimed at transforming the institutional forms of serious music. Although the experimentalists' technological discourse has been in accord with these critiques, the technologies are just as often employed devoid of any political connotations. It is worth noting, finally, that many politicized and practical elements of experimental discourse are redolent of the influence of certain popular musics, especially the advanced black jazz of the '60s — influences that are commonly unacknowledged.[29]

Placing the two traditions geographically and socioeconomically, the split between the postserialists and experimentalists was also one between the East and West Coasts of the United States, with Babbitt and followers based in the East, Cage and followers in the West. The Cageian postmoderns were thus susceptible to the Pacific and oriental cultural sympathies of the American West Coast and to the influence of Californian rock music in the '60s, while the East Coasters looked toward and identified with Europe, birthplace of the modernist avant-garde. And institutionally, they had different bases. Rather than seek tenured professorships in the WASP universities, experimental composers taught in liberal arts colleges, untenured, or performed for a living. Experimentalists often depended on their close associations with the visual arts, with dance or film and their subsidizing circuits, thereby gaining support from galleries, museums, and art centers.

A polemical article by Cage,[30] commissioned in 1958 by the director of the Darmstadt summer school and called "History of experimental music in the United States," epitomizes the tensions between experimental music and European (and East Coast) postserialist modernism. It reveals Cage's active rivalry with, and desire to supersede, the European tradition. In his subtle rhetoric, Cage describes experimental music as "*the*" American movement, and then equates "America" with "the world" in describing the necessity of America taking the lead from the old European discourse. Such a blatant bid for hegemony reveals the profound cultural rivalry that existed at this time, at least on the American side.

In conclusion, we have seen that the musical avant-garde is far from unitary. The antagonism between the two main movements — postserialist modernism and experimental postmodernism — can be summarized at three levels. They are distinguished, first, by their different relations to popular music and culture; second, by the absence or presence of a supraformalist concern with the social and political dimensions of cul-

Modernism/ Serialism, Postserialism	Postmodernism/ Experimental Music
Determinism	Indeterminism, nondeterminism
Rationalism	Irrationalism, mysticism
Scientism, universalism	Sociopoliticization
Cerebral, complex	Physical, performative, simple
Text-centered	Practice-centered
Linear, cumulative, teleological	Cyclical, repetitive, static

Within a unity of difference to popular music

Nonreference, absolute difference, nonacknowledgment	Reference, transformation

Within a unity on technology

Scientistic, theoreticist	Empiricist, artisanal
High-tech, institutional	Low-tech bricolage, entrepreneurial

Institutional base

East Coast universities	West Coast, art colleges, art institutions
Institutionally and state-backed	Self-employed, performance-backed

1.   The antagonistic counterpoint of musical modernism and postmodernism.

ture; and third, and related to this, by conflicting technological discourses and the use of different technologies.

The differentiation between the two movements involves a continuous counterpoint, an unfolding, antagonistic dialogue at times explicit, at others implicit. In this process, the postmodern experimental tradition is defined against postserialist modernism through a series of negations (Figure 1). And since the postmodern tendency to negation itself repeats a defining characteristic of modernism, it also embodies a basic discursive continuity. Thus the history of the two avant-gardes shows an internal pattern of simultaneous negation or opposition and continuity. We can describe the relation between the two factions abstractly as "*A* to *not A*": a relation of antagonistic or oppositional kinship; whereas the relation between these two traditions and popular culture and music has been one of absolute difference, in abstract terms "*A* to *B*," the other basic form of difference. Popular music is either unaddressed (by serialist modernists), or held as an "other" to be represented, drawn upon as a source or influence (by postmodernists).

We have seen that the "innovations" often attributed to postmodernism have earlier precedents. Neither reference to nor representation of the musical "other" are new, nor is a concern with the social functions of art; they are also evident in some early century musical modernism. The evidence of this analysis, then, is that postmodernism is defined in the first instance through a negation of modernism, that it remains locked into an implicit and antagonistic dialogue with modernism, and that throughout the century this has been the basis of its turning to the "other." The counterpoint of modernism and postmodernism may thus be conceived as a continuous and centripetal antinomy, a kind of mobile stasis. Two unities bind the antinomy: a belief in the necessity, and the exploration, of technology (increasingly evident from the postserialist period); but above all the assertion of difference from popular music and culture. In this sense, modernist abstention from any aesthetic reference to popular musics is the "stronger" and more absolute statement against which later postmodernisms rebel, but without breaking free completely from this defining discursive trope. Modernist aesthetic nonacknowledgment of popular music therefore represents the more extreme denial of the rival aesthetic discourse, its (persecuted and persecuting) obliteration as an object of reference or interest. By contrast, postmodern reference to and transformation of popular music involves a less extreme splitting. That is, although some postmodern composition evidences aesthetic and broader sociocultural awareness of the "other," this is no "neutral" acknowledgment of difference but, implicitly, another form of attempted control or domination — a statement that popular music, rather than being adequate in itself, must be brought into the ambit of art music for the full realization of its aesthetic potential.

Thus the most enduring, unchanging discursive feature uniting musical modernism and postmodernism — the assertion and determined maintenance of difference from popular music — is the one that is most imbued with varying degrees of splitting, denial and omnipotence. It may be conceived in terms of an antidiscursive denial that is both at times a purposeful and conscious offense, and a psychic-aesthetic defense. Popular music remains, for modernist and postmodernist composers, an "other" to be either ignored, or reformed, reworked, controlled at the composer's will.

We are now in a position to grasp, in advance, that many significant features of IRCAM culture and of Boulez's ideology — the founding principle, the "necessity" of bringing technology and science into music; the concern with new media, sound materials and forms; the self-conscious vanguardism and preoccupation with constant innovation; the theoreticism; the formalism, linked to an absence of critical concern with the social and political dimensions of culture; the notion of a necessary alienation from the general public; and the antagonism toward commerce and toward popular music and culture — all of these are prefigured both by the general historical character of artistic modernism, and by its mutated expression in the serialist/postserialist tradition of musical modernism as revealed by its counterpoint with musical postmodernism.

CHAPTER III

Background

IRCAM's Conditions of Existence

THE INTERNATIONAL CONTEXT: AMERICAN COMPUTER MUSIC NETWORKS

IRCAM is an institutional manifestation of particular forms of French cultural life, but it exists within and is part of a broader international context. The most significant element of this context is not European but transatlantic: IRCAM has been greatly influenced by and dependent upon the American computer music scene. Computer music developed in the United States in the 1960s in universities with large mainframe computing facilities. To gain access to these, composers had to ally themselves with electronic engineering, computer science, or cognitive psychology labs, the latter researching perception, information processing, and artificial intelligence (AI). Computer music thus grew up, usually unofficially, on the back of powerful academic and commercial interests that were in turn often linked to the defense sector.[1]

Two major American centers had an enormous influence on IRCAM from its inception. Stanford University's Center for Computer Research in Music and Acoustics (CCRMA) was the model for IRCAM's original infrastructure in 1975–76. CCRMA itself emerged from the Stanford Artificial Intelligence Laboratory (SAIL), a leading AI center heavily involved in defense contracts.

The decision to use Stanford was taken by Max Mathews, director of Bell Telephone Laboratories' Acoustics Research department, who is known in the vernacular as the "father of computer music." Mathews became, around 1975, IRCAM's first Scientific Director, from which time IRCAM and Bell Labs have also had close contact. Bell Labs is the research base of the giant AT&T telecommunications multinational, known globally for its basic communications research. Mathews had a major role in the early development of computer music, which he fostered at Bell Labs as an informal pastime and which became a passion in his research sector. He wrote one of the earliest computer music synthesis programs (Music V) and produced the first definitive text on the subject (Mathews 1969).[2]

Despite Mathews's input, IRCAM's early computing environment was perceived by some visiting Americans as unprofessional and bureaucratic. An apocryphal story illustrates what was seen as the inept attitude taken by the French bureaucracy and a clash of cultures. An American consultant systems programmer was brought over in 1976 to work on the main computer, the PDP10, and get it going. When he arrived at IRCAM, he found that the institute operated only during the office day, rather than a full twenty-four hours as do all self-respecting American computer centers. He also found the PDP10's memory size very limited. The story goes that the French IRCAM Administrator noticed the programmer sitting around reading sci-fi magazines all day long and asked finally, "Why aren't you working?" The programmer replied: "I don't have anything to work with!" He demanded more memory for the machine, and twenty-four-hour opening, until which time he would sit in his hotel room reading comics. After many battles with the Administration the programmer won, and IRCAM invested in more computing power and round-the-clock hours.

By the late '70s, IRCAM's computing environment had expanded to become one of the best facilities in France, so that French and American researchers were keen to come. Throughout the early period and until the mid-1980s, IRCAM remained heavily dependent on American computer music expertise and also on the technologies that these researchers brought with them. For example, in 1977 two of IRCAM's five sections — the Computer and Diagonal departments — were manned mainly by Americans. One was headed by a young American composer, and contained a Stanford researcher who soon became a leading figure in a rival commercial American outfit and a psychoacoustician from Michigan State University who later became the director of the Pedagogy department, a man who had been recommended to IRCAM by Babbitt. The Stanford CCRMA and Michigan State researchers brought over and installed invaluable software without which the computing environment could not have functioned properly. Important early help on IRCAM's real-time hardware project was provided by a senior Bell engineer and leading American music technologist, Hal Alles. In 1980, a Stanford researcher was still being used to write important software for IRCAM's 4C machine (Manning 1985, 253), while in 1984 American consultants to Bell were brought over to rework IRCAM's main computer operating system.

Cultural tensions and aesthetic, technological, and political conflicts abounded in the early period between the Americans and French. Mathews had been appointed over certain French directors' heads, and conflicts of scientific policy ensued. For example, Mathews and others proposed that IRCAM should not develop large hardware but should work on an area — real-time gestural control — neglected then, and largely since, by IRCAM (Mathews and Bennett 1978). They were defeated, and under its French and Italian directors the prototype hardware project continued apace. This signaled a debate that would remain central within IRCAM over the appropriateness of pouring resources into the development of basic signal processing hardware as opposed to more musically oriented hardware and software.

Mathews and Boulez had antipathies, differences of aesthetic and philosophy, that are related in stories that form part of IRCAM's mythology. For example, in the early days, Mathews was known to be obsessed with designing and making by hand an electronic, fretted violin that would interface to a computer. Eventually he built such an instrument (and also made one for postmodern pop star Laurie Anderson). The story goes that Mathews, bursting with excitement, rushed to tell Boulez that he had just succeeded in finding the key to the design problem of the fretted violin. Instead of sharing Mathews's pleasure, Boulez greeted the news with a certain ill-disguised *sang-froid* bordering on distaste. This was not Boulez's vision of inspired computer music applications. Mathews soon quit the job of Scientific Director, the first to experience its difficulties, and significantly, all Scientific Directors since have been French. Yet Mathews continued to be a consultant and to visit IRCAM.

According to another story, stormy relations between Boulez and a promising young American researcher blew up over a piece of the young man's music that Boulez dismissed as light. The researcher left after a couple of years, which caused some regret at IRCAM, since he blossomed into a leading talent in the field. This man became head of the computer audio division of Lucasfilm, an American firm working on similar technologies, and other ex-IRCAM researchers have since followed him there. By '84, the Lucasfilm group had produced the nearest, although more generalized and powerful, rival to IRCAM's hardware prototype: a machine called the ASP (Audio Signal Processor).

This points to another important and unlikely American link for IRCAM. Lucasfilm is the entertainment group responsible for the *Star Wars* and *Indiana Jones* film series. But rather than just producing mass entertainment movies, Lucasfilm also supports advanced computer audio and graphics research for application in its films, video games, and so on. The ASP, for example, is a real-time digital sound processor aimed at synthesizing, editing, and mixing together a complete film soundtrack. It was designed not only to be used in-house to produce the soundtrack of the movie *Indiana Jones and the Temple of Doom*, but also to be industrialized and sold to the film industry (Lehrman 1985). IRCAM's American circuit thus includes both academic institutions and commercial telecommunications and entertainment giants who are major rivals, and advisers, in the production of computer audio technologies.

But whether academic or commercial, a key difference between these American outfits and IRCAM is the smoother relations that obtain between basic computer-audio research and its industrial and commercial exploitation. For years, IRCAM's attempts to industrialize the products of its research were frustrated, and this proved one of the key sources of internal and external contention. In comparison, the characters of Bell Labs, Lucasfilm, and Stanford show the very different links between basic research and commercial applications in the United States. A significant example from the academic sector was the development by the director of Stanford's CCRMA, composer John Chowning, of a very powerful digital-synthesis technique by frequency modulation (FM) in the '60s and '70s. The FM technique was sold to the Japanese Yamaha corporation in a very profitable deal that effectively made the CCRMA self-financing.[3] It is this technique that underwrote the first generation of small commercial digital music technologies in the 1980s.

American personnel continued to be important to IRCAM during the 1980s. In 1984, five young Americans had significant roles, three as directors of projects — one of whom was also a key IRCAM composer, while another was informally Boulez's personal assistant. A Stanford graduate was IRCAM's main psychoacoustician, and a Michigan State graduate was IRCAM's most able computer scientist — known as a "wizard." By the '90s there had been a shift away from the dependence on American staff, no doubt partly related to the increased possibilities of finding suitably qualified French researchers. Yet throughout IRCAM's existence, exchanges with both the commercial and academic

American computer music research groups have continued. (Others include UCSD's Computer Audio Research Laboratory (CARL), and the
MIT Media Lab's Experimental Music Studio.) Commonly, IRCAM's
computer consultants come from one of these centers, and IRCAM researchers, when they leave, go to work in them. While working at
IRCAM allows Americans to enjoy a pleasant sojourn in Paris, the main
attractions of leaving IRCAM are not only that frustrated researchers
will be far better paid in the States but that they will be able to contribute
to technologies that may be commercially developed and reach a wider
public. Personnel exchanges thus link these institutions into a network
within which researchers whose skills are in demand can roam.

As the experience of American researchers at IRCAM testifies, however, it is the more immediate context of French cultural life, a constellation of discrete aspects of French national culture and cultural politics,
both historical and contemporary, that individually resonate with, and
converge to produce, the character of IRCAM. IRCAM culture is situated in a space that is crossed by both artistic and technological inflections of the rhetoric of modern French nationalism—a rhetoric that
uncannily unites the political Left and Center-Right.

ASPECTS OF FRENCH CULTURE
AND CULTURAL POLITICS

The existence of centralized, highly privileged institutions has long been
characteristic of the organization of French cultural life. More generally,
the French polity consists of a highly centralized bureaucratic administration centered on Paris, with local administration largely an extension of central government. The origins of this situation go back to the
French Revolution of 1789, from which time centralization and rationalization of administration, education, and so on came to be associated
with the progressive goals of ending inherited privilege and extending
equality of opportunity to all citizens. Thus the state has fostered centralized, bureaucratized, and privileged institutions in both the arts and
sciences (Avril 1969), even when it has acted in the name of popular
democracy.

Another feature of the modern period has been the important role
accorded to intellectual, cultural, and technocratic elites in French administration, and indeed the importance of technology in political self-
definitions of French identity. One source of these tendencies is the
theory of the avant-garde enunciated in the influential writings of the

utopian socialists Saint-Simon and Fourier in the 1830s (Manuel 1956, Shapiro 1976).

Saint-Simon first applied the term "avant-garde" to culture, referring to revolutionary "artist-engineers." In this he drew an analogy with the term's military use, for a scouting party that goes out ahead of the main force and initiates a skirmish. In his broader political vision, government was to be by an elite at once intellectual, industrial, and managerial, embodied by a Chamber of Inventions composed of engineers, poets and writers, painters, architects, and musicians. Saint-Simon's utopia thus centered on a dialogue between artists, scientists, and engineers, with artists having a leading role in the imaginative exploration of reality. His advocacy of the progressive social and political functions of the arts and sciences put them on equal footing and enjoined them to engage with each other and with modern industrial applications. Saint-Simon's ideas therefore led not only to the view of the artistic avant-garde as a leading force, and to a belief in its political role, but they also herald the fascination of modern artists half a century later with technology and science.

Elements of this nexus of beliefs have tended to come into play during periods of deep crisis in French society — following World War II and the events of 1968, for example. They were reconfigured in different ways by both Charles de Gaulle and Georges Pompidou as a means of reconstructing the national culture and unifying the nation (as before, prototypically, it had been unified in the Revolution). On de Gaulle's accession to power in 1959, an aggressive technological nationalism, at once civil-industrial and military, was his hallmark. De Gaulle's effort to rebuild France as a leading world power included a modernization program with three goals: military and economic independence and, central to both of these, technological leadership (McDougall 1985). Behind this strategy lay the nationalist desire to throw off the military, economic, and technological dependence upon the United States within which France had been enmeshed since World War II, but also the perceived threat from the Soviet Union and rivalries toward the rest of Europe, notably Germany. By the late 1960s these policies had generated the highly successful growth of the defense industry and of the civil nuclear power program, and both were implicated in the appearance, beginning in the 1960s, of a mass of spin-off, state-backed, high-technology research and development programs.

During the 1970s, Center-Right governments continued to give the highest priority to technology-led economic development, and under Mitterrand after 1981 the Socialist administration followed in the same

direction (Petras 1984). These policies have been paralleled by a profound restructuring of the political Left in the period since the crisis of
1968, including the eventual disintegration of the French antinuclear
movement and, at the same time, a decline in Left critiques of and wider
political debate about new technology (Johnstone 1984). All of this has
resulted in the dominance of a unifying technological and pronuclear
nationalism across the political spectrum, which in turn has had implications for the cultural milieu within IRCAM.

In 1959, de Gaulle set up the Ministry of Culture under André Malraux, with the nationalist task of promoting a leading role for the French
arts worldwide as well as nationally. A network of provincial "*Maisons
de la Culture*" was set up that, under Malraux's pedagogic policies, was
charged with taking great art to the people. By the 1970s, however, the
basic character of cultural policy was changing. The idea of promoting a
"national culture" came increasingly under attack as an alibi for state
subsidy of the elite arts, while at the same time the mass media were
charged with spreading cultural homogeneity and encouraging passivity.
The definition of "culture" was contested: in postmodern vein, it began
to be identified with cultural diversity and difference.

Under Jack Lang, Socialist minister of culture appointed in May
1981, the new cultural politics became official. Lang, who was previously the organizer of the innovative Festival of Nancy, proposed a
view of culture as involving the creative capacity of all, as experiential
rather than didactic. Culture was not to be conceived as a national entity,
but as consisting of different and incommensurable forms. Even as a
minister, Lang appeared to align himself with the margins in arguing that
"all cultural action must be against power" (Zeldin 1983: 365). It is an
interesting contradiction that as part of the Socialists' well-publicized
post-election gesture of doubling the budgets for education and culture,
Lang's Ministry continued to give great support to powerful cultural
institutions such as IRCAM, and that this continued throughout the
1980s.

We can discern in this history opposed cultural political ideologies
that align around the oppositions centralization and decentralization,
paternalism and populism, elitism and pluralism/difference — oppositions that themselves resonate with tensions between modernist and
postmodernist discourses. Yet the alignments are unstable, just as their
association with the political Right and Left is unpredictable.

The complexity is well illustrated by the cultural policies of President

Pompidou during his 1969–74 premiership. In the aftermath of the crisis of 1968, Pompidou brought renewed ambition to the Gaullist aim of reconstructing the national culture. Rather than decentralized yet pedagogic institutions, as under Malraux, Pompidou initiated a program of centralized cultural institutions that were to be forward-looking and contemporary but also aimed at a large public. The prototype was the Centre Georges Pompidou (CGP), the new National Museum of Contemporary Art, of which Pompidou and his wife took personal charge. Pompidou wanted the CGP to be a European innovation in the development of a centralized yet popular contemporary culture. Here we see a crucial shift within the polyvalent reigning ideology whereby it is proposed that centralization and fine art are compatible with populism. This policy continued throughout the '70s and '80s under governments of both Center-Right and Left, and produced several massive projects: the new national science and technology museum at *La Villette*, the new museum of French art — the *Musée d'Orsay* — and the new national *Opéra de la Bastille*.

The founding of IRCAM originates in these developments. The IRCAM idea came from Pompidou's invitation to Boulez, at the time that he was planning the CGP, to take part in the reconstruction of French artistic life after '68. IRCAM thus became the music wing of the new Centre. The institute was the result of personal contact between the president and Boulez as a leading artist-intellectual, of a convergence of their distinct visions, and of placing power directly into the hands of Boulez — an indication of the prominent role French intellectuals have been able to claim in public life and political office.[4]

There is another, related force common to both eras of nationalist policy: the desire to recreate a leading international role for French culture in the world at large, a role that is thought to belong rightfully to France and to have been lost or "stolen." This in turn depends on historical changes in international artistic hegemony.

The most important such change in modern times was the shift in leadership of the international art world from Paris to New York soon after World War II. Guilbaut (1983) shows the contribution of this shift to the broader establishment of postwar American hegemony through the policies of the Marshall Plan and the ideology of the Cold War. Although his analysis centers on painting, it concerns dynamics within modernism that, as I suggested in the previous chapter discussing Cage's rivalry with European serialism, also affected the musical avant-garde.

For the first half of the century, Parisian art had represented the height of Western culture, and Paris was considered the center of modernist thought. But in the aftermath of World War II, a series of factors — economic decimation, chronic political and social division — led to the extreme politicization of Parisian art and a chaotic fragmentation in which there was no space for the consolidation of a new avant-garde.

Meanwhile, during the late 1940s, leading American art critics such as Greenberg claimed that a truly national American style — abstract expressionism — had arrived in the work of artists such as Pollock and Rothko. This was simultaneous with the emergence of a large, new, American middle-class market for painting. Over the next decade, "ab ex" became the artistic spearhead for American culture at the same time that, in Cold War rhetoric, America began to be portrayed as the symbol of a universal Western culture, as the guardian of freedom and liberal human values. Gradually, abstract expressionism became the dominant international avant-garde.

Central to this shift was a subtle transition from the perception of abstract expressionism as a national American style to its perception as an international style representing a universal humanism and liberalism. This, in turn, was possible because of a second process: the depoliticization of the American avant-garde and its embrace of a purely formal artistic ideology.[5] The core of this was the notion, proclaimed by Greenberg and other champions of the style, that free, formal experiment itself enshrined the liberal values of spiritual independence and human freedom. This metaphorical reading of the relation between artistic form and politics, which as I argued in the previous chapter has recurred periodically in the ideology of the modernist avant-garde, was framed during the Cold War against the Stalinist suppression of modernism and imposition of socialist realism throughout the Soviet bloc.

In this way, in the immediate postwar period, America achieved an international hegemony in the arts to match its global political-economic power.[6] This history illustrates several issues. First, the mutual cultural fascination and rivalry, with shifting dominance and dependence, that has characterized modern cultural relations between America and France. Second, the depoliticization of the modernist avant-garde in the postwar period. And third, the tension within the avant-garde between nationalism (or localism) and internationalism, between the assertion of an authentically new, different voice and the expansive, almost imperialistic assertion of artistic leadership that respects no boundaries.[7] All of these are relevant to Boulez's own history, and to the analysis of IRCAM.

PIERRE BOULEZ AND THE MODERNIZATION
OF MUSICAL LIFE

Despite the postwar disarray of the French arts described earlier, the 1950s saw innovative developments in contemporary music. This was in line with the simultaneous growth of a postwar musical avant-garde elsewhere in Europe—particularly Germany and Italy—and in the United States. There were two important innovations of this kind in France, against the background of an essentially conservative musical establishment, and both were the origins of lasting developments. One was the rise of a school of electro-acoustic composition known as *musique concrète*, with an institutional base within the French Radio (RTF) that came to be known as the *Groupe de Recherches Musicales* (GRM). The other key development was the founding, by Boulez, of an organization called the *Domaine Musical* devoted to producing regular concert series of contemporary and twentieth-century composition.[8]

The first development centered on Pierre Schaeffer, a technician-turned-composer at RTF who, beginning in 1948, using the recording technologies and studios of the Radio, laid the foundations of the field of electro-acoustic music. Schaeffer's *musique concrète* compositions were based on the manipulation of taped natural sounds—vocal, instrumental, and other ambient, even industrial, sounds and noises—by editing, reversal, and speed changes. In the 1950s and 1960s the GRM became a focus for many young composers and fostered an important French school of electro-acoustic composition and research; for a period, this lay claim to be the main French avant-garde. Other approaches to electronic music were emerging simultaneously in Germany and the United States, yet Schaeffer was the pioneer of an influential technique and aesthetic.

Well-known composers visited Schaeffer's studio in its early days, including Boulez and Stockhausen. Both left dissatisfied and became in different ways rivals and critics. Stockhausen became involved in the GRM's main European rival, the studio of the West German Radio in Cologne, which generated an alternative approach to electronic music in this period known as *Elektronische Musik*.

Boulez, by contrast, did not continue an involvement in electronics and made known his strong reservations about the GRM. He created a stir by denouncing Schaeffer's approach to electronic composition as unsophisticated and inadequate. The main criticism was that *musique concrète* was untheorized and empiricist. The '50s were the period of serialist ascendance, led by Boulez, Stockhausen, and others, and any compositional technique not integrating these concerns was subject to question. The *concrète* technique took "ready-made" taped sounds and manipulated them empirically, manually, in the studio to make the piece. A score was produced, if at all, after the piece was completed rather than as a prior conceptualization — unlike the mode of the serialist avant-garde, who worked to preconceived and highly theorized plans and scores. Further, Schaeffer was trained as an engineer, not as a musician, and was thus vulnerable to the charge of not being a legitimate voice on compositional developments. This illustrates well the pronounced factionalism of the '50s and '60s avant-garde.

Despite Boulez's critique, Schaeffer was in fact a theorist. Beginning in the early '50s, he produced a great deal of research around *musique concrète* on issues central to the electronic and computer music fields, culminating in a formidable treatise, *Traité des Objets Musicaux* (1966). The research pursued by his group included the following: analysis of recorded sounds so as to be able to represent them visually in score form, documentation of the technical basis of tape and electronic music, and analysis of the timbres of nonmusical as well as musical sounds, which Schaeffer, following Schoenberg's concept of *Klangfarbenmelodie*, considered an important new structural dimension of music. Schaeffer proposed the notion of a "*solfège*," or basic syntax, of timbres that could provide a structural basis for *musique concrète*. The research therefore involved both acoustics and psychoacoustics, and although similar work was starting in other countries, Schaeffer's group were the originators in France.

By 1957 the various areas of research were brought together under the new generic term, "music research," and the studio took the name that it continues to hold, *Groupe de Recherches Musicales*. The Greek composer Xenakis, exiled in Paris from 1947, also visited the GRM studio. By the late '50s and early '60s, Xenakis and Schaeffer were following Stockhausen's lead — (Stockhausen's piece *Gesang der Jünglinge* (1955–56) was the first to combine natural recorded sounds with purely electronic synthesized sounds) — and producing works combining electronic and taped acoustic sounds. Xenakis, who like Schaeffer was trained as an engineer and was adept at mathematics, began to experiment with the computer as a data processor for musical composition and as a source of synthetic sound (Manning 1985). Thus Xenakis became the first composer in France to investigate the potential of computers for musical work.

We can now perceive the relations between the GRM and IRCAM as it came into being in the 1970s. On the one hand there are continuities largely unacknowledged by Boulez at the time. Thus, in many of the developments emanating from the GRM in the mid-1950s and early 1960s, major dimensions of IRCAM were already present. The concept of music research, the involvement of acoustics and psychoacoustics in the compositional milieu, the pursuit of timbre as a conveyor of structure: all became important to IRCAM. In this sense, Boulez's polemical rejection of Schaeffer and of the GRM is ironic.

On the other hand, IRCAM's approach has commonly been understood as involving a strong rejection or negation of GRM aesthetics and technology in line with Boulez's early critique, so that his antagonism toward the GRM has been seen as a prime motive for the emergent conception of IRCAM. Indeed, we will see in chapter 9 how techniques and technologies associated with *musique concrète* — tape recording, analog electronics — were subject to an almost irrational neglect and indifference within IRCAM culture.

The GRM was, then, the original French model for a music and technology center, and until the rise of IRCAM it retained a position as the leading center in France. However, the GRM has never enjoyed the status of IRCAM. It is not an autonomous and dedicated institution; it is smaller and more national in scope. Thus, when IRCAM came along in the 1970s, although the two institutions became rivals, it effortlessly surpassed the GRM.

In 1954 Boulez founded the *Domaine Musical*, and for over a decade the concert series promoted by this organization were the main arena for the performance of avant-garde music in France. Boulez remained both musical director and the main conductor until his departure in 1967. In 1968, as its prestige grew, the *Domaine* moved to a large venue, the Théâtre de la Ville, where it continued until 1973. Boulez's model for the organization was Schoenberg's Society for Private Musical Performances, which Schoenberg had set up in the context of extreme hostility to the new music of the Second Viennese School. The influence of Schoenberg on Boulez and others of the postwar generation, then, was not limited to aesthetic matters.

The following sympathetic account of the *Domaine* conveys its activities, ideology, and the respect which it gained within intellectual and artistic circles.

> Pierre Boulez created this organization in order to fight against the irresponsibility and uninterest of the public and private powers that be toward contemporary music. During the first fifteen years . . . the *Domaine Musical*

revealed to the French public a hundred major classic works of contemporary music that had hitherto been neglected (Schoenberg, Berg, Varèse, Webern, Stravinsky) and premiered more than two hundred new works by around sixty composers of the young generation. . . . The *Domaine Musical* concerts, at first criticized and mocked in reactionary circles, played a leading role in French postwar musical life.

(Menger 1983, 219, taken from C. Rostand,
Dictionnaire de Musique Contemporaine,
Paris 1970, my translation).

The *Domaine* thus began as an esoteric and elite meeting point of the avant-garde, countering established views and courting official disapproval. Yet by the late '60s and '70s it had become a central feature of high cultural life. Where Schoenberg's Society lasted only two years, Boulez's *Domaine* grew over the nineteen years of its existence into a well-attended and state-backed venture: it entered the cultural establishment.

Apparently set up against "public and private powers," the patronage upon which the *Domaine* depended indicates its far-from-marginal social and cultural milieu. For the first seasons, funds were provided by the Renaud-Barrault theater company, of which Boulez was then musical director. But soon the concerts were taken up by Mme Suzanne Tézenas, wealthy Parisian wife of an industrialist and patron of avant-garde artistic circles. Her salon drew together members of the haute bourgeoisie with a circle of intellectuals and artists who supported the *Domaine* by subscriptions (Menger 1983).[9] Tézenas, interviewed by Menger, evokes the scene thus:

> I knew Pierre Boulez in 1948, well before he became musical director at Jean-Louis Barrault's. It was P. Souvtchinsky, Russian *emigré* prince and musicologist, who brought him to me: Souvtchinsky was part of Messiaen's analysis class. . . . Boulez came to dinner here with some writer friends. . . . Souvtchinsky had a great influence upon Boulez, together they brewed up the idea of the *Domaine Musical.* . . .
>
> At the start . . . there were, as always, snobs who were looking for novelty. Many of these lacked nerve and dropped out. But there were Nicolas de Staël, Mathieu, the important abstract painters, Michaux, Jouve, Char, Mandiargues, all great friends, gallery directors. . . . There were gatherings here, at my home, to launch the concerts. . . . For ten years, after each concert, until Boulez left in 1966, I gave receptions. The composers used to stay talking until two in the morning.
>
> There were society people, writers, painters, art dealers . . . all visiting foreigners came through here. I was very close to Gaétan Picon who met Boulez here and who helped us when he [Picon] became director of Arts and Literature [a major section of the Ministry of Culture].

(Menger 1983, 222–23, my translation)

This quote conveys the operations of patronage by a social and cultural elite and Tézenas's self-conscious role as catalyst. An IRCAM director remembered Tézenas's receptions as "the last salons in Paris," and Menger notes (ibid, 223) that hers were the latest in a line of salons in which a mix of wealthy and intellectual Parisians came together to confer upon the current avant-garde — here upon Boulez, son of a provincial industrialist — a powerful social legitimacy.

The *Domaine* thus became a point of contact, merging, and conversion between cultural and economic power. By the early '60s, the state began to make a contribution — some 11 percent of funds for the 1963 season, while about 57 percent came from private gifts and subscriptions (Menger 1983, 232) — thereby adding to the legitimation of the organization. Menger argues that this was but the first step on the way to the official "consecration" of Boulez, a process consummated with the massive state backing for IRCAM.

The account by Souvtchinsky of his discovery of Boulez, which Menger calls wryly a "messianic vision" (ibid, 222), illustrates the pronounced mystification surrounding the notion of talent and its emergence, and shows Boulez as the recipient of projections of charisma and mystery:

> The appearance of a "new discovery" is always an unforeseen event. . . . The "new talent" never arrives alone: there are precursors, an entourage, promotion, rivals; but the lines, the historical currents alight in each epoch . . . with a curious self-evidence, upon a single personality whereupon the "discovery" is transformed into the "chosen" or "elect." Simply . . . Boulez was very quickly ranked at the highest levels of the hierarchy of musical phenomena of his generation. . . . One should never forget that all creativity, and particularly artistic creativity, is an eminently, mysteriously, hierarchical phenomenon.
>
> (Menger 1983, 222, my translation)

Boulez was therefore already in the early '50s, a few years after arriving in Paris as an unknown student, moving in exalted circles, meeting patrons and future cultural officials, and becoming known for his charismatic sectarianism. But as well as a platform for his own career, the *Domaine* became a gateway to success for other composers, an arena in which careers were made or broken, since a successful debut bestowed legitimation and recognition. One composer recalled the process for Menger: "The *Domaine* exercised such a fascination over people that, once a composer had been played there, they became somebody. I always remember the year that Betsy Jolas was played for the first time, it was as though she'd been given the *Légion d'honneur*. It was like being recognized" (Menger 1983, 226, my translation). Another described it thus: "At the time of the *Domaine*, the only sanction worth giving to a work was not the reaction of an anonymous public but the judgment of equals; the notion of success didn't exist, only recognition by one's peers" (Menger 1983, 225, my translation). Thus legitimacy came not from the positive response of the general public, which was disdained, but from the judgment of the elite circle of the *Domaine*. This process was complemented by another: the *Domaine* programs included older works selected by Boulez to represent the classics of the modern era. But this selection did not reflect extant judgments — (it was initially scandalous to the establishment) — so much as construct them, creating a canon of great modern works and composers in the postwar vacuum in which none yet existed. This strategy of complementary processes of legitimation, of the old and of the new, is also a feature of IRCAM.

The *Domaine* exhibits, finally, the tension between nationalism and internationalism characteristic of the avant-garde. Drawing on new music from different countries, electing a genealogy of international (mainly European) forefathers, hosting international celebrities as they passed through Paris, the *Domaine* set out to express and influence international musical currents, to imprint Boulez's canon upon the musical world, and to impress an international bourgeoisie and intelligentsia. But it did so on the basis of the strongest national foundations. In this sense, Boulez was a vessel for the broader cultural-political desires of the '50s and '60s. Compared with the relatively parochial horizons of the GRM in the same period, Boulez's *Domaine* had wider geographical reach and deeper historical ambition, and IRCAM was later to continue the *Domaine*'s tradition of internationalism.

BOULEZ'S CAREER

Surveying Boulez's life and work, two strategies stand out as having enabled him to attain great cultural authority, and so to accumulate the cultural capital necessary for the founding of IRCAM. One is his combination, unmatched by all but a few major figures of the postwar avant-garde, of productive and reproductive skills in distinct but interrelated areas of his work: as a composer, as a conductor, and as a theorist, writer, polemicist, and educator. In this way he has controlled every aspect of musical discourse: its production, but also the conditions of its production — its reproduction (performance, theorization, diffusion through education), and so its legitimation. In addition, Boulez has been active in cultural politics both nationally and at the highest international levels. He has had a pivotal role in linking France to international music currents, thereby combining national and international prestige.

Boulez's career can be divided into three phases.[10] The first is his rise to fame, from the mid-1940s to the early 1960s. Boulez is remembered in the late '40s and early '50s in Paris as a student leader who engaged in "terrorist" actions and wrote polemical articles against the musical establishment. His denunciations attacked many major figures, even those from whom he had learned much: Schoenberg, Stravinsky, Brahms, Messiaen. His most notorious polemic, "Schoenberg is dead" (Middleton 1978, 60–61, from 1951), accused Schoenberg of failing to carry through the revolution instigated with serialism, of having recourse to outdated romantic forms. Having purged the technique of Schoenberg's "mistakes," Boulez announced that serialism alone was the way forward for music. This laid the groundwork for what became the dominant '50s avant-garde development, total serialism, in which, as we have seen, the structuralist principles of serialism were extended to dimensions of music other than pitch. Boulez described his leadership of total serialism thus: "I momentarily suppressed inheritance . . . and went on to see how one might construct a musical language from scratch" (Heyworth 1973a, 61). In this way he constructs a complete break within music history: a crisis has occurred necessitating a new language. This remains the central theme in all his work.

Boulez's writings established a genealogy for his own work by portraying Schoenberg and then Webern, despite their failings, as the prophets of future music. With another text, "Eventuellement . . ." (1952), also advocating serialism, his early writings became quasi-manifestos for the young European avant-garde. The following quotes from these texts convey Boulez's polemical force: "It is not devilry but only the most ordinary common sense which makes me say that, since the discoveries made by the Viennese, all composition other than twelve-tone [serialism] is *useless*" (Boulez 1951, quoted in Middleton 1978, 61). And: "I assert that any musician who has not experienced . . . the necessity for the dodecaphonic [serialist] language is *useless*. His whole work is irrelevant to the needs of his epoch" (Heyworth 1973a, 59). Boulez's early polemics attracted public notoriety, augmented his charisma, and drew followers around him.

Between 1954 and 1967, Boulez was conducting and directing the *Domaine Musical*, while the late '40s to early '60s were his most prolific and successful as a composer. During the same period, he ventured abroad to the major European centers of the avant-garde, developing strong links with two important West German centers. The first came from his close relations with the director of the *Südwestfunk* German radio in Baden-Baden, Heinrich Ströbel, who became his main German patron. Ströbel also ran a new-music festival at Donaueschingen that premiered many of Boulez's (and Stockhausen's) works. The other was Darmstadt, site of the annual International Summer Courses for New Music, which became famous as the rallying point of the new postwar European avant-garde. Adorno taught there regularly during the '50s, which may account for the echoes of his thought in Boulez's writings. But in general the traditions of German music and philosophy had a strong influence on Boulez, and he came to think of Germany as a second home. Boulez became one of the main teachers at Darmstadt, and beginning in the mid-1950s, the leading figure of the European avant-garde. His lectures of 1960, published as his first book (Boulez 1971), consolidated his theory of a new musical language based on total serialism.

The second phase of Boulez's career, from the early '60s to 1977, mainly saw a great expansion in his conducting activities and increasingly prestigious international work, which culminated in Boulez being simultaneously the Chief Conductor of two of the world's leading orchestras — the BBC Symphony, and the New York Philharmonic. In London, Boulez was successful as a conductor and cultural figure, but in New York he was less so, both with the public and with others in contemporary music. He outraged composers in a 1969 interview by insulting many dimensions of American new music. In 1970 a group of well-known, mainly West Coast (experimental) composers accused Boulez of "imperialistic thinking" for not including any Americans in a forthcoming festival (Heyworth 1973b, 71). From this period stem Boulez's unpopularity in the United States and controversial relations with American music.

Back in Europe, Boulez achieved one of the world's most prestigious opera conducting jobs, at Bayreuth, the home of Wagner, and he conducted the entire *Ring* cycle there in 1976 on the occasion of its hundredth anniversary. Boulez has since remained closely associated with Bayreuth, and we will see that he is often compared, and evokes comparison, with Wagner. Boulez also became involved in several high-profile French cultural political controversies. In 1964 Malraux, then minister of culture, set up a commission to report on French music as a prelude to creating the new *Direction de la Musique* within the Ministry. A struggle for power took place between two factions: one led by the composer

Marcel Landowski, the other by Boulez, who produced a plan for major reforms. Malraux rejected Boulez's ideas, and in a newspaper article of 1966 entitled "*Pourquoi je dis 'non' à Malraux*," Boulez bitterly criticized the minister and announced that he was henceforth "on strike" against the official organization of French music. Himself under attack in the French press, Boulez cut ties with the *Domaine*, the Paris Opera, the French orchestras, and went into self-imposed exile in Germany (Heyworth 1973b, 53). (It is ironic, from the vantage of the present, to note that Boulez's main criticism was that the administration of music should not be in the hands of "failed composers" — implying Landowski, Milhaud, and others from the rival faction — but needed specialized administrators [Boulez 1986, 443]. In less than a decade, Boulez would propose himself as Director of IRCAM.)

A couple of years later, Boulez agreed to help plan major reforms of the Paris Opera. But in May '68, when de Gaulle called on leading intellectuals to publicly support his government, Boulez and others resigned from the Opera project, and he lent his name to a Leftist intellectual statement criticizing the government. In the context of these volatile relations with the French state and its music policies during the '50s and '60s, Germany above all, but also Britain, became alternative musical, intellectual and political bases for Boulez. The effect of such controversies was therefore to divide public opinion and to make Boulez an even better-known and more controversial figure at home while also strengthening his international ties and reputation.

The third phase of Boulez's career, from 1977 on, is the period following his return to Paris to direct IRCAM. After the conflicts described, this had the air of the returning prodigal son. President Pompidou was apparently unhappy with the hostile relations between Boulez and French officialdom, and with Boulez's virtual exile for a decade. Over dinner at the Elysée Palace in 1970, Pompidou offered Boulez a *carte blanche* to design the new music research center that he had spoken of in recent years, thus inviting him to take part in the renewal of French culture after '68 and specifically in the CGP. With a massive Parisian concert series called *Passage du Vingtième Siècle* throughout 1977 announcing IRCAM's opening, Boulez's return drew great public attention and IRCAM was launched with a major canonical statement.

After the opening of IRCAM, Boulez's conducting career continued, associated especially with the *Ensemble Intercontemporain* (EIC), an orchestra founded by Boulez in 1976, dedicated to contemporary and modern music and destined to enjoy a special relationship with IRCAM.

Yet as several commentators have noted, his compositional output declined sharply after the mid-1960s. This has led to the suggestion that his commitments to IRCAM and to conducting represent spectacular, but misguided, attempts to overcome a compositional block (Heyworth 1973b, 72, 74–75). Since the start of IRCAM, Boulez's only major composition involving computer music technology has been a large-scale work called *Répons*.[11]

IRCAM'S LEGITIMATION:
FRENCH CONTEMPORARY MUSIC POLICY

Once founded, IRCAM — and Boulez as its head — became subject to the tensions and contradictions of French contemporary music policy as it developed after the late 1960s. The desire to "modernize" French musical life and to win for France a prestigious position in the international musical avant-garde led to policies that, while they gestured toward populism and diversification, manifested overall the general tendencies discussed in chapter 1: increased scale, centralization, bureaucratization, and rationalization in the management of contemporary music.

As the Ministry of Culture's director of music from 1967 to 1973, Landowski made substantial improvements in the diffusion of contemporary music. He gave state funding to an increasing number of performing ensembles and festivals dedicated to new music. For a period in the late '60s, these festivals, such as the *Semaines Musicales Internationales de Paris* (SMIP), were popular with a young audience for whom avant-garde music became associated with radical politics. By the '70s this audience was already in decline.

Music policy in the 1970s under Jean Maheu (later, in the '80s, President of the CGP and of IRCAM) witnessed a massive overall increase in the funding for contemporary music. The total budget rose from about four million francs in 1974 to about thirty million francs in 1978: a seven-fold increase (Menger 1980, 15). This included small increases in support for festivals and composers' commissions, but enormous increases for specialized ensembles and for a new phenomenon: what were called, echoing the title of the GRM, "centers of music research." These centers aimed to foster interrelated scientific research and technological development around music, as well as the production of new music itself. The number of centers increased exponentially: in 1973 there were just two, in 1975 four, in 1977 in addition to IRCAM there were six, by 1982

seventeen, and by 1984 twenty-five centers. This rapid growth received
its biggest boost after the Socialists came to power in 1981.

There are two points to note. One is that the main reason for the
enormous jump in funding between 1974 and 1978 was the arrival of
IRCAM itself, which began operating fully in 1977, and of its close
collaborator, the EIC. In addition, during this era state funding shifted
from the support of cultural diffusion toward the support of centralized
music production and music research, a shift that benefited IRCAM.
Thus, the music research centers took between them in 1978 nearly
half the contemporary music budget, of which the vast majority went
to IRCAM. However, this was still a small proportion of the state's
total music budget — a budget centered squarely on the major Parisian
institutions.[12]

The new music research policy involved, then, an unprecedented degree of centralization and rationalization. This was apparent both in the
transformation of the creative labor of composition from an individual
activity into an institutional process, and in its rationalization within a
division of labor including not just composition but also related scientific
research and technological development. The policy fostered centralization in the absolute dominance given to IRCAM over all the other centers and similarly, in the EIC's dominance over all other contemporary
music ensembles. IRCAM received on average more than thirteen times,
and the EIC about eight times, the funds of their nearest rivals. By 1978,
IRCAM's subsidy was 40 percent and the EIC's 30 percent of the total
state budget for contemporary music. IRCAM's preeminence was also
expressed in its greater scale, the unusual administrative autonomy and
legal status it was granted, and, compared with the mainly national
scope of the other centers, its internationalism. IRCAM's privilege therefore involved an entirely different scale of resources, operations, and
ambitions than the other French centers.

But IRCAM shared with the other centers the rationalization of the
musical "language" inherent in the scientific and technological terms of
music research. We saw earlier how the concept of music research arose
to subsume the studies made by Schaeffer's group around *musique concrète*. These studies included acoustic and psychoacoustic research and
were closely tied to their electro-acoustic and tape-based compositional
experiments. In this period of expansion and consolidation, music research came to be understood as a double process involving the analysis
of musical materials using appropriate technology and scientific knowl-

edge, with the potential to feed back into composition by creating new sound materials and musical structures as well as new technologies. Clearly, several aspects of music research — its technological orientation, scientism, and more generally its basis in a proliferation of intellectual and theoretical discourses around music — link it with general tendencies in modernism. Under the new policies of the 1970s and 1980s, this became the dominant and institutionalized rubric for contemporary music in France.

When the Socialists came to power in 1981 and doubled the state budgets for education and culture, IRCAM's funds also doubled from about fifteen to thirty million francs a year. But rather than simply increasing the funds to existing institutions, the Ministry's new director of music, Maurice Fleuret, set up a number of new music research centers and augmented their funds at a comparatively higher rate than IRCAM's. They included a couple in Paris, notably two studios for the composers Eloy and Henry (cofounder of *musique concrète*). But the majority were in regional cities (Lyon, Marseille, Aix, Grenoble, and so on). The move expressed a desire on the part of the Socialist administration to lessen the "monopoly" enjoyed by IRCAM and Boulez and the dominance of Parisian centers. It also illustrates how music research centers were often created around well-known composers. These "*centres autour des compositeurs*," strongly identified with their composer-directors, rivalrous and factional, seem partly to have functioned as individual "empires" set up by the state to reflect a composer's stature.[13]

Thus, under Fleuret, the boosted music budget was apparently used for classic French Socialist (and postmodern) ends: decentralization and diversification. Fleuret's ideology espoused musical pluralism and populism, based on the equal validity of different musics, of "*les musiques.*" It was known as "*une philosophie d'ouverture.*" He expressed it thus: "There is no unity, no common language. . . . For the first time . . . the West lives without a dominant theory. . . . [The administration of art] must first of all give to the maximum, to those who have none, the means to express themselves. . . . Everything [that is, funding] has been multiplied by two for [music] research and creation, also for jazz, improvised music, traditional and popular music. . . . We are above all else preoccupied with reducing artistic inequalities" (*Le Monde de la Musique* July 1984, 98, my translation). A junior official of Fleuret's regime explained: "Fleuret's principle was that we are not capable of judging today, so we must create a greater diversity of music to be heard and played; but above all not limit the possibilities by a judgment. . . . It was above all the idea that there's no official art and that one should allow all."

While Fleuret's radical pluralism potentially posed a threat to the centralized, rationalized position IRCAM had successfully established for itself, in practice this did not prove to be the case. There were two wings to his policies, but they were unequal. Although he started the first direct state intervention in popular music — regional training centers for singers, help with record distribution — it was relatively minor. By contrast, Fleuret poured resources into serious contemporary music via the new regional music research centers. This was the main expression of his decentralization/diversification policy, and popular music fared comparatively poorly. Further, the "regional" initiatives, rather than representing local developments, were often set up around ex-members of the GRM or IRCAM. For example in 1980, when a number of directors left IRCAM after a major internal reorganization, some were asked by Fleuret's deputy, Michel Decoust (also ex-IRCAM), to run new centers. Notably, local musicians, including those working in popular musics (jazz, rock, pop, *variété*) whose composition is also dependent on electro-acoustic studio work, did not gain access.

Thus Fleuret's decentralizing policy had little to do with authentic regionalism or with allowing very different (popular) music traditions access to electro-acoustic studios. He "opened out" the field, but in many cases by resourcing associates and dissidents from the two dominant institutions. The policy was largely driven by hostility to IRCAM's hegemony. One of Fleuret's main criticisms was that IRCAM favored a certain aesthetic, due to the dominating personality of Boulez. So the new centers were seen by Fleuret as a means of planting the seeds for different ideas and aesthetics to bloom. However, manned by people steeped in the traditions of the GRM and IRCAM — both widely held to have fostered "house styles" — the social and the aesthetic diversity of the centers was constrained. Paradoxically, the policy reinforced existing networks and paradigms. The "risks" of too great a cultural difference were thus avoided. Moreover the music research sector remained ridden by inequality: financial differentials lessened but were still great. These developments illustrate the contradictions and limits of the Socialist discourse of cultural pluralism and populism. As I suggested earlier in this chapter, Socialist policy continued to support, and to placate, existing forms of cultural power.

We can see some of the mechanisms in the wider negotiation of cultural power in the following developments. They also illustrate the polemical press comment and public controversy that have surfaced periodically throughout IRCAM's existence. In the early 1980s, after the internal reorganization, criticisms of IRCAM were being articulated not only by Fleuret but in polemical public debate. Boulez was accused of concentrating his power within IRCAM, of banishing opposition. The most stinging critiques of Boulez's "regime" were twin articles by Xenakis and Eloy that appeared in the pages of the newspaper *Le Matin* in January 1981. They were also extraordinarily strategic: months before the election that brought the Socialists in, both Eloy and Xenakis — known as a stalwart Socialist intellectual and a close friend of Fleuret's — outlined programs for redressing the crises in policy represented by what they argued were IRCAM's failings and abuses of power.

Eloy's article exemplifies the harsh tone of the polemic. Called "The reign of lies," it consists of a series of denunciations. Boulez has "always shown a distrust, indeed a dislike, for electro-acoustics." His aim is for IRCAM to follow the path of the United States, where computer music has been the "ultimate refuge for academic postserialism. . . . IRCAM [is] nothing but a projection of the will for power" (Eloy, *Le Matin* 26 January 1981, my translation).

In another scathing article, Eloy praised Xenakis in order, by implication, to damn Boulez: "Xenakis . . . is an ethical man, unlike the usual custom of the Parisian music milieu. Computer music, for him, is not at all a matter of Institutions and of domination: it is a tool to put at the service of men" (Eloy, *Le Monde de la Musique,* January 1982, my translation). Eloy continued that IRCAM was technologically out of date, that Boulez's gesture at running an open-door policy toward other groups and composers was empty.

Fleuret's policy emerged shortly after and benefited both Xenakis and Eloy, at the same time that it also benefited IRCAM. Xenakis's computer music studio received much-increased funds, while Eloy got his own well-funded center. Socialist music policy was thus a curious compromise that failed to dismantle the centralization of resources upon IRCAM, and that "decentralized" by spreading the goods among rivals from within the same discourse, in order to quiet their complaints. Potentially a major source of opposition to IRCAM, Socialist cultural policy in this period balked at challenging IRCAM's hegemony.

It is instructive to examine the criteria by which the institute's legitimacy was assessed in this period by the *Direction de la Musique* — the public body closest to IRCAM. The *Direction* does not control or fund IRCAM, whose funds come straight from the Ministry of Culture via the CGP. Rather, the *Direction* manages and funds all other music research centers. So it has a semiadversarial and rivalrous relation with IRCAM — the one highly privileged institution beyond its control — while it is the main public body dealing in IRCAM's area of expertise. Powerless in reality to affect IRCAM, *Direction* officials nonetheless articulate informed views held within the Ministry.[14] Just as the policies pursued by IRCAM's critics when in power, due to the contradictions of French cultural politics, actually did no harm, the criteria of external evaluation and judgment applied by the *Direction* seemed at this time confused and irrelevant. The official view rested on a hopeful but fragile belief that IRCAM is ultimately subject to a process of self-legitimation — of self-monitoring and self-assessment.

During the mid-1980s, *Direction* officials saw the current music research sector as two-tiered: IRCAM, and then the rest — the smaller centers controlled by them. The relation between the two was described as complementary — the two having different functions and aims — but there was also a hint of critique and envy of IRCAM's dominance and a questioning of its legitimacy. There were three arenas in which IRCAM's legitimacy was discussed: its general cultural politics, technology, and music.

Regarding cultural politics, there was a dislike of Boulez's "absolute power" and influence at the highest levels of the state, a sense of democratic (and bureaucratic) outrage that "neither the Director of Technology nor of Music has the force to intervene at IRCAM, with a personality [Boulez] who is content to go to the most powerful." Officials spoke cynically of IRCAM as "official art" because of the dominance of Boulez's personality and aesthetic, whereas the small centers were considered more free, anarchic, and open: "they have no art directors." IRCAM was seen as institutionalizing and so as smothering creative individuality. "It's a bit dangerous that it's not an individual using things to make music, but an institution, a machine. . . . At IRCAM, as in movements like surrealism with a theory, manifesto, one loses a sense of different personalities . . . by manipulation into a theoretical position. There's something else than music at IRCAM!"

There were also doubts about IRCAM's management of its relations with the private sector, especially with certain large foreign corporations with which it interacts. There was unease that relations were informal, uncontrolled, so that massively state-funded research, for national ends, might find its way into foreign, and capitalist, hands — a ludicrous abuse, it was implied, of IRCAM's position.

However the prestige of technology among the French intelligentsia and officialdom tended to undercut these criticisms and doubts. Technologically, IRCAM and the other centers were seen by officials as having different aims and requiring different assessment. The small centers were expected to operate short R and D cycles, showing results — products, tools — after two or three years. They were supposed to work on applied technological research, to bridge the gap between basic research and commerce, to "find holes not perceived by the private sector . . . effective products. The private [sector] will not develop things like the 4X [IRCAM's synthesizer], the SYTER [the GRM machine], which are very powerful but correspond to a small market." The small centers were also enjoined to search for other funds, "to use their imagination to assure their survival." Thus, to gain the continued support of the *Direction*, the small centers had to show more immediate results and to operate a mixed economy.

IRCAM, by contrast, was seen as doing "fundamental" or basic research. It did not have to show short-term results or products, and was supposed to seek areas of research definitely not covered by the private sector. However, there appeared to be some confusion about precisely the legitimate position for IRCAM to take:

> They've resolved [the question] around the classical areas of research not done by the market: room acoustics, psychoacoustics. This legitimation is immediate. . . . I think some private companies take this research. [On the other hand] the products that [IRCAM] creates are not commercializable; public institutions don't have the economic necessity to need to develop commercial products. But the research is different: basic research can be applied industrially. . . . But this is not the aim of the institute — to develop things for the private sector — nor to develop products!

IRCAM did not have to seek other funds or sales of products. "IRCAM also has to do its budgeting, tighten its belt," but it was assured a basic continuity of largesse from the state.

Ultimately, an official expressed the question of IRCAM's legitimation in this interesting way: "They search themselves, year by year . . . to find their justification. 'What should we do?' they reflect. . . . They ask themselves for the justification of music research and computer developments. 'Is our work a little bit more sophisticated than that — software, for example — on the market?' When, in a few years, we find some good, cheap, high-performance products on the mass market — that'll be the justification!" In later chapters we will see that several oppositions implicit in the views described — of basic (pure) to applied research, long-term to short-term, research to product development — also recur strongly within IRCAM culture.

On IRCAM music, officials were equally evasive concerning mechanisms of judgment by the Ministry. Superficially, this could be seen as following Fleuret's dictat to avoid present judgment in promoting aesthetic pluralism. Pressed, an official spoke thus: "Boulez is someone who's very interested in *youth*. There have been some disasters but . . . there have also been good discoveries [of composers] — Manoury, Benjamin." Pressed again, the official again displaced the question of musical legitimation, this time by stressing Boulez's committed loyalty to IRCAM as a place for visionary work: "Boulez holds strongly to 'his institute.' He's had several other propositions, to direct the Paris Opera etc. . . . He resists and stays with IRCAM because he believes in it as a symbol. He sees IRCAM as the most important [project], a vanguard." Boulez's faith seemed convincing to these officials, as though in itself this guaranteed the eventual vindication of IRCAM.

When asked what Boulez had done musically since the premiere of *Répons* — his major IRCAM work, produced two years previously — officials laughed and answered "*Répons*! a new version." It is obvious, then, that *Répons* has borne a great deal of the weight of legitimizing IRCAM because music, and Boulez's music above all, remains the main arena for assessing the results of IRCAM. This gives further insight into the elusive and problematic nature of IRCAM's legitimation, since compared with the apparently instrumental character of technological or scientific research, music and aesthetics are far less tangible and "objective" spheres of value. Fleuret's philosophy, moreover, by emphasizing the right to produce (a diversity of) music, tended to obviate the whole issue of legitimation by reception, by audience response. In this, and despite other radical differences between them, Fleuret's views converged with Boulez's, which, as we will see, involve a rejection of the "mass public" and of legitimation by public "enjoyment" at all.

THE INFLATIONARY CYCLE OF CHARISMATIC AUTHORITY AND POWER

> I have absolutely no cultural authority. At IRCAM, we try to foresee. That's not an authority.
> (Boulez, *Le Monde de la Musique* no. 24, June 1980, my translation)

QUESTION:	"In the sense that you exercise cultural authority and power . . ."
ANSWER BY BOULEZ:	"Ah no! I have absolutely no cultural authority! You see . . ."
QUESTION:	"But after all, you have IRCAM!"
ANSWER BY BOULEZ:	"But that's not something one can call cultural authority. These are completely strange notions to me. At IRCAM, we try to foresee certain directions that music could take, and to give them a chance to manifest themselves. That's not an authority."

(The same passage unedited,
same source, my translation)

It has become clear throughout this account of IRCAM's conditions of existence that both public and informed official discussion of the ways in which IRCAM legitimates itself returns again and again to Boulez. The institute is, in France at least, closely identified with the man. By combining uncompromising interventions in French cultural politics with a prestigious international career, and by building his international stature until the French state could not afford not to use him, Boulez assembled the political means for the creation of IRCAM. The institute's legitimation within the world of French cultural life has depended in no small measure on Boulez's charismatic cultural authority. Yet the achievement of charisma and authority is not Boulez's alone. These qualities have been richly invested in him, constructed in mythic and heroic representations. Consider, for example, the two texts above: the first an edited highlight taken from an interview with Boulez in a major music magazine, the second the full transcript of the same passage. By editing, Boulez's statements are rendered an even more high-minded and provocative denial of his obvious authority than the original—making of it a charismatic challenge.

However Boulez has been complicit in the construction of his own charisma, not only by seeking a controversial public profile throughout his career but also through the minutiae of his self-representation. In chapter 1, I discussed Bourdieu's likening of the artist to a charismatic leader associated with youth, prophecy, iconoclasm, and asceticism. In another article (1981) he adds that the charismatic cultural function "spreads" contagiously outward from the artist (and art work) to key mediators: to the critic or impresario who "discovers" the talent, who has an "intuitive" sense of gift, and who, in consecrating a talent, confers charismatic authority both on himself and on the artist. But there is another form of "contagion" common in artistic networks: for established artists to patronize young talents, which critics then report, so condoning the patronage. I would extend Bourdieu's analysis and argue that charisma thus tends to be passed around a network of interested parties who each have an investment: that it tends to escalate, to be an inflationary currency. This is something which emerges clearly from Boulez's history, in which a network of older masters and critics have played a role in building his name, and in which the achievement of charisma, authority, and power have been mutually self-reinforcing.

We can see these processes at work in some common rhetorical strategies that have been used by critics and commentators to build mythic representations of Boulez. One is a strategy whereby Boulez is repeatedly compared to great composers, by reference to his genius or grand designs (for example Wagner, Mahler, or Richard Strauss);[15] another is to cite world-class musicians as supporters of his talent (for example Messiaen, Klemperer, or Stravinsky).[16] A further rhetoric commonly associated with Boulez employs concepts of revolution, vanguardism, prophecy, and indeed heroism—concepts imbued with charismatic connotations, and Boulez himself has often toyed with this rhetoric.[17] Boulez has also been the subject of hagiographic texts of different kinds that promote his charismatic authority.[18]

Two further aspects of Boulez's own work have helped to establish his authority. In his writings, he constantly refers to other realms of culture, thereby establishing for himself, intertextually, an impressive genealogy of musical and intellectual influences—composers, poets, writers, artists, philosophers—and demonstrating his wide intellectual scope. This making reference to the other arts, as I have argued, is a characteristic of both modernist and postmodern discourses.[19] Boulez has also, along with other leading French intellectuals in recent decades, expanded his media activities—broadcasting, writing for the newspapers—in the attempt to broaden the audience for his ideas.[20]

From roots in his youthful strategies for constructing charismatic authority, Boulez has increasingly converted this into power; and his growing links with French and international social and cultural elites, and with the highest realms of power in France, have themselves endowed him with both charisma and power. The process is self-reinforcing, since recipients of power themselves become mythicized. And the myth of Boulez's power now has great momentum, and is no doubt imbued with fantasy. Thus, when officials from the *Direction de la Musique* spoke of Boulez's "total power" concerning IRCAM, they did so with a mixture of outrage, envy and admiration in which it was difficult to separate the fantasy from reality. "He manipulates the Administrative Council, relations with the Direction of Music, the Ministry of Culture. . . . Management by the IRCAM Council is just formal, a show: it has no real power; nor the Direction of Music, nor the Ministry. It's all dependent on the personality of Boulez, who gives all confidence. . . . [But] he [also] helps relations between the musical sector and big politics, whether Socialist or Gaullist! He defends and promotes *La Villette*, the *Bastille* project."

BOULEZ'S SOCIOMUSICAL VISION

Hagiographers seize like vultures on . . . those who have contributed most to forming the character of an age. In their hands mortals become heroes and heroes become saints or gods. . . . A composer's biography must be made to match his works, and Titans have no weaknesses. The unity of the man and his work is one of the most persistent articles of faith. . . .

One [exception], however, is Richard Wagner, who remains the subject of passionate controversy. . . . The most striking thing about Wagner's life has always been the inextricable confusion of ambition, ideology and achievement. . . . [Yet his] artistic achievement [is] of such outstanding quality that it called in question and eventually overturned the existing language of music. . . . Wagner certainly saw himself as a prophet even more than an artist — a prophet who, having received illumination and grace, could claim the right to speak exuberantly and with authority on any matter whatsoever. . . .

There have been endless accounts of how his existence was transformed . . . from utopian revolutionary to sour conservative. . . . And yet it was the search for a total solution that was the real passion of Wagner's whole existence. . . .

[But] the worldwide response that Wagner proposed has remained isolated . . . lost in the general context in which there has been no fundamental change. . . . His plans were never to be realised because he died too soon to realise them. German art was never to know its first school, and Bayreuth was soon to become a blindly conservative rather than an exploratory institution.
(Boulez 1986, 223–29, "Richard Wagner: the Man and the Works," from 1975)

Boulez's ironic and perceptive comments on Wagner's charisma and career, which resonate so uncannily with aspects of his own life that they might be read as quasi-reflexive, also point implicitly to the profound parallels between his own holistic plans and those of Wagner. Like Wagner, he proposes with IRCAM a "total solution" in institutional form to the problems of contemporary music. Boulez's account of the fate of Bayreuth — Wagner's megalomaniac vision, his IRCAM — may be his prophecy of the eventual, or even appropriate, fate of IRCAM. It also hints at his extraordinary capacity for critical detachment.

Boulez's writings are extensive and complex, and contain unresolved tensions, just as his style of musical composition exhibits an antinomy between extreme control and (limited) aleatoric procedures. They range between the dogmatic, absolutist tone of his polemics and publicity, and the nuanced and reflexive quality of some theoretical texts. It is nonetheless possible to trace the key lines of argument that fed eventually into his plans for IRCAM.

In the late '50s and early '60s, at the time that he was leading the way with total serialism, Boulez stressed a new kind of rationalization of the musical system. "It is my belief that our generation will be . . . devoted to the expanding of techniques, the generalising of methods and the rationalising of the procedures of composing or, in other words, to synthesising the great creative currents that have made their appearance since the end of the last century" (Boulez 1986, 177, from 1958). He contrasts the present era with the previous rationality underlying tonality: "The rational appeal of tonality . . . and the new possibility of generalising — even standardising — musical relationships was essential to the further development of the art. . . . The serial principle, which is that of a hierarchy established anew in each work, and not a pre-existing system like that of tonality, has given the contemporary composer the ability to create musical structures that are constantly evolving. . . . It is worth observing . . . that scientific thinking has evolved in exactly the same way" (Boulez 1986, 37, from 1961). Thus for Boulez serialism allows a structural rationalization that is reworked for each composition so that the musical system itself constantly evolves. Yet this does not obviate his advocacy of the principles of serialism, which govern that "evolution" and remain a constant.

Citing Adorno, Boulez writes of the necessity of discovering the immanent laws of musical development and chides backward-looking neoclassicism. Also like Adorno, he propounds the avant-garde principle that innovation, by definition, involves a refusal of immediate gratification of the general audience: "It is in individuals who were in practice refused general admiration, and . . . even any corresponding social recognition, that we find the true portrait, or model, of an epoch" (Boulez 1986, 38, from same source, 1961).

In another lecture from this date there is a quasi-positivist stress on the interface of music and science by analogy with concepts from struc-

tural linguistics: "Music is a science as much as an art. How is it possible
to study the history of music except . . . through the evolution of its
forms, its morphology, and its syntax? . . . It is by this same study of
grammatical features that we can date a musical composition" (Boulez
1986, 33–34, from 1961).

Yet in a Darmstadt lecture from 1960, Boulez scorns "what is called
the 'mathematical' — and is in fact the 'para-scientific' — mania . . . [that]
gives the illusion of [music as] an exact, irrefutable science. . . . This is a
return to the medieval concept of music as a science demanding a scientific, rational approach: everything must be defined as clearly as possible,
demonstrated and formed on models already existing in other disciplines
based on the exact sciences. What a pious illusion!" (Boulez 1986, 73,
from 1960). These "number-fanatics" seek a "form of rational reassurance" (ibid.).

Despite these perceptive remarks on the tendency to reify scientific
method and analogy, ultimately, in a concluding Darmstadt lecture of
1960, Boulez makes a fragile compromise and refers to the relationship
between music and science as one of analogy. He states: "The argument
that music is sterilised if it is 'reduced to a formal self-sufficient system' . . . is invalid. . . . I have never established any direct relationship
between music and mathematics, only simple relations of comparison.
Because mathematics is the science with the most developed methodology at the present time, I have taken it as an example that may help us to
fill the gaps in our present system. . . . I have tried to establish an analogy" (Boulez 1986, 98, from 1960).

However this is an uneasy peace. Crucially, Boulez does not explain
how he distinguishes musical discourse from those he draws upon to
structure it by analogy — a problem concerning the status of theoretical
discourses around music that I discussed in chapter 1. In fact, rationalism and scientism recur constantly in his own discourse.

We saw in an earlier quote Boulez's reference to "evolution," which
accords with a modernist rhetoric of totalities, revolutionary progress,
and so on that he has also employed. Yet he often conveys a more subtle
and postmodern understanding of historical process, one tinged with
historical and cultural relativism. Thus, "Comparison of our own music
with that of other cultures must surely make us wary of talking about the
'eternity' or 'supremacy' of any of our musical laws. Their value is relative. . . . History is divided into periods of evolution and periods of
mutation, or, in other words . . . of conquest and . . . of stabilisation. . . .
There is no longer any place in a demonstrably relative universe for the

idea of progress as a kind of one-way movement" (Boulez 1986, 37, 35–36, from 1961).

By the late '60s, Boulez's rationalism was transmuted into a more mediated concern with technology and related scientific research; this is clear from his first speech in France touching on the IRCAM idea, given on 13 May 1968 at the height of the revolutionary events (Boulez 1986, 445–63). He speaks of the need for a renewal of musical sound materials to match the new post-tonal serial system and its forms. He calls for research using new technologies on three interrelated fronts: on new, particularly microtonal, intervals and scales, on new instruments, and on new sounds using the means of electronic music. In passing, he scorns the "takeover" of electro-acoustics by a "curiosity-shop aesthetics, this bastard descendant of a dead Surrealism" (Boulez 1986, 456), by which he implies *musique concrète* at the GRM.

In this and his famous article "Technology and the composer" (1977), often read as IRCAM manifestos, Boulez outlines broader historical problems necessitating this change: the need to transcend negation as the basis of the new musical language — a comment on his former adherence to an Adornian aesthetic, and on its limits — and the need to overcome the prevalent historicism of the musical world. In 1968 Boulez depicts the total serialist period as having laid the foundations of a new musical language, but one based necessarily on negation. He says that there must now be a shift to a period of "synthesis" (Boulez 1986, 463) drawing on the many musical, technological, and scientific currents of past decades. His use here of the term "synthesis" is significant, with its other meaning — electronic sound production — central to his vision.

Through these articles run also Boulez's more sociological analyses of the malaise of the musical scene. He criticizes the conservatism embodied in the "museum" culture of concert life, arguing that most major musical institutions — concert and opera halls and events, the orchestra, instruments — are outdated and have ceased to evolve. Concerts induce ritualistic experience; they make participation impossible and alienate the audience. Boulez calls instead for new "flexible" concert halls and programming, for visual interest and cross-media events that would attract the young and stimulate not contemplative but active reception. Boulez stresses issues of perception, proposing that contemporary music must demand a new active listening, the intelligent participation of the audience. On the one hand, this becomes a call for research into the nature of musical perception, which later feeds into IRCAM's work in psychoacoustics. On the other, Boulez simply restates what amounts to a classic article of poststructuralist faith: "Contemporary music in fact demands the intelligent participation of the audience, which is 'making' the work at the same time as the author. . . . [T]he work [has] multiple meanings that the listener can discover for himself . . . [by assuming] an active role, selecting from it what suits him" (Boulez 1986, 462).

In various ways these ideas resonate with the influence of Adorno, Benjamin, and poststructuralism—especially the later work of Barthes. Yet the reading of both Benjamin and Barthes is selective. While resembling Benjamin's critique of the reactionary and fetishizing cult of the artwork, Boulez's ideas absent completely Benjamin's positive theorization of mass-reproduced, commoditized popular culture. Barthes himself prepared the way for Boulez's confidence in the audience's active interpretation of serialism, which Barthes contrasts with mere "consumption" (Barthes 1977c, 163). Yet neither he nor Boulez specifies what distinguishes active reception—surely one of the most canonical and least-clarified poststructuralist concepts—from passive consumption, and for Barthes, at least, it is not primarily dependent on properties of the text.[21] Moreover, another of Barthes's well-known essays on music (1977b) contradicts this position. In it he stresses the difference between the music one listens to and the music one plays. Only the latter, "*musica practica*," involves active participation, which comes to mean here the sensuous activity of making music as opposed to listening. Barthes aligns this activity with popular and youth music, while technologically mediated and art music are denigrated as fostering passive reception. Barthes's writings are therefore ambiguous on postserialism. They have lent support to Boulez's own ideas about the possibility of active reception of his music. But they have been equally amenable to analyses highly critical of the postserialist avant-garde,[22] a music so complex that it could hardly be less open to the practical, productive intervention of nonspecialists.

On the actual small and elite audience for contemporary music Boulez is contradictory. He calls for composers to "set out in search of a public," not to be "content with the approval of a small group" or clique (Boulez 1986, 452); yet within IRCAM and more generally he chides those who seek to satisfy the mass public—"*le grand public*"—and appears to distrust the integrity of any event that draws large audiences. In Adornian fashion Boulez equates large audiences with commerciality, with easy listening and a lax aesthetic pluralism. Thus, in an interview from the mid-1980s that criticizes the minimalist and "repetitive" school of postmodernism, Boulez rejects what he calls the "supermarket aesthetic." He says, "I'm always astonished that composers speak in terms of quantity, i.e. 'music is valid if it has more than two thousand people listening to it.' For me, that's no criterion of validity" (Boulez 1984, 15). He argues that entertainment and enjoyment have nothing to do with value and artistic progress: "What remains in history — entertainment music or music that is more demanding?" (ibid.).

In the same interview Boulez sums up the composer's dilemma in terms of a deceptively naive choice: "The opposition, then, is really that of being understood or not being understood by the mass, being complex or not complex, having a vocabulary that is really very easy or one that is less easy to grasp" (Boulez 1984, 14). In this, Boulez epitomizes Bourdieu's analysis of "disinterestedness." His stress on the value of music residing in its being "demanding," "not . . . understood by the mass," "less easy to grasp": this all speaks to Bourdieu's analysis of the educated art perception that operates among the bourgeoisie and that distinguishes their "culture" from the immediately pleasurable experience of the lower classes. Boulez's approach therefore embodies an elitist cultural "distinction," yet it is in tension with his professed desire to create a larger audience. This makes his commitment to pedagogy as a way to broaden the audience more understandable.

Finally, in line with an Adornian view of the relation between commerce and culture, Boulez states bluntly: "The economy is there to remind us, in case we get lost in this bland utopia: there are musics which bring in money and exist for commercial profit; there are musics that cost something, whose very concept has nothing to do with profit. No liberalism will erase this distinction" (Boulez and Foucault 1985, 8).

Thus, autonomous music and related research involve, by definition, a negation of the interests of commercial success and of the mass audience. Boulez therefore exemplifies Bourdieu's analysis of the discourse of the avant-garde. This in turn indicates why his sociology remains highly circumscribed: concerned with halls and ritual, combining aspects of the Frankfurt School and poststructuralism, it evades consideration of the responsibility of "autonomous" aesthetic choices for the malaise that he describes with such concern.

IRCAM's existence is predicated on an extension of the same perspective. Boulez argues that electronic and computer music have so far evolved "irrationally" in commercial situations (such as Bell Labs), "under the ceaseless pressure of the market" (1977, 8) in both pop music and commercial telecommunications, and ignorant of long-term musical needs. Instead, they should develop in a speciaiized music institution where the search for "radical solutions" can be independent of "official powers." "An institute of this kind should enjoy a total autonomy and a very flexible internal structure despite its many external links. . . . With no immediate obligations it should be able to manifest a true *disinterestedness* and pursue objectives unattainable by any organization too deeply engaged in 'mundane' matters" (Boulez 1986, 465 and 466, emphasis in original). Boulez suggests that the institute should address sociological aspects of music — audiences, concert organization, "i.e. the relationship between the actual work, the performers and the public" (Boulez 1986, 465) — as well as new instruments and sound materials.

Several institutional models influenced Boulez's ideas for IRCAM: above all, the Bauhaus, but also the German Max Planck scientific institutes and the American university computer music centers, in which, Boulez says, there exists a "permanent alliance of musicians and scientists" (Boulez 1986, 484). In the article from 1968 cited above and "The Bauhaus model" (Boulez 1986, 464–66, from 1970), Boulez writes approvingly of the fusion of pure and applied arts, the laboratory atmosphere of invention and experimentation, and the collaborations between technicians/scientists and artists that were central to the aims and achievements of the Bauhaus. The parallels are deeper than Boulez pursues. In its second phase the Bauhaus became increasingly obsessed with progress, technology, and American influence, as summed up in its new slogan, "Art and Technology — a new unity" (Whitford 1984; Willett 1978; Gay 1968).

Above all, Boulez derives from the Bauhaus the notion of a "general school or laboratory" (Boulez 1986, 455) and a concept to which he refers repeatedly, the necessity for teamwork or collaboration between "researchers," musical and scientific, and technicians. The heart of Boulez's vision of IRCAM, then, is a "utopian marriage of fire and water" (Boulez 1977, 10) between music and science, art and technology, founded on interdisciplinary collaboration between musicians and scientists. Further, by this notion of collaboration inspired by the Bauhaus, by his stress on the collective nature of the undertaking (Boulez 1977, 14; Boulez 1986, 458), Boulez implies a democratic and egalitarian sharing of skills and ideas. This is the crux of his vision of the institute's internal social relations, and around it in his writings he scatters utopian and politicized terms reminiscent of various political rhetorics — socialist, Leninist, Trotskyist.[23] Thus, as in the quotes at the start of my introduction, Boulez calls for an end to private property and individual labor in creative work, for global ambitions, and for IRCAM to be a vanguard of long-term, future-oriented research.

The ideas behind IRCAM are thus intertextually complex and authoritative, and they raise contradictions and questions: how, for example, Boulez has reconciled his vanguard leanings and call for egalitarian collaboration with a hierarchical public bureaucracy, or his desire to avoid official control with IRCAM being a large state institution; and whether, or to what extent, his ideal of egalitarian collaboration between music and science has been achieved in IRCAM's work relations. It is time, therefore, to examine the relation between Boulez's utopian founding ideology and the actual functioning of IRCAM.

The Institution of IRCAM

Culture and Status

IRCAM is physically unusual: the main building lies underground on four descending levels below the Place Stravinsky, adjacent to the Centre Georges Pompidou. In 1984 IRCAM had two buildings: this new one and an old building, a red-brick former schoolhouse. In the late '80s a new tower was added neighboring the old building. Both overlook the kinetic Tinguely sculptures that adorn the Place. Next to the CGP's large, colored steel and glass, machinelike building, which stands out on the landscape, IRCAM's existence is discreet. Both it and the CGP are located on the Plateau Beaubourg, midway between the old Jewish quarter of Paris, the Marais, to the east, and the redeveloped commercial area of Les Halles to the west. To the south, bordering the Seine, lies the Place du Châtelet with its two national theaters: Théâtre du Châtelet and Théâtre de la Ville. This is the heart of cultural and commercial Paris.

In 1984 one approached IRCAM from the Place Stravinsky down a long, anonymous, descending flight of stairs ending in an automatic sliding glass wall. Inside, the reception area was flanked by electronic security systems. The underground building was designed by the neo-modernist architect Richard Rogers, also responsible for the CGP. The materials are concrete, steel, and glass, the interior modernist, functional, and bare, with muted, drab colors and few concessions to decoration or comfort. Like all high-technology centers, because of the need to keep its computers continually on, IRCAM operates twenty-four hours a day. Although the public can wander in during the day, they are not encouraged to move around freely, and outside office hours IRCAM is closed to all except staff and those with security permits. At these times, security is rigorously enforced by uniformed guards. IRCAM thus has more the look of a scientific research institute than that of a music or performance center.

The majority of technological, scientific, and musical work took place in 1984 on the four levels of the new building. The lowest floor, level -4, contains IRCAM's unique performance space, the *Espace de Projection* (Esp Pro). Level -2, the floor on which one then entered IRCAM, was the busiest. It contains a wide hall, areas for visitors and workers to congregate, and a long row of glass-walled offices. Hidden behind these are open-plan technical areas, the host computer room; and behind these again are a row of soundproofed studios, including an anechoic chamber — a totally soundproofed room for acoustic experiments. Level -1 consists of another row of glass-walled offices, above those on Level -2, which in 1984 were reserved for higher-status staff, including Boulez and department directors. Most offices had a vaguely chaotic air: they contained computer terminals and perhaps other electronic equipment, shelves of books, wipeboards with scribbled calculations, and desks strewn with papers.

IRCAM's history until 1984 falls into three distinct periods. The first, from 1970 to 1977, mainly involved planning, building, and development. By 1975 some research had begun in the old building, and in 1976 the EIC was founded. In 1977 both the CGP and IRCAM were opened. These events were celebrated by the concert series *Passage du Vingtième Siècle* in which seventy concerts took place throughout the year in venues all over Paris.

The second period, 1977 to 1980, was IRCAM's first period of full operation. The initial organizational structure was broad in orientation. There were five departments, each headed by a composer-director under Boulez's overall command. The departments were: Electro-Acoustics, Computer, Pedagogy, Instruments and Voice, and Diagonal (coordinating between the others). Electro-Acoustics was headed by the Italian composer Luciano Berio, equal in stature to Boulez, so that his "subordination" was largely formal. In reality, departments were substantially autonomous and followed their own interests. Berio, for example, invited a compatriot scientist to design him a real-time digital sound processor — which developed into IRCAM's major computer hardware project, culminating in the early '80s in the production of a powerful machine called the 4X.

The third phase was initiated by Boulez's sudden reorganization of

IRCAM in 1980. This followed a period of internal instability during which most of the codirectors left. The reasons were several. IRCAM was moving inexorably toward computer music and away from the broader concerns embodied in the five original departments. It was also rumored that relations between Boulez and the departing codirectors had deteriorated. Moreover, a major concert of IRCAM premieres at the Metz International Festival was considered a musical disaster by Boulez, and he determined to overhaul things. As we saw in the last chapter, this period was accompanied by much press speculation and polemic. Critics, external and internal, saw the change as Boulez consolidating his monopoly of power over IRCAM, and the autocratic manner in which he accomplished the reorganization lent itself to such an interpretation. Out of the blue, he suddenly called a rare general meeting at which he announced the new structure and allocated positions. Even those suddenly promoted were not warned of the "coup." But Boulez described the move as rational streamlining, making IRCAM into what it had essentially become: a computer music studio.[1]

After the reorganization, throughout the third period of 1980 to 1984, IRCAM's structure became that described here. Nineteen eighty-four, the ethnographic present in this account, is thus the culmination of this phase. Yet it was represented by management as in some ways an atypical, particularly difficult year. The dynamic of the institute was dominated by the lead-up to two major autumn events. One was the International Computer Music Conference (ICMC), the main annual computer music meeting, which IRCAM hosted for the first time. The other was the Parisian premiere of Boulez's composition *Répons*, the first night of which was also the opening concert of the ICMC. *Répons* ran for six packed nights in a specially prepared space in the CGP, and was designed to show off IRCAM's best music and technology not only to the elite of French culture, but also to the international computer music community. Much of IRCAM's scientific and technical resources were therefore directed toward preparing *Répons* and its technology for the premiere.

IRCAM had many uncertainties during 1984 concerning its technology. One source was the difficult negotiations over putting the 4X machine into industrial production (*"industrialisation"*), which was necessary to provide enough machines for the *Répons* premieres. Nineteen eighty-four was also an unstable period for the basic computing infrastructure. The year before had seen a transition from a DEC PDP10 minicomputer, which had served for several years, to the new generation of machines: a DEC VAX 780 plus the associated software operating system, UNIX. This VAX/UNIX combination was the up-and-coming system of the moment, increasingly widespread in the international research community. But for that reason the technology was also rapidly evolving and therefore unstable.

Partly due to technological instabilities, 1984 was a poor year for music production. Four commissioned visits were planned, but only three took place, one of which did not result in a piece. This was considered exceptionally unproductive, and the aim from 1985 was to have twelve visiting composers a year. One composer's visit was especially unsuccessful and caused an internal crisis in which some of the deepest problems of IRCAM's functioning came to light. This visit is detailed in later chapters.

Nineteen eighty-four was also unusual in seeing the departure of several of the most powerful, senior, and long-staying IRCAM directors, including the Administrator, the Scientific Director, and soon after, in early 1986, the Artistic Director. Thus 1984 was a culmination, but it was also a transition, as indicated by these departures and by certain major policy changes that occurred in 1985–86. For that very reason, however, 1984 was a period in which it was possible to witness key ideological and political conflicts and practical problems being worked through within the institute.

IRCAM began as a public institution, the music department of the CGP. However in 1977 it gained an unusual legal status: it became a semiautonomous private association with its own statutes, retaining some important links with the CGP. Its funds come direct from the Ministry of Culture via the intermediary of the CGP, while, as mentioned earlier, those of all other music research centers come from the *Direction de la Musique*. So IRCAM is unusually independent of the *Direction*. As a private association, IRCAM can employ foreigners, has managerial and financial flexibility, and is able to receive private patronage. Nonetheless IRCAM's main external executive — the Administration Council — resembles that of state institutions. It contains representatives from several related, key public bodies: the CGP, whose president remains IRCAM's president, the Ministry of Culture, the Ministry of Research, the *Centre Nationale de la Recherche Scientifique*, and so on. This legal and administrative autonomy is often depicted as a reflection of IRCAM's exceptional status and privilege as a body involved in creative origination and cultural production as compared with most state cultural organs, including even the CGP, which are confined to cultural reproduction (archives, exhibition, collection, performance). In this classificatory opposition of cultural production to reproduction, then, production is perceived as having higher status.

Internally Boulez, as IRCAM's Director, had overall management responsibility. He was aided by an Administration department. The original head of this department, who set up IRCAM with Boulez, was a high state official and a friend of Boulez's. It was during this man's period of office that IRCAM consolidated many of its privileges. An early IRCAM director saw IRCAM's position as linked to the personal status of this Administrator, whom he described as socially exalted: "He's a very upper class *fonctionnaire*, I mean *really* high class, *Conseil d'État* and all that. . . . Boulez wanted him because he'd done all the statutes for the big Opera scheme. That's how he knew [him]. . . . [He] was the Secretary General of a big company run by Claude Cheysson, who's now foreign minister." Talking of the way that IRCAM had been set up with the patronage of such figures, the director joked ironically thus: "They were with us from the start! If you're not friendly with Louis the Fourteenth, then you won't be able to sing at court! [*Laughing*] France is a monarchy, you see!" The original Administrator left IRCAM in 1982 to become a judge at the European Court of Human Rights. The next head of this department, incumbent in 1984, was a professional public administrator rather than a member of the haute bourgeoisie.

In proper bureaucratic fashion, the head of the Administration issues diagrams of IRCAM's formal organization and power structure, called "*organigrammes*." The 1982 diagram (Figure 2) illustrates the basic structure still current in 1984. It shows the division of IRCAM into two sectors — a music production or creation sector and a scientific sector — which contain several departments or teams, each headed by a director[2] or "*responsable*," and each apparently with equal status. It conveys IRCAM as consisting of a series of autonomous, functionally interrelated units: an "organic ecology," as one person put it.

The two sectors were overseen by two internal executive bodies: the Artistic Committee and Scientific Committee. According to the *organigramme*, each supervised the relevant sector of IRCAM, and each was composed of Boulez plus the directors of departments within that sector. The two committees appear to carry equal authority. However, in reality the Artistic Committee was more powerful; its meetings were regular and closed. The real politics of IRCAM took place here: invitations to composers and researchers, commissions, musical and conference events, long-term planning, public relations, and even some technology policy.

By contrast, the Scientific Committee had little power. It was an irregular discussion forum, and anyone could attend meetings. A researcher called them cynically "just a therapy session." In line with this, the role of Scientific Director, apparently equal or even senior to the Artistic Director and subordinate only to Boulez, was also relatively anomalous. IRCAM Scientific Directors have come and gone, usually lasting barely a year. The Artistic Director, on the other hand, was considered Boulez's next-in-command. Thus, the scientific side had relatively less power than the artistic, and in fact this is sanctioned by IRCAM's statutes, which imply that its scientific and technological work must ultimately serve musical ends.

ECONOMICS AND THE CIRCULATION OF PRODUCTS: THE 4X DEAL

IRCAM receives both public and private financing, but the overwhelming majority comes from the state. Its Ministry of Culture grant, distributed via the CGP, accounts for some 70 to 80 percent of annual funds.[3] Other income comes from small grants from the Ministry of Research and interest on IRCAM's own bank reserves. Between 1982 and 1985, IRCAM's total yearly income was in the region of 28 to 30 million francs. In return for state grants, IRCAM's statutes define it as a nonprofit research center obliged to do work of public benefit, and with this goes a ceiling on the amount of commercial development that IRCAM can engage in. Commercial income must not exceed 15 percent of annual income, so IRCAM is legally discouraged from developing profitable products, whether musical or technological. The statutes thus embody both Boulez's ideology and the view of IRCAM's role given by music officials discussed in chapter 3.

Private patronage contributes only a tiny part of IRCAM's income, yet it is proffered as a key cause for IRCAM seeking legal autonomy. It seems therefore to have primarily symbolic value in linking IRCAM to the tradition of bourgeois patronage and avant-garde salons also described in the previous chapter. A significant figure here is the Swiss millionaire Paul Sacher, a friend of Boulez's and for decades a champion of avant-garde music, who donates annually to IRCAM.

The circulation and sale of IRCAM's output may appear constrained by the legal limit on commercial income. But in 1984 there was little need for this, since as the statutes dictate, none of the potential sources of earnings made much profit. The income from sales of IRCAM products

Organigramme 1982 de l'IRCAM

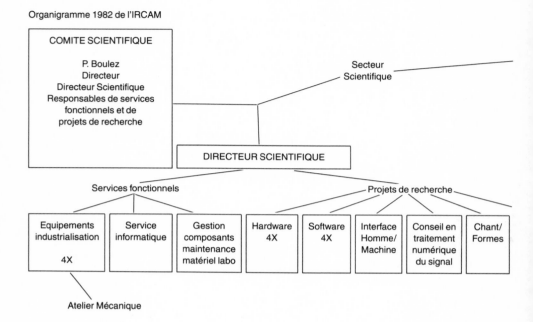

liaisons hiérarchiques ————————————
liaisons fonctionnelles — — — — — — — —

2. IRCAM's organization: *Organigramme* for 1982, indicating the basic structure and the hierarchical relations between parts of the institute that were still
current in 1984. (The only element that was different in 1984 was the *Comité*

(papers, concert and conference tickets, cassettes, videos, and so on) and
from IRCAM concert tours was small. Audiences for IRCAM concerts,
although large for concerts with Boulez and similar well-known figures
and for special "youthful" events, were not consistently so. Concerts
were thus far from self-financing.[4] IRCAM scientific work, as with all
academic and publicly funded research, was supposed to circulate freely
among the research community. IRCAM technologies might be thought

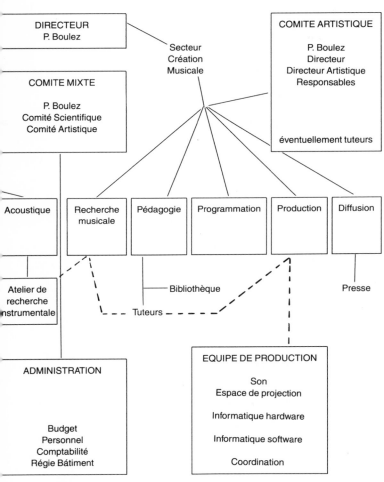

DIRECTEUR
P. Boulez

Secteur
Création
Musicale

COMITE ARTISTIQUE

P. Boulez
Directeur
Directeur Artistique
Responsables

éventuellement tuteurs

COMITE MIXTE

P. Boulez
Comité Scientifique
Comité Artistique

Acoustique

Recherche
musicale

Pédagogie

Programmation

Production

Diffusion

Atelier de
recherche
instrumentale

Bibliothèque

Tuteurs

Presse

ADMINISTRATION

Budget
Personnel
Comptabilité
Régie Bâtiment

EQUIPE DE PRODUCTION

Son
Espace de projection

Informatique hardware

Informatique software

Coordination

Mixte, which no longer existed.) (Source: IRCAM internal document, by permission of Laurent Bayle, Director of IRCAM.)

to have had the greatest earning potential. However in 1984 IRCAM's own software did not earn anything, since it was developed under educational licenses and so with the aid of a software environment provided without commercial charges, and IRCAM was also obliged to circulate this freely to other research groups. It was IRCAM's hardware that in 1984 appeared best suited to commercial development. Yet the story of setting up a production deal for IRCAM's hardware prototype — the 4X machine — is instructive in showing how, eventually, this also managed to avoid making profits for IRCAM.

From the beginning, the 4X "*industrialisation*" deal caused conflicts, pitting the Administration department and Boulez against two 4X team directors — VO (4X Industrialization director) and the designer BU (4X Hardware director) — who wanted to see the 4X reach a larger musicians' market beyond IRCAM. VO wanted to set up a commercial IRCAM offshoot to exploit IRCAM's R and D, following the American and Japanese models in which "enlightened" venture capital supports progressive research. But in the face of opposition, and of some ambiguity as to whether IRCAM could legally set up such a company, VO sought deals with extant industrial firms. A company called Sogitec expressed interest, and drawn-out negotiations took place in late 1983 and early 1984. Significantly, Sogitec was not interested in the 4X's musical capacities. It manufactured aircraft parts and was closely linked to the defense industry. VO sold the 4X to Sogitec by finding a way to use the machine to simulate aircraft noise, and the company bought it to become the basis of a flight-noise simulator. In July 1984 Sogitec was suddenly taken over by the giant defense company Dassault — makers of aircraft and high-tech weapons — which further set back the production timetable.

Eventually Boulez and management became persuaded, perhaps because several 4Xs were needed for the *Répons* premiere. IRCAM gave Sogitec the 4X prototype as the basis for production in return for just four 4X units and a small royalty. The 4X was thus taken up by a leading French company and valorized as industrially useful. Yet since Dassault/Sogitec had no interest in the music market, the 4X was never manufactured as a commercial music synthesizer, nor were enough produced even to distribute to other computer music centers.

The 4X-Sogitec saga was kept quiet during 1984 and was not spoken of freely within IRCAM. A very few workers mentioned confidentially that they were upset by the militarist implications of the deal, and equally by the failure of the 4X to reach a larger musical public, but most remained silent. The 4X designer, BU, was angry, and word had it that he refused to give Sogitec any written designs for the machine, so they had to work out its operations from scratch — just one factor in the lengthy delays that meant the 4X units arrived late from Sogitec, uncomfortably close to the *Répons* premieres.

In this period, then, IRCAM inhabited a contradiction. By statute it aimed to develop innovative research and technologies of the sort that the private sector cannot or will not produce. Yet paradoxically, the technologies were then of little interest to the commercial sector, so they remained almost a crafted technology — very few were ever made. They therefore had a tiny circulation, little wider influence, and little economic value. Given the dominant ideological as well as legal frame surrounding IRCAM, the likelihood of it earning from its prototype hardware was small. Certainly it earned little from the 4X.

But this is less contradictory once the ideological logic is grasped whereby the technology's lack of commercial validation is compensated by its retaining maximum symbolic value on the cultural scene because of its very uniqueness. By avoiding commercialization, the 4X was not debased by entering a large market. It remained an exclusive and pres- tigious "tool" that could be used only at IRCAM. It therefore added maximum prestige to the few pieces like *Répons* that, made at IRCAM, had virtual monopolies on its use. Without such exclusivity IRCAM might seem to have had few unique facilities to offer to composers.

Thus IRCAM's legal-financial constraints and the character of its cul- tural production converged in the mid-1980s so as effectively to avoid "undue" commercial profit. IRCAM's economic basis was defined by heavy dependence on public subsidy, but equally by willed negation of economic gain. It therefore accorded fully with Boulez's ideological an- tagonism to commerce, just as this, in turn, recalls Bourdieu's analysis of the sphere of cultural capital and its belief in the necessarily inverse relation between cultural production oriented to the future and for the public good, and commercial profit. In this sense IRCAM embodied in this era the sphere of cultural capital. We will see that by the turn of the 1990s, this basic ethos had been modified.[5]

ORGANIZATION AND ACTIVITIES

IRCAM's projects and activities in 1984 were as follows. The scientific sector included both applied technology and pure research projects. The main applied projects were five effectively related to the 4X (Hardware, Software, Signal Processing, *Industrialisation*, and Man-Machine Inter- face) and one team, called the Chant/Formes group, working on ad- vanced music software inspired by artificial intelligence (AI). (The pro- grams they developed were called Chant and Formes). There were also two small, temporary, applied projects not shown on the *organigramme*, both led by visiting American composer-researchers and both concerned with live interaction between computers and performers. One focused on the 4X, the other used small Apple computers. Finally, a new software project to design a musical expert system, again inspired by AI, was in the planning stages. The only pure research department was Acoustics, with its offshoot the ARI (*Atelier de Recherche Instrumentale* or Instrumental Research Workshop). It is notable that psychoacoustics, a pure research discipline central to computer music and to IRCAM's work, had no formal project and was fitted in by some workers around other work. The Computer Systems team (known simply as the Systems team), responsible for maintaining the main computer network, was attached to this sector.

Other technical groups — responsible for running the Esp Pro, for sound recording and amplification (the Sound team), and for hardware maintenance — were linked to a Production Office that ran the practical management of music production and performance.

The music production sector was involved in origination (composition, music research) and reproduction (performance, education, publicity). It contained four "departments" — Programming, Diffusion, Pedagogy, and Music Research — each consisting only of a director and an assistant or two. The domain of the Artistic Director was programming in the traditional sense: he took charge of invitations to composers, the twice-yearly Reading Panels (*Comités de Lecture*) in which scores were anonymously submitted for selection by a jury, and he also programmed IRCAM's main concert series. Pedagogy was responsible for the public lecture series, the educational courses ("*stages*") for visiting composers, the assistants ("tutors") to composers, and graduate researchers attached to IRCAM ("*stagiaires*"). Most psychoacoustic research also went on under the auspices of Pedagogy. Music Research had a less clear role. The director contributed to many of the above and saw his task as that of an *animateur*, but he also engaged in his own composition when possible. Diffusion, finally, took charge of publicity, of press and public relations. The four department directors made up, with Boulez, the core of the Artistic Committee, in which they together discussed many of the decisions on commissions and concert seasons.

Boulez and his three male codirectors from this sector had contacts in different areas of the contemporary music world on which they drew to people IRCAM. Boulez and the Artistic Director between them dealt with the elite of the European music scene, courting them when necessary — for example taking Stockhausen or Ligeti out to dine to encourage them to visit IRCAM. The Artistic Director, as well as Boulez, had the run of the highest levels of the contemporary music world: he is an impresario who had previously been the manager of a major contemporary music orchestra and of several leading European composers.

By contrast, the directors of Pedagogy and Music Research, both Americans, together filled out IRCAM's contacts on the American scene — particularly useful given Boulez's past alienation of elements of American contemporary music. The Music Research director, an ambitious young composer, mainly had contacts among the East Coast elite of "serious" music,[6] while the maverick director of Pedagogy was well known in American computer music and so had contacts with composers, scientists, and technologists from that scene, as well as some from the more "way-out" areas of West Coast experimental music, jazz, and even mainstream pop. The musical tastes and policies of these four men therefore differed, so Artistic Committee discussions could be experienced as antagonistic and as suffering conflicts of aesthetic and philosophy. However this "dissensus" was also, in practice, a functional complementarity since between them the four effectively covered all the powerful areas of contemporary and computer music.

IRCAM's official commissioning process normally involved selected composers coming for two visits of three months each, the first a "research" visit to learn about IRCAM's computer tools, the second a "production" visit to actually make the piece. The new works were then premiered in a concert season. Composers were assisted by the Pedagogy staff known as "tutors." But as well as the four official tutors, the tutor role was also carried out by young intellectual staff, on temporary contracts, whom I shall call "junior tutors" (although they had no official title). Tutors mediated between the scientific, technological, and musical sides of IRCAM and were supposed to be skilled in music, acoustics, and computer science. They taught composers about the technologies and research, and helped them to find ways of realizing their musical ideas with IRCAM's computer tools. Tutors did much of the "hands-on" work with the machines, developing and tailoring software to composers' specific needs. It is thus the tutor-composer relation, and indeed the role of tutor itself, that came closest to embodying Boulez's ideal of a fruitful and egalitarian collaboration between the musical and the scientific.

However there was also a great deal of unofficial music production involving IRCAM workers and "squatters" working in their own time. Although no staff — not even Boulez — were officially employed as composers, five of the permanent staff (Boulez, the Music Research director, and three tutors), many junior tutors, and even some technicians considered themselves composers, and some found ways to use the equipment

out of normal hours to produce pieces. This created anomalies and embarrassment for management, since it is important for IRCAM that it
should be seen rationally to control access to its facilities and so maintain
the quality of work being produced. Yet the implicit acceptance of unofficial production and the blind eye turned toward squatters betray two
realities.

First, it was commonly accepted among IRCAM intellectuals that the
best musical results came from those working more or less permanently
within IRCAM, who got to know the environment well. (In meetings, a
figure of several years was cited as the time necessary to become fully
adept with the technologies — clearly impossible for composers with
only six months.) Second, although most unofficial pieces were ignored,
when one was judged good, the official process took notice, the piece was
acknowledged, and the rewards could be high. This is because ultimately, as we will see, Boulez used musical judgments to assess both
workers and technologies, so that a good piece might suddenly promote
the composer and the technologies used, as well as feeding back prestige
to IRCAM itself. A squatter's tale can illustrate this process. A young
woman composer, the girlfriend of a junior worker and so able to gain
unofficial entry, produced a piece with IRCAM technologies that won a
prize at the prestigious Darmstadt festival. Word came out that she had
made it at IRCAM, and the artistic management looked foolish for not
being aware of the piece or of her talent. Yet after a mock reprimand,
they were pleased that she had won this important prize. Within a short
time, she was working officially at IRCAM.

Finally, closely related to IRCAM but with its own autonomous administration is the EIC, IRCAM's collaborative contemporary music
ensemble. Boulez often conducts the EIC, which takes part in many
IRCAM concerts and was central to his *Répons*; and some of the players
become involved in IRCAM acoustic research. So the links between
Boulez, the EIC, and IRCAM are strong.

POPULATION AND EMPLOYMENT

The IRCAM population contains people with very different kinds of
employment status. It centers on the salaried, permanent employees.
These positions are strictly limited and number about fifty-five to sixty.
They are controlled by the Administration, and cover the full spectrum
of jobs, from Boulez to the postman. In 1984 they were unequally dis-

tributed among the institute's parts: they comprised mainly administrative, clerical, and technical staff, the directors of the various departments, and a core of research staff. The latter centered on 4X projects, with ten, while pure research and non-4X technology projects lacked permanent workers: Acoustics and Chant/Formes had just one each. Staff on the music side were few and were not employed as composers. Musicians were in fact the workers who most often had temporary and insecure positions at IRCAM, whether as junior staff or as commissioned composers. The distribution of permanent, salaried positions, then, was very uneven and favored 4X-related projects over both pure research and music — surprising given the stress on permanent collaboration between musicians and scientists in Boulez's founding vision.

In addition to these employees, IRCAM has a large number of workers on temporary contracts, people working unofficially and unpaid ("squatters"), and visitors. In all, during 1984 this floating population numbered about sixty-five people, of whom some forty-five stayed for a substantial period.

There are two forms of temporary contract for IRCAM workers, known as *vacations* and *honoraires*. *Vacations* or fixed-term contracts last for between three months and a year. In 1984 they involved low pay, no security of employment, and compulsory layoffs of one-third of the duration of the previous contract in between recurrent contracts. These were the most exploitative form of contract, and they were often used sequentially to hold junior staff in a kind of semipermanent limbo. A good proportion were held by young, foreign musicians and researchers keen to get a toehold inside IRCAM, especially those working as junior tutors.

Honoraires are fixed-term contracts lasting a few months, better paid than *vacations* by a total fee, and task-specific. *Honoraires* were given to two kinds of visiting workers considered to have particular expertise: to invited researchers and computer scientists and to commissioned composers. *Honoraires* computer scientists, who were usually American, came to work on the computer system or specific research projects as consultants. Their labor was restricted to the period when they were physically present at IRCAM. Commissioned composers received a fee and expenses for their time living in Paris. Financial terms for composers varied, although IRCAM policy was to pay them within a close range of fees according to their age and renown. Given their labor before and after the IRCAM visits, composers' fees were moderate compared with those for computer scientists. However, it was implied that in practice certain "star" composers were paid well beyond the normal range; certainly, differences of treatment were apparent.[7]

In 1984 IRCAM's squatters worked unofficially and were the object of much grumbling by the Administration, yet they were also joked about, and except for the occasional purge, tacitly accepted and left alone. Squatters were let in informally through the friendship and patronage of certain directors, notably the Pedagogy director. Most squatting was done in the evenings, nights, and weekends because in the day a squatter's presence was conspicuous, there was little space to work, and the computer system was congested. But to get into IRCAM outside the office day one needed a security pass, which required a high-up patron to persuade the Administration. Squatters included both computer scientists and musicians. There was, for example, a tradition of squatters from the Computer Science department of Vincennes university, where they were short on computer power. Musician squatters included young composers who were friends of IRCAM staff and those who had attended an IRCAM *stage* but had not (yet) got full official backing.

A stream of international visitors comes through IRCAM each week. Many have past and continuing connections as researchers, composers, or people from the computer music or contemporary music worlds. Quite a few turn up by recommendation or simply out of interest to look around and possibly to start a bid for a formal relation. Composers who have past and future commissions visit in order to discuss their requirements or to do short bits of work on a tape or piece. Periodically, commercial computer music technology firms come through to give a demonstration or to make formal contact with IRCAM research: for example, Synclavier and Yamaha both visited in early 1984, while most companies in the field attended the autumn ICMC.

Certain groups within IRCAM constitute themselves as subcultures — a group "for itself" with a cohesive internal identity. In 1984 all the technical teams — Systems, Sound, Esp Pro — had such collective identities, as in different ways did the Administration, the Chant/Formes group, and to a lesser extent the 4X projects. These were constituted both through common antagonism to other parts of the institute and by different kinds of positive collective labor, ideology, and mutual affection. The one marked subculture that did not derive from a formal team — and so was not represented on the *organigramme* — was that constituted by a series of voluntary, biweekly "musicians' meetings" that began at the start of 1984. Held under the auspices of the director of Music Research,

the meetings involved collective reflection on the general direction and
higher goals of IRCAM. They brought together those of IRCAM's music
and research intellectuals from various projects who considered themselves most concerned with IRCAM's deeper and future orientation, or
felt that they should be seen to be. The group was IRCAM's own, self-
constituted intellectual vanguard: I shall call it the "musicians' group."

In terms of nationality, IRCAM was in 1984 mainly French, with a
secondary presence of Americans, plus a scattering of western and eastern Europeans and Australians. Most permanent positions were filled by
French workers, while Americans came as short-contract workers and
visitors. As we have seen, the dominant French-American polarity has
been there from the start, and in 1984 Americans continued to play a
major role.

IRCAM attempted its most rigorous international coverage in its artistic policy of invitations to composers, whether for commissions, sub-
missions to the score reading panel, or selection for the composers' *stage*.
Yet the range of IRCAM commissions over its first decade centered on
just six countries, with France and America receiving by far the most,[8] so
that in fact the "international" policy has favored a few culturally dominant nations. The French-American axis, then, had strong effects musically as well as scientifically and technologically.

In 1984 IRCAM had a classic sexual and racial division of labor. All
of the low-paid, low-status clerical staff were women, while women
were barely represented in the higher sphere of research and production,
whether technological or musical. There were few nonwhites at IRCAM.
The most numerous were the North African men and women cleaners
seen for brief periods in the early mornings and evenings. They came
from a private contractor via the CGP and were the only unionized
workers to enter IRCAM (belonging to the Communist CGT). The
IRCAM accountant was also of North African descent, the only such
permanent member of staff. There was one black American composer on
temporary commission in 1984. He saw himself as a "token black man"
among IRCAM intellectuals, and was self-conscious and uncomfortable
in this role.

The age profile of the institute was young in 1984. The majority of the
population were aged between their mid-twenties and late thirties, with
just a few over-forties. The overall impression was of a young population, especially among the male research and production staff, and of
older authority figures gambling, taking risks, on what they considered
to be dynamic young workers on the make in their field.

PRODUCTION AND REPRODUCTION:
UNEQUAL STATUS AND THE DIVISION OF LABOR

The production of music at IRCAM, bringing together scientists, technologists, and musicians, supported by administrative and clerical staff, involves an institutional division of labor more extensive than any previous historical form. We can now look more closely at these internal social relations. The question is: how differentiated and stratified are they?

Within IRCAM, it is widely believed that the staff associated with research and production have high cultural status, since they are directly involved in the institute's main, public work. This status extends beyond those with obvious executive and cultural authority, as the position of staff such as the junior tutors makes clear. These people, who do the same work as tutors — assisting composers, writing software, doing psychoacoustic research — but who are not employed as such, have high cultural status despite their low pay and insecurity. By contrast, administrative and clerical staff concerned with basic institutional services — with reproduction — have lower status. The Administration itself is concerned primarily with the institute's bureaucratic and physical functioning, while clerical staff are attached to different units, for which they perform servicing tasks.

This delineates a basic division of IRCAM culture into two spheres: a lower-status administrative and clerical sphere associated with reproduction, and a higher-status research and production sphere associated with production. This is a variant of the fundamental classificatory opposition of production to reproduction mentioned earlier this chapter. In the external arena of French cultural politics it referred to IRCAM's greater prestige, as an institution engaged in cultural production, than the rest of the CGP, associated only with cultural reproduction. Within IRCAM culture the concept of production refers primarily to music production, but it also has the inclusive meaning of "intellectual origination in general" (whether of music, research, or technologies). While this concept of production is explicit, its opposite — reproduction — is an implicit category referring not to cultural reproduction but to the broader sociological meaning — that is, servicing and maintenance of functioning. But once again, production is perceived to have higher status and prestige than reproduction.

There were many expressions of the two status domains within IRCAM culture in 1984. The most obvious was a close correlation with

IRCAM's sexual division of labor whereby the lower-status sphere of reproduction was associated with women and the higher-status production domain almost exclusively with men. Figure 3 outlines the sexual division of labor. It shows that there were far fewer women than men in the IRCAM population and that just four women worked in research and production, none of them in full-time positions.

As for women with higher office, they were confined to reproduction even when working ostensibly within the sphere of production. Of the three women directors, one was the Administrator, one the coordinator of music production, and one the head of Diffusion. Significantly, the position of IRCAM technicians was precisely the obverse. The technicians were all men (with the exception of one Systems technician); and although ostensibly in servicing roles, they were closely associated with musical and technological production. The Esp Pro and Sound teams assisted all performances and went on IRCAM tours; the Sound team supervised recordings, while the Systems team was vital to the functioning of the computer research environment. The technicians were, then, considered essential to the success of production. Both of these groups — women directors, male technicians — thus represent transitional positions, poised between production and reproduction.

The sexual division of labor was sanctioned by sexist hostility aimed at women who defied the "natural" order of things by taking on higher or skilled roles associated with production. This surfaced in certain men's attitudes, hinted at directly or indirectly when women were not present, or reported by women, and it took one of three classic ideological forms: the view that the woman at issue was a hysteric; that she was being hired or tolerated because of her attractiveness and/or because of her sexual relationship with a man at IRCAM; or that she was lesbian, uninterested in men, or somehow aberrant.

The division of spheres between reproduction and production was echoed by symbolic temporal, spatial, and technological divisions within IRCAM culture. Spatially, it was most clearly expressed in the location of the Administration department in the old building, separate from the rest of IRCAM; and technologically, in the Administration's totally independent microcomputer network, while secretaries had no access to computer facilities at all, so that their separation from the research culture was complete. Similarly, secretaries never attended the various open meetings to do with research and production, while technicians and administrative directors sometimes did. These meetings were for the dissemination of policy and ideas. They constituted IRCAM's internal

Full-Time Permanent Salaried Staff:

Total	=	54 (100%)
Men	=	38 (70%)
Women	=	16 (30%)

Women:

Total	=	16
Clerical	=	12: secretaries, assistants, receptionists
Directors	=	3: Administrator, Production Office, Diffusion
Technician	=	1: Systems team

Regular Temporary Workers:

Total	=	44 (100%)
Men	=	36 (82%)
Women	=	8 (18%)

Women:

Total	=	8
Clerical	=	3: secretaries, assistants on *vacations*
Research	=	2: computer scientists, one 4X *vacation*, one systems *honoraire*
Composers	=	2: one commission/*honoraire*, one squatter
Postgraduate	=	1

Other occasional visitors during 1984:

Total	=	20 (100%)
Men	=	20 (100%): composers, musicians, scientists, researchers

Within whole population:

Total population	=	118 (100%)
Total women	=	24 (20%)

Of all women workers:

Total	=	24 including 15 clerical, 3 directors, 2 computer scientists, 2 composers, 1 technician, 1 postgraduate

3. IRCAM's sexual division of labor in 1984: women's jobs and employment status.

forum: the public space in which adults engaged in democratic debate. Secretaries' office-bound nonengagement with this space demoted them, by implication, almost to the status of nonadults.

Temporally, the population kept two different timetables: the normal office weekday and the rest — evenings, nights, and weekends. The office day was kept strictly by all administrative and clerical staff. Secretaries felt that their timekeeping was being monitored by the Personnel director, who sometimes hung around the entrance hall, fetching a coffee and chatting amiably. Directors and research staff were less reliably available. They wandered in later, had long lunch engagements. Meetings and consultations filled their office days.

By contrast, the unofficial evening, night, and weekend culture contained exclusively production-related workers. Within this, and informally, different workers took different shifts. Technical teams and all involved with performances stayed into the evenings whenever performances occurred. The Systems team had maintenance duties to carry out each evening: they changed over the computer tapes and disks upon which all the day's programming was recorded, and made backup copies as a security against loss. Working regularly around the clock were the projects using the 4X, which had a twenty-four-hour timetable to gain maximum use. Less routinely, and less tied to specific tasks, were the composers and computer researchers who could be found working into the evening, and some throughout the night. This included the more ambitious computer scientists who stayed, relentlessly pursuing their programming, among them some from the Chant/Formes group and IRCAM's two "hackers." One hacker could often be glimpsed working into the night in his darkened room, his hair and grubby anorak disheveled, sometimes with a half-eaten baguette in his hand dripping crumbs into the keyboard, until he fell asleep slumped over his terminal.

Those using the evenings and nights to compose included, occasionally, directors and tutors, but more often those with commissions, junior tutors, and squatters. They worked at night for different reasons. All wanted to avoid the endless, mundane interruptions of the office day, which precluded creative work. All wanted also to work out of peak hours to avoid computer congestion on the VAX, and so to work faster and without constant "crashes" (breakdowns) of the system. The peak time for congestion was weekdays between 11A.M. and 5P.M., when the VAX was stretched to capacity, and when overstretched it would crash. So visitors, learners, and squatters were barred from using the VAX during those times (although in practice some still did). Musicians on

staff used the "offtime" to bypass their lack of official status as composers. For example, tutors did their own composition work—when not
engaged with a visiting composer—late at night and on weekends. One
commissioned composer worked only at night because he so disliked the
bureaucratic routines of the day. Squatters worked at night to avoid
official notice, and to gain maximum computer freedom while they
learned the ropes of computer music and produced their first, inelegant
sounds.

The night and weekend culture thus had the sense of being open-
ended, with no immediate goals. Composed of bohemian juniors and
squatters, it constituted a sort of self-styled intellectual and artistic vanguard: those least tolerant of bureaucracy, most ambitious and/or as yet
unrecognized, and wishing to get concentrated work done uninterrupted
or unseen. All-night workers were spaced throughout the house, logged
on to the VAX at different terminals, and might never meet. Periodically,
they would use the computer to check who else was logged on, giving a
mediated sense of companionship. A spontaneous camaraderie might
arise as, every few hours, on-screen messages and jokes would pass between workers asking how things are going and whether anyone would
like to go out, above ground, for a coffee and cognac at one of the all-
night bars. But there was no lasting group identity here: it was a small,
fragmentary, changing, and competitive collectivity.

However, there were two additional forces behind the two-timetable
system. The first concerns secrecy and privacy. IRCAM had an interconnected system of loudspeakers linking most offices and studios, and
through them the sounds being produced by anyone using the computer
network could be heard by all around the house: an enforced "democracy" of aural information. Similarly, programming on the central VAX,
since it linked together all using it, meant that others logged on to the
system could attempt to gain access to one's files and look at one's work.
Both of these technologically potential "democracies" of information
created ambivalence in composers and programmers. By working at
night, intellectual staff tried to circumvent them and to retain greater
privacy for their work-in-progress, whether from fear of embarrassment
at crude early work or from fear of rivals' spying.

The second force expressed by the two timetables returns us to the
distinction between productive and reproductive staff. The motivation
for night work for intellectuals was not at all pay, but the pursuit of
art/science/knowledge; and with this the added status and charisma that
accrued by disdaining the limits of the office day and being seen to ex-

ploit themselves (differentiating themselves from the merely exploited) by working extraordinary and long hours. Cultural status thus appeared to vary directly with the degree of self-exploitation[9] in intellectual labor — at least, that was the implicit belief of IRCAM's intellectual vanguard. By contrast, for reproductive staff there was no incentive to work beyond the office day. Theirs was an entirely different symbolic economy of time in which accurate time-keeping was under surveillance by those in authority and in which snatching an extra half-hour for lunch embodied dissent. Thus, while intellectual workers vied to devote a maximum of antisocial time to their creative labor, lower-status workers engaged in a symbolic struggle to wrest time back from that paid for by the wage.

THE "CULTURED" AND THE "UNCULTURED"

The status division between production and reproduction was also expressed by subjects' different cultural dispositions, especially by their attitudes toward avant-garde and IRCAM music. In chapter 1, I discussed Bourdieu's analysis of two basic kinds of art perception. We find within IRCAM culture examples of those two forms, whereby the cultural attitudes in IRCAM's lower, reproduction sphere correspond to the "naive" and "uncultured," and those within the higher, production sphere to the "cultured" and "knowing." But the situation is more complex — a complexity that extends Bourdieu's analysis rather than refuting it.

Bourdieu sees "education" and "culture" as the distinguishing factors between his two kinds of art perception, with culture the more obviously inherited and unconscious class trait. He also considers educational achievement to be structured by class (Bourdieu and Passeron 1977), yet with education he leaves some space for the acquisition of cultural capital. Within IRCAM, we will see that the concept of a "need for education into understanding" avant-garde music was the main form in which lower-status workers expressed their sense of lack of cultural mastery, of "not knowing about" or "not understanding" the music.

Overall, the social distribution of cultural capital within IRCAM followed, in 1984, the three structural positions outlined above: that is, workers associated with reproduction, with production, and those workers transitional between the two. Whereas workers from the reproduction sphere considered themselves without any substantial involvement in art and intellectual work, it is striking that those poised between reproduction and production — the male technicians, and two women artistic directors — shared a background of work in the arts, or engaged in external professional cultural activities.[10] They were thus far from culturally naive and professionally and pragmatically involved in artistic work. So they did not express the mystified reverence for all things artistic that was characteristic of reproduction workers.

Lower-status administrative and clerical workers were united in believing that they did not have the educated kind of "culture" that IRCAM's music and intellectual sphere embodies. The only exceptions were the very few with family or other background links to. contemporary music. For example, one secretary had a brother who was a well-known French concert pianist, a specialist in contemporary music. "Contemporary music was always in the family: my brother began to play Messiaen before he played Mozart. He won the Messiaen prize at Royan." She came to IRCAM through her brother's contacts with the Artistic Director. Urbane and knowledgeable, she arranged to work with Berio: "It was fantastic! . . . I loved Luciano [Berio] . . . as a person, and also [his] Italian culture and language." By contrast, the Personnel director's father was a provincial orchestral leader. Speaking of his less exalted musical roots he said: "We always had music in the family. . . . That's why I'm glad to be here at IRCAM—even though the music practiced by my father wasn't the same music that's made here . . . [laughs nervously]. But anyway, one still lives with artists, music . . . things that please me." These background links to music, for workers from all levels, cut across other divisions and provided a strong sense of identification with IRCAM's musical mission.

Beyond the broader unity, however, there were three different attitudes discernible among reproduction workers toward the "culture" of IRCAM's higher sphere, embodying varied degrees of awareness, mystification, and resistance. Most common, and most consciously self-deprecating, was the enchanted attitude of reverence expressed by workers who believed that they had no understanding of avant-garde music, so that they must submit themselves to a process of gradual education or socialization—signaled mainly by going to concerts and talks—in order to appreciate IRCAM's musical and intellectual raison d'être. These workers attributed their lack of "culture" to family or education, or to a lack of "gifts." Their attitude was imbued with a strong sense of moral self-improvement, and undergoing a process of education became a mark of good faith in the institute and of commitment to their job. Indeed, in IRCAM's earliest period this attitude was institutionalized: weekly educational seminars on IRCAM's musical philosophy were pro-

vided to coincide with the *Passage du Vingtième Siècle* concerts for all
levels of staff, who were expected to give up their lunch time for them. A
secretary recalled these events with an ecstatic nostalgia: "Everyone was
supposed to come: it wasn't high level. The atmosphere was so good! We
all learned together, and I was so happy to discover that the music I heard
on the radio, that I didn't like, could *attract* me. And then I was very, very
motivated and went to concerts many times. . . . This was so good for me,
it was the right music at the right time for my mood." Another secretary
said of her cultural background and the effect of her entry to IRCAM:
"My parents weren't rich, we had no theater, no concerts. There were
just records and radio: music was a bit secondary — not of the first order
of importance. We didn't learn music, except through a local choir. . . .
Since I've been at IRCAM, I've gone much more often to concerts, at
IRCAM and elsewhere. I've discovered Stravinsky. It sounds idiotic, but
I *listen better*, I buy more modern things, whereas before I knew absolutely nothing about contemporary music. I have little judgment, because I have few [musical] gifts."

Although many lower-status workers talked of going along to IRCAM
concerts to learn about the music, in reality only a few of them could be
seen at most concerts. The sense of obligation thus appeared stronger
than the desire.

Another reproductive worker, one of several Administration department directors, stressed the process of education into higher culture as a
pleasurable adventure. On IRCAM and avant-garde music he began:

> Well, my education didn't at all predispose me to this kind of music. [How-
> ever] I am [now] very curious to *discover* this kind of music. . . . But until now
> I have lacked — whether it be other people, or the culture, or an approach —
> that could help me to *understand* or to like this music. . . . Since coming here,
> I've had much advice [*laughs*] . . . about how to try to *enter into* this music. . . .
> Yes, I go to concerts — this evening I go to PL's . . . [*as though countering his
> own skepticism:*] No, in any case I *want* to get into it. I have a great openness
> of spirit for this kind of thing.

We can see here ambivalence beginning to peep through. Other Administration directors represented the second position among reproductive workers: a combative attitude of resistance to cultural mystification,
a thinly concealed skepticism toward the self-evident value of IRCAM
music, and even plain dislike. One such director, a professional state
bureaucrat, when asked if he was interested in contemporary music,
replied with some irritation:

The music that interests me above all is classical music; not that it interests me especially, but I received an education that was very classical for some years. . . . When I arrived here, I knew absolutely nothing about contemporary music. I must say that I find that to understand contemporary music, or even to listen to it . . . it's a question of *education*. And a classical [music] education isn't sufficient. When I first went to concerts here, I was *incredibly, profoundly bored* and annoyed. Whereas now — but I've been here a number of years — I go to concerts out of my own interest: I understand the evolution, I understand things . . . [*prevaricating, automatic, circular*] that's to say that I like the music, so it interests me a lot more. Whereas at the beginning!! [*exasperated, annoyed*] . . . it was completely hermetic!

Another Administration director said of his relation to IRCAM music:

WS: I go *very, very rarely* to concerts here!

GB: Is it the aesthetic of avant-garde music that you don't like?

WS: No, not really, that doesn't bother me — there are many musics that are not easy to assimilate. No, what I don't like. . . . [*equivocally*] On the other hand, I went the other day to PL's Workshop [concert by the black American composer], and that I liked a lot. . . . But thinking of works like Radulescu [commission premiered earlier]. . . . Phew!!, [*frustrated, angry*] it's hard. I'm also upset when I see that we're giving a concert, and I know how much it has cost, to see the result! I'm really brought down! . . . All the concerts are expensive for IRCAM. And generally, in my opinion, very few of them are good.

These workers also felt confident to express less personalized and emotional and more intellectually detached views, sometimes as though representing "the general public." They took the form of different critical assessments of the social context of IRCAM music. One Administration director argued that IRCAM was failing in its duty to provide educational links with contemporary music, without which the general public would remain annoyed by and uninterested in the music. In speaking about this, his critical attitude barely concealed his own personal dislike. Following IRCAM music, he said, is "about education, and that's annoying . . . I mean, in relation to the public; it takes a certain time for them to get used to it."

GB: You have sympathy with the public's problems with contemporary music?

TY: [*Laughs ironically, as though to say "Do I!"*] I've already spoken of this to Boulez, but [*exasperated*] . . . without success. I'd like to see, for the public, all the links explained — between the classical school, the period at the turn of the century, the Viennese school, and then today. . . . If we talk of the general public, of which I'm a member, I'd like it if they'd explain to me some of the many things I don't understand — dodecaphonic music, for example, things like that . . . how today we've arrived at Stockhausen, Boulez. . . .

GB: You mean, about the revolution after tonality?

TY: Yes, all that! which they don't teach here. Boulez's response was, "No, we mustn't, because here we're an institution for *creation*, so we must only show and explain creation." . . . [*Outraged*] In concerts, they only do IRCAM pieces! It's a bit tough. That doesn't work for the public: for them, it's important to give some carrots.

A different Administration director enunciated a critique of the size and character of the IRCAM audience, linked to an appraisal of the networks of patronage surrounding IRCAM's composing elite:

Very few people go to the concerts. I find that strange: very big expenses to touch a very small, strictly Parisian public. . . . It's always the same types: "B.C., B.G." [*bon chic, bons gens*: slang meaning very chic, very classy people] . . . the "*nomenclatura*" — what you in English call the "establishment." . . . My impression is that only a small clique comes. . . . In the *Espace Libre* you find that epitomized. For publicity they put a little piece in *Libération* [the Leftist newspaper] — and who reads *Libération*?!! Exactly the same crowd! There's been a change the last year, though: they've made videos that explain what IRCAM is, contemporary music . . . and they're shown on TV. That's a better way: [at least] some new people [will] come across the music. [Whereas for] the *Espace* . . . well, it's the mates of a friend of [the organizer] who bring along their tapes, their little films. It's not some *unknown*, anonymous guy who's made something and who gets to come along.

It is notable that these critical attitudes of rebellion against cultural domination were held by the most powerful workers within the sphere of reproduction — by Administration directors. They were aware of cultural difference, and they resisted it. Only they were sufficiently confident, in private, to be insurrectionary, to dissent.

A third position, the opposite — being unaware of the significance of cultural difference and not resisting — could be found among the least powerful and lowest status reproductive staff. These workers appeared quite unconcerned by the issue of cultural distinction and unaware that the higher culture of IRCAM had any relevance for their own lives: the two were simply not brought into juxtaposition. IRCAM's espousal of absolute cultural values did not concern them. They were unaware both of the implicit denigration of their own culture and of the meritocratic option of cultural "self-improvement." This position of "otherness" did not preclude a reverence for IRCAM intellectuals and particularly for Boulez, the "*patron*."[11] Thus a very few of the lowest-status workers did not even profess the desire to be "educated into understanding" the

music: they were content without, and had other kinds of relationship to
other kinds of musics.

HOW MUSIC IS EXPERIENCED BY THE "UNCULTURED"

I have shown that many lower-status IRCAM workers—in the shadow
of high-cultural production—were quite anxiously aware of the "understanding" that they lacked, and that they hoped education could improve. The ways in which they related to musical experience betray variants of the unmediated cultural pleasure that Bourdieu has described.
Asked about their musical tastes, most were concerned first simply to list
music that they "like" or "don't like," without explaining why, so that a
personal consumer choice stood as sufficient justification. Crude classifications were used, hesitantly, to aid identification of the different musics enjoyed. Thus, two secretaries expressed themselves as follows:

> I listen to a lot of classical music. The music that I love is nineteenth-century.
> . . . The ones I prefer are Beethoven, Wagner . . . mmmm, Stravinsky, De-
> bussy. . . . Oh yes! I love jazz. I listen to a lot of different music. But I like some
> more than others: for example, I like some jazz musicians—I like best people
> like . . . [fishing around] er, John Coltrane . . . er, phew! . . . I forgot earlier,
> about classical music, I like Richard Strauss. But, OK, I also listen to modern
> music—the Beatles . . . well, I don't know if they're modern [laughs], but. . . .

> My mum liked classical music—Beethoven, Bach, Haydn. My dad liked jazz,
> above all gay and amusing—Sydney Bechet. I discovered Gershwin's Rhap-
> sody in Blue—ravishing! I was eight. . . . The radio wasn't very important—
> just for variété—we liked it OK. . . . Rock or pop? No, I'm not very "rock/
> pop." I love very much Ella Fitzgerald, Jessye Norman . . . singing the blues. I
> don't like "violence" at all, I like some harmony. [I last listened to] Fabien
> Thibaud, a French Canadian singer—d'you know him? I think he's got a very
> pretty voice. Apart from that, I recently bought Pulcinella by Stravinsky, and I
> adore that record . . . [shyly] conducted by Boulez!

The person with the most sophisticated and encyclopedic awareness
of classification, but applied only to popular music genres and as if
learned by rote rather than by inner understanding, was one of IRCAM's
lowest status service workers, KR:

> KR: Pop, jazz, reggae, "black," disco, country: I listen only to foreign
>   pop. . . . I love hard rock—Judas Priest, Iron Maiden. . . .
> GB: . . . Led Zeppelin?
> KR: Led Zeppelin? I don't know whether that's hard . . . Black Sabbath:
>   that's hard rock . . . Deep Purple isn't . . . no, no. It's good, but not [hard
>   rock].

Asked to explain why they liked something, to expound further or to exemplify a taste, these workers were insecure and could become inarticulate. When I pressed KR to be specific about the music he last listened to, for a couple of minutes he went absolutely blank and could not tell. Then he blurted out at a run: "Elvis Presley, Little Richard, the Shadows, Buddy Holly, Chuck Berry . . . Beatles, Rolling Stones, the Pink Floyd . . . Jazz: I have lots. I have Duke Ellington, Stan Getz, Django Rheinhardt, Louis Armstrong . . . Fats Domino. . . ." These workers had two ways of expressing their relation with music, extending from the "like/don't like" consumer judgment. One was emotional and sensual: about feelings, mood, the pleasure of discovery. Reference was made to the "right music at the right time for my mood," to "discovery," to "the music that I love" and "adore," to "gay," "amusing," and "ravishing" musics. When asked whether she strongly disliked any IRCAM music, a secretary replied: "It's like . . . *candy!* Some are good, some are bad, some I like, some I don't." The other way, extending this further, dwelt upon the material forms in which musical experience is embedded: the commodity or technological forms, their costs and quantities, the process of buying them, the physical or emotional state of the listener. KR had the most elaborate awareness of the role of music in his life. He hoarded music on cassette and was acutely aware of quantity, cost, and commodity form. He was also intensely concerned with the physical state that he needed in order to listen to music. He explained:

> I have six to seven hundred cassettes: it's a collection that's not complete . . .
> they're arrangements, a mixture. . . . I buy cassettes because they're less
> expensive, I watch for things coming on sale. . . . I buy more cassettes than I
> listen to! I buy them when they're on sale because I may not be able to find
> them again in a month. . . . That's good to do. . . . I can listen to them in future
> years, my collection. . . . I listen to music on the weekends because I play
> sports nearly every night: combat sports, like karate or judo. . . . I feel like a
> cassette, so I put on a cassette . . . and then I'm away, and that's it! I listen only
> to cassettes: I make a selection [from the radio], I choose the pieces that please
> me and I erase the rest. . . . Me? to listen to great music [*la grande musique*:
> he means serious music] I must be in a room all alone, and only listen to that.
> If not—if there's noise, the telephone, the doorbell—if one's disturbed, it
> doesn't work. The only piece of classical music I've got is the *Sword Dance*—
> Khatchaturian? Rimsky Korsakoff? I can't remember. . . . Beyond that, only
> Ravel's *Bolero*. Those are the only two—quite modern.

These ways of talking illustrate the relatively simple, sensual, and unmediated nature of lower-status workers' vocabulary for their musical experience—as Bourdieu argues, an absence of the knowledgeable codes and categories through which the "cultured" are supposed to experience music.

The three positions outlined among reproduction workers reveal the cultural differentiation of IRCAM's nonintellectuals, those without cultural capital and servicing the dominant institutional expertise, a differentiation ranging between the rebellious assertions of the powerful, the compliant aspirations of those socialized into a cultural lack, and the complacence of those altogether "other," powerless even to sense their exclusion. Of these, only the second involves a process of subjectification to the dominant aesthetic system, one imbued with an ethical program of enlightened self-improvement. It is, however, this position that subsumed the majority of IRCAM's reproductive workers.

ACHIEVED AND INHERITED CULTURE
WITHIN THE HIGHER PRODUCTION SPHERE

The "need for education into understanding" avant-garde music was not expressed by lower-status workers alone. IRCAM intellectuals and production staff also commonly held this view. However, they considered themselves to have already been through this education process, and so to have attained an affinity with contemporary music. The process was often described in mythic or heroic terms: as one of gradual revelation or enlightenment, or as a trial by fire overcoming obstacles and so a mark of determination and commitment. Whatever, the relationship was achieved and now assumed. One composer described his enlightenment in terms of a repudiation of his parents' (lack of) culture. He placed great importance on the classical music radio stations that had introduced a higher musical appreciation into his life — also spoken of by other French IRCAM intellectuals:

> My parents were always against me doing music. They thought that musicians didn't earn a living — the mentality that musicians always screw up their lives. So they forbade me to do music! I had to wait twenty years, till I left home and went to Paris. . . . There was no music in the family house; the cultural milieu was not very elevated. . . . My mother was from Corsica, a woman with very little education. And my father had a normal education, but for him culture wasn't a part of his life that could be intellectually stimulating. It was something around, but he didn't understand that culture could be enriching. . . . No records, no; but there *was* the radio: and that's how I came to know about music. When I was thirteen, I listened all the time to *France Musique* [radio station]. . . . I discovered a *world* of music that I had known

nothing about! I found it completely extraordinary and so that's what I decided to do, at thirteen years. Before that, I knew nothing: I was in a milieu, basically, that was culturally very, very empty.

The American director of Pedagogy also described his emergence from the cultural surroundings of his family, in Belleville, Illinois, a lower-middle-class white suburb, and how his parents began to stimulate his interest in both science and music; but in rather different terms:

> My dad was very "scientific oriented"—a manager on a local air base. I got science from my dad: I got interested in space—this was the '50s—when I was a kid. My mother brought music to me: she was a pianist, popular music mainly. She had a lot of sheet music, collections of Gershwin tunes. She didn't play too well. . . . My first musical experience was Tex Ritter [*giggles at the absurdity*]—a country 'n' western singer. At four or five years old I liked to listen to certain *licks*. There was a Tex Ritter lick—"Frog he went a courtin'"! [*cracks up laughing*]. . . . In grade school I wanted to be in the band. I wanted to play trumpet, but the band manager said that my lips weren't thick enough!! [*laughs at the implied racism*]. So he told me I had to play drums! Just like that! [*laughs*]

It was a rare IRCAM music intellectual who professed to a "natural" and inherited rather than primarily "achieved" culture. Contrasting with the Pedagogy director's sense of cultural "legacy" was that of another American, the Music Research director, the one IRCAM intellectual to claim inherited cultural capital in relation to both music and computing. From a New York Jewish background, his father set up one of the first computer-graphics businesses, while his mother was a concert pianist, trained at the Juilliard, who became a successful music teacher. The director spoke of his mother devising stimulating cognitive musical games to teach her children. In these ways he conveyed a feeling of rich inheritance in relation to his vocation as a computer music composer.

The result of the majority experience among IRCAM intellectuals of achieving, sometimes against odds, a close relationship with contemporary music is that IRCAM's higher production sphere was imbued with a strong sense of classless meritocracy and of cultural commitment, rather than inherited cultural privilege. The classlessness was also supported by the sense that since research and production workers were judged on their creative merits, workers from humble backgrounds could prove themselves and be promoted. And in fact, workers with both humble family backgrounds and a lack of relevant high educational qualifications had done well. Thus, as well as the French composer and American

director of Pedagogy discussed above, several other key music-related
intellectuals came from lower-class origins, and some lacked formal education both in music and in computer science.

But against the meritocracy and "humble origins" thesis, there were
also IRCAM intellectuals who clearly came from culturally and/or socially privileged backgrounds. For example, the Artistic Director enjoyed both familial and educational privilege. He was educated at Cambridge and apprenticed at Glyndebourne. His family, upper-middle-class
Jewish Londoners, had dealt in art, jewelry, and antiques for genera-
tions, so becoming an impresario was hardly a departure. Yet despite his
evident cultural privilege, even the Artistic Director felt that since he had
struggled to overcome a lack of musical background and a family preju-
dice against contemporary art, his relationship with contemporary music was personally achieved. Other workers had either one or the other
kind of privilege. For example, American workers with lower-class roots
tended to have been through elite American universities — Stanford,
Yale, or Harvard.

Thus the meritocracy thesis must be modified by regard to these shifting dimensions of privilege. Nonetheless, the fact that all higher-status
production staff, whatever their background, sincerely believed that they
had meritocratically and individually attained their particular attach-
ment to contemporary music countered the potential within the institute
for a sense of cultural domination of nonintellectual workers — a sense
hinted at only by the critiques of the two Administration directors.

STATUS DIFFERENCES WITHIN THE SPHERES OF
PRODUCTION AND REPRODUCTION

The analysis above suggests the existence of hierarchies within each
status domain, hierarchies that generated resentment. Within the reproduction sphere, Administration executives had higher status and power
than the lower clerical and service staff. Different groups of workers
expressed hostility toward the higher Administration differently. Secretaries, directly subordinate, experienced it as unmediated policing about
which they remained largely mute. Research and production staff, from
their "other" sphere, channeled their hostility through a disdain for the
Administration's bureaucratic Philistinism.

The production sphere also contained a hierarchy of status. On the
one hand, formally and publicly, IRCAM's music-related intellectual

staff had the highest cultural status. On the other, Boulez's vision had stressed long-term research rather than short-term market-driven technological development, suggesting that IRCAM subscribes to the wider ideology in which pure research has higher status than applied. The key to how these forces intersected in the production sphere is provided by membership of the informal musicians' group, those attending the voluntary meetings called together by the Music Research director. The meetings were held in a central seminar room over some months. They delineated a group of IRCAM intellectuals who aspired to the role of IRCAM's ambitious vanguard and who considered themselves the most music-oriented workers within IRCAM: the two were linked, as in Boulez's vision. As well as the regular attenders, others would occasionally turn up when interested (Boulez, the Artistic and Scientific Directors, programmers and technicians), so membership was self-elected. But the group's core consisted of the directors of Music Research and Pedagogy, the 4X Software director, the Chant/Formes director, two junior tutor-composers, a junior tutor-psychoacoustician, a composer-researcher, and three official tutors. Of these eleven men, although none were officially employed as such, nine were composers or musicians. The group thus contained almost all the self-defined serious musicians from IRCAM's higher sphere.

It is striking that after music intellectuals, the musicians' group consisted primarily of software researchers or programmers. Two were the directors of software projects, two were closely associated with Chant/Formes, while the tutors and junior tutors engaged in a great deal of programming when assisting composers to provide them with custom-built software environments for their pieces. Thus in all, nine of the group were regularly involved in ambitious programming. But there was a further twist to this logic of status, since the Chant/Formes group asserted themselves informally as the most farsighted and fundamental technology researchers within IRCAM. Their software work, related as it was to AI, was considered, at least by allies and sympathizers, closer to pure, long-term research than to short-term technological development. Hence in the musicians' group, software came to be identified with long-term research oriented toward IRCAM's musical ends. It was, then, this informal and ideological coalition of interests in the musicians' group that embodied the institute's major bid for its highest cultural status as a vanguard. We will see, however, that this was hotly contested by others, so that status was more volatile and less assured here than in the rigid

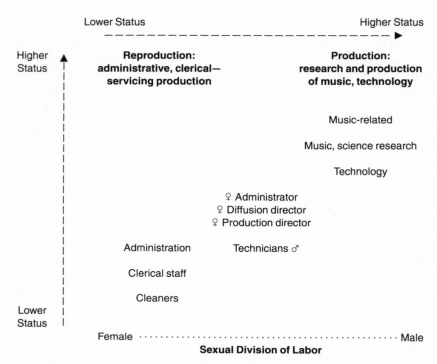

4. Production and reproduction: two status domains within IRCAM culture.

hierarchy of the sphere of reproduction. Figure 4 summarizes the analysis of status differentiation.

STRATIFICATION AND STATUS

A great deal of secrecy and mystification surrounded finances and salaries within IRCAM. It was difficult to get information on IRCAM's annual budgets, even though as a state-funded institution they are meant to be open to public inspection. Salaries were generally not discussed between workers, so they remained ignorant of their relative positions. The Administration was felt by workers to use this to play people off against each other, which may partly have been due to the Administration's difficulty in dealing with the staff given Boulez's quixotic interventions, which I discuss shortly. But it was also a way of maintaining control, which added to the distrust of the Administration.

Officially, salaries were set according to a hierarchy of twelve categories derived from the public-sector pay scale operating at the CGP — that is, for *"fonctionnaires"* (public sector employees). These categories, according to the Personnel director, reflected the degree of skill, training, and responsibility of the jobs in each, and within each category a worker's age, experience, and time on the job were taken into account. But because of IRCAM's independent status its workers were not in fact *fonctionnaires*. The Administration therefore had flexibility when negotiating salaries and used it differently for different workers. Lower-status workers were told that they could not rise a category without a position opening at the next level up. In practice, such rigorous controls operated for some and could be disregarded for others. By contrast, the salaries of the top three executives — Boulez, the Artistic and Scientific Directors — were *"hors grille"*: completely beyond the scale of categories.

Pay differentials varied across the scale. Between the lowest and highest categories — between the most unskilled administrative worker and the highest paid directors within the scale — they were in the region of one to four. Although I was not given access to the wages of the top three directors, it was possible to estimate their pay. From this, it appears that IRCAM's top salaries were of the order of twenty times the lowest and five times the next highest salaries. Clearly, IRCAM was an extremely stratified institution.

The pay of temporary workers was even more differentiated. *Vacateurs* — temporary, junior staff in research and production — received, on average, pay similar to the bottom of the salary scale. With their compulsory layoffs, they were thus the worst paid and least secure of IRCAM's longer-term workers. For commissioned composers on *honoraires*, the average and range of pay were close to those for permanent, salaried positions; but composers had no security or benefits, were paid for just a few months, and often worked well beyond the official commission period. With the exception of the top three executives, computer science consultants were by far the best paid workers at IRCAM, with pay almost twice the highest category. It is possible that their pay entered the range of the top three directors'; however it was sustained only for a short visit. To complete the picture of the population, the majority of persistent squatters were musicians and composers hoping to find an entry into IRCAM.

We can now begin to discern the character of stratification at IRCAM and how it related to status differences. Overall, the pay scale sanctioned the sexual division of labor by comparatively and systematically devaluing both the sphere of reproduction (administrative and clerical staff) vis-à-vis production, and all women workers. The uneven distribution of

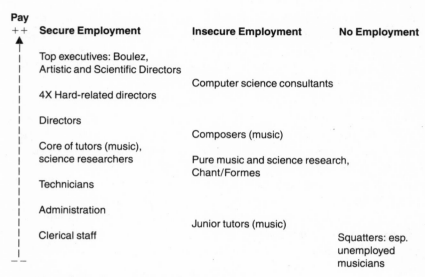

Pay ++	Secure Employment	Insecure Employment	No Employment
↑	Top executives: Boulez, Artistic and Scientific Directors		
		Computer science consultants	
	4X Hard-related directors		
	Directors		
		Composers (music)	
	Core of tutors (music), science researchers		
		Pure music and science research, Chant/Formes	
	Technicians		
	Administration		
		Junior tutors (music)	
	Clerical staff		
––			Squatters: esp. unemployed musicians

5.   Pay and security among IRCAM workers.

salaries and conditions, then, closely paralleled IRCAM's status hierarchy as shown by the stratification of and between the spheres of production and reproduction, in turn associated with the institute's sexual division of labor. To this extent, status and stratification were directly correlated.

But there were two striking exceptions within the higher production sphere in which status and stratification were inversely correlated. Although music-related work had the greatest status within IRCAM, and scientific and technological research had lower status by virtue of servicing musical ends, music fared far worse in terms of pay and conditions. With very few people employed specifically as musicians, the musicians in the population were filled out by eight junior tutor *vacateurs*, their pay the same as low clerical staff, the few commissioned composers, and unpaid squatters — all with little or no security. Thus, by comparison with the staffing of science and technology projects, music-related workers were both less well paid and less secure.

Stratification also reversed the dominant, if contested, status hierarchy within the scientific sector. Computer science consultants were paid better than all others, although they had no security, while the numerous 4X-related staff were both well paid and secure. By contrast, pure research and Chant/Formes — part of IRCAM's intellectual vanguard — fared poorly in terms of staff numbers, pay, and security, despite

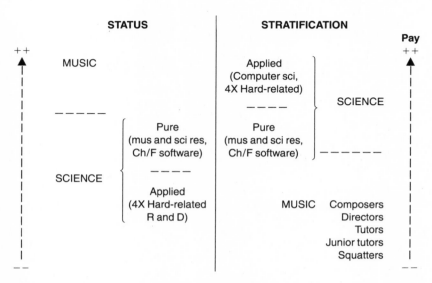

6. Inverse correlation between status and stratification among research and production workers.

their high cultural status. Thus hardware-related research and development was better resourced by all measures than both pure research and high-level software. Figure 5 depicts the different pay and security of groups within the institute; while Figure 6 shows the inverse correlation between status and stratification among workers in the higher production sphere.

The main question arising is why status and stratification were inversely correlated in this way for research and production. I suggest this occurred partly because of the different labor markets, partly because of the different forms of evaluation operating within the domains of music, pure research, and technological development, and partly because of the ideology of vanguard workers. The "rewards" received by different workers had the effect of achieving an uneasy peace mitigating the rivalry between them.

The extremely favorable labor market for the (mostly American) consultant computer scientists meant that, given IRCAM's dependence on them, and despite the Administration's resistance and nationalist rancor, they bargained their way to very high pay. But the situation for IRCAM's French computer science staff was also favorable, so that disaffected ones had little trouble obtaining jobs at other prestigious research establishments.[12]

Musicians were in a far weaker position since, crudely, apart from the well known, IRCAM did not need them. Rather, they needed IRCAM for prestige and career advancement. Of course, IRCAM required a constant supply of composers to produce the musical goods that justify its existence, and it sought some kind of international coverage. Moreover, IRCAM was dependent on the patronage of "stars," internationally well known composers, to affirm its status. But generally there was an oversupply of artistic labor, and composers competed with one another to come to IRCAM.[13] Because of the economic strictures of commissions, and just as within the profession at large, many composers added to their income by teaching or by commercial work — a strategy kept quiet because of IRCAM's Boulezian dominant ideology. More importantly, for those experiencing degrees of self-exploitation in the present, the promise was held out, by Boulez's own career as much as anything, of potentially higher rewards for their work than for any other kind of intellectual labor within IRCAM. That is, for the very few there was the potential to achieve great economic as well as cultural success. For musicians, then, the risks and the self-exploitation were higher, but the potential rewards also appeared greater, than for all other IRCAM workers.

However, these labor market factors do not explain the generally higher security and pay given to technologists, and especially those in 4X projects. There were mundane reasons: the 4X was one of the oldest projects, predating Chant/Formes, and its two highest-paid directors were two of the longest-serving; yet it did not precede the relatively impoverished Acoustics department. Then, the 4X was tied closely to Boulez's own *Répons*, in which so much of IRCAM's high status was invested. But these reasons were bolstered and rationalized by management ideology as articulated by two senior directors. According to them, IRCAM's permanent positions should provide the institute's basic human infrastructure, consisting of administrators, secretaries, technicians, directors, and key technologists. By contrast, they argued, IRCAM's musicians and higher researchers should not enjoy a permanent or secure relation with IRCAM. As creative and intellectual workers they should be contracted so that they remain on their toes and have to prove themselves with results of artistic and scientific value. One of the directors posed the dilemma thus: "We need composers at IRCAM, but do we need them actually running things? . . . How do we find a system where the composer does more than just a research project and yet is less than a permanent fixture?"

This management notion contains a double irony: first, in rehearsing the view advanced by Boulez at the time of the Malraux debacle, and second, in its self-evident exemption of Boulez himself. It also raises the management's problem of evaluating scientific and musical results, and with it a basic contradiction between IRCAM's functioning and Boulez's founding ideology. According to that, IRCAM's work must be future-oriented, of long-term value rather than finding immediate markets. But in fact, and despite the deference of Ministry officials, IRCAM management had to judge artistic and research results in the short term to maintain both internal and continuing external legitimation. We will see that this was resolved by Boulez's judgment reigning in questions involving music; while the Artistic Director seemed to oscillate between an elitist confidence in his instinct for spotting talent (enunciated here in terms of his ideological opposition to Fleuret, the Director of Music), and an occasional and revealing self-doubt:

> And I spotted very quickly, [and] very cynically, what my grandfather told me years ago: all these people who think they're creative and they aren't. . . . If you're a crummy composer, it's much better to listen to music rather than try and do it. . . . [Whereas] the fashionable tradition now is "everybody's an artist, everybody can speak." If you read Monsieur Fleuret [*mocking*] there's this idea, which he actually announces, that *everybody* should make music, *every* discipline is equally worthy — whether it's rock, jazz, folk — all "*les musiques*," plural. *No*, they're *not* equal, I don't agree. I believe in fine art, I believe in aristocracy, and I believe in elite [culture]. . . . Yes, my job is [on] the missionary side. It sounds pretentious, [and one must] not be sadistic, but it's to ask for the very highest standards you possibly can. Very soon, for example, I spotted the conductors who were any good. . . . [About talent:] So how do I think I "know"? Well, I don't know that I *do* "know."

Technological validation was, however, even more problematic, since Boulez was not equipped to judge that sphere. Hence the apparent continuing search for a suitable Scientific Director for IRCAM. But in fact the problem was circumvented by Boulez resting the internal legitimation of technologies, and of the people responsible, on his judgment of the quality of music produced with them. Researchers were well aware of this, as exemplified by the Chant/Formes director:

> I had asked [junior tutor] WOW to come in order to make real musical use of all the materials that we had already made [with Chant], like the [simulated] Tibetan voices, the oboe. . . . We had those materials, [but] I had no confidence and no time to make a musical object with them. And it was very important because otherwise it's not possible to demonstrate the power of the [Chant] system and the interest of the materials. If it's not in a musical con-

text, I can extrapolate but other people *cannot*; and especially *Boulez* cannot. If you present [a technology] to Boulez that's not in a musical context, he's not interested, even if it's a very deep and interesting thing. You have to put it into a musical context: that was WOW's job. Boulez is interested in having real musical output.

The 4X project had done well and had been relatively immune from this kind of judgment since, historically, it had been closely implicated in Boulez's own *Répons*. Earlier 4X prototypes were used by the Music Research director on pieces that were clearly well received — as shown by his rapid promotion by Boulez within IRCAM. By contrast, the Chant/ Formes group's credibility had been badly damaged by a piece that was made using Chant in 1979 that Boulez considered risible. Thus the 4X, developed symbiotically with *Répons*, had been inherently favored in terms of resources while Chant/Formes had suffered. Yet the key 4X-related workers were not subject to the same extremely favorable labor market as international computer consultants. Nor were the higher resources and pay for 4X workers justified by its commercialization, as we have seen. Thus the privileging of 4X hardware-related work is not fully explained by any of these factors. I suggest that it was supported by a more primitive and "concrete" ideology, which I describe further in chapter 7, in which large hardware technology was perceived by some, including management, as a more substantial, tangible, "real," and "productive" result than high-level software or pure research, which were considered experimental, ephemeral, and risky.

Finally, another level of analysis comes from examining the ideology surrounding and perpetuated by the musicians' group, IRCAM's music-oriented intellectuals. Although some of the poorly paid and insecure members of the group complained of their marginality, they also chronically exploited themselves; and in this way, through signs of devotion and of the ascetic pursuit of art and knowledge, justified their role as IRCAM's intellectual vanguard with its attendant high-cultural status. Indeed, some perceived these conditions as inextricably tied. In the following, a software researcher in the group, one very important to IRCAM, appeared to welcome his weak contractual position as a means of greater intellectual freedom. Asked, "Has it never been reasonable to expect to be given security and a better contract?" he replied:

If I haven't got it, it's probably because I haven't asked for it enough. . . . Somewhere, I like the position where I [can] say: "Well, I don't need you [IRCAM]", at least, to live. That's not bad because it means that when I say something in IRCAM it's not for my own purposes, in the sense that if they don't pay me any more, well it's very sad, but I can live. I have a more *impartial* view because I'm not dependent. . . . [A close ex-colleague] was rather conscious of that. He told me, "You should keep your position [job] elsewhere, otherwise you will never be able to do *real* research at IRCAM. You will be too involved in production and the necessities of the house."

The researcher links his part-time contract here not only to intellectual independence but to "real," unmotivated (pure) research, which he opposes to baser "production": another opposition characteristic of IRCAM culture.

The musicians' group's heady mixture of self-exploitation with concepts of cultural leadership and pure, disinterested research reveals a layer of mystification reminiscent of Bourdieu's analysis of the avant-garde. For Bourdieu, this position rests on the belief that the highest cultural capital and the best strategy for its long-term accumulation come from disdaining immediate economic reward or a large market by adopting the marginal, prophetic role associated with youth, iconoclasm, and asceticism. Hence for the musicians' group, IRCAM's internal avant-garde, self-exploitation became a sign of dedication to higher values and of self-belief. The gamble for all who adopt this bohemian strategy of willed marginality is that asceticism and devotion to the unrecognized now may later win recognition and "consecration." At IRCAM this generated ambivalence. For some, marginality and self-exploitation became imbued with the hope that, eventually, accumulated cultural status would convert into economic value — that artistic or scientific success would bring high rewards. Others clearly wished to remain marginal by deferring endlessly or disdaining altogether this more profane validation.

Thus IRCAM's vanguard musicians and researchers were tempted into self-exploitation through collusion with an ideology in which, for the present, cultural and economic capital were inversely correlated: high cultural status accrued to those who were seen to exploit themselves the most and whose economic position vis-à-vis the "established order" was weakest — (hence also their collusion with the management ideology outlined earlier). In return, the vanguard were compensated by the reward of the highest cultural status.

We can now see how the inverse relation between status and stratification within the higher production sphere rested on two ideological moments: a primitive privileging of hardware over software and pure research, and a belief in the inverse relation of cultural and economic capital for IRCAM's musical and intellectual vanguard. The analysis also substantiates a contradiction between Boulez's original vision and the functioning of IRCAM. Those workers closest to Boulez's ideal — tutors, junior tutors, music-oriented pure researchers, that is, IRCAM's vanguard musicians and scientists — rather than being the best-supported core of IRCAM workers, were the least secure and most moderately paid of production staff. However, they were compensated by high intellectual status and, given accumulated authority and charisma, a few were able to benefit from internal patronage with ample rewards.

CHAPTER V

Power, Institutional Conflict, Politics

On the surface, IRCAM was in 1984 a highly bureaucratized institution. With written statutes, a hierarchy of departments and salaried officials, an elaborate management structure, and plentiful documentation and memos, the institute appeared both rule-bound and routinized. Centralized French bureaucracy penetrated the very language used. IRCAM periodically received instructions from the Ministry of Industry and Research designating the latest official French computer terms to be used in all state-related bodies.[1] Yet despite rigorous attempts at translation and resistance to linguistic imperialism, English — standard in the international computing world — was often the pragmatic language of choice for IRCAM's cross-nationality collaborations.

Just as it is commonplace in industrial sociology that informal associations and actual operations run counter to formal bureaucracy, so the reality of IRCAM's functioning undermined the surface since it was permeated by "irrational" and highly imperfect bureaucratic processes, with both serious and trivial consequences.

THE ILLUSION OF BUREAUCRACY

Despite IRCAM's *organigrammes*, it was in fact difficult to ascertain the various departments, people's functions and interrelations. *Organigrammes* were hard to find in the building. Some three months into fieldwork, and still confused by who was what, I finally found an *organigramme* by venturing one evening when nobody was around into Boulez's office.

There, on the wall over Boulez's desk, as though to remind him of bureaucratic functioning, was the diagram that many had mentioned and
none had been able to find. This illustrates the practical invisibility of
official guidelines to jobs. Instead, the internal phone directories were
used, which listed people by name, annulling differentiation by offices —
symbolic of an apparent social "leveling" that was common (and popular) within IRCAM. Thus the culture as lived preferred to forget its
implicit, official hierarchy.

I was able to wander into Boulez's office because, although security
maintained strict boundaries to the outside world, there was in 1984 a
strange absence of security within the institute. Most research labs, computer rooms, offices, and cupboards were kept unlocked.

Exemplifying a deeper absence of rational management, there was a
common awareness that IRCAM lacked adequate documentation of its
research and production and also lacked rational planning, clearly defined goals and timetables, for its scientific projects.

But the clearest expressions of nonbureaucratic functioning concerned
employment and work, and at several levels they contradicted the official
ideology as visualized in the *organigramme*. Most obviously, there was a
mismatch between what workers were officially supposed to do and what
they actually did. Many did several jobs at once or contributed to several
areas. This was especially true of musicians' group members, the interdisciplinary vanguard. The gap between junior tutors' official low status
and pay and the centrality of the work given to them — the guidance
of commissioned composers — illustrates a further anomaly: staff doing
work of higher status and greater importance than their official position.

Another hidden and surprising level of "irrationality" was workers'
lack of educational criteria for their jobs, and so the ubiquity within
IRCAM of people working on things that were not their main area of
expertise. For example, neither of the two software project directors had
formal training in computer science. One, originally a professional flau-
tist, gradually taught himself over his first few years at IRCAM: "I realized that the key to working with computers was programming. When I
started to work around the 4X with Pierre, I got into it more seriously,
and I started making little programs, and then big programs. . . . Then I
started making up for the programs that weren't available." The other
director, known as an AI expert and software designer, explained: "I've
never learned computer science. . . . I've learned it by experience and
because I need it for this and that, and for my courses."

On the music side there were people with important roles who were not musically trained. For example, one junior tutor who produced a piece that led to sudden high promotion and Boulez's patronage was musically an autodidact and had trained in philosophy. Similarly, people qualified only as scientists found themselves given important music-related, and especially tutoring, work. One official tutor had trained in computer science, another junior tutor in mathematics.

The Systems team also contained anomalies. The new Systems manager, an American who took over in mid-1984, was a composer rather than a computing specialist. Lower down the group, an eastern European *vacateur* trained as a composer had gained a place inside IRCAM by teaching himself enough computing to be hired as a Systems technician. Other such misqualifications and overqualifications included another eastern European, himself a composer and the son of a famous composer, who was given only technical and junior tutoring work; while one of the building caretakers told me that he had studied physics up to Ph.D. level — for which reason, he explained, he found IRCAM a fascinating environment.

It is clear that many of these varied employment realities arise from the nonstandard, complex, and interdisciplinary nature of IRCAM's work, the difficulty of delimiting job boundaries, and the temptation for workers to cross them and to extend their capacities. However, it was equally clear in 1984 that they acted also as a cover for the exploitation of junior workers, who were keen for their skills to be recognized and who hoped eventually to be given more appropriate work, usually as a composer, through advancement and patronage.

Above all, the institute might have been expected to organize job appointments and promotions according to proper bureaucratic procedures: that is, particularly for a high-level research institute, it might be expected that these would be rationally meritocratic. We have already seen a common mismatch between qualifications and employment. It is in relation to these areas that we begin to glimpse the importance of patronage within IRCAM and Boulez's power to override bureaucratic procedures. In short, when a permanent, full-time position became vacant in 1984, it was used freely for whichever worker or function Boulez considered necessary. As a by-product, crucial functions might remain unfilled for long periods. Most promotions also involved Boulez's intervention, and workers, seeing this was the way to gain promotion, tried to go direct to Boulez. If they could not or were prevented, and were fobbed off on the Administration, it meant that the process was far tougher, the rewards were likely to be lower, or they would be entirely unsuccessful.

Directors from the Administration talked of Boulez's interventions. One said, concerning a controversial promotion, "It was a promotion, but there were a few problems with the tutors who thought he wasn't competent and were jealous because we didn't ask them. In the end, it's Pierre who decides these changes!" Another senior figure in the Administration was not happy with Boulez's encroachment on his managerial territory through his exercise of patronage. He complained, "He descends into the running problems, and that's wrong. He has no idea of policy on salaries — that's not his competence! . . . It annoys me. People think they don't need to talk to me because Pierre has decided. Pierre protests, 'But I just listened!' . . . But psychologically, people think they've got it in the bag, so I take them back a few steps. I prefer him to leave things alone. If people go to Boulez first, it's an error of functioning."

Access to Boulez's patronage was markedly unequal. Research and production staff and technicians being brought into the *Répons* production orbit were able to call on his intervention. But with few exceptions it was not considered appropriate for lower-status workers to approach Boulez over employment problems. The form was to go first to their department head and then with backing to the Administration. A long-time secretary commented cynically on this situation, and on the apathy of higher status workers who lacked the incentive to take part in the political channels available to them: "[Those] people much prefer to deal directly with 'God' [Boulez]! They don't want to be represented because they can go straight to 'God!' " Reproductive workers were thus well aware of the inequality of access to Boulez and its effects on internal politics.

CHARISMA AND PATRONAGE IN THE HIGHER PRODUCTION SPHERE

The respect accorded to Boulez's patronage was much strengthened by the obvious authority that he commanded within IRCAM. In other words, his patronage was legitimized by his position as the institute's charismatic leader. It would be impossible for IRCAM workers to be immune to Boulez's international reputation and his place as a national culture hero. In 1984 the only open disenchantment about Boulez within IRCAM was voiced by a visiting but marginal American musician. We saw above one secretary's reference to Boulez as "God," a sardonic comment on his absolute power and apparently benign presence. An Administration executive also spoke critically of Boulez. But neither would have dared to criticize him intellectually. Other than these, Boulez appeared to be held in near universal respect, as shown by the following string of comments, all of which responded to questions about what attracted people to being at IRCAM:

> It's all Pierre!
>
> Boulez was the *King!*
>
> Boulez did some talks. I was totally struck by [them], I mean like lightning — I felt that this was my future. So I dropped university, I asked Boulez what I had to do. He told me to study, then stay in touch with IRCAM.
>
> It means that [my] research cannot stay confined in its own rhetoric, because of this . . . side of Boulez saying "Is that musically interesting?"
>
> [Boulez] analyzed the *Rite of Spring* and Webern's Opus 21. I was fascinated, by his charisma . . . this crazy guy. I was just bowled over by these beautiful sounds! I'd never heard anything like his music, it was just breathtaking.

Two mythic incidents from 1984 illustrate further the character of Boulez's authority and charisma and his role as musical leader. An informal seminar of IRCAM's music intellectuals was called to discuss junior tutor WOW's new piece *Chréode 1*. For several hours WOW discussed the piece at a blackboard in terms of the computer programs that he had helped design — Chant and Formes — which were used to compose it. He described in minute detail the underlying philosophy, the transformations of material, the encoding and notations used. After this, we adjourned to the Esp Pro to hear the piece and then returned again for more discussion in the seminar room. Eventually Boulez, who had quietly come in earlier, spoke. He said that WOW had told us plenty about the programming and scientific basis of the work, but had neglected to tell of its implicit musical ideas, of the "architecture of emotion" consisting of tension, climax, dispersion, change of timbres, and so on. Boulez ended by noting that the problem of composition was "to give meaning to the structures." This was the only intervention to break out of the programming mode of talk and raise specifically musical issues.

A major commercial computer music company came to IRCAM to give a demonstration of their latest big synthesizer. In due course the moment came when the automatic music transcription facility was to be shown in action. After repeated requests for someone to volunteer to play a tune — (the hapless demonstrator said naively "I'm sure *someone* must know a tune or two here!") — a reluctant tutor sat at the keyboard and played a few bars of sleazy cocktail muzak. The audience rushed to the front of the room to watch, with awe, as the music crystallized into a score on a small VDU in front of their eyes. Suddenly Boulez, who had unobtrusively entered the back of the room, said: "But it's got it *wrong!* It should be in triple time . . . in 6/8!" At this there were cries of "He's right!" The machine had transcribed the music into a 4/4 duple meter, so making a very simple rhythm appear extremely complex, rather than the 6/8 or 12/8 triple meter that was appropriate. The demonstrator was dismayed, and the synthesizer became a laughing matter among IRCAM researchers. Boulez's "Emperor's New Clothes" intervention made him appear as the "true seer," as the fastest and most perceptive skeptic in the room, in line, moreover, with his skepticism toward commercial tech-nologies. It is interesting to note in passing that Boulez's observation was not very profound; I had been on the verge of perceiving the mistake, and anyone with musical aural training could have done so. This suggests that in a situation with few musicians present, Boulez's skills may be experienced in an exaggerated way. In fact at this time, as the Pedagogy director informed me, the problem of computer recognition of basic mu-sical meter was far from trivial, but a major psychoacoustical puzzle akin to that of semantics for speech-recognition and transcription programs.

While Boulez was often experienced as benign, when exercising power he could be thoroughly, if productively, autocratic. The way that crucial decisions and crises were dealt with in the following three meet-ings can serve to illustrate.

The first was a musicians' meeting, several months into the discus-sions, that concerned the future of the Music Research department given the impending departure of the current director. Previous meetings had been occasions for free speaking, and the group had discussed a new democratic structure, without a head, for the department. However, an hour into this meeting, having first allowed those present a say, Boulez began a monologue in which he entirely redefined the structure of the de-partment, including a new rotating director or "secretary." To a stunned room, he summed up: "We've agreed, I think, on the idea of a rotating secretary. . . . I propose WOW [a junior tutor] as the first. . . . We'll decide all this democratically, and work on the question of how to implement a democratic structure. So you must decide for yourselves if my proposal of WOW is OK." However Boulez's suggestions were taken as faits accomplis, and those present relished the irony whereby, despite a rhet-oric of democracy, nothing — not the way the decision was made, nor the structure, nor the person selected to be new head — was democratically agreed.

The second meeting, a Scientific Committee meeting, was held in the wake of a disastrous three-month commission visit by the composer AV (see chapter 8). Boulez used it also to announce the forthcoming departure of several senior staff. It was therefore a crisis meeting. Many problems had dogged AV's visit, and the meeting was concerned with tracing the causes. But the blame was shifted around between petulant parties, and Boulez's temper rose until he erupted into a monologue. "Things are never properly planned in these meetings! This discussion should have happened a year ago, ahead of AV's visit! . . . Composers are always put into impossible situations and cannot produce, so we can't meet our commitments. . . . We might as well shut up shop! We need a *manager* to make sure that people produce results at a precise date — an *autocrat!* Autocrats aren't idiots!" Pressed further, Boulez exploded: "We're not a laboratory here! We have *absolute imperatives* to fulfill, quotas of production."

The third meeting was partly concerned with Boulez's resolution of these problems. A rare general meeting, he used it to introduce some new directors. While discussing budgets for the coming year, and in reply to a question from his personal tutor, Boulez suddenly elected this popular man as the equivalent of a new Scientific Director. The whole room, including the tutor, seemed shocked. Later, the future of the *Espace Libre* experimental concert series was raised, and Boulez was damning: "They're awful! Mortally boring, amateur." Just one voice was raised against the diatribe, although many thought the series worthwhile. It was gradually terminated. Boulez's handling of power was thus abrupt and autocratic, despite his awareness of and toying with issues of internal democracy. This may indicate why the delegation of power, for example to Scientific Directors, was always problematic.

DESIGNATING "HEIRS": THE DIFFUSION OF CHARISMA AND PATRONAGE

Patronage and the use of personal contacts have played a role since the beginning in some of IRCAM's higher level appointments, as could be expected in a new and complex field; and in the musical world, in which, like the artistic world in general, patronage plays a major role. But the most striking patronage phenomenon at IRCAM was closely linked to issues of charisma. It consisted of a pattern whereby Boulez lit upon a hitherto unknown young composer in whom he then invested great authority and power, either by promotion or by external recruitment. The young man enjoyed a period in which he became a kind of divinely elected "heir," as though being tested as Boulez's successor: a crucial problem, in line with Weber's classic analysis of charismatic leadership.[2] The task of the heir designate, consonant with Weber's analysis, seemed to be to exhibit and accrue as much charisma — consisting at IRCAM of musical and scientific talent — as possible in order to prove a worthy successor. More interestingly, the heir had a second task: he had to exhibit a similar "talent" for spotting and fostering talent by bringing in other young men (and women) of high artistic and intellectual quality. In other words, he had also to develop a skill for bestowing patronage and thus creating a nexus of talent. Sadly, the pattern sometimes ended with the heir's fall from grace and the young man leaving, disillusioned and bitter.

We can now see the importance in this general charismatic economy of Bourdieu's linking of charisma and artistic talent and of the strategies discussed earlier whereby IRCAM's young vanguard musicians and intellectuals attempted to bolster their talent and charisma by ascetic displays of devotion. Their ideological equation dictated that to be a "successor" they must demonstrate a prophetic, rebellious creative talent, marginal and against the current order. As we saw at the end of the previous chapter, some of IRCAM's vanguard sought to remain marginal, preferring this position vis à vis power within IRCAM; but others "did not resist" being plucked out of obscurity and recognized by the IRCAM authorities, who could validate the truth of their work — and promote them. This strategy of accumulating charisma and seeking patronage was diffused throughout the music-oriented intellectuals, who were, in varying degrees, ambitious young men. Among them, several exemplify the role of successive heirs elect. Moreover, we can trace links between them, since, paradoxically, in proving themselves they "elected" and patronized each other in turn.

In a sense, the Artistic Director was the first young man given a chance to excel by Boulez. He was no composer, but an up-and-coming impresario who brought with him a great deal of accumulated cultural capital. The Director was himself well aware of the phenomenon: "XX [another 'heir'] was given a lot of power [in 1980]: too much power too young. That's one of Boulez's things. He did the same to me, actually. . . . God! I was a kid when I was brought here! . . . It's always a risk. And he's always on the side of the young, rather than the proven. I think it's a generous fault." Four young composers — WL, HY, WOW, and NR — epitomize the phenomenon of the elected heir. WL directed one of the original IRCAM departments. Boulez brought him to IRCAM in his late twenties from a senior job in a European conservatory. The main project fostered by WL was what became Chant/Formes. He brought the director, MC, into IRCAM; but also others, including HY, who later replaced him as heir. The collaboration between WL, a composer, and MC, a scientist, was described by MC as the utopian prototype of all such work (see chapter 7). MC recalled nostalgically the fruitfulness of the collaboration, which was enabled by WL's musical and scientific skills, and hinted that Boulez was envious: "WL was himself involved in research very deeply. He programmed, he made experiments. So he had insight into that, and results, somehow, that Boulez could *not* have. . . . Boulez was not able to do that at all: a question of time, courage, of involvement." Boulez soon after began his own long-standing relationship with his personal tutor, perhaps modeled on WL's dialogue with MC.

However WL, who had been seen as Boulez's "golden boy," fell out very badly with Boulez around 1980, with the result that WL left — an incident so painful in the collective memory that people were loath to speak of it. The turning point was a piece that WL produced, using the new Chant software developed with MC, that Boulez greatly disliked. MC described the incident ambivalently: "I think the results of the research *were* poor and disappointing. It's true that, at that moment, our [synthesized] voices were, as Pierre said, 'plastic voices' and 'like spaghetti.' . . . Pierre Boulez was certainly impatient to get some results; but really, musically, an outcome in the direction that *he* wants, and nothing else! [*laughs*]" Soon after, when WL left, it was apparently because of this aesthetic conflict. WL's view was that Boulez had not found him sufficiently strong as a manager, which he thought was the role Boulez had in mind for him. Aesthetic and technological disagreements, he felt, compounded this.

In the 1980 reorganization, at the time of WL's fall, Boulez suddenly announced HY as the new director of Music Research. HY was widely seen as the successor to WL in the role of Boulez's favored heir. He was in his mid-twenties, a young American composer with no such previous position, but he had been at IRCAM for several years and had developed a relationship with the 4X team. In this period HY had worked for very little on short contracts. Suddenly, with the promotion, which was also a surprise to him, he was given a certain power and authority. He became a member of the Artistic Committee and organized major conferences and publications. He also continued to compose, bringing in other promising young composers to work as his assistants. Among them were WOW and NR, later his successors. But HY introduces another significant development: he was very strong theoretically and rhetorically and proved himself a fine speaker, writer, and publicist. He could thus command authority at international conferences. HY's eventual fall was signaled not so much by a piece of his own (although his aesthetic had begun to shift in a direction that was to prove unpalatable to some at IRCAM), but by the experimental concert series *Espace Libre*, which he started in 1983. His power on the Artistic Committee declined, and his lack of favor was marked by Boulez's instructing him to undertake a relatively mundane documenting task — to write a database of composers' visits. HY thought that his experience indicated the dual reality of the position of heir elect. Although some power was delegated, the heir was at the same time totally dependent on Boulez's overall control, and the power vested in the heir could always be wrenched back or undermined. By 1984 HY was looking for other work, and within months he had secured a good job at a major American university.

WOW was the next heir designate. He first came to IRCAM on the composers' *stage* and was noticed by MC because of the interesting sounds that he produced during the course. In this way, the *stage* functioned as an informal talent-spotting ground, although to discourage *stagiaires*' ambitions IRCAM staff routinely disclaimed that the *stage* had any relation to working at IRCAM. MC and HY brought WOW in as a junior assistant and composer to work with MC on Chant/Formes. Like all junior tutors, WOW also helped others with pieces, including HY. Before his sudden promotion he was on two-month to six-month contracts in the lowest wage bracket. There is no doubt that the key element in WOW's promotion by Boulez in spring 1984 was his piece *Chréode 1*. The piece, made with the Chant and Formes sofware, also had the desired effect of finally legitimizing the programs and the Chant/Formes group in Boulez's eyes. This was, then, a striking example of a well-received piece legitimizing a technology. The Chant/Formes director recalled Boulez's reception of WOW's piece with excitement: "It seems that [Boulez] found WOW's piece really something: one of the *first* and one of the *rare, rare, rare* examples of music done at IRCAM that has some interest! . . . I asked Boulez one day, 'What of interest has been done at IRCAM?' And the only one he mentioned was Höller's *Arcus*! That's all, since '76 or so . . . and *now* he talks of WOW's piece too." By the time WOW took over as director of Music Research, patronage had become the job's more or less legitimate concern: seeking and bringing to IRCAM interesting young researchers and composers with projects to be done, cheaply, under the department's auspices. Parisian born and bred, WOW was well placed to draw in local talent and saw this as his role. One major success was his association with his wife-to-be, also a composer, whom he encouraged as a squatter and helped to learn programming. They could be found together late into the night at adjacent terminals, studying new programs and AI languages and preparing their pieces. From this, his wife produced the unofficial piece that was highly acclaimed at Darmstadt, and the glory reflected back on WOW for his astute patronage. WOW's skills were wider still than HY's, since in addition to being a composer and a theorist he was also a good programmer. By 1986 WOW was becoming disillusioned, and his place as Music Research director was taken by the next young heir elect, NR. However, WOW survived the transition, remained at IRCAM, and later consolidated his position by becoming a highly adept director of Pedagogy.

NR had taken the IRCAM *stage* at age twenty-three, where HY had noticed him and plucked him out as an assistant. From that time he became a junior tutor on very low pay, working long hours yet all the time learning and producing pieces in his own time. NR had earlier been trained in computer music in Italy. Like WOW, he was known to be very capable theoretically, scientifically, and as a programmer, as well as being a composer. NR had a significant musical success in 1984 with a piece for piano and computer tape, and this was affirmed by his being commissioned to make a piece for the IRCAM tenth anniversary concerts in 1987. From IRCAM, with HY's help, NR went as a postgraduate to a prestigious American college and then returned to succeed WOW as heir elect in the position of Music Research director.

These four men, and their interrelations, therefore exemplify the successive phenomenon of Boulez's quasi-heirs. They were themselves socialized into becoming patrons; and while musical success was central to gaining Boulez's support, it was not sufficient, since it had to be buttressed by strong theoretical and scientific skills.

The main alternative patronage system to that around Boulez flowed through the Pedagogy director, RIG. He was responsible for allocating tutors, organizing the *stage*, and for choosing graduate students and occasional researchers. He thus had ample opportunity to offer work to young people whom he found interesting and brought many people into IRCAM, especially as junior tutors and squatters. Most were on low pay or unpaid, and he encouraged them to feel this was an exciting break. The Chant/Formes director MC had a similar, if smaller, role. He brought in young composers and scientific graduates to fill out his group and, himself a night worker on an insecure contract, exemplified the ideal of negation and material ascesis of the vanguard intellectual. He was therefore himself a charismatic scientific leader within IRCAM.

RIG's committed approach, like MC's, gained strength by his own example. Like MC, he often worked late and was rumored almost to live at IRCAM. RIG's informal, "laid-back," friendly, and anarchistic approach was the opposite of Boulez's. He gave the impression of being on the same level as those who worked around him, while at the same time he maintained running battles with both Boulez and the Administration. RIG thus appeared the leading American bohemian dissident within IRCAM. Yet his identification with the young and marginal was partly illusory inasmuch as he was a powerful figure, and while providing them with breaks, he effectively encouraged them to collude in their own economic marginalization.

We have seen that charisma and patronage went hand in hand and systematically imbued the production sphere and that patronage was legitimized and appeared natural and benevolent by being linked to the concept of talent. The narratives of key individuals' IRCAM careers stood as dramatic, exemplary myths to the young musicians and intellectuals who entered IRCAM, alerting them to the high potential rewards, and the high risks, of collusion in this system. However, we have also seen the chronic volatility and fragility of the position of the heirs elect, the tendency for an eventual downfall, perhaps because there was nowhere in reality for them to go with Boulez still in office[3] and, ultimately, no one could be allowed to usurp him.

This may go some way to explaining why it was that when the issue of succession to the Directorship of IRCAM after Boulez became unavoidable in the early 1990s, it was not one of the composer-heirs who emerged as front-runner but IRCAM's second Artistic Director—a French contemporary music manager widely liked within the institute and thought to run a benign administration. Yet notably, this man maintains close relations with the long-staying composer-heir WOW, who remains a director, so that together they "take care" of both intellectual/artistic and administrative leadership. This relationship appears to be an ideal resolution of the antinomic opposition of composer-philosopher to professional administrator that has characterized Boulez's thoughts on artistic management since the Malraux debacle of the 1960s, as well as the actual functioning of IRCAM.

POLITICS AND INSTITUTIONAL CONFLICT: THE DUAL STRUCTURE OF POWER

In 1984, the politics of workers in the lower-status reproduction sphere concerned the basic parameters of their jobs: pay, hours, conditions, the attitude of bosses, and the threat of sanctions and sackings by the Administration. For some, this translated into a concern with the political processes through which they could express grievances, while for many it did not. The formal channels for worker representation were a body called the *Comité d'Entreprise* (company committee) and several positions called *Délégué du Personnel* (staff representative). The *Comité* had the highest profile of the two. It consisted of several elected staff, the Administrator, a representative of the Director, and the Personnel director, who convened it every month or so. But the *Comité* had no actual power and was for consultation and negotiation only. It existed to air workers' problems, to explain changes brought in by management, and to dispense little "extras" provided by the organization (sports facilities, outings, holidays, discounts). *Comités* have become widespread in French industry and represent an attempt to provide in-house consultative bodies that will discourage cross-enterprise unionization. The *Délégué* position, again elected and requiring volunteer candidates, appeared anomalous at IRCAM since only one existed in 1984 and no one else had come forward.

Of all the staff interviewed, only two low-grade administrative workers who had been active in the *Comité*, and the Personnel director, chose to speak about in-house politics. One worker had been at IRCAM from early on and had been instrumental in starting the *Comité*. The following portrays his views on the *Comité* and on what he perceives as a dual power structure within IRCAM.

> I gave information to everyone informally [about the *Comité*], or no one would have been elected, as the Administration didn't tell any workers! The people involved were all lower workers, not *responsables*. . . . It's not taken seriously, the people in high positions don't want to be involved. Why? It's not politics: it's basic human rights, humanitarian! . . . Here it was no unions, just people talking without any politics; this was interesting. And yet still the higher people did not want to be involved. . . . Those people are *not interested* in politics, in power. . . . You know, in IRCAM something is very clear: it's difficult to have a homogeneous group. The reason is that people are very independent; they always want to fight [or] deal on their own, to speak directly with Pierre Boulez! They don't want to be supported by anyone. . . . *They* can manage; *they* have some power! And in the other group [low-status

workers], they can't manage, because they have no power, so [there must] be several to fight, to get some explanation. [But] it doesn't work: [there's] no sense of general interest. Higher people go straight to Pierre; lower people have no such chance.

It is significant that this man's reference to "politics" combines two different meanings, revealing his own ambivalence. He seemed to mean, first, organized union and Left party politics, which he wanted to distinguish from "basic rights" and "humanitarianism" and to disown. But later, he talked of "politics" in terms of a critical attitude toward and awareness of "power," and as a constructive and necessary force. His attitude toward unions was in fact positive, and he was deeply frustrated that IRCAM workers did not see fit to get unionized. During early 1984 the only unionized workers at IRCAM—the cleaners from the CGP, members of the Communist CGT—were engaged in a chronic dispute that led to occasional strikes. On those days both IRCAM and the CGP buildings were strewn with leaflets that argued passionately the local CGT case. At IRCAM they lay around apparently unnoticed and drew no reaction from workers.

The same man provided a convincing analysis of why IRCAM was difficult to unionize:

LK: To have a union inside IRCAM, we would have to have a leader, and no
        one in here wants to be a leader. Many people would like to have a
        union here . . . because they realize that in case of problems, injustices,
        the Administration and Direction—Pierre Boulez—are very power-
        ful. . . .

GB: No one will tell me about the injustices. . . .

LK: It's difficult, phew! [*pained*]. . . There have been lots! [*Defeatedly, very
        reluctant to talk*] Those bad events, [*vaguely*] I will let you know. . . .
        There are more reasons why people don't join unions: first, they are not
        all French, and I'm not sure that foreigners can belong to unions. Then,
        the people working here for short periods want to be well thought of—
        to get new contracts! And third, there are many different [kinds of
        worker]: fifteen in such a small place, little groups that can't get to-
        gether to fight with the same aim. The *Comité could* be more
        powerful—it is in big companies like IBM. It's meant to solve injustices,
        deal with social conditions, and so on. But it doesn't have voting power
        or backup externally, unlike unions. . . . When injustices have come up,
        the Administration has often said [to the *Comité*]: "You shouldn't be
        involved—stay in your place!"

This worker's political awareness, his evident pain and cynicism, were surprising since he generally appeared far from angry or politicized and was, rather, a sunny, popular, middle-class person. His reluctance to instance "injustices" may have derived from his current desire to revoke his former politicization, but it also seemed tinged with fear — a fear of the Administration expressed also by other low-status workers.[4]

The kinds of grievance that such workers may have feared can be illustrated by two stories of past "injustices" meted out to women clerical staff. The less extreme story concerned a longtime secretary whose work relations with her director boss began to deteriorate for no apparent reason, which began a cumulatively punitive process against her centered on *avertissements* — official cautions. The secretary fought. She saw a solicitor, the Administrator, and finally Boulez, who eventually produced a compromise and overrode the Administration. The secretary emerged enormously grateful for Boulez's humane and enlightened intervention and appeared charmed by his attention.[5]

This secretary had also been active in the *Comité d'Entreprise* and spoke of past attempts to unionize IRCAM. "We went to a couple of meetings at the CGP, with members of the CFDT, not the CGT — it's less violent. . . . We went to get information. They said, 'You're not protected there at all, you're sitting ducks.' I think we had a little meeting [at IRCAM]; but people were basically against it. They seemed worried about militancy, politicizing the situation. I think they were scared. [Involved in this were] some research workers, the technicians, secretaries: not the *responsables* or higher level researchers, no, no." The second story of injustice done to lower-status workers circulated among them as a notorious myth. The story was told by a clerical worker and concerned a past secretary who had been sacked, it was believed, maliciously. The secretary had been extremely active in her own defense and had tried to get help from the unions at the CGP, to no avail, and tragic personal consequences had followed her sacking.

In both narrators' eyes, the stories ultimately delineated a managerial division of labor in which a malign Administration stood opposed to Boulez's charming and humanistic leadership. Further, unionization was perceived as a force that might provoke Boulez and so endanger the potential for asking for his patronage. The stories were interpreted to show that even for lower workers, rather than unionizing it is better when in dire straights to appeal to Boulez's favor. As we have seen, not all lower-status workers shared that opinion; but at least they were commonly aware of and concerned by the possibility of unionizing — an awareness that was notable by its absence among higher-status workers.

Higher-status workers at IRCAM did, however, have conflicts with the IRCAM Administration. Junior tutors and tutors, for example, clashed with them over pay and conditions, while others engaged them in more purely ideological battles. Yet despite this, we will see that IRCAM's research and production culture was remarkably nonpolitical. This should be grasped in light of the fact that of those French IRCAM intellectuals who told me of their party political affiliations, almost all had voted Socialist in the 1981 general election.

Among higher-status workers, the most exploited (junior tutors, *vacateurs*) had to deal with the Administration in the period when they were proving their value to IRCAM. One battle arose out of the musicians' group deliberations on a new democratic structure for Music Research. For some, this included the desire to equalize the substantial pay differences within the group: in particular, to raise junior tutors' pay to near that of the official tutors, who were paid about twice as much. One junior tutor spoke of the benefits of a new openness within the group about pay and linked this to his own past struggles with the Administration over low pay.

HM: Nobody's ever had this knowledge before, so you were always operating in the dark. You didn't really know against what to make your demands; because you could say "I want this much," and [the Administrator] would say "Nobody makes that much!" She doesn't come clean!

GB: When did you learn about each other's salaries?

HM: I still don't know what everybody's salaries are. I just know what WOW's salary is, and he knows mine. Nobody knows what HY's [the past director's] was. No, I don't know the tutors' salaries. . . .

At one point two junior tutors, in their frustration, threatened to try to publicly expose workers' pay levels. But in fact they did not, and it would have been inappropriate for their intellectual charisma had they been seen as overly concerned with such issues. In effect, the promotion of one of them by Boulez in 1984 ended the plan for a united front on pay and the end of secrecy. His promotion was divisive and caused resentment. By 1986 the other militant junior tutor had also been promoted to a directorship. Thus Boulez's interventions helped to fragment attempts to coordinate the negotiation of pay and promotions among higher-status workers.

Another major struggle between the Administration and high-status staff during 1984 centered on the official tutors. Tutors' contracts described them as assistants to visiting composers and had no word about them also being composers. But three of the tutors considered themselves

serious composers and decided to fight for the right to set aside a substantial period each year for their own composing within IRCAM. One
tutor became the organizer and tried to negotiate a document with the
Administration, rather than coming to an *ad hoc* and personalized understanding with Boulez. The key issue was highly emotive: who is defined as a composer within IRCAM and who is not. The tutors, subordinate to the directors in the music-production sector, felt that several of
those directors saw them as only second-class composers. Given these artistic rivalries and their formal qualifications, and unusually for IRCAM,
the tutors considered it more likely that they would receive a productive
and reasoned hearing from the Administration.

The Pedagogy director RIG was notorious for conflict with the Administration. But its character was very different. He was known to be
ideologically opposed to bureaucracy, rules, and "policing." The objections went both ways. RIG acted in many ways that the Administration
experienced as anarchic and that provoked their censure.[6] The broad
sympathy with RIG's attitude among researchers was expressed in the
following gentle satire. In written guidelines on how to present bibli-
ographies in the annual report, RIG's junior and friend gave the following imaginary reference to exemplify the form: "RIG (1999) – '*Le chaos
bureaucratique*,' in: Marx, K. and Marx, G. (eds.), *L'Approche Stocha-
stique dans la Bureaucratie Française*, 10/18: Paris."

Other political clashes within the production sphere in 1984 concerned the nature of senior scientific management. They included the
controversies over the 4X production deal outlined in chapter 4 and
conflicts about the Scientific Director's role. Apart from these, the main
political clashes among IRCAM's production staff rested on discursive
conflicts and oppositions stemming from their work, which I describe in
later chapters.

There is one final feature of the broader political character of
IRCAM's research and production culture to be noted. It lacked a significant political dimension that it could have been expected to have: a
concern with, or awareness of, the politics of high technology. Given the
4X production deal with major defense contractors, the proximity of
IRCAM's technologies to military applications was clearly an issue in the
air. Yet only one junior tutor, uncomfortable about the deal, spoke of it
briefly in private, as well as informing me of the 4X designer's despair. Of
all the population only two American visitors spoke openly and fully of
the issues: one (ID) a West Coast music software researcher, the other
(NI) a marginal computer music entrepreneur.[7]

When I raised the militarist links of the 4X deal, the researcher ID
responded with an eloquent, self-explanatory discussion of the practical,
moral, and political dilemmas at stake.

ID: Oooh! [*Sighs*] It's a very, very thin layer that separates the technological
          base of computer music from that used in advanced radar systems for
          things like cruise missiles. Typically work like that gets done at Law-
          rence Livermore Laboratories and Los Alamos Laboratories in New
          Mexico. They build and design the missiles, the bombs, the delivery sys-
          tems. . . . [*Upset*] And, you know, we're on the same [computer] net-
          work with them. And I get requests from time to time from Los Alamos
          and Lawrence for CARL software.

GB: You mean they just send you computer mail . . . ?

ID: Mmm! "Send us a [computer] tape."

GB: How do you feel about this?

ID: Well, very queasy. You know, I'm a *pacifist*, a Quaker! [*laughs at the
          irony*] So I had to determine my position . . . well, if I took a classical
          pacifist line I wouldn't have anything to do with the field. Because it's
          just too close. On the other hand, I made the following—I hope not too
          devious—argument: that what really counts the most is how these
          things get *utilized*. And if we abandon this technology to the military,
          then we can guarantee that it will be used without any humanist ra-
          tionale whatsoever. I like to think of what I'm doing as a way of *recap-
          turing* the technology for humanist considerations. . . . The user
          interface has been very unfriendly. . . . What's that wonderful saying? "It
          suffices for evil to triumph that good men do nothing" [*laughs sadly*].

GB: Could you just say "no" to requests for software from Los Alamos?

ID: I *could*, since we just *give* it away—we're not under any obligation to
          give it to anyone on the education network. Los Alamos are on that net-
          work: it's the standard UNIX "uucp" network that connects the VAX
          here at IRCAM to us in San Diego.

GB: But it's not just a technological linkup because it's also this network of
          exchange of knowledge and information . . . ?

ID: Yes, and actually I have *not* said "no." There's only a few ways to get
          through to those people and confrontational techniques are not going
          to work. [*Abruptly*] I *do* go on marches, you know: I walk up to the
          front gates of General Dynamics and tell them to stop producing cruise
          missiles. But when I'm dealing with people from General Dynamics who
          are interested in CARL software, I'm basically trying to *lure* them away
          from their activity—by proposing alternative utilizations of the technol-
          ogy. There's another good reason for keeping the exchange going: [peo-
          ple in the defense industry] are very technologically astute. And to an
          extent micro and desktop computers are there because of the armament
          industry.

GB: So how much do you get back from them?

ID: Exactly! A lot! [*laughs*] Well I think you'd have to say that the whole
        [computer music] field is there in its present state as a result of the inter-
        est the military has in it! They have such *vast* resources to command
        that it's certainly helped accelerate the technology. . . . I do feel like a flea
        on the back of a monster, it's true. . . . It's a kind of meditation to be in
        this position: to be confronted with what are the major driving forces of
        American industry and technology, and to try and see the directions it
        might be taking, and to use my humanistic judgment powers to try to
        influence it where I possibly can. . . . [But] I *am* aiding and abetting at
        this point, there's no question about it. . . .
           We sent out a [computer] letter describing the CARL software, and
        one of the letters we had back was from Los Alamos, and we sent them a
        tape [of the software], and I haven't heard from them since. I suspect
        their use of it is related to speech research with a view to allowing
        fighter-bomber pilots to give verbal commands. Perhaps also for under-
        water acoustics, sonars, submarines. . . . The same thing can be used
        equivalently without any modifications whatsoever to either help make
        bombs or help make *music*. . . . A lot of the defense establishment runs
        UNIX. The latest Berkeley UNIX release [4.1a] was sponsored in part by
        defense — one of the ARPA projects.[8] So they sponsored this UNIX de-
        velopment for military applications, which meant of course that it was
        also a wonderful environment for making music! [*laughs at the irony*]

GB: Should these things be debated in the computer music community? Are
        they?

ID: They are *not*. It's *utterly unconscious*: this is probably the most ex-
        tended discussion on the subject I've ever had. . . . I've thought of raising
        it; but if you would just focus consciously on this as an issue, it would
        just *consume* you! As perhaps it should. . . . I'm not sure but quite a lot
        of people in the computer music community don't actually support the
        relationship with the military-industrial complex, because they uncon-
        sciously see the fallout for computer music! Mainly pure AI research-
        ers. . . . But if you're engaged in computer music, and you consider
        yourself a liberal, then there's this strong *cognitive dissonance* that
        must exist between your liberal leanings and the technology you're
        utilizing — the way that technology got into your hands!

   This man's account not only of the militarist links pervading computer
music and computer science but of the lack of conscious debate about
them among researchers suggests that the phenomena were far wider than
IRCAM. The second American visitor, NI, volunteered his views on the
subject unprompted and in a very different personal and emotive style, as
befitted his position as a nonintellectual computer music entrepreneur.

   I can appreciate what the 4X is: it's a *tremendous* accomplishment! I'd never
   seen such a powerful piece of hardware in my life! Never seen a machine that
   could even begin to do what it can do in real time. . . . [*Jokes sardonically:*] I

heard you need a letter from the Pope to get near it, but . . . I mean I'd *love* to work with the 4X, the way I worked with the Alles machine at the [Bell] Labs — but that doesn't seem likely. No, [*countering his own criticisms*] I don't even care what the limitations are: a machine that powerful is fabulous. [*Change of mood:*] And it saddens me greatly to hear how proud they are of its use, its commercialization. A *tremendous* irony! [*Incredulous:*] They're proud! I was in a roomful of scientists and engineers and they were boasting about it: "It's now being manufactured for a flight simulator!" They should be ashamed — not proud, *ashamed*! — that the world's most beautiful and powerful musical instrument is being used to train people to *kill* other people. And they don't even see! I was so amazed: I was the only person in that room who saw death around! I could have cried.[9]

The contention that computer music researchers within IRCAM, as elsewhere according to ID, suppressed the issue of links to defense industries is supported not only by the almost total absence of any mention of the issue in 1984, in public or private, during exactly the period of negotiating these links for the 4X, but also by the following. In this interview a key IRCAM researcher discussed his training in high-level, AI-related computer science at a major French nuclear research establishment.

RESEARCHER: I had zero [computing] experience. I had to do something to learn it. Somebody told me: "The thing to do is to go to the Nuclear Energy Research Center in the south of Paris. Maybe they can teach you." I went there and they took me for a *stage*. I learned a little, and they asked me if I wanted to work on the subject that they were interested in, which was speech synthesis — there was a research group on speech transmission and recognition. . . .

GB: Why on earth was there such a research group at the Nuclear Energy Research Center?

RES: Because at that time the nuclear energy field was not expanding but declining, so all the people had to find new domains of research or applications. And as they had a good background in signal processing, speech was a good way to experiment with their knowledge.

GB: More generally, has there always been a strong tie between research around the nuclear industry or nuclear energy and computer science, historically?

RES: I have no idea. . . .

GB: I just wondered when you say you went there to learn, whether. . . .

RES: No, it's just a question of *opportunity*. I found someone, and he knew about that place where I could find a job, a position. That's all, nothing else.

In this narrative the researcher fends against his own responsibility for his decisions. His almost excessive stress on the purely pragmatic and instantaneous considerations behind his entry into a nuclear research center and then into speech synthesis served to defend against any other possible considerations about these links.

Thus, while the presence of politics in IRCAM's higher research and production sphere consisted mainly of informal rivalries for intellectual prestige and charisma and for the patronage which flowed from these, this sphere was equally characterized by two significant absences of political consciousness or practice: of the politics of institutional and organized labor (whether the *Comité d'Entreprise* or unionization), and of the politics of high technology. Both must be understood in the context of broader historical shifts in French political culture outlined in chapter 3; in particular, the decline of critical perspectives on new technology among the French Left and intelligentsia. According to ID, a telling absence of engagement with the politics of high technology — with the close relations between this research and the military — is also characteristic of the wider fields of computer music and computer science. From his account, it seems that denial — the tendency to obliterate from consciousness such problematic and, indeed, potentially violent and persecuting realities — is an apt term to describe this phenomenon of the collective unconscious of computer music.

CHAPTER VI

Music

Uncertainty, the Canon,
and Dissident Musics

IRCAM was characterized in 1984 above all by a chronic musical and aesthetic uncertainty revealed in its everyday work and music-production culture. By contrast, the institute's concert programming embodied an extremely coherent and forceful canonization of twentieth-century high-musical modernism consistent with Boulez's own genealogy of music history. In the light of profound musical insecurity in the present, I show in this and the following chapter how IRCAM's resources were channeled into three powerful and legitimizing displacements: first, an unassailable interpretation of the musical past; second, the development of technology and pure science around music; and third, and central to IRCAM's intellectual identity, the assertion of a realm of utopian and scientistic thought and theory closely linked to composition, and concerned with IRCAM's unique role in the future of music.

THE ABSENCE OF MUSIC: AESTHETIC UNCERTAINTY

Empirically, music was strikingly absent and "unheard" in the institute's daily working existence, except in its role as an occasional evening performance center. Walking around IRCAM in the day it was rare for one to hear any music. Sometimes, when a *stage* was in progress, students' initial, often crude attempts at computer-synthesized sounds could be overheard through the interconnected speaker system, set within IRCAM's commonest soundscape: the constant, arhythmic tip-tap of the computer keyboard as someone programmed away. Music was sometimes practiced, sounds produced or tapes played, behind the closed doors of the IRCAM studios. But generally, for those expecting IRCAM to be a musical environment, there was a sense of simple musical deprivation that could breed "rebellion," as shown by these two anecdotes.

Visiting composer AV was working as usual late into the night on sound-synthesis files that took some hours to deliver up a sound. He tapped away at the computer keyboard and rewrote the parameters of the files while I sat and watched. After several hours, he called over to me with frustration: "Hey, Born! Play me some *real* music!" and commanded me to sit at the grand piano parked in the studio to sight read a book of Bach chorales lying nearby. Elsewhere at IRCAM in a tiny attic room, American composer PL also regularly worked nights. Stumbling into his room in the small hours, I found him playing loud music on cassettes to entertain himself as he programmed through the night. Contrasting starkly with the laborious and cerebral activity, he played pop star Michael Jackson's *Thriller* album, then at the top of the pop charts and his favorite, or music by the notorious New York improviser John Zorn, with whom he sometimes played.

Music itself was also largely absent from the *stage* for computer music beginners in early 1984. The first lecture with taped music examples, one of very few, came a full month into the course. Compared with the strong emphasis given to learning the theoretical foundations of computer music, music and sound themselves took a low priority, which students found taxing.

Musical and aesthetic questions were very little discussed openly or debated in meetings. This can be illustrated by the significant meeting described in the last chapter in which junior tutor WOW discussed the composition of *Chréode 1*, and which ended with an insightful intervention by Boulez. My diary about the meeting included the following reflections, which raise many of the central issues around the place of music at IRCAM:

> WOW discussed the piece for several hours entirely in terms of the programs (Chant and Formes) that he had helped to write which were used to compose it. The language used both to discuss the programs, and of the programs themselves (programs being the new codes used to construct the music), was that of science and structuralism ("syntax," "frequency," "phase," "quantum"). This was fascinating because I was observing the social process of constructing and negotiating a new language, notation, and mode of analysis (the computer program) deeply implicated in the compositional process, since it controls the new medium (the computer). Boulez's intervention had raised the question of the limits of this language, what it did not seem able to

discuss — i.e. specifically musical questions; and the dangerously seductive determination, the autonomous rationality, of languages and notations around music. The seminar encapsulated the uneven development of media and aesthetic. The institute is primarily united around its technology, but seems uncertain about how to use this, and how to create means of communication (an analytic language, a notation) that do not take over and dictate aesthetically. I think a further uncertainty is the aesthetic itself, i.e. the "musical decisions" that the young composer was so anxious to avoid discussing until Boulez made his point.

It is striking that Boulez's intervention in this meeting was experienced as a ray of light piercing the technical and scientific discourse, as though only Boulez could risk talking directly of music.

We will see later how aesthetic discussion became sublimated into the issues of music research and psychoacoustics that preoccupied IRCAM's music vanguard, so that IRCAM composers, when they gave introductory theoretical lectures or wrote articles on their music, defined their aesthetic primarily in terms of these scientistic conceptualizations. More generally, the impression of how the aesthetic was raised within IRCAM's daily culture was through intellectuals' sudden infatuations with new scientific, especially biological, analogies for music: a kind of constant, arbitrary, conceptual foraging. Thus, walking along the top corridor of offices one afternoon, I passed an American composer, a squatter who was keen to find a place within IRCAM. He talked with excitement of a new branch of genetic biology that promised to provide beautiful conceptual models for composition. Another day, I noticed in a tutor's room a large glossy book on Mandelbrot's fractal geometry, a fashionable area of mathematics concerned with formulating the "logic" behind the apparently random shapes found in nature (for example, the shape of coastlines). The tutor was learning about this with a view to importing it into his compositional schema. I learned later that it was being referred to more widely by artists trying to bring science into their work. This same tutor was quite conscious about the phenomenon of conceptual borrowing and spoke warily of "science envy." At a musicians' meeting called to discuss the Formes program, a music director digressed enthusiastically as follows: "There are also very important and interesting *biological* models now: Lindermayer — his work on how a leaf grows, functions of growth generation. . . . I've been thinking of [a biologist] as a possible scientific adviser here. His work is very exciting and may have applications to musical structure. In fact much of Pierre's work reminds me of growth processes." Less elevatedly, an elderly composer taking the *stage*

told me one day at length about his aesthetic vision. He spoke of wanting
to develop a way of generating the total form of a piece from the internal
microstructure of its component sounds: "So the apple will have the same
internal structure as the tree it's hanging on, and as the molecules in the
apple! All the levels of the musical structure will be perfectly unified!
Don't you think that'll give a marvelous result?"

The repeated turn to biological analogies—those of growth, of the
germination of a seed into a full-blown plant, of the unity of micro and
macro forms—has an important precursor: that is, they are redolent of
the organicism that was the central metaphor of the tradition of German
musical romanticism and that found expression not only in composition
but in music analysis. It is this tradition, traced through Beethoven, that
Schoenberg saw himself as continuing and that major twentieth century
music theorists such as Schenker and Reti endorsed; indeed, it is a dominant lineage in twentieth century musical thinking.[1] What is surprising,
is that this kind of conceptualization of music appeared to be experienced within IRCAM's research culture as innovative or unprecedented.
Rather than new ideas, it was perhaps the belief in the potential for
improved scientific bases for these analogies that caused such intellectual
excitement. In other words, postserialism and its extensions into computer music have generated new possibilities for both scientizing and
technologically modeling the earlier organicism, and for ensuring that
the structural principles of organicism are followed rigorously (even
deterministically) through.

It is clear, then, that in comparison with the inarticulacy and sensory
immediacy of lower-status workers' discourse, IRCAM intellectuals did
not in fact enjoy sophisticated and articulate musical-aesthetic forms of
talk. There was a lack of specifically musical and aesthetic discussion,
and in its place a proliferation of scientific and technological theory and
talk. I explore this in greater detail in the following chapters.

Other phenomena confirm the sense of chronic aesthetic uncertainty
and dissatisfaction. There was a deep rivalry between IRCAM's internal
composers, expressed in constant private put-downs of each others'
work. Close colleagues would confess to me that they thought so-and-so
was really a better philosopher, or programmer, or researcher, than a
composer. Thus, one composer said to me that so-and-so (a junior tutor
aspiring to be a composer) was not really a composer. A second composer, having seen the recent premiere of a third, dismissed the new piece
as a mess. A junior tutor-composer said of a visiting composer, "I don't
like his music, though I must admit it's clever technically." The same

person spoke with frustration of a fellow tutor's piece: "This was very atonal, lyrical, self-conscious — nothing new, not what IRCAM should be doing, and irrelevant to his work here." No internal composer's piece was immune from harsh private criticisms by his peers. These judgments happened so often that they became a fragmenting undercurrent of doubt beneath what appeared on the surface to be close collegial relations centered on optimistic theoretical, scientific, and practical exchanges.

Privately divided among themselves, IRCAM music intellectuals colluded in putting down outside composers, a classic form of reinforcing community by uniting against the outside. Tutors, for example, maintained a flow of mocking comments on the progress of visitors' pieces. Sitting down to a musicians' meeting, the group joked about the recent IRCAM premiere of a major GRM composer whom they considered to have still produced a *musique-concrète*-like piece, despite having access to the advanced technology of the 4X. Laughing, they ridiculed the premiere as boring and the composer for his omnipotent pretensions: he sat on a raised dais with a spotlight trained on his head and hands as he controlled the mixing desk. Continuing the theme, a tutor joked that the 4X designer had produced a 4X program called MusCon, at which all present collapsed with mirth. This "MusCon" was densely packed with meanings: both "*musique concrète*," implying that this music is so routine that it can be churned out automatically by machine; and "*con*," meaning "bloody stupid," implying that such a program churns out "bloody stupid music" — and therefore that *musique concrète* is bloody stupid.

Visiting composers were commonly seen by IRCAM music intellectuals as willing victims of the commission process, inexperienced with the technology and therefore impotent to produce good pieces and utterly dependent on their tutor as a "nurse." A tutor mused that the visiting composer he was assisting was being very quick: "He's turning it out by the meter, and as soon as he's finished the piece he says 'OK, *now* can I have a job at IRCAM?'!!"; at which, again, all in the room fell about laughing with derision at this composer's naive audacity.

Aesthetic uncertainty both fueled and was reflected in the classification conflicts that expressed struggles between IRCAM workers over who was defined as a composer and who was not. In this classification system, to be defined as a composer conferred the highest cultural status and confirmed artistic talent, while not to be implied lack of these. Although almost no one was officially employed by IRCAM primarily as a musician, among the few who were there existed a further hierarchy between those considered, or who insisted on being defined as, a "real composer" and those who were (or did) not. Boulez was most securely "a (real) composer," followed by the Music Research director, who attracted envy and criticism for his assertion of the right to spend time on his own composing. Less securely, certain junior tutors were classified as composers: one, WOW, because of the successful piece that had "proven" him; another because his compositions had a high profile and because he stubbornly defined his contribution strictly in music-theoretical and compositional terms. It is notable that the young men who managed to assert their status as composers within IRCAM were also those in the running as Boulez's heirs elect.

The hierarchical classification was revealed equally in the dissatisfaction of those musical staff who were not institutionally defined as composers, especially the tutors and junior tutors who considered that they ought to be. That a hierarchy existed and had powerful evaluative effects is illustrated by this casually contemptuous remark by a music director: "I wouldn't want to be a tutor here! Why don't these guys leave and take the risk of being musicians if they want to? I wouldn't stay and be an assistant at IRCAM till I'm forty! How awful! That's my definition of academicism."

But hierarchical classification worked to elevate as well as subordinate, and subsumed a further hierarchical ideology of the composer as superior to the instrumentalist. Thus, when one IRCAM visitor, known to me primarily as a performer and improviser, was considered by a director to be doing innovative work, the same director redefined him, upwardly mobile, as "a composer."

The deepest classification conflict, however, was not overt. It concerned the low-status IRCAM workers who themselves composed, but who were defined neither as composers nor even as musicians within IRCAM. The "double lives" of three such workers — the Sound director, a Systems technician, and a junior tutor (who was also at times a squatter) — were publicly revealed only when their music was played in one of the *Espace Libre* concerts. Hearing these workers' pieces, the room was full of surprised comments: "But I didn't know that XX made tapes!" The public airing of these "illegitimate" compositions was controversial. It alarmed one key music intellectual who might have been expected to support such an open event. He was deeply troubled, saying that the concert was dangerous in exhibiting an uneven diversity of musics within IRCAM, which he thought would be fuel for IRCAM's critics. By contrast, the director in charge of the *Espace Libre* held the concert to

symbolize IRCAM's lack of a "house aesthetic," in his view a positive
strength and likely to have quite the opposite effect on external critics.
This man was soon to leave IRCAM.

Finally, musical uncertainty was most clearly expressed in the chronic
dissatisfaction with most IRCAM music that was pervasive even among
IRCAM's music intellectuals and that seemed to exist back-to-back with
an uncritical reverence for Boulez's *Répons*, so that his music alone was
exempted from the general gloom. Typical of the comments on IRCAM
music were the following, from an exchange with a Chant/Formes researcher when I asked him "What's your attitude toward the music
that's produced with your software tools?"

RESEARCHER: Ah, *extremely disappointed* most of the time. It's very rare that
              I find something really interesting musically. I admire Höller's
              work, but musically I don't like it. On the other hand, I think
              that Harvey's piece is the best that has been done at IRCAM.
              But it's not something that will last into the future because it's
              more on the end of [certain developments] than something
              new. It's amazing, musically wonderful, but probably it could
              have been done anywhere else as well as at IRCAM! [*laughs*] I
              mean, it proves nothing for IRCAM.

        GB: Do you mean because it's basically *musique concrète*, a treat-
              ment of existing musical objects?

       RES: Yes, yes exactly. So Harvey has a fantastic intuition and
              ear. . . . But [the unique resources of] IRCAM [were] used for
              nothing in that [*laughs ironically*], except for having the com-
              puter and tapes!

The composers and pieces mentioned here were among the four often
cited when subjects were asked to name their most valued IRCAM
music. The four were: Boulez's *Répons*, Jonathan Harvey's *Mortuous
Plangos Vivos Vocos*, York Höller's *Arcus*, and WOW's *Chréode 1*.
Höller and Harvey appeared to be most respected by the IRCAM establishment, including the Artistic Director, WOW by IRCAM's younger
and vanguard population.

But the researcher's comments reveal a further significant level of
critical doubt expressed by subjects from within IRCAM and outside
about the three most praised IRCAM pieces, by Boulez, Harvey and
Höller. That is, the view that these pieces could just as well have been
made without all the technological resources of IRCAM, with existing
music software or even simple analog devices, and did not really utilize
the unique computer music possibilities of IRCAM. The same criticism
was made after the premiere of a major IRCAM piece in comments by an

American computer musician that refer to an ancient rival of IRCAM's: "I think *YY* was a bad piece done very well, in which the 4X was *incredibly underused*. You could have produced the same results with just a few analog devices and filters! I think that was a pretty general response. It was a farce, all those technicians sitting there! [*With irony:*] Xenakis said to me, 'Is this contemporary music?' " A few pieces were exempted from this technological skepticism, such as WOW's piece, which was taken by some to demonstrate the musical power of the Chant and Formes programs. But it was the weight of such technological as well as aesthetic criticisms, threatening to collapse IRCAM's whole rationale and voiced by both external and internal critics, that was a stimulus for the coming into being in 1984 of the musicians' group vanguard, with its remit to purify and renew the institute's highest ideals.

CONCERT PROGRAMMING AND THE CANON: CERTAINTY ABOUT THE PAST

By contrast with the aesthetic uncertainty of the culture of music production, IRCAM's concert programming and courses, publications, records, and video cassettes — everything that contributed toward musical reproduction — constructed and maintained an extremely consistent and forceful perspective on the modern musical past. In other words, they embodied a canon: a view of the sacred landmarks in modern music, a genealogy of modernism in music. We have already seen the earlier processes whereby Boulez institutionalized his own view of history and how, beginning in the 1960s, it came to be acknowledged as a dominant one. With IRCAM, Boulez's genealogical statement took on a far grander scale than before, in the *Domaine Musical*. In effect, the modern canon enunciated by IRCAM is one that, not least through Boulez's own historical efforts, has been largely accepted both by the musical establishment and by musicologists. In reproducing it, then, IRCAM risked nothing and gained status by giving this orthodoxy its most intensive and prestigious international statement.

The massiveness, the cultural megalomania, of the canonical statements that IRCAM produced from the start can be illustrated by the concert series *Passage du Vingtième Siècle*. The series, commemorating the opening of the CGP and IRCAM, took place throughout 1977 in major venues all over Paris. With around 115 modern composers played in some seventy concerts over twelve months, the sustained scale of the series is quite unique in the history of contemporary music: a bid to gain for France, by this founding statement, the key legitimizing role for future music. In light of the range of composers represented, IRCAM's canon may at first appear aesthetically broad and eclectic. But this impression is undermined by the absence of certain areas of contemporary music, by the very uneven quantitative distribution of pieces — that is, whose works were most played, and by the nature of packaging and publicity.

Figure 7 is an approximate analysis of the distribution of composers according to the number of their pieces played in the *Passage*.[2] The table shows the main characteristics of IRCAM's genealogy. Implicit in the programming is a classification of modern composers into three groups, by generation and by valuation: first, the "classics" of the early century, those elected as the forefathers of the contemporary avant-garde; second, those considered the leaders of the generation that rose to eminence after World War II, dominant beginning in the late 1950s; and finally, the rest — both the less successful from that second generation and younger composers.

Among the "classics," the table shows the preeminence of three composers, Schoenberg, Webern, and Berg (the Second Viennese School), with a secondary presence of Stravinsky, Bartók, Ives, Debussy, and Varèse — a genealogy utterly consistent with Boulez's own, centered on the modernist serialism of the Viennese with the addition of other important early modernists. Predominant among the mid-century leaders are Boulez's colleagues from the Darmstadt school — Berio, Stockhausen, Nono — and his teacher Messiaen, also an early teacher at Darmstadt, all in their time proponents of a generalized extension of serialism. At the head of this group is Berio, who was in 1977 an IRCAM codirector, while Boulez himself appears in a retiring fourth place. Added to this is a judicious mix of other leading composers of the generation, including two — Ligeti[3] and Cage — who, in very different ways, have been powerful dissenters from serialism; and two others often considered the leading composers in America and (after Boulez) in France, respectively: Carter, and Xenakis — the latter a concession to Boulez's rival on the French scene.

The third category confirms the tendencies analyzed above, in that two of the six composers leading this group, Maderna and Pousseur, are also important ex-Darmstadt figures while three are early IRCAM figures. The group also includes a major recent teacher at Darmstadt, the British composer Ferneyhough. In this last group we see other forces coming in: both an attempt at a range of nationalities (as with IRCAM's

Composer	Approx. no. of works played

"Classics": Early Twentieth-Century Masters

Composer	
Schoenberg	16
Webern	15
Berg	9
Bartók	4
Stravinsky	4
Ives	3
Debussy	2
Varèse	2

"Leaders": Midcentury Generation

Composer	
Berio*	9 d,c
Ligeti	9
Stockhausen	8 d,c
Boulez*	7 d,c
Carter	6
Nono	4 d
Messiaen	3
Xenakis	3
Cage	3 d,c

Others: Including Younger Generation, Less Successful, and IRCAM Composers/Directors

Composer		Composer	
Maderna	2 (Ital) d	(continued . . .)	
Pousseur	2 (Belg) d,c	Zimmerman	1 (Germ)
Kagel	2 (Argentina)	Henze	1 (Germ)
Globokar*	2 (Yugoslavia)	Holliger	1 (Switz) c
Decoust*	2 (Fr) c	Ferneyhough	1 (UK) d,c
Chowning*	2 (US) c	Birtwistle	1 (UK)
Babbitt	1 (US)	Maxwell Davies	1 (UK)
Crumb	1 (US)		
Rzewski	1 (US) c	. . . etc. (all other composers had	
Bennett*	1 (US) c	just 1 work played)	
Risset*	1 (Fr) c		
Manoury*	1 (Fr) c		
Grisey	1 (Fr) c		
Amy	1 (Fr) c		
Eloy	1 (Fr)		
Jolas	1 (Fr)		

* = Past or present IRCAM director or worker
d = Taught at Darmstadt International Summer Courses for New Music
c = Past IRCAM commissioned or visiting composer

7. IRCAM's canon: approximate distribution of composers by number of their works played in the *Passage du Vingtième Siècle* concert series, 1977. (Information taken from program books, *Passage du Vingtième Siècle*.)

commissions, with strong representation of Europe and the United States), and a good number of French composers — the kind of mix of nationalism and internationalism characteristic of the attempt to reconstruct avant-garde cultural hegemony. Finally, the group contains many of the lesser-known composers who were, or later became, codirectors or workers at IRCAM (Chowning, Bennett, Risset, Manoury) or who have been commissioned by IRCAM (Amy, Grisey, Holliger, Birtwistle, and others). Together, the three groups portray a canonical genealogy leading, in essence, from the serialism of the Second Viennese School through the mid-century generalized serialism and postserialism of the Darmstadt school, centered on Boulez himself, to IRCAM: a trajectory that exemplifies high modernism in music.

The packaging and publicity of the *Passage* also conveyed the canonical aim and demonstrated a keen awareness of the importance of sophisticated marketing that has increasingly characterized IRCAM. For example, the very first concert of the *Passage* was called simply "Today," a statement of music of the present containing works by Boulez, Ligeti, Xenakis, and two others including the young composer Manoury, later an IRCAM junior tutor. More common were concerts presented as "classics," conferring canonical status on the past. The third concert of the series was called "Classics of the Twentieth Century" and included works by Schoenberg, Webern, Stravinsky, Ives, and Varèse. Similarly focused on early modernism, and marking their centrality, were several concerts devoted exclusively to "The Viennese School" (Schoenberg, Webern, Berg). Highlighting the major developments of the next generation were concerts called "Darmstadt and After," including the work of Boulez, Stockhausen, and Nono. Clearly these marketing strategies aimed to establish a powerfully legitimate and universalized interpretation of music history.

Other aspects of the *Passage* publicity pushed home the genealogy in case the point had been missed. The series' book-length program contained long historical essays such as "The origins of the twentieth century: the Second Viennese School," "Crossing the twentieth century: beyond the Viennese" (by Susan Bradshaw), and others called "Technology and music in the twentieth century" (by John Pierce), and "Invention/research" (by Boulez himself), the latter essays conveying the turn toward technology and scientism in postwar Boulezian modernism. This turn was confirmed and naturalized by the inclusion at the end of the program of a totalizing overview called "The twentieth century: music — arts — literature — science: A synoptic table." In the table, for each year between 1900 and 1970 key historical developments in each of the four domains are laid out side by side, as though to assimilate them all within a grand evolutionary intellectual scheme. For 1913, for example, the Parisian premiere of Stravinsky's *Rite of Spring* on the left of the table is posed against Niels Bohr's founding of quantum theory on the right, with Freud's *Totem and Taboo* in the middle; while for 1954 the start of Boulez's *Domaine Musical* and the premiere of his most successful piece, *Le Marteau sans Maître*, are posed against the first American nuclear-powered submarine, and so on. As though to detract a little from this universalizing rhetoric, the *Passage* program also contained a disarming, poetic preface by Boulez that dissolves the sense of historical givens into a more poststructuralist rhetoric of diversity and contingency.[4]

IRCAM's artistic policy after the *Passage* and into the later 1980s remained remarkably consistent and unchanging. In the concert seasons the same canonical names repeatedly recur: from the early modernist "greats," Schoenberg, Webern, Berg, Stravinsky, and Bartók; among the contemporary leaders, Boulez, Stockhausen, Berio, Messiaen, Nono, Xenakis, and so on. More diverse series also sometimes occurred, such as "Contemporary Polish Music" (1982–83) and "Music Theater" (1978–79). Thematic marketing became increasingly common during the mid-1980s, unifying the programming as well as making it more didactic. New concert series appeared that took place in the CGP and attempted to draw a wider audience.

Overall, despite Boulez's sometime critique of traditional concert-hall ritual, IRCAM's main concert series remained traditional, formal, and reverent occasions, based doggedly around the canon. The highly elite audience drawn by IRCAM's major canonical concerts can be gauged by that of the Parisian premiere of Boulez's *Répons* in October 1984 in a special large hall of the CGP. A row of reserved front seats remained empty until just before the start, when a group of figures swooped to the front to fill them, among them the leading right-wing politician Jacques Chirac — then Mayor of Paris, later Prime Minister — and Mme Pompidou. Days later, in the Sunday morning session of the International Computer Music Conference (ICMC) to which IRCAM was playing host, the crowd filling the Esp Pro was alerted by an unexpected police presence to the grand entrance, moments later, of Boulez accompanied by the glamorous Jack Lang, Socialist Minister of Culture, and his entourage.

IRCAM's musical reproduction, then, has constructed an extremely forceful canonical genealogy of modern music, focused on high modern-

ism and its legacy, and unchanging. This strategy of stasis has reinforced
its universal and timeless legitimacy, since "classics" must by definition
be seen to be abiding and beyond the fluctuations of fashion.

But beginning in the early 1980s, this core stasis began to be accompanied by a growing number of events related to computer music that
attempted to broaden the narrow canon by adding a parallel commentary with reference to this new musical field, and to younger composers.
The broader programming was at first influenced primarily by the two
American music directors, HY and RIG, and within computer music it
too was canonical. There were courses and occasional conferences, such
as "The Composer and the Computer" (1980–81), "The Concept of
Music Research" (1982–83), "Perception and Composition" (1983–
84), "Artificial Intelligence and Creation" (1984–85), and concert series
with works by composers such as Harvey, Höller, Chowning, Murail,
and Risset. Unlike the composers of the main canon, all of these composers are known particularly for their work with the technologies or conceptual issues of computer music. All have had, in addition, some association with IRCAM. After 1986 the new Artistic Director reinforced
this trend, so that in 1987 the concerts held to commemorate IRCAM's
tenth anniversary contained only works by six recently recognized
young IRCAM composers. Thus began the attempt to engineer a generational and discursive transition in the canon: from the older, postwar
generation of leading figures whose heyday had been defined by serialist
discourse, to a younger generation brought up in the postserialist tradition of everyday involvement with technological and scientific expertise,
raised also in an environment in which postmodernism had become
ubiquitous.

DISSIDENT CONCERTS:
ESPACE LIBRE AND IMPROVISATION

The broader conception of IRCAM's mission was epitomized in 1984 by
some "dissident" concert series organized by the American music directors HY and RIG, which caused controversy within IRCAM by combat-
ing in different ways the established artistic policy. These were HY's
monthly *Espace Libre* series and RIG's two series, one called *Musique au
Centre*, the other colloquially known as the "Off Festival" of the ICMC.

The *Espaces Libres* were sprawling, informal, "experimental" multimedia events held in the Esp Pro and lasting from 6:30 P.M. until after
midnight. They attracted a large, young, intellectual, and bohemian Pa-

risian audience. The evenings began with a theoretical discussion for an hour or two, normally about a composer's work — Boulez, Harvey, Manoury, HY himself — or introducing aspects of IRCAM's computer music and scientific concerns. There followed lengthy interludes of live performance, tape music, and video screenings, often interspersed with more theoretical talk or question-and-answer sessions between audience and panel. People would come and go throughout the evening, and some of IRCAM's intellectuals were available, if often remote. HY saw the series above all as a strategy to open up IRCAM to the outside community of young, interested musicians and artists: a function he felt the main concert series, with their stiff and formal, orthodox format failed utterly to fulfill. In addition, HY was very committed to multimedia work and saw the *Espaces* as the only forum in which this area could be addressed at IRCAM.

RIG's series were also informal affairs, devoted entirely to improvised music, itself closely related to free jazz. The *Musique au Centre* series was held in a modern art gallery of the CGP, where a small improvising group would play in front of the abstract paintings for an hour to an audience sitting on the floor. The audience came and went, also looking at the paintings. The "Off Festival" of the ICMC coincided with the conference's formal concert series and aimed to show the live, performance-oriented developments in computer music: how small, portable, real-time technologies could be used for improvised music. It took place in the main Parisian free jazz club to an audience of forty or so mostly American computer music and IRCAM people. It is significant that, in fact, RIG organized both the official ICMC concerts and the supposedly rebellious, anti-establishment "Off," an irony that was not lost on RIG himself.

These series contradicted IRCAM's dominant artistic ideology in several ways: most obviously by their relatively unstructured informality, their "unseriousness" and lack of focused, reverent ritual; by their inclusion of musics — jazz, improvisation, and rare references to pop — not deemed legitimate; and by their openness to amateur and professional musicians from outside IRCAM's usual network and aesthetic. The technological bent of the concerts was also mildly subversive in focusing on live uses of small, often commercial technologies and on video — a medium developing a strong amateur culture as well as professional uses and associated more with pop music and experimental art than with concert music. The series came, then, to connote "youth" and offered different expressions of a postmodern alternative within IRCAM.

In the *Espaces*, the theoretical discussions mainly involved well-known IRCAM figures; but the performances and tape and video sessions brought in both less-known IRCAM members and works from unknown, "way out" or amateur Parisian and American musicians and artists who had come to HY's attention by writing or sending in tapes. Such an open artistic policy was clearly antithetical to the authoritative proponents of the canon. But the openness was limited. In 1984 just one *Espace* had an entirely open section, called "*Programmez-Vous,*" for the public to bring in their own tapes.[5] Normally, all works presented were preselected by HY, who was in no simple sense an aesthetic populist.[6] Nonetheless, during its brief flowering HY's *Espace* series came to be perceived by interested outsiders as one route into IRCAM.

The degree of urgent desperation stirred up by the *Espaces* in outside musicians wanting to gain an IRCAM hearing for their music is illustrated by the following incident from a concert, as noted in my diary.

> HY and I sit together in the audience. We hear a violin sonata of a young American composer, introduced by HY as "a pupil of Roger Sessions, more and more known." As we listen, a young Japanese man suddenly appears and inserts himself between us. He asks HY in a loud whisper if he will listen to a cassette of his music and thrusts it with a scribbled envelope into HY's lap. He continues to talk to HY over the violin playing, and his hands are shaking very nervously. When the piece ends he demands of HY that he should be allowed to play violin improvisation *now*, because his music is much better than this sonata. HY says, "Wait, not now, we'll see about it later" and skillfully deflects the guy's aggressive approach. About ten minutes later, the man gets up and stalks out very obviously, dramatically.

In terms of multimedia, the *Espace* series included performance art as well as video. One evening, for example, included a highly emotional performance using sounding objects and sculptures, movement, and poetry by a Hungarian woman artist, friend of a Hungarian within IRCAM. The video component ranged from work by obscure Parisian artists and youngsters to the latest fashionable video art from the American scene, to (more rarely) the recent mainstream pop videos, such as those by Michael Jackson or Culture Club, admired by HY. The aesthetic conflicts provoked by these events are indicated in my diary. "Watching a young Parisian's music video this evening — with a loud, heavily rhythmic soundtrack like industrial rock music, to which some dazzlingly bright, abstract patterns made with computer graphics rhythmically change shape — I hear the Artistic Director say to HY: 'What is this *dreadful* stuff? This awful music?'; to which HY responds: 'It's a bit messy, but promising.'" This young man became a client of HY's. Yet he was, in a sense, far from being an "outsider." His father, an internationally renowned visual artist, was an acquaintance of Boulez's, which helped to smooth the way for the young man to take the composers' *stage*.

RIG's improvisation series included jazz and improvising musicians known to RIG from his own wide contacts in those areas. As a student, RIG was himself a jazz drummer, and since that time he had retained contact with many leading black American jazz musicians. It was well known that Boulez disliked free improvised music, as well as the frivolities of pop music and pop video. Thus, HY's and RIG's series were destined to be opposed by him and the Artistic Director.

One *Espace* caused particular controversy within IRCAM and exemplifies the ideological conflict generated by the events. Early in the evening, after a discussion of a major IRCAM composer's work, came a showing of the Michael Jackson *Thriller* video, then the most talked-about phenomenon in pop. It was followed by a set of pieces by IRCAM workers, all of them unofficial composers — both tutors and "unknown," "secret" composers. Among these were a passionate tape piece by the main sound engineer, dedicated to Allende's Chile and evoking the sounds of torture, and a tape and free saxophone piece by a squatter-technician. The evening ended with the first free improvisation by IRCAM musicians (including myself) and scientific workers, with real-time transformations of the playing by the 4X machine. The concert was experienced as defiant and exhilarating, the hall was full and the audience lively.

But it caused great disquiet. An outside musician commented, "That was a political gesture, because Boulez has always been against improvisation. It was very brave of HY." By the following day, HY looked grim and explained that he had been told off: "The Administration didn't like it. It cost too much money!" HY seemed skeptical that this was the real motor of criticism, understandably, since the *Espaces* depended mainly on unpaid, voluntary labor. But the strongest criticisms, by the Artistic Director and Boulez, took the form of censuring the unprofessionalism and "heterogeneity" of the events. They were expressed in muted official terms in the minutes of an Artistic Committee soon after. HY was due to leave IRCAM within months, and the minutes clearly signaled a reassertion of control.

CHAPTER VII

Science, Technology, the Music Research Vanguard

From its inception, computer music aimed to transcend the limits of tape and electronic music and their analog techniques, whether those of the French school, *musique concrète*, or those of the German *Elektronische Musik*. The former school was thought to use rich sound materials with poor control, while the latter applied sophisticated controls to poor sound materials. This trade-off between richness of sound and complexity of control appeared irresolvable until computer music technology promised an integration that could overcome it. In fact, hybrid technologies — using both tape and electronic synthesis — provided more satisfactory electronic music results. But throughout the history of these fields, their proponents have — often polemically — rejected mixed technologies, preferring to adopt purist stances and to proselytize for one kind or another. This was also characteristic of IRCAM in 1984. It was hoped, then, that computer music could enrich the quality of sound materials by its capacity, in theory, to simulate "any imaginable sound" as well as completely new timbres, and at the same time improve the modes of controlling musical structure and process, from the shape of individual sounds or phrases to whole pieces.

IRCAM'S MAIN TECHNOLOGICAL RESEARCH PROJECTS

Early computer synthesis in the late 1950s and early 1960s produced disappointing results for two reasons. There were technical problems due to the limits of computing speed and power, given the extremely heavy computing demands made by current sound-synthesis techniques. More importantly, there were also conceptual problems, since digital synthesis revealed the lack of adequately subtle acoustical analyses as models for the synthesis of musical timbre. This led to a growth in psychoacoustical research, in particular on the perception of timbre, with the aim of this informing improved synthesis. For example, pioneering work by Risset on trumpet timbre involved a feedback between computer-aided analysis and attempted synthesis (Risset 1965). This signals the heightened interdependence that arose in computer music between research on computer analysis and on computer synthesis of timbre and other musical parameters — an intensification of the earlier discourse of "music research" associated with analog technologies at the GRM. Thus, scientific analysis of music/sound, much enhanced by the computer, and the problems of contemporary composition came to be seen as inextricably linked.

By the 1970s and early 1980s, two major developments had occurred. The first generation of computer music synthesis languages, known as "patch" languages, had become established (for example Music V, Music X, and so on, that were based on Mathews's work at Bell Labs). These required the rigorous and detailed specification of each acoustical parameter of the sound. The patch languages produced improved sonic results, but they were far from real time and involved lengthy delays between the input of data and the eventual emission of the sound (the "turnaround time"). The IRCAM Pedagogy director recalled how, back in the early days of computer music, he would take a batch of punched computer cards to his university computer center and wait a week for them to be processed so as to hear back the encoded sounds.

As we saw in chapter 3, a technique of digital synthesis by frequency modulation (FM) had also been developed by Chowning at Stanford. Digital FM brought efficient ways of generating rich and complex timbres in real time and became the basis of the new Japanese consumer digital synthesizers starting in the early '80s.

But the dominant computer music developments prior to IRCAM, such as the patch languages, rather than simply transcending the limits of electronic music, also involved the loss of some of its positive characteristics. First, the use of sophisticated patch software depended on access to large, powerful computers and so was confined to major institutions (universities, radio stations). This contrasts with the earlier wave of small, cheap, portable analog technologies, both commercial and self-made, that were widely available to musicians for composition and live performance and that were used both in popular music and experimental music. Second, patch languages involved a loss of real-time synthesis compared with analog techniques. Thus, even with later patch languages such as Cmusic—the basis of the 1984 IRCAM *stages*—turnaround times of forty or fifty to one (forty or fifty minutes' delay to hear back one minute of synthesized sound) were common.

This problem subsumes other important losses: of an empirical work method, and of gestural control of the sound-producing devices. Analog music technologies took the form, crudely, of boxes with controlling devices that could be played around with — knobs turned, faders moved, different patches made — while sound was being produced or with a slight delay. Instead, computer patch languages were characterized by profound abstraction, complex scientistic conceptualization, and delay: in other words by extreme mediation, both temporal and conceptual. From this stems a further limitation inherent in earlier computer music. Given the exhaustive acoustic information required by patch programs and the time delays before playback of a sound, it was very difficult for the user to isolate precisely which parameters were responsible for which aspect of the resultant sound. Not only was it therefore difficult to judge which parameter to change in order to improve the sound, but the programs treated each acoustic parameter independently and did not lend themselves to exploring the interplay between them. So in addition to the programs being abstract and laborious, users found them unpredictable. This was paradoxical, given the appearance of a totally rationalist and scientistic method. By contrast, analog synthesis allowed just such an empirical, gestural exploration of the interplay of different sound-affecting parameters in real time.

These observations contest the view that patch languages offered a thoroughly rational and complete control of sound. The gap between this ideology of their potential and the character of their actual use is illustrated by the following incident. During the IRCAM *stage*, a young composer learning to use the Cmusic patch program synthesized an interesting and complex sound — by far the most musical result produced by a student so far, as the teacher commended him. On checking how the sound had been made, the teacher was surprised to discover that the young man had unwittingly written erroneous amplitude values into his file, which would produce "foldover" and distortion in the sound. So the most aurally interesting result produced by the program had come from its technically incorrect use. Just as significant was the follow-up: that evening, the student tried to reproduce the same rich sound by resynthesizing using exactly the same (erroneous) values as before. But try as he might he could not recapture it and found instead that each attempt produced slightly different aural results. The program was unpredictable: it did not reproduce identical output given identical inputs.[1] The notion of digital synthesis involving the total, rational, and predictable control of materials — a positivist scientific model of repeatable experiments giving identical results — seems in this case to have been questionable.

In the early '80s, the motor of development in computer music became the commercial Japanese sector, which produced increasingly sophisticated real-time consumer synthesizers based on digital FM. From the crude Casio range, to the Yamaha DX range, to the more ambitious Fairlight synthesizer, these were oriented toward nontechnical users and offered a range of preprogrammed and programmable, discrete, synthesized timbres controlled by a keyboard. A significant development in the mid-1980s was MIDI (Musical Instrument Digital Interface), an industry-wide standard that allowed users to link up different digital synthesizers and personal computers into powerful networks of musical instruments and controls, limited mainly by the skills of the user. Digital recording technologies also expanded, and gradually the price of commercial technologies declined. By the late '80s many composers and musicians could afford to set up variably sophisticated digital synthesis and recording studios at home based on music and recording software developed by Apple, Atari, and similar companies for use on their personal computers. Commercial developments therefore brought major changes in the means of musical production for both professionals and consumers.

IRCAM's technology projects in 1984 apparently aimed in various ways to overcome the limitations of earlier high-tech computer music, and to recapture some of the characteristics of good musical instruments that had been lost in the transition from analog technology: real-time response, less conceptual abstraction and complexity, and empirical control — that is, a more appropriate interface for musicians. But in fact most of these remained undeveloped, and the projects focused on the more unique and unprecedented musical possibilities of powerful computers. The two main projects, the 4X and Chant/Formes, aimed respectively to advance powerful real-time digital synthesis at the level of hardware and to provide increasingly sophisticated high-level music software for synthesis and control.

It is striking that within IRCAM in 1984 the commercial computer music developments described, which focused on real-time response, improved empirical and gestural control,[2] and so on, were rarely mentioned. They were a vague background, occasionally surfacing in discussions, and brought into IRCAM by "dissidents." Thus, one of the more or less implicit principles of IRCAM's dominant ideology at this time was a hostility and contempt toward all commercial developments and especially "low-tech" or small consumer technologies. Consistent with Boulez's own ideology, it was held that IRCAM had nothing to learn from commerce.[3]

A variant was voiced by tutors on the *stage*. When asked about IRCAM's relation to commerce, they described the two sectors' concerns as totally distinct. The commercial industries were, they said, oriented toward "the pop or mass music market," while IRCAM and other basic research institutions were concerned with "more subtle, abstract musical uses of technology . . . [with] computer science and music research, for contemporary music." They proposed a "trickle down" model whereby basic research comes only from autonomous research institutes and then diffuses to commerce, so that commerce becomes dependent upon and derivative of institutions such as IRCAM, which have the major pioneering role.

Another incident, however, suggested both mutual suspicion and industrial tension between the two sectors, and at the same time a growing respect from some IRCAM researchers for what could be learned from commerce. A representative of the Yamaha corporation, in 1984 the leaders in commercial technologies, came to visit IRCAM to demonstrate their latest CX synthesizer. The senior Japanese executive took the machine through its paces. The breakthrough with this machine was size: the extraordinary miniaturization of a digital FM unit. Bemused and admiring of this tiny, powerful toy, the researchers gazed at its black casing. Finally, the American composer PL (who alone worked seriously with small commercial systems), defying the implicit etiquette of the occasion, challenged the man to tell how it worked: what was in the box? A pause, and the representative replied, "Ah . . . Japanese air!" The room broke into polite, ironic laughter, and mystery was maintained. The story hints at how IRCAM's dominant anticommercial ideology concealed both rivalry with and intense curiosity about the commercial technology sector — a curiosity that was, for the most part, well repressed.

Thus, IRCAM's technological research culture in 1984 could be understood in terms of IRCAM's assertion of difference from the commercial sector, oriented as that is above all toward consumers or users. Despite lip service, we will see that IRCAM's main research at this time tended to neglect issues of user friendliness or man-machine interface. These were not given priority since they were not perceived as basic or fundamental research.

The aim of the 4X project was the production of the most powerful real-time digital synthesizer, with a strong emphasis on real time, the capacity that had been lost with earlier kinds of digital synthesis. The project also centered on innovative hardware design: pioneering new signal-processing techniques and, simply, building a big machine.

The 4X project originated when the designer, physicist BU, was brought to IRCAM in 1975 by the composer Berio who, the story goes, wanted "a real-time synthesizer with a thousand oscillators." The 4X was more powerful and more flexible than its earlier prototypes, the 4A, 4B, and 4C machines. It was capable of both real-time synthesis and analysis of sound. The range of processing techniques available on the 4X included known digital techniques and digital simulations of important analog techniques: additive synthesis, subtractive synthesis by numerical filtering, FM synthesis, synthesis by sampling of acoustic sounds and processing them, ring modulation, harmonization, echo, reverberation, phasing, frequency and spectral analysis, and so on. The 4X was, therefore, unique in its power and generality in 1984, although its position was in some ways being threatened by a more powerful commercial rival—the up-and-coming Lucasfilm ASP.

The design intention of the machine was to provide a basic signal-processing hardware architecture that could be used flexibly for different synthesis techniques. But one of the major weaknesses of the project lay in the fact that hardware alone is not sufficient to provide this. It also requires the development of appropriate software and peripherals to add to the basic hardware for it to be fully, and musically, usable, and this next crucial stage was neglected in the early years of the project. BU was not interested in software and had little time for what he saw as the pretensions of IRCAM's software intellectuals. So in 1984, a full three years after the final hardware had emerged, the main 4X-related work was the development of software and of peripherals such as the DACs and ADCs and various gestural control devices. The 4X Soft team was developing both the basic operating programs required for the 4X to run, and higher-level programs to enable users to configure the machine in the desired way and to link up to other machines. All of these were meant to contribute to realizing the eventual aim of developing a "4X musical workstation."

In 1984, all the work of the several teams engaged on the 4X project went toward preparing for the *Répons* premieres, in which the 4X had a starring role. By 1985 the earliest form of the 4X work station had been produced and four were in use within the institute. However, no 4X work stations were distributed to other computer music centers. The history of the 4X reveals a stress on real-time digital processing power based on innovative hardware, but a relatively weak awareness of the necessity of developing both software and peripherals, and so of the musician end of the R and D process.

The composers who used the 4X most successfully were those resident at IRCAM, such as Boulez, certain tutors and junior tutors, and HY, the Music Research director. HY praised highly the 4X's flexibility and instantaneous response, which he felt allowed for empirical work and for trying out compositional ideas in a responsive environment. Indeed, for HY it was the 4X rather than IRCAM's advanced software that embodied the more utopian experiment. It fostered real-time composition methods, and with the completion of research in progress it would be amenable, like earlier analog technologies, to gestural control, and could be readily adapted for live performance uses. The 4X was thus, according to HY, exemplary of a technology that could weigh against the high-tech tendency to displace live performance. On the other hand, the 4X's few internal critics spoke of it as far too generalized, simply a grandiose and primitive simulation of analog techniques — "a glorified patchboard with a thousand oscillators." Among these critics, the Chant/Formes group was the most vocal. They argued that the 4X technology was out of date, that it lacked musically appropriate controls and neglected the computer's potential for higher-level music-conceptual development — concerns that were the basis of their own software work.

The Chant/Formes project was concerned entirely with high-level software and aimed to innovate both in synthesis techniques and in the structuring and control of sound for composition. Yet the software was not real-time, and in 1984 it remained dependent on a high-tech computing environment. The research was carried out, and the programs ran, on the VAX.

The Chant/Formes group saw themselves as the most advanced computer science project at IRCAM. They linked their work conceptually to recent developments in AI and its application in fields as diverse as speech recognition and synthesis, computer graphics and animation. Both the Chant and Formes programs were informed by AI developments such as the language LISP, and object-oriented and interactive programming. The links to AI, in the mid-1980s the fashionable leading edge of computer science, signaled the group's aspiration to the role of IRCAM's computer science vanguard, their sense of themselves as the most "radical" computer science ideologues within IRCAM. This was supported by their earnest articulation, for example in *stage* lectures, of the utopian philosophy behind their work.

According to this philosophy, Chant and Formes aimed to transcend the previous generation of patch languages and, more broadly, prevailing software design, in several ways. In contrast with patch languages, the programs took the form of a branching tree of options. The group saw this as user-friendly since in theory any inexperienced user could follow a list of options supplied with default values and produce a sound as a result. As the user learned more about the program, she could engage at a deeper level and experiment with different values.

Second, Chant and Formes were supposed to evolve through interaction with the user, so that ambitious users could create their own "personalized environment" within the programs and feed back ideas into their ongoing design. The programs were to be produced through collective use. This in turn invoked two further utopian principles: a belief in the responsibility and creativity of the user, and a critique of the program as closed and definitive and as the private property of the designer/author. Instead, the program was conceived as an open text.

Third, the programs were object-oriented. Two genealogies converged on this concept, one from AI and the other from *musique concrète*. "Objects" are defined in AI programming terms as processes in time with a unified coherence. The dual manipulation of objects (themselves processes) into organized hierarchies, and sequentially (in time), thereby constructing multilayered and recursive structures, are the basic principles of LISP. In *musique concrète*, a "musical object" is a unified sound entity — a sound extracted by tape recording from the total sound world — used as a building block for a larger tape piece.

Fourth, both programs centered conceptually on time, whether the microevolution of the frequency spectrum characteristic of a particular timbre (Chant), or the formal structuring of a composition in time (Formes). In contrast to the laborious and abstract specification of time values in patch languages, the new programs aimed to provide elegant means of manipulating these temporal dimensions.

Chant was a synthesis program based on simulating the physical laws of sound production in the human voice. It originated in research on speech synthesis undertaken by the project director, MC. By manipulating these laws, Chant allowed a higher-level control of acoustical parameters than the patch languages. Control of timbre was achieved by moving simulated "formants" — peak resonances — against each other in time. In this way Chant could synthesize not just vocal sounds but a variety of other timbres. Most importantly, it also allowed the synthesis of transitions between timbres, of continuous timbral change. This was a major interest of IRCAM's musicians' group vanguard.

Formes was a control program aimed at structuring sound materials for composition that centered on the manipulation of musical objects. But compared with *musique concrète*, objects could be defined far more widely — from a single sound, timbre, or amplitude envelope, to a musical phrase or complete compositional structure. Formes manipulated objects in two ways. First, objects were organized hierarchically: each level of the hierarchy controlled the next level down. Objects could be reused at different levels and moments in the structure, fostering thematic and material unity. Second, Formes enabled the hierarchy of objects to be ordered in time. A piece was built up by constructing a "syntax" of objects controlled at the highest level by a command process that embodied the overall syntax or form.

Chant and Formes were intended to be more intuitively appealing and musically meaningful, less complex and scientistic than the prior generation of patch languages. The group's antagonism to patch languages carried nationalist overtones: a rejection of the limits of American software and a desire to supersede it with more advanced programs inspired by French AI. The degree of nationalist ideological division can be illustrated by this tirade by a (French) Chant/Formes researcher against the (American) Pedagogy director for his continued advocacy of patch methods for teaching: "How can you trust a man who's never touched the most important tools in this house? He doesn't know anything about Chant or Formes! . . . It's an ideological battle. His position's very dated, his practice is out of touch."

Yet contradictions surrounded Chant/Formes. Despite their rhetorical support for collaborative and knowledge-sharing enquiry, the Chant/Formes workers were seen by others in IRCAM as secretive and protective of their own research. For example, they actively excluded a former researcher who left the group to work elsewhere in IRCAM. Further, despite user-friendly aims, and like the 4X, the main skilled users of the programs in 1984 were composers resident at IRCAM or regular visitors. The programs remained opaque and recalcitrant in inexperienced hands. Unlike the 4X, Chant was later distributed to other computer music centers. It was also, in the late '80s, adapted to run on commercial machines such as the Apple Macintosh. Chant therefore had a longer, wider, and more influential life than the 4X.

The programs received some criticism within IRCAM. A junior tutor-composer complained of Chant being slow, overcomplex, and resisting musical use — not so different from the patch languages; and he much preferred to work in real time with the 4X. Formes was claimed as the first program to provide lucid means of conceptual control for composition. But its critics saw all this as ephemeral, a mind game of no real use to anyone. These criticisms came from high in the scientific sector, including some in the 4X project. They also, therefore, marked a mutual antagonism between the two main technology projects.

DISSIDENT TECHNOLOGY: A SMALL-SYSTEMS PROJECT

The two main projects, both oriented toward high technology, contrasted with the one temporary project in 1984 devoted to small systems or low technology: that of PL. With its implicit advocacy of small systems and of their commercial sources, both contradicting IRCAM's dominant ideology, PL's project was the prime example of a dissident research project in 1984.

PL was the only nonwhite intellectual worker at IRCAM, and the project was his alone. He was employed at IRCAM on temporary contracts for about two years until the summer of '84. He was both a composer and a professional performer in many areas of music: avant-garde and experimental musics, improvised music, jazz, rock, and funk. PL was unique among IRCAM composers in continuing a busy performing career, which in '84 included tours in the United States, Japan and Europe, around which he slotted IRCAM work. His work outside IRCAM, then, involved musics that were well known to be disapproved of by Boulez, and although PL was discreet, no other IRCAM worker engaged so blatantly in officially unacceptable musics.

PL's project was based on Apple II microcomputers, for which he wrote software using common and commercially available languages such as BASIC and low-level assembler code. The project aimed to create an interactive system based on small personal computers linked by MIDI to commercial synthesizers whereby musicians and microcomputers could "intelligently" improvise music together. It worked as follows. The musician played into a microphone linked by an ADC to an Apple II. This Apple's "ear" program, designed by PL, analyzed the musical input according to certain preprogrammed underlying musical principles (such as pitch, register, duration, rhythm, loudness). Having analyzed the input, a "player" program, also written by PL and running on another Apple II, constructed a musical response, again according to various principles (elaboration, contrast, inversion, and so on). This output was fed to a digital synthesizer that "played" the computer's musical response. Finally, the musician responded by improvising, so initiating the interactive network once again. PL was able to get this to work in real time: the computer's musical responses occurred so fast that they appeared instantaneous. His final version for the IRCAM premiere had three Apple IIs linked up to three Yamaha DX7 synthesizers, improvising with four musicians.

PL was an autodidact in computing, and he wanted his system to be portable, practical, cheap, and yet conceptually and musically sophisticated. He believed strongly that the two were compatible and was scornful of those "snobs" who equated size of technology with quality of musical result. PL's interests in intelligent systems and interactivity, as with Chant/Formes, linked to ideas currently fashionable in AI. A philosophy graduate from Yale, PL was well aware of these implications and his work was far from intellectually naive. His project existed to celebrate small-machine power and also the bounty of the "start-up" commercial sector — small companies such as Apple that, growing from nothing, had challenged the dominance of manufacturers like IBM and DEC. In this David and Goliath worldview, the force of progress rests with small, innovative venture capital that breaks the sluggish monopoly of the giants, and in PL's eyes the character of each sector was concretized in their technologies. With his good friend the Pedagogy director RIG, PL was an ardent proponent of the philosophy of small technology and of the adventurous and enlightened commerce that produces it, a position echoing with classic American free market liberalism.

PL got his IRCAM commission with the backing of American music directors HY and RIG; his project had little appeal to the Artistic Director. As well as being PL's patrons, both HY and RIG were personal friends of his. In their life outside IRCAM, RIG and PL shared an immersion in the social and cultural milieu of Parisian black American "jazzers." But in general PL felt patronized by IRCAM and thought that people treated his work condescendingly as a piece of fun. In return he was highly skeptical of IRCAM's musical, technological, and scientific pretensions. He was especially critical of the 4X and *Répons*, and he scorned the institute's bureaucracy and politics.

PL expressed his willful marginality through symbolic spatial, temporal, and physical means. Early in '84 he avoided coming into IRCAM at all by working on his system in his cramped apartment. He boasted of his freedom and independence, that he didn't need any of IRCAM's resources in order to work. However, in February he decided to move inside IRCAM and was given a small, disused attic room in the old building. As he put it, this was spatially "the furthest away one could be inside IRCAM and still be in the place!" PL eschewed office hours and worked at IRCAM from late evening until early morning, a choice that rather than resting on the usual technological alibi of overcrowded resources clearly derived from his bohemian lifestyle. PL later began unofficially to use his attic room as a place to stay as well as work and left personal effects there in addition to his equipment—clothes, books, a mattress. Exceptionally for IRCAM, he locked the room to protect what was his own precious property—a concession from the building manager.

Another expression of marginality was PL's avoidance of the musicians' meetings, his self-estrangement from the vanguard musicians' group, to which he might have been expected to belong. This showed his utter disdain for IRCAM's internal politics. He did not want to depend on IRCAM beyond the present commitment—unusual for visiting composers, most of whom sought continuing relations with IRCAM and its associated prestige. PL was cynical about the careerist implications of working at IRCAM and said that there was more to learn and better music to be made outside.

Throughout the spring of '84 PL worked away at the "ear" and "player" programs, refining their musical principles and smoothing out programming bugs. He tried the system out in his solo improvising gigs in Europe and the United States. Taking just one Apple made the system portable, and he could rewrite the programs, recorded on small floppy disks, as he traveled. He also asked musicians, including myself, to improvise with the programs for feedback. The project culminated in an IRCAM premiere in May. Four free jazz musicians played in various combinations with the system while PL controlled the overall network from the back of the hall. The concerts went down well with the audience. But the reaction of IRCAM directors was less warm, as this excerpt from my diary of the first night conveys.

Re. PL's premiere tonight: the gig is full. As often around PL, a festive and gay
atmosphere — his perception that he's the in-house clown/entertainer.
I sit next to two music directors, AA and BB.
PL starts slowly by talking vaguely through the system: three Apples, three
DX7's, MIDI interfaces etc. Says he's not interested at all in voicings/timbre
synthesis, but in discovering and working with "rules" and "structures" of
musical process in improvised playing.
AA comments: "The free improvisation sounds dated. I don't like [the guitar-
ist's] playing."
BB: "Is there a score? [*Dubiously*] It sounds like there is: *something* must be
directing it! [*Half joking*] I'm not sure what the contractual situation is if
there isn't a score!"
AA: [*Jokey, disparaging the playing*] "Bringing your instrument tomorrow
night, BB?" meaning, "you could play just as well."
PL asks of the room after a few pieces: "Shall we have an intermission?"
AA and BB shout back imperiously, "No, PL!" PL calls one.
In the intermission, AA and BB, usually rivals, exchange opinions: that it's a
"mess," not "professional," "tight," or impressive enough. Once again, it
seems that the judgment of "not being professional" is leveled at a concert
whose aesthetic was a source of disquiet and disapproval.

In terms of musicians' experience of playing with PL's system, despite
having arrived some days earlier to get the "musical feel" of the machines, the guitarist of the group did not enjoy the computer's responses.
He remained antagonistic and played in an intransigent way, trying to
give the machine a "hard time." This shows that the aesthetic embodied
in PL's improvisation "rules" did not suit all players equally well. My
own experience, playing improvised cello with the system, was that it
was difficult to make musical sense of, but interesting. One weakness of
the "ear" program, for example, was that it required the player to hit a
pitch very precisely. Its pitch-following device could not make sense
either of notes that were slightly off pitch, or of glissandi — slides between pitches used by instrumentalists for expressivity and common in
many nonwestern and popular musics. So the programs could not deal
well with analog or continuous pitch phenomena — one of the inherent
difficulties with the discrete bias of digital technology.
    More significant were the insights gained into PL's concept of the
"rules" of improvised music. From playing, I suggested some ideas to
him that, surprisingly, he hadn't thought of. The main idea was that
the "ear" program should "listen" not for individual but for repeated
rhythmic and pitch patterns, for grouped or patterned events, a feature
of many musics and kinds of improvisation. Before this, PL had programmed the "ear" to search only for discrete parameters or their differ-

ence from the previous event, a very fragmented model of musical process. He followed my suggestions and eventually found ways, months later, to program the recognition of certain "basic musical patterns."

This story emphasizes, first, how crude were the initial musical "rules" that PL was working with; and second, how writing these "rules" depended upon a prior selection of the key aesthetic characteristics of the musical genre in question or desired, and could not avoid being aesthetically charged. PL's selection of "rules" dictated from which aesthetic standpoint the sounds coming into the "ear" program would be "heard," just as his "player" program would elaborate those sounds according to similarly aesthetically imbued "rules." PL's own perspective on this issue revealed contradictions. In individual discussion he portrayed a sophisticated understanding of the aesthetic differences between musics, without which he could hardly have played successfully in so many. Yet he also had little time for what he dismissed as "musical relativism." In this vein, he claimed that his programs were based on the musical principles of improvised music and in doing so he employed the universalizing rhetoric, common at IRCAM, of "rules" and "structures," implying that his programs expressed general principles of improvised music rather than just those of one genre or aesthetic of improvisation.

At base, PL appeared uninterested in taking up the issue of the inevitability of implicit aesthetic biases in his and other musically "intelligent" systems. He preferred ultimately to present himself in a scientistic way that ignored aesthetic questions in favor of quasi-universal "rules." Thus, despite his very different and diverse external musical work, for his IRCAM work and at the level of rhetoric PL retained a universalist view of musical structures and "knowledge." While subverting many aspects of IRCAM and its technologies, PL did not contest the dominant forms of rhetoric around music and the aesthetic.

MUSIC RESEARCH AND PSYCHOACOUSTICS

The related domains of psychoacoustics and music research also had a pivotal ideological position in 1984 within IRCAM, and they were propounded by the musicians' group as the way forward for musical composition. The musicians' meetings were initiated in urgent response to a massive planning document for the future of IRCAM, written by the incumbent Scientific Director at the start of '84, which hardly mentioned music or music research at all. That autumn he left IRCAM and his plans were never realized; but internal conflict between the scientific side and those who saw themselves as upholding IRCAM's musical ideals appeared to be chronic. As the musicians' meetings developed, they worked on defining two levels of future music research: the main research themes, and the social organization of research, for which they proposed new collaborative teams reminiscent of Boulez's Bauhaus model. This was a bid for more autonomy, power, and resources for music research, which the group felt to be under threat. By insisting on the centrality of IRCAM's future and long-term orientation, its musical goals and social organization, the group embodied a fundamentalist return to Boulez's original vision.

Central to the musicians' group engagement with music research and psychoacoustics in 1984 were interrelated concerns with timbre and with musical form. This must be understood in the context of historical developments arising from the impasses of musical modernism earlier in the century and their contemporary legacy.

The functional tonal music system upon which baroque, classical, and romantic music was based centered on manipulations of pitch, while timbre was a relatively neglected parameter of composition. With the gradual dissolution of functional tonality in late romanticism and early modernism, composers showed increased awareness of timbre, whether in Debussy's exploration of tone color or Varèse's extension of the range of sound materials. However, Schoenberg was the first to theorize timbre as a major musical parameter with his 1911 concept of *Klangfarbenmelodie*: a "melody" defined by successive changes of timbre rather than pitch. Webern, in his pointillist works, pursued this by experimenting with timbral contrasts as a structuring device.

As we saw in chapter 2, the main thrust of the postwar avant-garde under the ideology of total serialism was the scientific extension of serialism to control all musical parameters, including timbre. But attempts to control timbre in this way by electronic synthesis, such as those by Stockhausen, produced poor, monotonous results. This was not the only postwar expression of an interest in timbre. Perhaps in reaction to the rationalist excesses of total serialism, during the '60s an eclectic range of composers—from the Poles Lutoslawski and Penderecki of the *Klangfarbenschule*, to Xenakis, Berio, and indeed Stockhausen—evinced a looser, sometimes mystical concern with sound color. At the same time Schaeffer was taking further the idea of timbre as a structural dimension with his aim of constructing a *solfège* of timbres for *musique concrète*. But it was the failure of early electronic synthesis in the service of total serialism, and of the acoustic analyses informing it, that led to efforts by scientists such as Risset to gain better analyses of timbre. I noted before how important computer technology became in allowing a new kind of feedback between timbral analysis and digital synthesis, with the idea that, in theory, digital synthesis could produce any timbre, given appropriate information.

This generation of researchers came to believe that physical descriptions alone could not explain the perceptually or musically meaningful aspects of timbre, so psychoacoustical research was deemed necessary to find the most perceptually important dimensions. These analyses helped to achieve a more organic range of synthesized timbres, revealing at the same time the extraordinary complexity of timbre for both analysis and synthesis — something that we will see continues to pose problems for computer music.

Some psychoacoustic research was employed, however, in a harsher critique of total serialism. Composers and researchers hostile to serialism and concerned with the audience's bewildered incomprehension of this music turned to perception studies to explain it. They argued that serialism transgressed the perceptual limits of the listener and was too complex and fragmented to be musically meaningful. In some cases, the scientific refutation of serialism was allied to a postmodern call for a return to tonality. This research did not simply criticize serialism as music, then, but offered a scientific critique based on purported universals of human perception.

A final factor in this history concerns another major problem in twentieth-century composition: the absence of any coherent approach to musical form since the advent of modernism. This refers to the high-level organization of musical sound horizontally, through time, but also vertically, as with tonal harmony. Classical musical form had continued into late romanticism, but with the break from tonality around the turn of the century came the question of new forms to match the new musical systems of atonality and then serialism. Boulez in 1951 chided Schoenberg for the "contradiction" of retaining classical form despite his invention of serialism, and Boulez's view — that musical modernism must seek new forms to suit new sound materials — became orthodox. Yet over the century no sustained modernist approach to form emerged, so that the problem of new musical forms has remained central to debates around modernism and its limits and has been high on the compositional agenda.

More recently two important developments have occurred, both dependent on the computer. The first links issues of form with timbre and time. We have seen that throughout the century composers have considered whether timbral change can structure music in time. Computer synthesis offers ways to further this, since unlike *musique concrète* and electronic synthesis, every component of a digitally simulated timbre is built up completely from scratch so that the timbre is no longer inviolate but, in theory, infinitely malleable. The technology has therefore come to be seen as a means of taking two such simulated timbral objects and, through an analysis of their components, building a "bridge" or "transition" between them. According to this approach, timbral objects need no longer remain discrete, but may be transformed, melted into one another, thereby creating unprecedented possibilities for structural movement by timbral change. Hence, while at the micro level each partial in the timbre is rapidly evolving in time, at the macro level the transitions construct higher-level musical time — a "timbral syntax."

One possibility of timbral transition, then, is that the microtemporal processes within the timbre and the formal macroprocesses constructed by timbral syntax could be related. The composer could derive macromusical forms from microtimbral processes — generate the whole from the seed — or vice versa, and so create unity. This is a highly sophisticated version of the notion of unifying micro and macro that we saw in chapter 6 was a rhetoric widespread within IRCAM and that continues the organicism of the tradition of German romanticism as reinterpreted by Schoenberg. In 1984 this approach was the pinnacle to which IRCAM's musicians' group vanguard in various ways aspired: an organicism doubly consecrated through its mediation by the latest, most astute scientific analyses and by the unique musical possibilities of advanced computer technologies. Since in 1984 the Chant and Formes programs were considered by many in the group to come closest to offering tools to pursue these ideas, the destinies of the Chant/Formes group and that of the vanguard were closely entwined.

The second development around musical form has involved a different level of computer applications. The work of writers such as Meyer (1956) indicates the parallels that have been developed in the past between information theory and music analysis. In disciplines related to computer science we can trace a development from information theory through cognitive science to artificial intelligence, a kind of applied cognitive modeling with the computer both as analytic tool and means of simulation. AI is based on the analysis of forms of knowledge to extract their essential content and logic or "rules," which are then redescribed as a structure of inference and written as an "intelligent" computer program, such as an "expert system," that represents a simulation of that knowledge system. Similarly, in music there has been a development from music analysis as a purely analytic field to one that, employing the computer and in conjunction with the rise of cognitive music studies and AI, aims to provide both computer analyses of musical structure and also computerized models of "musical knowledge" or "rules" as aids to composition. The computer has therefore come to be seen as a tool for analyzing the deep structures or "cognitive rules" characteristic of certain musics, but equally for simulating these rules — and indeed for generating entirely new abstract structures as frameworks for composition.

There are two observations to be made. First, we can see in these developments, due to the mediation of the computer as both analytic tool and simulator, a subtle but profound elision between analysis and composition: the two are close to becoming as one. Thus, at IRCAM in 1984 the main psychoacoustician, HM, constantly entertained the desire to compose since he saw his cognitive analytical work as generating compositional ideas, yet other composers' use of his research disappointed him.[4]

Second, the computer's ability to produce elegant abstract models has meant that its generation of new conceptual schemes for music, in particular mathematical and cognitive structural models, has become quite autonomous from the analysis of extant musics. This lay, for example, behind the AI-influenced approach of IRCAM's Formes program, with its generalized and abstract, hierarchical ordering of objects and events in time.

Both of these developments, along with the constant conceptual foraging for scientific analogies to structure composition that I described in the last chapter, evidence a continuity with deeper characteristics of musical modernism. They should be grasped as an extreme contemporary expression of modernist theoreticism, the tendency for theory to become prior to, prescriptive of, and constitutive of compositional practice.

In this genealogy the scientific study of cognitive universals takes a central place, both psychoacoustic study of microtimbral and temporal processes and cognitive study of musical structure. We have seen a convergence from several directions of interrelated concerns with timbre and sound material, timbre and temporality, timbre and form, and timbre and perception. All were considered to be enhanced by the computer, since in theory it enables "any imaginable sound" or musical structure to be both analyzed and simulated. Yet it is also obvious that timbre becomes a rhetorical catchall subsuming many diverse preoccupations, and that "timbre," "temporality," and "perception" become generalized discursive themes. Motivated by major problems of musical modernism — the sense of sterility attached to composition techniques such as serialism based originally on the primacy of pitch, the lack of an approach to musical form, the errors of midcentury rationalism and scientism, the conceptual weakness of *musique concrète* — research on timbre and perception has been held, at IRCAM and more widely, to offer ways forward.

Overall, it is striking that the response to the deep musical and philosophical impasses that arose around early and midcentury serialist modernism has been to amend and improve the rationalism and scientism through increasingly sophisticated scientific and technological mediation. Far from rejecting the deeper epistemological character of modernism, postserialism has refined and complexified it, for example in the elision of computerized music analysis with compositional genesis. As we will see in greater depth, the discourse within which IRCAM is situated is a scientistic refinement of the classic concerns of modernism.

This legacy, with little overt hostility to serialism, lay behind the continuous reference to perception, timbre, and form by the IRCAM vanguard, for whom the study of musical perception and cognition would lay the basis for new sound materials and new musical forms. In 1984 there were, by consensus, two main psychoacousticians at IRCAM, neither employed as such: Pedagogy director RIG and junior tutor HM, both of whom had trained in cognitive music psychology.

IRCAM's psychoacoustic research at this time examined how listening organizes the physical world by differentiation and integration. The issue of aural integration can be illustrated by pitch perception, which involves the unconscious integration of many different harmonic partials (frequencies within the harmonic series) into a single sound object. This psychoacoustical phenomenon is called "fusion," and it was a theme of HM's research.

Work on harmonic fusion has fed into study of the contrasting perception of "inharmonics": those sounds, like bells, that are not based on a single harmonic series. Research has shown that we do not hear inharmonics as fused single objects; rather, we search unconsciously within them for the patterns of the harmonic series and hear them as a set of overlapping, incomplete harmonic pitches. In fact, when we perceive a pattern of higher harmonics within an inharmonic but the fundamental harmonic frequency is physically missing, the brain projects a phantom fundamental to replace the missing one, a phenomenon known as "virtual pitch." These apparent details were major interests of IRCAM's vanguard, since digital synthesis has the unique potential to construct infinite numbers of inharmonics and to change over time their "internal" structure of frequencies (or spectrum) so as to produce interesting senses of movement "within" the sound — another kind of timbral transition, known at IRCAM as the "evolution of spectral form." Thus research on inharmonics, virtuals, fusion, and the "internal evolution" of sounds was seen as potentially valuable for composition.

The phenomenon of aural differentiation can be illustrated by RIG's studies of timbre. It is known that listeners have the capacity to differentiate relatively between pitches, so that they hear pitch intervals as relatively the same (for example a fifth, an octave) even if at absolutely different registers. RIG's work in the 1970s examined whether subjects have a similar cognitive capacity to differentiate between timbres, which are both physically and perceptually multidimensional. He focused on the "multidimensional scaling" of timbre and the notion of perceiving "timbral analogies." Subjects were asked to judge the similarity or difference between instrumental timbres (oboe and cello, clarinet and voice) sounding the same pitch. This gave a distribution of timbres according to perceived likeness and difference, though little understanding of the parameters underlying these judgments. From this, RIG drew up graphic representations of timbral perception in terms of two-dimensional and three-dimensional spatial distributions. These were meant to provide predictive maps of how to create perceptually interesting new timbres, as well as to serve as guidelines for the simulation of perceptually valid timbral transitions. The research aimed to inform both the synthesis of new sound materials and, through timbral syntax, new compositional forms. The implicit message: "where pitch was, let there be timbre."

Composer AV's project in 1984, described in the next chapter, was an attempt to put some of this psychoacoustical work on timbral transition into compositional practice. In the following dialogue, HM, who was involved in the project, discussed the aims as well as problems that arose. But the exchange also conveys well the strategy whereby issues of perception are brought in as a hopeful way out of what has been, essentially, an aesthetic failure. The failure was an attempt to create a musically meaningful "interpolation" between two distinct timbres by synthesizing glissandi (slides) between their component frequencies. Rather than reconsider whether such an aim is unmusical, HM preferred to think of the aim — a key principle of the music vanguard as informed by psychoacoustics — as correct, but the method used as perceptually at "too low a level." The answer, for him, was therefore not to think of a new musical aim but to be more scientific.

HM: In his first visit in '82, AV wanted to work on timbral transition — from an oboe to a soprano voice sound — and we did that using Chant on the PDP10 with MC's help. Then he wanted transitions from very complicated inharmonic sounds like a gong or tam-tam into a soprano. But the problem is: even at the level of physical modeling, there's no similarity at all between those two things. I wrote him some [software] instruments that would allow him to take any given set of frequencies and have them interpolated in some bizarre fashion with another. It was a total failure. All we got is this large glissando which was not at all satisfactory for timbral transformation. So we started to think of other ways. . . .
        We learned that it's not just to do with the frequency dimension. It's much more complicated. I've been playing a lot recently with this notion of the coherence of the behavior of sound objects, and what coherence means in one case is totally different from another case. So for that to be successful you'd have to be making the interpolations at a much higher level of behavior of the elements, because simply thinking at an acoustic level is not satisfactory. We did get some partially satisfactory results, based on a notion I came up with of a sort of pivot — a period of time in which things decompose and recompose into other objects. That was much better: we'd totally disintegrate one sound and then have it re-form over a specified time into the other sound.
GB: What you seem to be saying about timbral transformation is that the idea of interpolation as a continuous process is contradicted by realizing how precise are the coherences of timbres as discrete objects? . . .
HM: I wouldn't say it's contradicted: I think it *is* contradicted at the level we were dealing with it. But that's like trying to talk about social organization at the level of molecules — we were trying to deal with it at too low a level. It implies having a much better knowledge about what we mean by coherence in each case; so that when transformation takes place, it's at a *perceptually relevant* level, so that coherence is maintained, or incoherence if that's desired, at a level that's *believable* to the ear.
GB: So you're still convinced of the idea that there could be a syntax of timbral transformations that could in itself be some kind of syntactic language?
HM: Yes, I think so.

The absences in IRCAM's psychoacoustics are also significant. As well as being central to the *stage*, psychoacoustics was the subject of IRCAM's main public lecture series in 1984 called "Perception and Composition." Both courses dealt with timbre, inharmonics, and so on, but neither dealt at any length with rhythm as a musical dimension. Only the public lectures had a session called "Rhythm and Time Perception," which looked at issues of time, memory, and duration rather than rhythmic issues of pulsation, beat, repetition — phenomena associated aesthetically with jazz and popular musics. Musical time in total serialism is conceived in terms of calculated durations that construct extremely complex and irregular rhythmic structures. RIG, who gave the lecture and who we have seen was keen on jazz, nonetheless spent all his time on a critique of this serialist approach and its lack of perceptual validity. He talked with relish, as follows.

> Boulez was a guinea pig in an experiment in complex rhythmic perception at Bell Labs. The idea was: can a composer really hear the differences if a performer of his music plays very complex rhythms right or wrong? For example, in 6/8 a 7 over 6, or 19s over 13s, and so on — such as one finds often in the music of Carter or Ferneyhough. The results? Boulez and a well-known avant-garde violinist both showed great *errors*, and in opposite directions! So this shows that the ideas of rhythmic perception of someone like Carter are *wrong*! They are impossible to realize on two levels: that of production by a player and that of perception by a listener, even a highly skilled one!

RIG ended the thirty-minute talk: "I was going to talk about another level — why one jazz drummer will have 'swing' and another won't! But I guess I'll leave that for another evening." He therefore managed only the briefest reference, amounting to an evasion, of the issue of sophisticated rhythm in other musics such as jazz; and this, on the tail of an elaborate perceptual critique of serialist rhythm that signaled his ongoing ideological battle with Boulez.

This incident highlights the specificity of the musical terrain that IRCAM's psychoacoustic research addressed and upon which it erected "universal" models of human perception. In fact, during 1984 there was one research project devoted to analyzing the "rules" of jazz improvisation, which may seem to contradict my point about the aesthetic limits and the universalizing character of IRCAM's psychoacoustics. But the project was weak, its status low, and it was bugged by illegitimacy, above all because it was seen as not sufficiently generalizable by contrast with the rest of IRCAM's psychoacoustics, which was presumed to be.[5] In his lectures, HM appeared to have a sophisticated grasp of the issue of musical-cultural differences, admitting that "our cognitive abilities are experience-based, culturally specific." Yet challenged by a student who posed the extreme cultural determinist position — "But I hear no sound, nor any music, outside a certain aesthetic and historical context: it's all in these contexts!" — HM said nothing and the issue was never elaborated. Rather, on another occasion HM opted for a different perspective that evades cultural or aesthetic specificity, this time by dissolving it into an extreme individualism: the poststructuralist idea of music as a radically "open text." HM talked of "listeners [recreating] music by their own taste structure, so there are a multiplicity of different meanings or readings in a certain music." As we have seen, this rhetoric was also at times characteristic of Boulez.

Finally, it is worth noting that RIG's experiments in timbral perception involved just nine subjects: of these, all were IRCAM workers and one was Boulez. It is on the basis of these thin experiments employing very culturally specific subjects that RIG drew data to be interpreted in terms of universals of timbral perception and intended in turn to generate apparently aesthetically independent techniques of timbral syntax. This throws into relief the claims of the research to embody culturally independent perceptual or musical universals, and it emphasizes the ideological nature of the scientific claims to universality.

THE MUSICIANS' GROUP VANGUARD

With psychoacoustics as a framework, the musicians' group saw as their common purpose the definition of future areas of research that would be of maximum musical use to composers. Over several months of meetings, the group's main interests were aired, scrutinized, and then formulated as documents to show Boulez for approval. These were written in commanding and utopian language, a sort of internal marketing targeted at Boulez. The five main themes proposed for future music research were: timbre as a conveyor of musical structure, timbral transition, timbre as a musical concept based on the interdependence of previously distinct parameters (pitch, evolution of spectra in time, and so on); formal generation of musical structures and their relationship with time; an "inharmonic musical expert system" (or "computer environment as an aid to composition"); real-time computer/performer networks for interactive performance; and information transfer of IRCAM software from the big machines to small systems. However the themes were very unevenly supported in meetings: the first three received wide backing, while the last two were proposed by RIG and gained only weak and rhetorical support.

A glance at the external writings of members of the musicians' group continues the themes. The first issue of a new international contemporary music journal in 1984 contained a collection of theoretical exegeses on composition and related music research by key composer-intellectuals from the group.[6] All combine accounts of their work that are philosophical, analytical, sometimes technical, and influenced by computer science. One junior tutor-composer gives his theoretical exegesis of a large composition that was well received by the IRCAM establishment. He writes of perception and memory as they relate to musical time and form. Once again he employs the rhetoric of unifying micro and macro as the conceptual basis of the piece: "In the end the sound and the sound space are the microcosm and macrocosm of the same formal idea." However, others from the group dismissed this man's concerns — permeated by information theory, and weak on computer expertise — as dated, far from IRCAM's cutting edge.

An article by the future Music Research director WOW concerns the rationale for *Chréode 1*. Sophisticated in both philosophical and computer science terms, it emphasizes that what is new to computer music is the extension of composition to sound material itself. With reference to AI, WOW notes that the simulations provided by programs such as Chant (voice, timbres) and Formes (structures) are not simple mimesis but "rather the formalization of an implicit or explicit knowledge. . . . When knowledge is 'realized,' it becomes available for compositional treatment and manipulation. Through . . . modelling, which makes explicit everything that was implicit . . . musical knowledge tumbles into the universe of 'explicit control processes,' and enters arithmetical space." WOW uses scientific analogies from genetics and morphogenesis as metaphors for musical form, and also makes reference to Thom's mathematics and catastrophe theory. The article ends with a series of visually elegant graphs representing aspects of the work that convey scientificity and rigor: WOW's model for a new visual representation of music.

The departing Music Research director, WOW's rival, has an article explaining several of his IRCAM works. Within a nuanced account fully aware of the excesses and misuses of metaphor — (he writes, "although nature suggests the spectral structure as a fundamental tool for musical uses, the composer must take this 'reality' only as metaphor' "; and "my musical spectra never copy natural spectra . . . and only use these as a base . . . for freely composed structures") — he nonetheless makes mandatory reference to "the use of timbre, and of spectral quality and transition to define musical structure."

Finally, throwing light on the character of music making at IRCAM, there are twin articles by the composer Höller and his (ex) tutor CX on the making of Höller's piece. The articles epitomize the division of labor between composer and tutor: composer as philosopher-theorist and tutor as technician-servicer. While Höller's essay concerns high conceptual matters, CX's focuses on pragmatics and the work method: it is a blow-by-blow account of his hardware and programming innovations that went into the actual making. Höller's article is a philosophical treatise on "organic form," "sound gestalt" and "time gestalt." He writes that his composition method is driven by a theory that "begins with a 'cell,' but the cell is organized in such a way that it contains the plan of the whole. . . . It is comparable to a 'genetic code,' which as we know from microbiology, contains all the essential information for the organism. The organism as a whole is the result of an evolution, which may best be described as a process of projection of a microstructure onto a macrostructure." Höller again draws on genetics, here for scientistic legitimation of his "micro-macro unity." Meanwhile, CX gives an account of creating digital sound files, customized computer programs, programming subroutines, and so on. Interestingly, CX is even left to outline Höller's actual compositional scheme for the piece, a variant of total serialist procedures; while his article ends with long, detailed, technical appendices, including dense programming language. Höller is thus freed for pure, untrammeled philosophical-theoretical exegesis. Comparing the two reveals the extraordinary difference in the forms of text and knowledge considered appropriate to the roles of composer and tutor.

The tutor CX ends his article with two veiled criticisms of the production and his servicing role in it. First, he says that Höller's piece had "been conceived very much with analog sound transformation processes in mind . . . [and] could have been realized equally effectively and much more simply in a traditional [electronic] studio." Once again this expresses the criticism that the piece did not really utilize IRCAM's technologies. CX then notes that to create a piece "more idiomatic of the [computer music] medium . . . requires either some fairly intimate experience of the system or very detailed briefing." He suggests that "In principle, it is much better that the composer should have his own hands on the apparatus, in that this theoretically permits him greater freedom to experiment and achieve the effects he wants" and that composers should be encouraged to gain greater self-sufficiency. Given that CX is himself a composer with "intimate experience" of the medium, and the one who did the "hands on" work for Höller, these muted complaints speak not only of a profound dissatisfaction with the hierarchical division of labor between visiting star composer and tutor, but also with the misuse of

IRCAM resources and the resultant, necessarily compromised musical results.

The themes that emerge from the musicians' group's internal recommendations to Boulez and from their external writings also appear in the rhetoric of their meetings, where they discussed and evaluated work in progress. One project being debated early in 1984 was psychoacoustician HM's "inharmonic musical expert system," which had just begun. The following speech from a meeting shows how he explained the idea.

> This will be an interactive environment, but musical . . . with well defined knowledge formats. It will follow branching options: either by default or by user specification. We need a historical mechanism to be able to retrace the steps of decision making, back to before things went wrong! Rule specification will be derived from aural-perceptual research. The system will be organized as a hierarchy, like Formes, but additional to Formes you can make inferences by a logic, compositional and perceptual, within the system. For example, we'll have the possibility of manipulating inharmonic spectra to bring out certain virtual pitches. So we need rules of transformation, complex multivariable rules. The system will be interfaceable with all the synthesis systems in the house — 4X, Chant. Now, we'll have inferences of pitch, inharmonics; later, other aspects too. For example, you'll be able to follow the interior polyphony of an inharmonic spectrum. . . . Eventually we'll work on the organization of inharmonics into "scales," *like* harmonicity but *of* inharmonics.

This monologue combined psychoacoustical and musical interests, here around inharmonics, with ideas concerning the structure of expert system software, an important dimension of AI. Expert systems, as I have mentioned, are interactive programs based on bodies of knowledge that are written into the programs as rule-following chains of reasoning. They have mainly been developed for industrial purposes and more controversially for medical diagnosis: certainly, areas of knowledge in which interpretation and moral or aesthetic judgment are considered to play a minimal role. The idea of a creative musical or artistic expert system was therefore a departure.

In fact, the expert system project did not survive the year. However it illustrates the importance of high-level software R and D and of programming for the musicians' group, since they were seen as researchers' means of producing both the most sophisticated general technologies and also the particular customized "solutions" for the musical problems posed by composers. Much music research concerned the interdependence of psychoacoustic and music research with the development of new software tools.

A later meeting, at which researchers outlined their proposed projects to Boulez, gives a sense of critical exchanges. It was the crucial decision making meeting: the talk had to convince Boulez.

> Boulez comes in early, with only five of us here. He shakes us each personally by the hand, lays out his watch on the table. It is all quite ritualized. HY comes late, looks cynical, fed up.
>   Boulez starts: "Who speaks first? HY or WOW?"

HY:	WOW! [Symbolizing: transfer of power from HY to WOW as director of Music Research accomplished].
MC:	[Starts with the project "Generation and Manipulation of Musical Forms," involving Chant/Formes workers MC and WOW] We want to establish certain rules and constraints: to give choices to the composer within which to produce a piece. The structuring will happen out of the material developed by the composer.
WOW:	They will be tools for realization, very general and abstract, like Formes. This is the first time such a thing has been realized. . . .
BOULEZ:	[*Interrupts*] What exactly do you mean by "generation and manipulation of musical form"?
MC:	I mean to allow a series of aesthetic choices for the composer: for example, "Do I want a certain attack or articulation here? What kind? What timbre here?" and so on. . . .
HY:	You mean a library of possible effects and musical choices? I'm worried by such an attempt to set up a series of rules and constraints. It might in fact *limit* composers' musical decisions.
HU:	[Composer-junior tutor, involved in expert system project] I'm not interested in "abstract structures." I want structure to develop from the knowledge of the material, so if one changes the material the structure changes.
BOULEZ:	But HU, one creates a certain material with a certain internal structure in mind: the material used and structure envisaged are totally interrelated! [*Teasing, rhetorically*] Surely no one here chooses material with no structural idea in mind, do they? No followers of Cage here, are there?!

They move on to another project: HM's expert system, now also known as "Evolution of Spectral Form."

HM:	The basic questions here are to do with understanding perceptual categorization, musical memory, cognitive bases. To describe processes so as better to synthesize them. We need information on the evolution of spectral form, to make inharmonics work in more musically complex ways. . . .
BOULEZ:	To be frank, I really don't see the musical significance of these ideas. . . .

The two projects begin both to vie and to unite before Boulez.

> MC: Actually, your project and ours are very similar, overlapping in their aims.
>
> WOW: The difference is really one of methodology. Ours gives choices, rules, and constraints; yours [expert system] is more cognitive, about basic knowledge, and more normative. . . .

These exchanges indicate an openness to mutual criticism, but also intense rivalry within the group. They show Boulez's playful policing of the correct organicist doxa, as well as a peremptory skepticism toward the proposals on his part.

UTOPIAN PROJECTIONS: THE NEEDS OF THE USER AND OF THE OUTSIDE WORLD

The musicians' meetings were imbued with an implicit utopianism expressed most obviously in the open and egalitarian character of debate, but also by two aspects of the content of discussions, both touching on the social. The first was the concern with small systems and real-time networks for live performance. This had utopian leanings in revealing an awareness of IRCAM's relations with the outside world, through projections of the needs of users beyond IRCAM and of the institute's potentially wider progressive effects. The second dimension was internal: the proposal for a new social organization of research as a "musical think tank." The quality of communal utopian projection — of predicting necessities or desires — was shown by the common use in meetings of the phrase "*Imaginez que . . .*" ("Imagine that . . .").

Although, as I have shown, both the 4X and Chant/Formes projects originated in critiques of the extant limits of computer music, both projects depended on a high tech computing environment that by definition excluded the majority of musicians. Also, in 1984 and despite intentions to the contrary, neither project had successfully met the challenge of user-friendliness or an improved man-machine interface. It was against this record that some in the musicians' group argued for research on information transfer to microcomputers, gestural control, and real-time performance systems. The ideas were justified as follows by one of the leading advocates of this approach for music research. (The author himself had recently bought a Yamaha DX7 for compositional sketches at home.)

> In the future, more and more composers will have access to inexpensive systems for computing and music synthesis. Although most composers will

probably continue to prefer the sophisticated and costly technology of major
research institutes like IRCAM, their small systems will be perfectly well
suited for many levels of testing, sketching, and exchanging information. It is
essential that IRCAM strive for total compatibility between small development systems and its own production facilities. But this is not enough! We
suggest that IRCAM sponsor a long-term project which involves the information transfer of programs from its large systems to a form that can work on
small systems. IRCAM could conceive a working tool for commercially available small systems and in this way fill a strong need on the part of users . . .
and [so] retain practical and conceptual compatibility with an ever-growing
group of composers and researchers.

The aim of working on real-time computer networks for performance, as
in PL's project, was advanced by his friend RIG in these terms: "What I'm
interested in now is live computer groups, a performance laboratory."
This caused controversy. Proponents saw it as another move toward
closer relations with the larger community of musicians. By contrast, the
4X Soft director argued that it was not basic research, simply an "applications problem": that work of this kind did not make use of IRCAM's
unique means and expertise, and so was not legitimate IRCAM research.

A meeting to discuss the small systems proposal led to a polarized
argument between members of the musicians' group and the Scientific
Director, FOL, who spoke for the scientific sector. Those for the proposal gave two main reasons. First, pragmatically, because they thought
that the Japanese were now so advanced that it would soon be impossible to stay ahead of them technologically; rather, IRCAM should concentrate on its unique music research resources. IRCAM would "become
a fossil in the next ten years unless we fundamentally change direction."
Second, as implied in the long quote, there was the wish to "open up"
IRCAM by making links with small systems so as to feed innovations
to the larger musical community and give outsiders greater access to
IRCAM's technologies. This was partly a desire to popularize the institute, partly a response to perceived demand, as the Music Research
director — gatekeeper for the *Espaces Libres* — eloquently explained:
"Essentially it's about external people's access to what we're doing here,
making relations with the rest of the world. . . . Every day we get hundreds of people phoning, coming in, sending stuff, asking about projects,
suggesting ideas. We can never deal with the potential demand: hundreds
of composers! So we have to redirect ourselves, make a structure of
relations with the outside." The proposal also embodied a commitment
to or belief in the future decentralization of information technology: as
with PL, an optimistic vote for the future power of small systems.

Those arguing against the proposal made three points. First, FOL appealed weakly to tradition and said that IRCAM had "always been developing large systems" such as the 4X. Second, he said that large system development was the unique responsibility of IRCAM because of its scale of resources. This was supported by the 4X Soft director, Boulez's tutor, who added the Boulezian view that IRCAM's proper role was to develop things that the market would not, the "Rolls Royces of computer music technology." Third, FOL answered a criticism of the 4X implicit in the previous point: namely, that it had been extremely hard to find a production deal for the 4X and that once produced the price would be very high, so that it had not found a market. FOL's answer was simply that when the software was complete, if the 4X "proved fit," the price may well drop and it may find a market. (As we have seen, this did not happen.) In short, the argument revealed underlying conflicts and rivalries between music research on the one side and the scientific sector and 4X project on the other. FOL conveyed the fear that IRCAM's production of large-scale hardware was under attack, while hostility from his side toward music research was equally clear in its marked absence from his grand planning document.

It is interesting that embedded in the small systems debate were covert struggles of a different kind: for the appropriate character of IRCAM and for the control and character of projection. The debate was characterized by an oscillation between subjects' idealism and realism, revealing a deep tension over who were the "idealists" and who the "realists" — a tension present as a continuous subconscious in many IRCAM dialogues. Thus the views for or against big or small machines were phrased either as what IRCAM should do in an idealist sense — for example, because small systems are the way forward in the democratization of technology — or as what IRCAM had to do in a realist sense — for example, because there is no market for the 4X. The opposing view could also be put either way: "IRCAM should build big machines/do high level music research because it is uniquely placed to do so" (the idealist, defending noncommercial freedom and responsibility), versus "IRCAM should build big machines because the Japanese are way ahead on small machines and it is foolish to compete" (the market realist).

The debate resonated with issues concerning which of the public sector or market is most progressive, where the power is between the two, and where IRCAM should situate itself. The "idealist/realist" duality was partly rhetorical strategy. but it spoke also of a deeper moral tension about the appropriate character of IRCAM and its legitimation. Must

IRCAM be realist, and is realism in fact more material and "better"? Or should IRCAM use its unique privilege to be utopian, to aspire to idealism?

"COLLABORATION" AND "CREATIVE FLUX": SKEPTICISM TOWARD THE VANGUARD

The other utopian axis of the musicians' group involved their imagining a new social organization of research, which they saw as closely implicated in its success. From the discussions arose the notion of a musical think tank: several well-supported, long-term, collaborative, and egalitarian research teams, democratically managed and unburdened by immediate production needs. The meetings themselves were held in this open-ended, "knowledge-sharing" spirit, thus prefiguring the proposal. A draft document put it this way:

> During our discussions, much effort was made to define the proper organizational structures that would make it easiest to achieve our goals. [This led to] one concept that we all felt very strongly about: the concept of IRCAM as a *musical think tank*. We should strive to find an area where confidence and freedom are given to composers and researchers on a long-term basis, so that exchange and conceptual fantasy can be encouraged. Only in this way can new musical ideas be born, and can that creative reflection . . . which deserves to be called Musical Research be nurtured.

The think tank was partly a pragmatic plan — the closest the vanguard came to labor relations — motivated by the wish to improve the poor security and pay of the junior tutors in the group. It was also striking as the only attempt by IRCAM intellectuals to reform the institute's own social relations.

Advancing the idea, Music Research director HY drew on the models of Bell Labs, MIT, and Xerox's basic research center, Xerox PARC, whose director, Alan Kay — a leader in the field of small systems development — he had just visited. Directly contradicting IRCAM's charter, HY argued that commerce succeeded in supporting long-term research better than IRCAM. His description in a meeting, without Boulez, of Kay's organization, and the discussion that followed, illustrate many of the issues around the social organization of research.

HY: The reality of work at Xerox PARC, Bell Labs too, is that someone like Kay can support a research project for ten years, let it develop slowly and eventually produce results. . . . It's the kind of commitment to intellectual freedom and long-term development that's *completely missing* at IRCAM!

HM: I agree. If I talk of the environment I want for my work on the bases of musical organization, it requires different tools, entry into synthesis, acoustic analysis — moving around freely between different areas, dialogue with different people.

JDK: [Tutor, scientist, not a composer] But we need better definition of what you [HM] mean to do. . . .

HM: It's work on inharmonics: HU [composer] is interested in it, and it fits in with [a postgraduate's] thesis. We've had a few meetings, FOL too. It begins to be a research group, but delicate as yet.

RIG: So it begins to be an *équipe* [team] with different talents, skills: that's what we want to happen. But when a composer's involved, as they should be, it shouldn't end with the production of a work. It's hard to get composers to extract, after finishing a work, what's *generally useful* to the community to learn from the project behind the work. Someone should be there to theorize that, if not the composer.

JDK: [To HY, who was thought not to document his work] When will you write up the work on inharmonics which you've used in recent pieces?

HY: Well, I suppose after I've finished the piece I'm doing now. . . .

JDK: It seems to me that you composers writing up your musical aims, and the acoustic techniques used to arrive at those ends, would be a very important input to our psychoacoustic research here! . . . [To HM] How will you isolate the musical parameters of inharmonics? It seems to me you need the input of a composer to inform you of these.

HM: [*Fed up*] But I've already formulated this, by talking to many composers!

HY: [Defending HM, to JDK] What do *you* think are the musical effects of inharmonics? We'll use our ears! You have to begin somewhere!

JDK: [To HM] You see your project, finally, as a sort of secret garden. To develop your work, you need to clarify, open up, discuss exactly what you're going to do."

The tutor/scientist, JDK, was pressing here for better communication between researchers and composers. He questioned whether psycho-acoustician HM was aware enough of the specifically musical possibilities of his research, implying that HM was not himself sufficiently a composer. He also gently prodded the Music Research director for not having written up the technical and research bases of his IRCAM pieces: one example of the major IRCAM problem of lack of documentation of research. This tutor had recently suffered exclusion from the Chant/Formes team and felt bitter at their secrecy, hence his heartfelt plea for researchers to "open up."

Collaboration between researchers and composers to advance music research was in itself a utopian principle of the musicians' vanguard. This is exemplified by the following discussion with Chant director MC, in which he touched on his collaborations with three composers: AV, WOW, and especially WL, the composer-director who first brought him to IRCAM and with whom he developed Chant. MC depicted the good composer-researcher dialogue as the driving force for progress in both software design and music research, which are seen as for the common good rather than the individual glory of the composer.

MC: WL was at the point where he was unable to compose any more, because the globality of music in the century was . . . [*searchingly*] where would it go? He decided to do music research [to make] building blocks for the future; so that music is no more the [sole property] of the composer . . . and to have progress in that sense.

GB: In terms of providing a whole new series of tools?

MC: Not only tools but concepts, research and so on. And in a very *nonindividual* way. Since the beginning I have been working with WL. We understood each other very well and did really fantastic work. . . . WL was hoping that I could do something [for him] in real time, good quality, and with a simpler computer. . . . WL conceived everything, and then the piece was physically realized by XX [American programmer]. XX was really the tutor for WL: he did the tedious work of repeating the synthesis — not in the sense that tutors here are making things that composers cannot do, because WL [himself] was able to do everything, learn any language. . . . When WL was no longer here at IRCAM, I felt the lack of a composer. I knew that each time I'd worked with a composer, something new happened. And that has been verified *every* time: the last time with AV.

GB: So you learn more about what you want to do with the system?

MC: Yes, I discover things that I cannot discover without their needs. Typically, [composers] want something and so I'm obliged to find a solution to the problem. Otherwise I can think and think but no precise solutions come. That's what happened with AV. He told me, "Here's a listing of what I have with the Fairlight. I like it, it's very simple." So I said, "OK, I'll do it: not like that but much better." [This produced] a way of considering Formes that was really one of the best. . . .

      [A few years back] we had a *stage*, and WOW attended. I always like to hear the music done by people; my "sound" is always open.[7] During that *stage* I listened to people. One interested me, and it was WOW. I thought, "A guy who makes that in a fortnight is really great." I was working with the [Chant-simulated] Tibetan voices at that time, and WOW said: "I like that, how do you do it?" So we began to talk. I said I'd like some help from a composer's point of view. . . . Finally we decided to ask WOW to stay for a year.

From this it becomes clear that some in the musicians' group saw aspects of their present work as already embodying the collaboration ideal; so the think tank proposal was more a bid for legitimation and support for this approach from Boulez, who, we will see, appeared skeptical. Others from the group depicted the development of Formes as epitomizing the ideal of collaborative research, as articulated here by HM:

> Formes was developed a little by MC and JDK [scientists], who tried to put in certain musical capabilities. Then XU joined, who's a computer scientist, and he started developing these incredible ideas. It reached a first stage of development and then the musicians came in: HY's used it, NR and HU have used it. They all found there were a great deal of problems, things they needed it couldn't do, which were *implied as possible*. And so they started firing all this stuff at XU, and it went into an incredible state of flux — because there was this very fast turnaround loop between a [musician's] suggestion and its implementation by XU. In a sense [the musicians] were serving as developers, by *imagining possibilities* that weren't yet implemented. It's the musicians — especially NR — who dove in there and understood at a very basic level "what is this program doing," so they could then suggest concrete things to XU. So there's a constant movement between stability and instability, the fixed program and creative flux.

The issue that HM ends by raising, that of stabilizing research (including new programs) so as to make it both communicable and usable for production, was contentious at this time within IRCAM. Internal and external critics argued that much IRCAM research was too "in flux" or "in process" to be usable, and so effectively meaningless. HM's account hints this may, in part, have been related to the open and collaborative research process — one negative consequence of the utopian ideal — although this link was not explored by vanguard researchers. When I pursued the problems of stabilization and of bringing long-term research to fruition, HM responded as follows:

GB: Do things ever stabilize in research, so they can be used widely, even within the house?

HM: That's a real problem. For instance, in the early stages of Chant it was always evolving, so it was very hard to use it as a tool for production. There came a point when they decided they'd gone far enough, that any further things they would move into another project — and that became Formes. So after a few years Chant got sort of fixed, and at that point it really entered into production. But that took a number of years. And meanwhile people are saying, "Well, it's been a year, you know, and we don't have any tools that are useful!" It doesn't work that way! You have to get to a certain level before you make a version people can use. It's the same problem with Formes: it's been evolving constantly, and it's been a real frustration for people using it.

GB: So that's why there's been tension about Formes, with people saying it hasn't been stabilized enough to communicate?

HM: Exactly, it hasn't been stabilized yet because it's a bit too young. There's an agreement that they'll make a version in the next few months that'll be fixed and usable, and that should be documented. But first it has to get past a certain threshold. If you do it earlier, it wouldn't be as interesting as a tool because it wouldn't have the musical power that you want.

HM ended by commenting with frustration on the misunderstanding of this process by management:

> The musical production wing over there, Boulez and [the Artistic Director], refuse to understand what this process is because they haven't been in there struggling with development themselves. They don't want to know about all that [research] "garbage," only the musical end. There's a kind of impatience, and I understand. But I know that to get there, you have to go through certain steps. I *could* make a tool that goes straight to immediate [musical] demands. [But then] it's good for nothing except that immediate demand. Whereas, if I'm more careful about the path I take, and the possible spin-offs along the way, then this becomes a much richer domain and generates knowledge, in the sense of coming to know how to create a system as well as gaining an end goal.

HM's argument must be understood in the context of Boulez's increasing skepticism toward this vision of research and, more deeply, toward the whole concept of music research that, despite public pronouncements, he had begun to betray at internal IRCAM meetings. On several occasions, Boulez had chided researchers for failing to orient their work sufficiently toward music production and for indulging in unproductive research, as shown by this characteristic monologue from one of the last musicians' meetings.

BOULEZ: I don't want IRCAM to become like the CNRS where researchers hide in corners for thirty years! I want tutors and researchers to divide their time between research and production. And I want *all* research to be tied to problems of production and realization; so when a composer arrives. . . .

RESEARCHER: [*Interrupts critically*] This is the short-term perspective!

BOULEZ: [*Brushing him aside*] I've just started. For example, when Stockhausen came, he needed research on tools for his piece, didn't he, WR [the tutor]? I want the artistic year and research year to be the same, to underline the tied nature of these two processes: interaction between realization and reflection. This is the main thing I want to stress. We have a responsibility to keep in touch with the outside world! Everyone's following what we do here, so we have to have results to show for our work.

The sense of a major gap in "understanding" between Boulez and the musicians' group, and of the exasperation this caused, was expressed by two members in a meeting by this joking exchange:

AA: We need to translate all these ideas into *"les catégories de Pierre"* [Pierre's categories]!

BB: *[Laughing, with frustration] Mais qu'est ce que c'est, "les catégories de Pierre"* [But what *are* Pierre's categories]?!

The group was, then, fully aware of Boulez's ambivalence toward music research. A researcher put it thus: "Pierre is hard to figure out, he's ambivalent. He agrees there should be the research, but he gets impatient if he doesn't see results soon enough. One minute he's saying, 'What's being done doesn't serve for anything at all!' The next minute he's got his *'utopie de la recherche musicale'* [music research utopia] idea going on! *[Doubtfully]* He *says* he's committed to it. . . ."

The quote from Boulez above implied that his attitude stemmed primarily from the responsibility to show results, for themselves, but also to legitimize IRCAM and to appease critics. Yet his doubts about music research seemed to be deeper, and to be shared with other senior directors, a fact satirized by the following joke bibliography entry in an internal memo: "BU [4X designer] and Boulez, P. (1985) — '*La recherche en musique?*,' *Revue de Neurospeculation*, 69: 123–145."

Boulez was therefore not alone in his criticisms of the musicians' group vanguard. Similar criticisms were made in meetings by the Scientific Director, FOL. In a meeting to discuss the group's proposal document, he charged them with being too abstract, impractical, and unreal, but also with ignoring the 4X project, with creating boundaries between themselves and the scientific sector (although several were in fact scientists), and with sheer elitism.

FOL: In such a document, outlining the main axes of research, you must include the research around the 4X!

HY: But we've been trying to say for fifteen minutes that these are the *musical* research themes [implying that the 4X is not music research].

FOL: But these goals should be stated *practically*! They are too abstract, high up in the sky.

BYV: *[Ironically]* Maybe as a *scientist* you have problems, FOL. . . . You're setting up your watertight compartments between music research and scientific research again. We're trying to get beyond that!

FOL: It's this document that's reinforcing the watertight compartments, not me! Anyway, how many people from the house have taken part in the meetings that drew up this document?

[*Angry groans*]

HM: Anyone and everyone could have come! They were publicized as open meetings to discuss the future of music research.

FOL: Look, I've never seen a "research document" that's as impractical as this! It's inadequate. The majority of people not present here would think so too. The themes are too big, vague. You must think about how they develop in reality.

The same conflicts continued at a later meeting, and the sense of a division between the musicians' group and the scientific sector became even clearer. They were debating a proposal concerning which people could constitute a music research committee. In the debate, of all the musicians' group, only the Pedagogy director RIG held to the utopian ideal of "effacing" the by now highly charged "frontier" between music and scientific research.

FOL: It's too homogeneous: there's no one who can consider the musical utilization of the 4X, such as BU [4X designer]. There's no one from the "other culture!"

BYV: [*Contradicting FOL*] It's heterogeneous!

WOW: But come now, is BU really interested in music research? Does he ever come to our meetings or go to concerts?

FOL: Yes he does, but there aren't many concerts that use the 4X!

BYV: Well, he does "little pieces" to amuse himself on the 4X. . . .

RIG: My main point is that we must *efface the frontier* between music research and scientific research. We must get beyond this boundary!

HM: But now we're back to the fundamental argument again: whether there are specific research problems that are primarily *musical.*

BYV: Otherwise, we'd see all the people working on software, the 4X and so on as doing music research.

RIG: [*Exasperated*] It astonishes me sometimes that we identify something as "musical"; and then if another person [i.e. someone not defined as a musician—a scientist] makes a contribution, about using a certain tool or whatever, then everyone says "Oh that's not a *musical* perspective"!

We see here, then, a basic conflict between the vanguard group, who saw themselves as fighting to defend IRCAM's specifically musical goals, and the scientific sector, who perceived the vanguard's high-level music and software ideas as impractical and elitist. This opposition between the musical and scientific sides of IRCAM took other forms; most notably, aesthetic differences and the antipathy that followed.

Thus, while one of the musicians' group was patronizing about 4X designer BU's "little pieces," BU in turn intensely disliked IRCAM music and resented that his machine was used to make it. BU was keen on easy listening music and had himself used the 4X to produce some jazzed up Corelli, hoping eventually to make a record like Wendy Carlos's *Switched On Bach* to show off the "real" musical possibilities of the 4X. BU told me a story that epitomized his contempt for avant-garde music. He said that one day, for fun, he had used the 4X to churn out a pseudo avant-garde piece in just twenty minutes — a "piece of cake," he said. A senior visiting composer had come into his studio, listened to it, and was most impressed, asking who had made it, how, and so on. BU laughed hilariously at this and ridiculed the hallucination of avant-garde music with me. Symbolizing his hostility to IRCAM music and musicians, and joking but with serious undercurrents, was a sign fixed to his studio door, shown in Photo 3: a musical note covered by a red "no entry" symbol, implying "Musicians keep out!" Nor was BU alone. His partner, the 4X Industrialization director, was equally hostile to IRCAM music — a major reason he had fought so hard to find a commercial deal to produce the 4X for outside musicians.

The conflict pitting the vanguard and the scientific sector against 4X Hardware groups took another related form: an opposition between mental and manual labor. While the vanguard music and software researchers considered their work to be the most intellectually advanced, they were disparaged by the 4X Hardware and Scientific directors for producing abstract and ephemeral work of no real scientific or musical value: "just so much intellectual hot air." By contrast, the 4X Hard directors presented themselves as artisanal, manual workers. 4X Industrialization director VO spoke ironically as follows of his position within IRCAM and vis à vis Boulez: "Boulez is fond of citing the Bauhaus, Mies van der Rohe. . . . But I ask you, what about the little guy who built the building with his own hands, who worked for twelve years, ran the budget? He's not even mentioned by Boulez! I wonder about that when I read about the Bauhaus. . . . I'm the *éminence grise* here!"

VO, who was soon to leave, was resentful that when the history books about IRCAM came to be written they would mention only Boulez and would neglect the role of "little guys" like him in building the place from scratch, as well as the practical power he had wielded behind the throne. BU, as we have seen, was devoted to hardware design and skeptical about software in general. He believed, he said, in solid mechanical skills as the basis of scientific research, and he belittled the practical illiteracy of computer science hackers. He spoke of their work as insubstantial,

ungraspable, and portrayed himself by contrast as a mechanic who enjoyed working with his hands, making things that you could get hold
of. At the end of our talk he drew some photos from his wallet to show
me with pride. They showed several large, wooden, remote-controlled
model sailboats that he had crafted by hand for his sons.

We can now understand the character of status conflicts around the
institute's central division of labor: between those identified with music
and those with science. Publicly, as we have seen, music and related
research had the highest status. Musicians saw IRCAM's machines (especially hardware) as tools for their expression, and the scientists and
technologists who produced them as servicing their needs. Thus, the
musicians' group held an implicitly hierarchical view: although they affected to respect the top hardware scientists, they saw them as "not
musical" and not engaged in the most important research. But in their
turn, in rejecting IRCAM music and the software research, high theory,
and intellectual pretensions that surrounded it, IRCAM's hardware scientists dismissed also the whole basis of the status hierarchy in which
they were meant to be implicated. This was nowhere better expressed
than in VO's contempt for Boulez's "Bauhaus" hypocrisy.

THE STRUCTURE OF OPPOSITIONS IN IRCAM'S
INTELLECTUAL WORK CULTURE

From this analysis we can discern a set of basic oppositions in IRCAM's
intellectual work culture: between the musical and scientific sides of
IRCAM; between software and hardware, as in the mutual antagonism
between the Chant/Formes project and, more broadly, the musicians'
group and those aligned with 4X Hardware; and between mental and
manual labor.

The think tank debate raised other significant conflicts within the
intellectual culture: those of long-term versus short-term research cycles, of the open-ended progress of pure research versus its stabilization
and use in an actual musical work. The musicians' group argued that
IRCAM must support long-term fundamental research that is independent of immediate music production needs, and that it currently failed to
do so. In contrast, Boulez and the Scientific Director argued for research
being tied to production, to showing results in a specified, shorter time.
Here, within IRCAM's high status production sphere, "production" and
"research" had specific meanings defined by opposition. While "research" was conceived as an ongoing process of experiment and knowl-

edge seeking, "production" was reserved specifically for the actualization of research, for work that stabilizes the ongoing flux of the research process and becomes allied to a result, either musical or technological.

This delineates another set of semantic oppositions within the intellectual work culture, organized as an associative chain whereby "long-term" was associated with the idealism of the musicians' group and with "fundamental, pure research" that can disdain immediate results, while "short-term" was associated with "production"-related or applied research that has more immediate ends in mind, seen by its defenders as "realist."

From all this, we can trace a structure of basic classificatory oppositions that constituted the differentiation of IRCAM's research culture in this period. Figure 8 is a schematic summary of this structure. We have seen that the oppositions represented tensions and conflicts of ideology, legitimacy, and practice regarding IRCAM's own work. They were not all identified one-to-one with specific groups or positions, although some did represent the affiliations of certain subcultures. Most clearly, the musicians' group linked a chain of associated binary poles, so that the set [music : research : long-term : idealism : software (Chant/Formes) : mental labor] together formed a charged semantic field. But the opposite poles were not brought together in as monolithic or coherent a way; although there were similar, shorter chains of association such as that for Boulez linking [music : production : short-term : realism], or the chain [science : production : realism : hardware (4X) : manual labor] linked with the 4X Hard directors. Thus while Boulez, the Scientific Director, and the 4X directors shared doubts about IRCAM's music research and high-level software, their positions were far from identical.

The binaries delineate, then, a map of discursive positions that IRCAM intellectual subjects could adopt or move between, and the chains of association are discursive strategies, alignments. The strength of the vanguard musicians' group lay precisely in their appropriation of a discursively powerful and ideologically charged set of associations, and in this set representing a return to Boulez's fundamental values for IRCAM, apparently despite his own loss of faith — (a move to regenerate the discourse similar to that attempted by Boulez in relation to Schoenberg). We can see now that IRCAM culture contained, and was constituted by, a complex logic of oppositions. The unity of the field was produced by a play of difference, and by containing dissent: a phenomenon that, as Bourdieu (1971a, 183) and Williams (1981, 225) suggest, rather than weakening the culture may work to increase its authority.

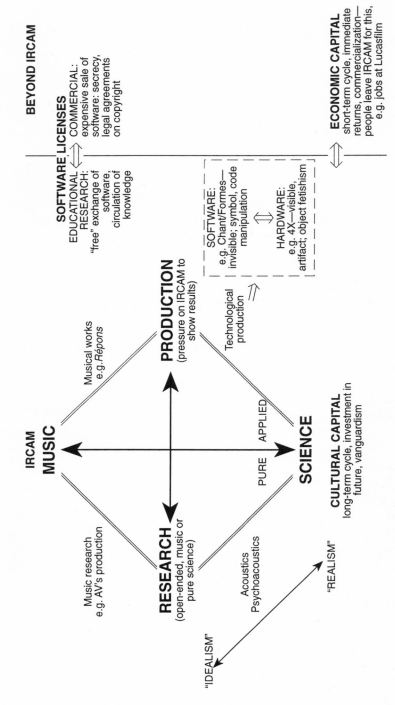

BEYOND IRCAM

SOFTWARE LICENSES

EDUCATIONAL RESEARCH: "free" exchange of software, circulation of knowledge ⇔ COMMERCIAL: expensive sale of software: secrecy, legal agreements on copyright

SOFTWARE: e.g. Chant/Formes—invisible; symbol, code manipulation ⇔ HARDWARE: e.g. 4X—visible, artifact; object fetishism

ECONOMIC CAPITAL
short-term cycle, immediate returns, commercialization—people leave IRCAM for this, e.g. jobs at Lucasfilm

IRCAM

PRODUCTION
(pressure on IRCAM to show results)

Technological production

Musical works e.g.*Répons*

MUSIC

Music research e.g. AV's production

RESEARCH
(open-ended, music or pure science)

PURE   APPLIED

Acoustics Psychoacoustics

SCIENCE

CULTURAL CAPITAL
long-term cycle, investment in future, vanguardism

"IDEALISM"

"REALISM"

8.   Structure of oppositions in IRCAM's intellectual work culture, 1984.

The ideological character of the sets of associated binary poles is shown by certain implicit distortions and irrationalities thrown up as classificatory byproducts through the operation of implied opposition. For example, if we trace through the implied oppositions to the terms of the first chain above, it is untrue that IRCAM hardware development required less research, that it was more short-term than software development, or that it involved primarily manual labor; just as, if we trace them for the last chain above, it is questionable whether IRCAM software necessarily had a privileged relation with music, or that it was less "science" than hardware. However, as significant as the actual associative content of the binary oppositions is the splitting that they embodied on both sides: the constant polarization, bouncing between excessive idealization of one term and excessive denigration of the other — a splitting engendered, at one level, by mundane institutional rivalries, yet with wider discursive ramifications.

In discursive terms, the debate around the vanguard played out the broader contemporary questioning of the legitimacy and value of long-term, noncommercial basic research, equated here with music research. The meetings represented a constant search for the means to legitimize this research internally while it was still in progress, as if to counteract an underlying uncertainty and loss of confidence. In their high seriousness, the meetings seemed to be experienced by those taking part as a way to answer the broader erosion of legitimacy — as though, microcosmically, IRCAM's vanguard bore this full weight. The vanguard was therefore involved at the same time both in research itself and in a search to formulate its legitimation. This recalls Jean-François Lyotard's observation that, in general, science is always also involved in constructing its own legitimation (Lyotard 1984, 38).

Moreover, the attack on the group's support for future-oriented knowledge seeking was made in terms of short-term cycles and, most importantly, productive results — both technological and musical. And this proposes a new kind of legitimation, by results or performance. The debate within IRCAM thus also rehearsed the shift in forms of legitimation analyzed by Lyotard (1984, 37–47) whereby the old form of "speculation" in the quest for truth has given way to a new kind of scientific self-legitimation based on performativity — the "best possible input/output equation" (1984, 46).[8] The two positions taken in IRCAM's research debate, then, epitomize the conflict between modern and postmodern discourses of legitimation.

Given the symptoms of aesthetic uncertainty, despite the institute's combining within itself the hitherto most unquestionable spheres of post-Enlightenment cultural value — aesthetics and pure science — IRCAM was rehearsing the crises of their self-evident value in its own intellectual culture. Even without embarking in a commercial direction, IRCAM management felt defensive and under pressure to produce results similar to those required by commerce. Thus, while IRCAM objectively inhabits the state subsidized, noncommercial sphere — the domain of cultural capital — management was beginning to favor the production of short-term, "hard," visible and audible results and performance-related contractual status for creative staff. IRCAM was showing signs of potential transition.

The outcome of the musicians' meetings was uneven. Of the research themes, those involving timbre and form continued to develop. The group staged a large international conference on timbre in mid 1985, and timbre remains a broad organizing concept for much high-level computer music work at IRCAM and beyond. However, the more utopian themes touching on the social — those concerning small systems and the reorganization of research — met with hostility in 1984, so that the dominant technological discourse and orientation of research remained intact while the think tank idea as a whole was dropped.

A final irony of the musicians' meetings was revealed by the comments of a musician who took a leading part in them. Despite being, in public, a fine theoretical proponent of music research, this man told me that he was skeptical about too much theory — that it was lifeless academicism, irrelevant to his music. He said, "I don't believe in music 'researchers': we all do music research as part of our work process at times toward our pieces." Privately he was ambivalent, like Boulez, about the value of "pure," "autonomous" music research. This hinted at a disjuncture between his private and public selves, his practice and his theoretical rhetoric.

1. IRCAM: external view.

2. IRCAM: entrance, 1984.

3. "Musicians keep out!" sign on 4X studio door.

4. The 4X prototype.

5. Flight cases in corridor.

6. Mechanic's workshop.

7. Technicians' area.

8. Experimental clarinet.

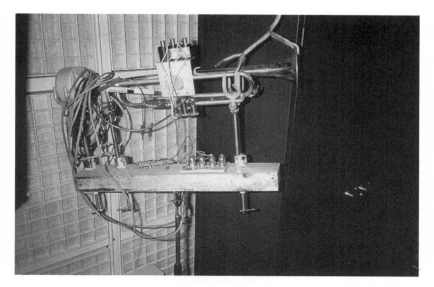

9. Trussed up trumpet.

10. Interconnected speaker system in a research office.

11.   Main corridor with glass roof and two rows of glass-walled offices.

12.   Outside glass-walled office looking in.

13. Inside glass-walled office looking out.

14. Terminal: VDU and keyboard.

15. Collaboration: socializing the technology. (With the permission of the subjects.)

CHAPTER VIII

A Composer's Visit

Mediations and Practices

In the previous two chapters we saw how the rhetoric of IRCAM was imbued with more and less arbitrary intertextual reference to science and computing, including biology, maths, physics, and structural linguistics, but especially to the overlapping domains of cognitive music psychology, cognitive science, AI, and computer science. The implicit principle was that these areas can provide a metalanguage not only for music analysis but for composition: the basis of a new aesthetic. We have seen also that although a few individuals admitted to the metaphorical quality of these discourses,[1] they did not provide an alternative and continued to employ the same rhetoric themselves. I want now to extend the analysis of mediations in IRCAM's intellectual work by examining its texts and codes, objects and machines, and its sociality. I show later how these come to be employed in music production through an account of composer AV's commission visit to IRCAM in 1984.

TEXTS AND CODES

IRCAM's intellectual culture is marked by an extraordinary antinomy: by a vastly multiplied textuality on the one hand, and its character as an oral-aural culture on the other. These are both in contradiction, and yet also interdependent. Computer music at IRCAM involves a multiplication of mediating texts and codes, knowledges and authorities around music, both laterally and vertically. With its retention of the conventional musical score alongside the new textuality of computer music,

IRCAM is characterized not by a search for notations and codes to supersede orthodox music notation, but rather by the addition of many more new codes and texts. IRCAM is, then, strongly text-centered. Yet this proliferation of texts and codes fails as yet to solve a central problem in computer music inherited from electronic music: that of finding a specifically musical textual representation, a musically appropriate and expressive notation, for tape-based musics.

At IRCAM the musical score, with its strong visual form, remains the central authoritative text, often buttressed by theoretical exegesis. This contrasts markedly with the displacement of the score in electronic music history, in which existing music notations were often considered inadequate for the complex new soundworld. The primacy of the score at IRCAM can be illustrated in several ways. The kind of piece most fashionable and prestigious among IRCAM composers was one mixing the resources of a live orchestra or ensemble, requiring conventional scoring, with computer-generated tape or live computer transformation, as with Boulez's *Répons*. This kind of piece was prestigious both in commanding vast resources and in retaining the authority of the score. Scores were also the focus of the judgments of the twice-yearly Reading Panels, IRCAM's attempt at open competitions to discover compositional talent. Despite composers' choice to submit either score or tape, and despite computer music being primarily a tape-based medium, the Panels overwhelmingly received and judged by scores.

Further stories convey the importance within IRCAM of the visual look of the score. Early in 1984 a music director told me bemusedly that Boulez was to conduct the orchestral music of the avant-garde rock musician Frank Zappa in a concert of American music. He said, "I haven't heard it, but the score's good: it looks like a real score!" Implicit here was the belief that the music's legitimacy rested on its *looking* like a "real score." After the concert the same director's judgment was that the music was "pretty boring really." Issues of the valuing of visual scores over the aural, of the judging of music by its look, its visual hypercomplexity, are more widely contentious within contemporary music. A visiting IRCAM composer commented cynically that he knew this score-centeredness well, that composers were steeped in it by their training. He told an apocryphal story to illustrate the hypocrisy surrounding the issue. A few years back, a well-known contemporary music quartet was playing a concert at Darmstadt. They decided to alter the order and played a piece by composer XX earlier than printed on the program. This composer was late for the concert and missed the announcement. After the quartet had finished his piece, the audience applauded and called for him to go up on stage. The composer refused, pointing to the program note and saying, "It's not my work!" The moral: the composer did not know they were playing his piece because the score was so complex that even he could not imagine the sound of his own piece; he knew only the look of it from the score.[2]

However, a story told by another IRCAM composer indicates how for composers dedicated to difficult scores, computer music can appear a salvation. Early in his career this man had written a string quartet, but he found no quartet able to play it. Having become involved some years later in computer music, he was finally able to hear his quartet "accurately" for the first time by programming the computer to play it in its full complexity, a task that had defeated human musicians.

The power of the visual within musical modernism is not limited to the fetishism of the score or technical texts. It derives also from the longer-term mutual fascination in modernism and postmodernism between the visual arts and music that I discussed earlier in the aesthetic theory of Greenberg, in which music came to be the paradigm of all the arts and especially of abstract expressionism, in the work and philosophies of Cage and experimental music, or in the marked presence of abstract visual artists in the salons of the *Domaine Musical*. It is nowhere better exemplified than in Boulez's reverence for Klee and Kandinsky, artists who drew analogies with music in their concern with color and form. All of this points to a blurring of the boundaries between different media in modernism, which may encourage the visual qualities of the score to be read as indicative of musical value.

A recent example from computer music takes this tendency further. In the mid-1980s the computer music studio led by Boulez's rival Xenakis had produced a digital machine called the UPIC that worked by the user drawing visual designs with a special pen onto a computer screen. These visuals were immediately translated into synthesized sound: the visual became the aural. The UPIC raises starkly the question of to what extent visual signs deployed to produce the aural are musically appropriate.

The contents of the *stage* indicate the lateral extensions of knowledge involved in computer music apprenticeship. There are four specialist areas of knowledge considered necessary to becoming adept at computer music: general computing,[3] acoustics and psychoacoustics, electronic music techniques, and the area of computer music itself. Beyond all this, a knowledge of orthodox music theory and notation is assumed. Those taking the *stage* in early 1984 were supplied with an enormous amount of written material on basic computing, on acoustics and psychoacoustics, and above all on Cmusic software—the patch language that was being taught, for which there was a three-hundred-page teaching manual. There were, however, no materials or formal teaching on electronic music or studio techniques, areas considered by IRCAM to have an aural-empirical method and in which notation remains problematic, just as there were few actual sound or music examples. The *stage*, then, neglected the aural, as well as non-notated electronic music techniques, while immersing students in the burgeoning textuality of computer music. Textual fetishism accompanied a lack of priority given to sound itself and to music not grounded in the authority of the text.

In terms of the multiplying vertical mediations in computer music, we should first note the multitextuality inherent in all computer software, a key characteristic of this medium. The use and the development of software involve the writing of coded instructions within a software language, or the creation of a completely new language, within the context of a hierarchy of such languages. At each level of the hierarchy, a translation occurs between any two adjacent languages or levels of code. Instructions from the language at a higher level must be translated into a form whereby they can be "read" and executed by the lower-level code or language without any (or with minimal) loss of "meaning."

The hierarchy of codes that normally operates in computer software includes, at the lowest level, machine code, the instructions that drive the hardware, written in binary form; at the next level up, assembler code, made of mnemonic abbreviations of machine code; above this, the general operating system that provides a basic framework and set of services; and above this, any of the major languages such as FORTRAN, Pascal, C, or LISP. The point about these higher-level languages is that they provide condensed ways of expressing many thousands of lower-level operations in assembler or machine code; thus extremely complex instructions can be encoded with economy. The rationale is also that compared to assembly language they provide more conceptually meaningful forms of expression. Thus the history of software development has apparently been a search for increasingly technologically and conceptually economical and powerful languages for different kinds of applications.

Computer music software such as that used and produced by IRCAM adds yet a further level of mediation, hierarchy, and translation, since the music languages are themselves based upon, or written in, established

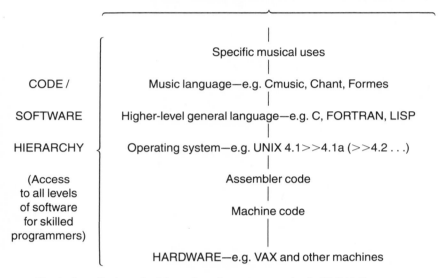

USER INTERFACE

(Access limited to "surface" interface for naive users)

CODE /

SOFTWARE

HIERARCHY

(Access
to all levels
of software
for skilled
programmers)

Specific musical uses

Music language—e.g. Cmusic, Chant, Formes

Higher-level general language—e.g. C, FORTRAN, LISP

Operating system—e.g. UNIX 4.1>>4.1a (>>4.2 . . .)

Assembler code

Machine code

HARDWARE—e.g. VAX and other machines

9. Vertical mediation: the hierarchy of computer codes in IRCAM's computer music system.

general languages. Thus, Music V is written in FORTRAN, Cmusic in C, IRCAM's Chant in FORTRAN, and Formes in LISP. Figure 9 gives an impression of the hierarchy of encodings.

These are not passive levels of mediation, since in order to become a skilled user of Chant or Formes it is also necessary to be knowledgeable in FORTRAN or LISP. For example, in setting out to learn how to use Formes, composer-squatter NP first had to spend some months learning LISP programming. The problems this may cause are indicated by the following diary note from a *stage* session one month into the course, in which we were learning how to use Chant.

We're working with the Chant Manual on "user subroutines" — sections of the program amenable to user manipulation. WOW writes up a new kind of syntax on the board, and before we've written it down he rubs it out! Everyone gasps, laughs, looks baffled. "Leave it up till we've copied it down!" But WOW has moved on already. *Stagiaire* VT protests: "But you've written it in FORTRAN! How can we learn how to use FORTRAN so quickly? It's impossible." WOW explains that we need to know FORTRAN to use some Chant

subroutines. This is the first we've heard. Comment: WOW baffles us by
giving us too much to take in, a completely new language, and rubs it out
before we've even taken it down, as though aware that it's impossible for us to
learn this level of control.

What is the character of the texts and codes involved in computer
music? Looking at these texts one is struck, first, by the way the condensed mnemonics of programming sometimes spill over into the ex-
planatory texts, revealing a carelessness with the language of explanation. But above all, one is struck by the condensed complexity and
unintelligibility of the codes themselves. This is exacerbated by the way
that the technical codes and syntaxes of programming are teasingly reminiscent of, and yet distort, natural language. Because of their basis in
signifiers and terms drawn from natural language, programming languages create an illusion of closeness to natural language. This illusion
seems to deceive some programmers themselves, who find it difficult to
perceive the intransigent opacity of the programs to the layman.[4] Despite
the claim above that high-level software employs expressions appropriate to its functions, it is hard to see how computer music languages can
be seen as appropriate forms of expression for musician users. Rather,
they necessitate lengthy apprenticeship into complex technical knowledges and codes with only extremely mediated relations to music. It
is notable that the skeptical composer-programmer PL, working with
small machines, decided to program not in higher-level languages but in
assembler. He did this, he said, because the programs ran faster and he
could control them more directly and easily in assembler than when they
were mediated through higher languages. He found assembler just as
amenable to encoding his musical needs.

Beneath computer music's surface textual complexity, then, lies a
great density of lateral and vertical, conceptual, technical, and technological mediation. To use the patch languages and other computer
music software for even the simplest exercise requires knowledge of
several domains. These enter directly into the description of the sound
desired, or into the manipulation of parameters, such as simulated formants in Chant, that produce the sounds. And skilled use requires programming knowledge of the computer language underlying the music
program.

Let us look in greater detail at what is involved in using a patch
language. To produce sounds, the user must build up complete acoustical
and psychoacoustical descriptions from scratch and then encode them
into the language. The user writes a computer "score" utilizing a code

with a very precise syntax in which every tiny detail — spaces, lines, commas — must be correct. The smallest error of code or syntax creates a bug and prevents synthesis taking place. The "score" file contains two kinds of information: an "orchestra of instruments," that is, coded instructions that simulate analog sound generators or transformers (oscillators, filters, and so on), and a list of "events," that is, code for a sequence of sound events to be produced by the generators. For each event, all basic parameters — starting time, duration, frequency, amplitude — must be specified and each "instrument" fully "described."

In the Cmusic teaching manual that was used in the *stage* in 1984, there was an introductory section on how to write the simplest possible "score" file that began with a disarming disclaimer: "This example is so simple that it wouldn't even sound very good." It then took two full pages to explain the information required behind the coding and the code protocols. The coding was dependent on a prior conceptualization of the electronic instrument patch to be simulated, which in turn depended on a prior understanding of electronic music patching as well as a sophisticated knowledge of acoustics. Overall, this introductory section was both extremely dense and unclear, exhibiting a massive disproportion between exegesis and code. The sense of the explanation was far from self-evident, and the meaning of terms wavered and multiplied; for example, later on it was mentioned that five terms — "function," "stored function," "function table," "wavetable" and "lookup table" — all "refer to the same thing," but this was simply asserted without explanation of the looseness of the definitions.

Even in this attempt at a careful pedagogic exercise, then, there was a curious oscillation between extreme precision and imprecision in defining higher functions, as well as absence of explanation and even some faulty explanation. Faced with this kind of text, apprentices became bewildered by the combined excesses of trivial technical information and the highly mediated nature of the medium. Of a cohort of twelve on the *stage*, two dropped out within the first two weeks, while another *stagiaire* confided, four weeks in, "I haven't understood anything for days!" Very few seemed able to make much use of the teaching. This recalls the realistic view of tutors, mentioned earlier, that to begin to be truly at home with IRCAM technologies took several years' full-time application. They cited this figure in discussing the unlikelihood that visiting composers on three-month or six-month visits could do interesting work, which must also throw doubt on the educational function of the six-week *stages*.

There are several interrelated problematic effects — concerning opacity, instability, constant debugging and retranslation — of the complex character of mediations and the vertical hierarchy of codes in computer music. I will outline them briefly. They return in the substantive case of music production that I describe later.

In 1984 the problem of opacity seriously affected both skilled and naive software users. Skilled IRCAM programmers complained that, looking back on programs they had written in collaboration with several others, the complexity of the codes made it extremely difficult for them to reconstruct afterward from the codes themselves exactly what was done and how in the bits of code authored by colleagues, without asking them. Programs at IRCAM were often put together over a period of months or years by several collaborators, a gradual, collective bricolage. Software was, then, characteristically a result of multiple authorship. Moreover, the process was very far from being totally preconceived, so that programming solutions to problems and aims that arose in the course of development were tried out, altered, and kept or discarded often without any record being kept of the why and how. One tutor-programmer described his fantasy of a program as a sort of monstrous baroque or rococo construction made up of many fussy incrustations added on to the main body until the original body becomes almost indecipherable. In other words, due to social and temporal mediation, programming code — despite its image of transparent logic — is far from open, self-evident, and transparent to decode, even for the highly skilled authors themselves. However IRCAM programmers seemed to delight in this intransigent opacity since, despite the many difficulties that it caused, it made programs appear artful and unstandardized expressions of collective imaginative labor.

For unskilled users, we have seen that it was impossible to intuit the implicit logic of the codes, so that their use required guidance and lengthy application. Even then, unlike skilled programmers, naive users learned to control and interact with only the surface level of the hierarchy of codes. Thus, if there was a bug they were powerless to enter lower levels of the hierarchy to work out and correct what was wrong, just as they were relatively powerless to alter or improve the system as a whole as they might wish. It is this problem that lay behind the AI aim to design interactive systems that would allow users to create custom-built software environments for themselves. However, this aim cannot itself escape the material character of software: even with an interactive program (such as Chant) there are still layers of code underlying the program that naive users have no skill to enter and modify. The density of technological and coded mediations is therefore far greater here than in either traditional score-based musics or the empiricist techniques of analog electronic music. Figure 9 indicates also the different relations of naive and skilled users to the vertical mediations of the technology.

Further problems derive from the link between the dense vertical mediations of computer music and the chronic instability of the wider technological environment. Computer technology changes constantly and rapidly, so IRCAM's environment in 1984 was very unstable, which caused a continuous process of adjustment to new variables. Each individual (especially infrastructural) technological change had repercussions within IRCAM's total technological configuration; with every significant change of hardware or software, all other levels of software had also to be adjusted. Thus, when the UNIX operating system software was upgraded from the extant version, 4.1, to the new 4.1a, all the programs in the house had to be rewritten or retranslated in terms of the coding of the new version. For this enormous task, two American consultants were brought in full-time for several months; and one expressed the opinion, even while bringing in 4.1a, that in order to keep abreast of wider developments IRCAM should really be investing in the next generation of UNIX, 4.2 — which was already being introduced in the United States. The retranslation of programs into 4.1a — the rewriting of every bit of higher code into the lower code of the new operating system — caused severe problems, as we will see. Each new translation raised the risk of new bugs, which necessitated much work debugging the system. Because of bugs, the computer system became very fragile during this time and the VAX crashed constantly, often many times a day.

But retranslation, and the risk of bugs and need for debugging that it caused, were not simply enforced by the revision of external technological standards. They occurred also because of voluntary experiments in bringing in new hardware and software when researchers were tempted by new possibilities to adapt their programs to run on new systems. (For example, Chant and Formes, designed initially for the PDP10 and then the VAX, were rewritten in 1984 to run also on the 4X.) Thus researchers themselves courted the constant retranslation of programs for new contexts. They seemed ambivalent about the phenomenon and in some ways blind to the effects of their own actions. Programmers avowed that each such process yielded useful "knowledge," yet they railed against the chronic weaknesses of the system. We will see that because of opacity and IRCAM's related problem of lack of documentation of software R and D, programming adaptations were often ad hoc and remained "one-offs" rather than being fully analyzed and documented for general use. The inherent vertical mediation of software, then, can induce a constant tinkering by skilled programmers, a constant play of retranslation between codes, of readjustment to challenging new circumstances — the longer-term productivity of which is questionable.

OBJECTS, MACHINES, SOCIALITY

Not only IRCAM's texts and codes, but its characteristic objects, machines, physical environment, and sociality are key mediations through which IRCAM culture is constituted and its music produced. Photo 4 shows the 4X prototype machine, with a protective wax seal. The 4X was quite small, less than a meter tall. Its rather ordinary surface — just a small steel box with some controls — belied the intense interest stimulated by its inner workings. The story goes that when the Sogitec company, which was to put it into production, came to see the 4X, the designer BU refused to let them know the machine's secrets, so Sogitec had to build up their understanding of the machine from nothing. BU's reluctance may partly have been caused by his dislike of the company. But it also derived from his refusal over the years to document the workings of the 4X: there were no written accounts of the technology. This, in turn, recalls an early IRCAM myth. Berio, who first brought BU to IRCAM and asked him to build what became the 4X, had decreed that IRCAM should be an oral culture, passing information from person to person, centered on sound. Paradoxically, what had started as an anarcho-utopian principle became, around the 4X, a preservation of secrecy encouraging a fetishism of the machine's mystery.

Photo 5 shows the IRCAM lower corridor in 1985 filled with the flight cases used to take the 4X and other computer and audio equipment on *Répons* and other tours. A visiting Canadian researcher, seeing the many well-built and expensive flight cases strewn along the corridor, commented dryly that with the money spent on them he could have equipped an entire computer music studio. That so much money was spent simply on protective casing for the 4X rather than on musically productive machinery was, to this man, indicative of its fetishization and of IRCAM's irrational budgeting.

This links also with the advocacy of manual and mechanical values by the 4X Hardware directors, values that were held to be embodied in these machines. These values, and a corresponding admiration for machinery, were held more widely in IRCAM, especially by technicians. Photo 6 shows IRCAM's own mechanical workshop, kitted out with a full range of industrial metal and wood lathes, sited in the bowels of the institute. The workshop was home to a craftsman-mechanic who was supposed to be able to build any physical object: for example, he had crafted an extraordinary microtonal keyboard for Boulez. Photo 7 shows part of an electronic technicians' lab. These areas were strewn with tools, cable, and wiring with which technicians built and repaired equipment. It was in terms of these manual/mechanical aspects of IRCAM culture, in which physical objects were held to embody mechanical values, that the software dimensions of IRCAM culture were denigrated for having no such physical embodiment, no object form, for being insubstantial and ephemeral. The discursive conflict between hardware and software was thus played out at a material level — the materiality of hardware bestowing a literally objectified legitimation.

Photos 8 and 9 show two ordinary acoustic instruments — a clarinet and a trumpet — bound up in electronic wiring for acoustical experimentation. The clarinet was one of several currently being measured in an acoustics studio, while the trumpet was long since experimentally obsolete and stood around unused, a pet object of delight and a butt of jokes. The story was that it had been elaborately wired to measure the acoustics of trumpets, but that the setup had not worked, so it was a pathetic reminder of experimental failure. The instruments — trussed up in wires for measurement, pierced by intrusive electrodes and electronically monitored, the trumpet sacrificed to failed experiment — represent a kind of torturous binding of the musical body, an attempt to capture and so rationalize their complex, organic aural workings. Nothing epitomizes so well the penetration of IRCAM's rationality into the very musical body, a symptom of power to which Foucault advises us to attend (Foucault 1977).

Photo 10 shows a study containing a suspended loudspeaker that forms part of the interconnected speaker system operating throughout the institute. Photo 11 shows the main corridor on level -2, with its skylights at ground level and the two rows of glass-walled offices to one side, while Photos 12 and 13 show different views, from outside and inside, of the glass-walled offices. These features embodied the IRCAM principle of aural and visual openness. Thus, anyone could hear sounds being made using the main system over the interconnected speakers, and anyone could look into the studies and see what was going on. But, like the inmates of the Panopticon (Foucault 1977), this "democracy of infor-

mation" was also experienced by workers as a form of permanent surveillance. So they often closed off the speaker system and worked at
night to avoid others hearing their sounds over the speakers; they put up
posters, moved cupboards in front of the glass walls to block them and
prevent people from looking in.

Photo 14 illustrates the physical objects used most continuously for
all IRCAM intellectual work: the computer terminal, a keyboard and a
VDU screen linked up in '84 to the VAX or 4X systems. The objects are
designed for solitary work, the user engaging with the system by tapping
into the keyboard and gazing into the screen. This work involves no
aural stimuli, a very reduced and unspecialized gestural control (compared with musical instrument playing), and the impoverished visual
stimuli of the VDU. If we compare working long hours in this way to
previous ways of producing music, it comes close in terms of sensory
deprivation only to the act of composing simply with pen and paper.
Even this involves a form of mediating visual imagination and graphic
skill as part of the compositional process (Cook 1990), whereas terminal
work is almost purely conceptual. Also striking is the chronic isolation of
the long hours of conceptual work necessitated by learning and using the
complex mediations of computer music.

Workers maintain their actual isolation while indulging in the computer's enjoyable form of pseudosociability, its substitute for direct human contact: computer mail. In '84 all workers, when they first logged
on to the VAX in the day, read the computer mail or messages that had
been stored for them. Messages came throughout the day from people at
other institutions to which IRCAM is linked by national and international computer networks, and from individuals within the house. They
would often interrupt work in progress by suddenly appearing on the
VDU screen. Mail was either purely informational or more commonly
also fun; the language was often colloquial, the tone joking, teasing, and
between the sexes flirtatious. There were also ritual communications
shared by all members of the VAX "community": systems messages sent
out every morning by the systems manager or one of his team. Having
logged on to the VAX, users deployed a command that listed all the
people currently logged on to the system, and where they were located —
at which IRCAM terminal. These forms of computer-mediated sociality
became substitutes for direct contact: a worker could go in to the house,
log on to the system, work at his terminal all day, exchange computer
mail with others in the house and know exactly who was there and
approximately what they were doing, and yet never physically meet

another person. Terminal work thus involves extreme physical, sensory, and social discipline, balanced only by its cerebral challenge and its capacity for distanced and mediated sociality.

But workers had other ways to combat the isolation and socialize the technology. The work culture involved much informal, spontaneous oral consultation, as well as sustained collaboration. One such social moment, from a long-term music research collaboration between a psychoacoustician and a composer-squatter, is shown in Photo 15. These two would meet and work alongside one another for some hours at a time, one bringing scientific and programming skills, the other posing problems arising from her compositional work. The mutual engagement is palpable.

A COMPOSER'S VISIT

To convey the social and technological character of music production and how the various mediations that I have described enter into musical work, we can examine the production visit of the commissioned composer AV. It cannot be considered a typical visit, since it was dogged by many problems. Yet there is no typical composer's visit to IRCAM, and each necessitates particular computer music "solutions" to unique compositional aims. AV's experience nonetheless illustrates some characteristic features and problems of music production at IRCAM.

AV's three-month visit to IRCAM in mid-1984 was his third. He had taken the IRCAM *stage* in 1980 and had made a "research" visit of two months in 1982 to learn about the technology and prepare for his later production visit. AV is a composer based in Britain. He was well liked within IRCAM following the *stage*, in which he showed an aptitude for computer music. He had a strong background in electronic music, having trained in electronic studios in London, one in his music conservatory, and he had worked extensively with the Fairlight digital synthesizer. Most important for IRCAM management, AV had recently won first prize in the major European electronic music competition at Bourges. AV was thus highly regarded as a promising composer who already had some knowledge of computer music. For all concerned, this was to be an ambitious project.

During the '82 visit, AV had worked with Chant on the PDP10. After two months he had produced one minute of music based on timbral transitions between a simulated voice and Chinese oboe. The '84 visit was supposed to extend this work with more powerful technological means so as to allow a far longer piece to be made along the same lines, exploring timbral transitions as themselves carriers of form — creating a syntax of timbral changes. This was an attempt to put into practice the research of AV's friend, the psychoacoustician HM, whose ideas for the project were quoted in chapter 7. AV himself described the aim thus:

> I wanted to work with recognizable timbral identities modeled on known sounds — voice, gongs, oboes or whatever. . . . I believe that it's the particular behavior in time of those instruments that conveys eighty percent of the identity of the sound. So I wanted to model this type of behavior and then interpolate between [them], and find if possible some kind of *syntax*: some way of evolving in time that would belong inherently in the process, not borrowed from another type of music. . . .
>
> For example, the musical syntax of polyphony is related to the way that the voices interact with each other, and each note is a self-contained timbre. But if you're working with timbres that are continually changing in time, then obviously the syntax has to be related to that process inside the note, as it were. I wanted to experiment with those changes to see if it was possible to extract some common *rules* — maybe "rules" is too intellectual a statement — that could somehow be generalized. . . . Therefore I didn't just want to have timbre A and timbre B, and just play a succession of transformations; I wanted to see if there was any way of creating a structure, a syntax, taken from the [sound] wave behavior.

We see here again the search for a "language" unifying material and form, a syntax derived from the "wave behavior" of timbres. But for various reasons, the 1984 production visit was a frustrating failure and produced only abortive results. After three months' work, rather than a full commission AV had produced only seventy-two seconds of sound.

Because of his aim of making a piece consisting of timbral transitions, AV's project was extremely demanding of computer resources. In many synthesis-based pieces, each discrete timbre or small section can be digitally produced and then transferred on to analog tape to be gradually built up into the overall piece. But working with continuous mutations of timbre is a far more demanding task for digital synthesis. The synthesized timbres must first themselves be sufficiently complex and organic, already demanding of computing power, and as well as this, the computer must be able to produce time sections of the piece long enough — perhaps several minutes — to convey convincingly the gradual, continuous timbral changes. In '84 the amount of computing power and memory required to sustain such long and complex synthesis files was enormous, and the synthesis time could also therefore be lengthy. Each time the composer wanted to alter something and resynthesize, it would take a

great deal of time. So the technical aim of the production was to provide
AV with a less lengthy, closer to real-time working environment. At the
end of his '84 visit, bitter about its failure, AV recalled the technical
aspects of this as compared with his earlier visit as follows.

AV: When I did the research period in 1982, I worked on the PDP10. It was
        clear that I could not produce an entire piece on that system, because af-
        ter two months I came up with only one minute of sound that was really
        together. There's no way that Chant could produce on the '10 or any
        such system a large-scale piece with enough feedback to modify things
        as you're doing them. We had some very lengthy experiences with files
        running for one, two, or even two and a half days just to turn out a min-
        ute and a half of sound that was eventually wrong anyway!

GB: Even this morning NP took two hours to get ten seconds of sound
        through with Chant and Formes on the VAX. . . .

AV: Yes! It's still the same! The VAX is not sufficiently faster than the '10 for
        my purposes, even with the Array Processor.[5] So it was clear that it
        would have to be real-time if I was to work with heavy calculation and
        be able to change things quickly enough to make something really artic-
        ulate. In real-time systems, the 4X was the new thing around. So I
        waited till the 4X was installed and running. And then reports started
        coming back to London that in fact the 4X wasn't as magical, or as real-
        time, as everybody thought.

GB: You say you couldn't work with Chant running on the '10 or the VAX
        and get enough control. But then how did WOW do *Chréode 1* with
        Chant on the VAX, *non* real-time, and get such good results [also of
        timbral transition]?

AV: But it took him a year and a half, working in the house all the time!
        Which is the ideal situation. If you live here, you run a job, like on the
        '10, and it runs for two hours or a whole day: [*with irony*] you go to
        your meetings, it's still running, so you go to a second meeting! So fi-
        nally, before coming, I said let's have a meeting to decide what I need. I
        came over for a week and we had a meeting with all the people con-
        cerned except the Systems people — which was a shame, because now I
        see they're the only people objective enough about the load of the sys-
        tem. They could maybe have said that certain things wouldn't work —
        like the fast link. . . .
            There was a lot of pressure from the [IRCAM] environment of this
        kind: [*cynically*] "We [IRCAM] cannot afford another [commission]
        failure . . . because it would mean to the world that our all-mighty, all-
        powerful doomsday machine, the 4X, is not able to do the jobs we
        thought it was able to do!" And so they wanted to give it a go anyway.
        They were prepared to work very, very hard. But they were overly op-
        timistic. They gave me a demonstration of the 4X with Chant when I
        was here, and I wasn't pleased with it. Its system of filters is a bit like the
        Vocoder, not so flexible. I said, "Why don't we wait till the Array Pro-

cessor is ready," which it only is recently, "and I could use my old Chant
programs with it?" But they said: "Look, there's another possibility:
we'll have Formes on the VAX, with a setup almost identical to what
you had before on Chant. And that could be transferred into data for
additive synthesis instruments, and we could have the 4X patched as an
additive synthesis instrument, taking this data. And at the composer's
level you'd be dealing with a file system that would look almost the
same as Chant, and would use the same criteria. So it would be like
working with Chant on the ' 10."

So the idea was that MC and other people that know Formes inside out would write very quickly, theoretically, a program just like
Formes — which is very flexible — in the VAX, and that data would be
transferred by another program into additive synthesis data for the 4X,
which would have a configuration inside — which is what HM wrote, a
patch — to behave like an additive synthesis instrument. MC and XH
were writing, when I came, the Roc program and the new Formes program. Roc runs on the PDP11, takes the data from the disk, gives the
data from the VAX to the 4X, shoves that data into the 4X in real time,
and the 4X plays it. But there's another Roc program before that transfer, in the VAX, that changes the data from Formes into additive synthesis form.

GB: Who thought this system up?

AV: RIG, and he was overly optimistic; but he made some general argu-
        ments. There was the need for an efficient and powerful additive synthe-
        sis machine. It could be developed for my piece, but it wouldn't just be
        used for my piece. The scale was rather gigantic: the amount of work
        and number of people involved were out of scale for one piece! But the
        idea was it would stay as a general instrument to be used by other peo-
        ple, *stagiaires* and so on. So they said, "Let's do it anyway!" I was cau-
        tious. I said "OK, as long as at the end of the day if I say it's not working
        we cancel the concert, and you bring me back to IRCAM when a more
        suitable environment is working." They agreed, so when things started
        to go wrong I thought, well, I'll come back another time, but I'll experi-
        ment this time. . . . I don't want the same things to happen again: next
        time everything will have to be working before I get here, because next
        time [*fed up*] a piece *has* to be produced!

This quote also illuminates two central dimensions of the work process: time, and collaboration between the composer and tutors. The time
involved in AV's production can be divided into macro and micro aspects. At the macro level, we have seen that in three months' work, with
the part-time help of three tutors, he produced just seventy-two seconds
of music. This represents, crudely, an overall production ratio in the
region of 54,000:1: that is, it took about nine hundred hours to produce
one minute of sound. Functionally, the time was divided between bouts

of software writing by the tutors and then AV's use of the system and feedback on problems and improvements that he needed. Because of the technical ambitions of the project, much production time was taken up by writing, rewriting and debugging programs.[6]

At the micro level of daily working, there were revealing discrepancies between AV's and HM's accounts of the turnaround time. HM told me that AV was getting a 30:1 ratio — that it took thirty minutes to synthesize one minute of sound — and he contrasted that with the "bad old days" of computer music a few years back in which ratios of 300:1 were, he said, common. But it is clear from AV's description above that he actually experienced far worse ratios. In his previous visit he talked of ratios of some 900:1 (1 day for a minute and a half of sound) or 600:1 (ten hours for one minute), while for this visit he described a ratio of 180:1 as common (three hours for one minute). In the quote I interrupted him to mention NP's experience of waiting two hours for ten seconds of synthesized sound: a ratio of 720:1. Thus the delay involved in complex synthesis in '84 was still lengthy and very far from real-time. This was so even for certain uses of the 4X, contradicting the aims of that machine, as well as for IRCAM's three other main pieces of hardware: the VAX, PDP11, and new Array Processor. However, it is striking that in-house researchers and tutors such as HM perceived that time as far shorter than visiting composers — in fact, a distorted perception.

AV's project tapped the utopian spirit of the musicians' group in several ways: in its technical and musical ambition, based on the latest psychoacoustical ideas; in its aim of being not individualist but of use to the whole music research "community"; and in those ideals being embodied in collaborative, supra-individual practices. We saw earlier that collaboration between composers and researchers to advance music research was in itself a central principle of the musicians' vanguard. For AV's project there were three tutors involved, only one of them employed as such: HM (junior tutor and psychoacoustician), MC (Chant/Formes director), and XH (a visiting American computer musician acting as a tutor). Here is AV's grateful account of his fruitful collaboration with MC. As he admits, MC was responsible for designing the overall architecture of his work environment.

> Basically MC did most of the Formes stuff, and XH's job was to write the conversion from Formes to the 4X into additive synthesis; and after that, he was also involved in rewriting some of the stuff that MC wrote in LISP into C to make it faster. Let's say the architecture and the conception of it was produced by MC. . . . [The first month] I was just following MC's work and

would say: "I would like certain parameters and I would like to control them this way," and he would say "I think it's working," and I would try it and say "It's not doing it," or "It's doing it but it's crashing." So he'd get deep into the system to debug it, and I would sit next to him watching and eventually learn what the system was all about.

So from the point of view of writing software, I had nothing to do with it except to [posit] specific musical needs, put as technically precisely as possible. That's the good thing about MC: if it's possible he will find a way of doing things. He's always very receptive. He'll say, "Are you sure you really want that much control? That's a helluva lot of work!" And you say, "Yes, I need it for that and that reason," and he'll say "OK, that's a *composer's* decision, you must have a good reason," and he'll go and do it and be *excited* about solving that problem.

The work done by AV's three tutors was, then, programming: writing new programs so as to construct an entirely new configuration of IRCAM software and hardware in order to achieve greater real-time power. It was in fact the first attempt to unite Chant and Formes, running on the VAX, via various links with the 4X. The system and its development, involving close coordination between the three tutors, is described here by HM.

I did the additive synthesis instrument for the 4X. [For that,] AV had to think what he wanted musically. We started out with forty-two partials, with amplitude and frequency control on each one. It was limited to that because AV wanted everything at a 32K sampling rate. . . . It turns out you can control the ramps at 16K and still run your oscillators at 32K. So then we had much more resources, and ended up getting an eighty-four-partial version going. . . .

The *new* thing was driving additive synthesis on the 4X by the Roc program hooked up to Formes: the combination of Formes and the 4X. Formes makes a file [on the VAX]; you transfer the file to the PDP11 and feed it to Roc, who feeds it to the 4X. MC wrote the Roc program. Roc doesn't do anything intelligent, just shoves information into the 4X. . . . XH wrote the thing that prepared stuff for Roc in Formes, and then MC actually built the environment in Formes for AV. Right at the start I had to make the 4X additive synth instrument, a patch, because all the rest of the stuff had to depend on what the 4X had to receive, what its limits were. So there was really close coordination between me and XH, XH writing the Formes to Roc file translator and me writing the [4X] instrument. . . .

MC came up with some routines that allow you to describe things in the same language as Chant, spectral forms that evolve in time, but then you can add other things like how many partials you want. It took those spectral forms derived from Chant algorithms and applied them to partials in an additive synthesis instrument. So there's a translation from the formant shapes [of Chant] into a spectral envelope that can move in time. . . . So AV could use his prior knowledge of Chant and yet do it in an additive synth fashion. He also had the control over the imaging process from additive synth that you can't get in Chant — discrete control over each partial.

Figure 10 outlines the baroque configuration, involving several new links and versions, that HM describes. The point was to allow AV to use the same Chant and Formes user interfaces that he had used before and knew musically how to control — but by linking them up to the 4X to have them more real-time, and by having them drive an additive synthesis patch on the 4X to have greater detailed control over each component partial than was possible with Chant.

The quote also touches on the character of debates during the work process: the musical "needs" posed by AV for his tutors to meet by finding solutions. HM mentions an early issue: AV wanted to have as large a number of synthesized partials as possible so as to be able to produce really complex and organic timbres. They started with only forty-two (each produced by one simulated oscillator) but some weeks in discovered a way to let him control eighty-four partials at any one time. Another question was the amount and quality of organicity. AV discussed these issues as follows.

> HM's instrument was something to be discussed. It depended on certain choices I had to make, and the limitations of the 4X: whether I wanted maximum oscillators — eighty-four — with much less control, or forty-two oscillators with more control. Or what kind of global control I wanted. And then, of course, noise. . . . HM worked on the preliminary version that was only forty-two oscillators, but then someone suggested a way of doing it bigger, so he had to do it all over again. [Then] the program doing the conversion from Formes to the 4X patch also had to be changed — and every time you change something there's a bug, which takes time. So I started with forty two and ended up with eighty-four partials, with added noise.

Other key issues during the production process concerned the quality of attack — the very beginning of the sound, and a crucial timbral variable — that AV could get with the software. This related in turn to two technological variables: first, the "quantum" of the synthesis program, that is, the time between each update of information. The shorter this time, the finer the "grain" of the material and control and the more demanding of computing power. This was set at thirty milliseconds, which was, apparently, quite slow. The second variable was the transition time between two notes, depending on a subprogram called TTR (*temps de transition*). The slowness and quality of the quanta and TTR were unsatisfactory to AV, since he believed that they produced sluggish attacks, which dampened the brilliance of the timbres as a whole.

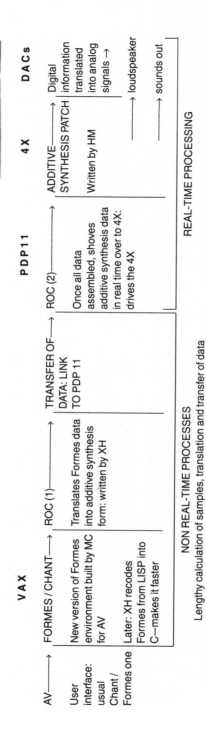

10. AV's project: technological configuration and main contributions of tutors.

The following notes from my diary covering two days of the production convey the character of the work in progress halfway through AV's visit.

16.4.84, 5:00 P.M.: AV and XH [tutor] on 4X in Studio 3. WR [another tutor] comes in to advise them of his inharmonics program.

Question is: how to work with inharmonics. AV wants to be able to specify inharmonic partials at both the bottom and top of the sound, not all clustered at the top end.

WR suggests: "I have a code in Cmusic where you specify three variables: the fundamental frequency, the "distance" between partials, the subdivisions of the octave. For example, to get a series of inharmonic partials all a minor third apart you'd put in: 100Hz (for the fundamental), 3 (for 3 semitones apart), and 12 (for semitones or divisions of 1/12th of the basic octave space). You can also do it with non-octave space, then you need a fourth variable."

AV and XH discuss how to rework WR's program in LISP for the 4X and how to make more disk space to allow this.

AV goes out to get a sandwich: "It's breakfast time for me!" He was up last night working till 7:30 A.M. XH and I stay, XH programming.

XH: "I'm working on getting more partials out of the 4X for each sound: previously we could get only forty-two partials, now we can hopefully get eighty-four. Also, I'm trying to get each to have a *noise* surround. But either the machine crashes, or nothing happens at all! — another form of death!"

XH manages after an hour to get a complex noise around his partial: first one oscillator to try it out, then to be applied to many oscillators/partials. We hear it, and he alters the degree of noise. Then we have to leave the studio at 6 P.M. for WR's turn with the 4X.

17.4.84, 4:30 P.M.: AV, XH and WR in 4X studio 3.

WR: "Roc causes the PDP11 to crash more. Have you noticed the '11 is crashing more often these days?"

AV and XH laugh knowingly and say: "Yes, as we told you!"

AV teaches WR about the TTR subprogram: it controls the transition between two notes; AV and XH have used it in AV's sounds. WR calls in BYV [4X Software director and Boulez's tutor] to sort out a problem with the DACs, which are producing a *chord* — a tritone of course![7] — as the test tone rather than the correct single tone. After ten minutes BYV has sorted it out; he and WR leave.

AV asks XH if he can speed up a process running as a sound file.

XH, annoyed, snaps back: "I'm *not* a computer scientist!"

AV and XH equalize the mixer and arrange the patch board linking it to the 4X to hear the sound out: eighty-four oscillators, sixteen audio channels at around six per channel.

AV jokes ironically about how computer music is the highest state of human experience because one has just to engage with and enjoy the actual process of work, rather than it being about the end result of a piece: renouncing the gratification of a result.

We chat about the music research meeting yesterday in which Boulez stressed the need for research to be directly tied into production and musical results, to which AV says unhappily: "Well Boulez should come in here and try producing a piece and see how long it takes him to get good results! If only. . . ."

AV and XH spend about an hour tracing a strange problem. The amplitude meters on a couple of channels in the mixer show a fluctuation: the needles are waving around at us wildly but regularly when no sound is emitted. Why? They try to trace it. A phasing problem? Or because of the noise they've put on each oscillator? They try to isolate the problem. It changes each time we try something. It seems to be caused by the noise, because empirically it gets better when they get rid of the noise effect, but they cannot understand why.

6:30 P.M.: MC comes in. He and AV immediately discuss a problem with how the TTR transition seems to affect the attack on each note following it. AV is unhappy with the current state of the program and asks MC how they could achieve a more variable start to the envelope. So he draws on paper what he'd like to be able to get, and MC tells him how he can already. AV complains that he can't get a powerful sharp attack now, except on the first note of a phrase. MC thinks and comes up with a way but they leave it agreeing that the current possibility is too slow for a sharp attack.

AV and XH work together on the idea of a transition (frequency-wise) from an inharmonic spectrum (e.g. with each partial a minor second apart) to a harmonic spectrum.

AV keeps posing the questions to XH and MC from his compositional desires: "How do I get this?" "What if I wanted to get a sharper or more variable attack?"

AV leaves for half an hour; XH and MC discuss possible variables in the recursivity of the noise program and negotiate programming possibilities. Here, XH poses the problems and MC answers with what's "easy" or "not possible" to do.

AV's work schedule meant his coming in every day for about ten hours. He was given six timetabled hours a day with the 4X during which he could actually try to hear the sounds. This was usually at night, either 6:00 P.M. to midnight or midnight to 6:00 A.M. In these night periods he sat alone, or with my company, in the 4X studio at a terminal, using the Chant/Formes interface to rewrite his files for many hours at a time. When the files were rewritten with new variables, he would launch the synthesis program, setting the program in motion to produce its millions of sound samples. Due to the length and complexity of his files, the samples would be ready some hours later, at which time he could hear what he had done, remodify the files again, and start all over.

In a day I could try out about three or four changes at most. That means you really have to work out everything in your head beforehand, get your data theoretically right, not expect to get feedback from sound itself but do it preconceived from theory — which is not the right way of doing things. I prefer the real-time aural environment, much more empirical, flexible, where you can try things, retry and retry as with the Fairlight. That's still not possible here.

During the day, AV would spend a few more hours at the VAX terminal preparing his night's work. He could not launch his files during the day and had to work at night because his files were so big and demanding on the system, including the VAX, that they overloaded it in the day, causing it to crash. This was seen as antisocial to the community as a whole. So he could work only when no one else was running programs on the system. AV drew criticism for his "megalomaniac" files; yet, as he replied, he had been commissioned to work with timbral transition and this necessitated very long and complex sound files.

AV's main work, then, was sitting at a terminal for many hours rewriting files, and waiting while the hardware churned out the sound samples. Only a very small proportion of the working time involved hearing back the sounds. During the long hours' waits AV would work on other musical dimensions, for example the harmonic score of his piece, which flowed in and out of polyphonal harmonicity, or he would amuse himself, when frustrated, by asking me to play piano. The quality of AV's experience, and frustration, can be gauged by computer mail messages that he sent me during the visit, shown in Figure 11. They convey, with witty desperation, his annoyance with the recalcitrant slowness and unmusicality of the system. One is set up as a "race" between AV and the VAX "till the end of time or the VAX crashes."[8] Another takes the form of "a nice chat" between AV and the intransigent automaton, the "Vaxo Unmusical," which ends with "System going down [crashing] in 30 secs." One speaks of his sense of being "nailed to" a terminal. Most eloquently, AV quotes from Conrad: "silence was being murdered by the atrocity of those vulgar sounds." The technology comes across almost as a willful adversary.

LOCAL CONCEPTUAL AND TECHNOLOGICAL PROBLEMS: NOISE, AND THE ABSENCE OF "RATIONAL" TECHNOLOGICAL EQUIVALENCE

I discuss in the next chapter the larger technological difficulties that were ultimately responsible for AV producing only seventy-two seconds of sound. Here I outline the finer conceptual and aural problems that arose, and that point to the limits of the technological system he worked with. The most significant involved the simulated noise that was supposed to

From: vin Sat May 5 20:45:38 1984
To: born
Subject: CONRAD
``..silence was being murdered by the atrocity of those vulgar sounds''
Joseph Conrad (from 'Victory')

From: vin Sat May 5 21:07:56 1984
To: born
Subject: Vax 11 vs. Alejandro
think: a Vax 11 can on average do operations 1 million times faster than
Alejandro, yet
        if the Vax gives Alejandro 1 second advantage it will never
        catch up again.
Don't believe it?
        listen carefully:
        We said that the Vax gives Alejandro 1 second advantage.
It's the Vax's turn now! It does an operation that lasts 1 second. The
Vax and Alejandro are neck and neck now.
        but! Alejandro being 1 million times slower has covered 1
        millionth of a second....
        and so on till the end of time or the Vax crashes....

From: vin Fri May 18 18:56:54 1984
To: born
Subject: a nice chat....
A.V.:   Hi there it's me again!
V.U.:   Vaxo Unmusical
       IRCAM login:
A.V.:   I said it's me!
V.U.:   password:
A.V.:   MEEEEE!!!!
V.U.:   login incorrect
       login:
A.V.:   look here, we haven't got all day, you know..
V.U.:   password:
A.V.:   (ok...OK...) vin
V.U.: $
A.V.:   That's better!!
V.U.:   systems message: system going down in 30 secs!!!

From: vin Mon Jun 4 01:45:37 1984
To: born
Subject: ``..... but with a nail..''
       The Concise Pocket Ircam Encyclopaedia
       page 874 second paragraph
``nail''—analogue device made of metal or other resistant material.
       Figure of speech: ``nailed to'', as related to terminals.

11.   The frustrated author: AV's computer mail messages. (By permission of the author.)

enrich the timbres and make them more organic-sounding. AV found the noise provided by the complex additive synthesis setup inferior to and cruder than what had been possible on previous visits using Chant. He expressed it thus at the end of the visit. "From the very beginning we knew that I needed noise, because my preliminary research used a very specific type of noise that Chant can produce which is nicely modeled on some formant shape; and that means it really follows the model of the sound itself, so it's not detached from the sound. While the noise that we've got now on the 4X is not shaped in the same way, and is therefore kind of *detached* from the image of the sound you're producing. It sounds together with it, but it doesn't *fuse*."

In the last days of AV's stay an informal "postmortem" meeting took place in the 4X studio between him, MC, and junior tutor WOW to discuss the problems with the project's deeper research aims. The discussion illustrates again the positive aspects of the tutor-composer interaction: MC asks for feedback on how AV experienced the technology with a view to future improvements, and AV conveys, sometimes brutally, the failures in what they provided. AV was fed up at this time and anxious that he had been made to look bad in front of Boulez and IRCAM management, and his annoyance shows toward the end of the discussion. Overall, he oscillates between thinking of the visit as providing some useful general knowledge or as a total failure. Despite the technical character of this discussion, it nonetheless contains some of the most musically nuanced exchanges that I heard within IRCAM.

AV: The seventy-two seconds only achieve fifty-five percent of what I wanted.
[*AV plays the seventy-two seconds of taped sound. After playing it:*]
[*Grimly*] That's about it!

MC: OK thank you. . . .

AV: I still prefer Chant. . . .

MC: What are the forty-five percent missing?

AV: Ah, noise. . . . [*Starts from the top*] Well, at the level of syntax, I would have liked to be able to run this twenty times, and change things all the time instead of spending ninety percent of the energy on getting it to work and ten percent on the actual syntax — by that I mean the process of transformation, the ways to apply dynamic and all the other parameters, to enhance that [syntax] and make it develop as some kind of language. Although I'm quite happy in a general way with the [syntax research] direction, I don't think in this example it comes across one hundred percent as I would like. [*Exasperated*] But each run, when I want to change something, it takes so long that . . . ! At the level of sound: that's where I think it's weaker, the actual timbre itself. I don't mind so much not having the kinds of attacks I would like — which is due to the fact that we've got those thirty-millisecond quanta and the 4X has that delay — because I could *mask* the attacks very easily: either with Chant or a Fairlight I could make a mix and mask it, it could be a mix trick — I don't mind. But the *lack of noise* in the evolution of some sounds makes them really, ah, too compact.

MC: Ah. . . .

AV: If it weren't for the extremely different vibrato rates that I've used — which isn't natural because voices don't sing with such different vibrato rates, but OK, maybe that doesn't matter. But if I would have wanted to use voices that were sort of straightforward, like in the previous version of Chant, close-miked voices, then you would have heard just a mass of sound with no identity whatsoever. I've tried it. You hear one voice on its own, and . . . it's a synthetic voice but it's a voice. You put four together and it's no longer a voice, and that's because they *fuse* — you use several additive synthesis instruments and they fuse. Unless you've got noise that evolves in some characteristic way with its own envelope, like in Chant — in my earlier Chant example I hardly use vibrato, and when I use it it's certainly not to create the voice image, I used to just play around with it — but here, without the vibrato it's nothing, it doesn't work. So I think that straight additive synthesis may be very powerful to create single sounds, but to create evolutions it has the problem that . . . [it] turns very easily into a *mass*, just a thick layer of partials. On the other hand I have done mixes where if you take steady-state voices and mix them like that, they start sounding like [*laughs*] electronic sounds! But you can always get that breath image from very close, which has a definite contour, and it gives you a close-up presence that *this* hasn't got. These voices sound like they don't have enough energy in the top, and in fact they have plenty, more than they need!

MC: They don't seem to have. . . .

AV: Exactly, and that is [lack of] *noise*, there's no question about it. You can have some noise at minus 70dB, a little bit, all the way up to 16K [KHz] and. . . . Because it's true, you analyze a real voice and, sure, it doesn't go above 6 or 7K in any significant way; but you record a voice and you cut off above 8K and you *kill* the voice completely. You do a spectral analysis and there's nothing up there; yet you. . . .

MC: I believe you, yeah! . . . Microevolutions. . . .

AV: It's not partials, it's *rubbish* [i.e. noise: he means it positively]. But you get rid of that rubbish and . . . it moves in some way that's *greatly effective*. Then one can say: so what? Why should we be so hung up on having biological [i.e. organic] sounds, why not just explore? So I have in a way accepted that, OK, I'm not going to get that quality; so maybe I should explore the actual sounds that this system can produce. That's why in the end I've been concentrating more on the syntax, because at least if that's strong then. . . . But it's such a long process! The old idea of having a few faders to play with on every run and say "More of this" [doesn't exist]. What do you think they [the sounds] lack that could be easily implemented on the system now?

MC: [*Stumped*] I dunno. . . . We could look at every detail of the variations within the 4X in order that they run really fast. . . . It was impossible to use noise on the 4X. . . .

AV: It doesn't seem to be a relevant parameter. That generalized 4X noise was just hovering wildly around the partials without any [possibility of] control. . . .

MC: [*Contradicting AV sharply*] You *have* control over it!

AV: Well, you only have control of the proportion of it. . . .

MC: And the bandwidth, and the location. . . .

AV: [*Frustrated, forcefully*] And the quality of that noise is . . . it's a *really shitty noise*! It hasn't got any warmth at all. It adds *garbage*: when you add that to a voice, what you hear is a voice with some noise in the background, like you've got some *interference*. I mean: "Have you got a radio on?" or something, you know, that's how you feel: "Can you turn that noise *off*!" It doesn't fuse at all, it has no . . . it's definitely not the kind of noise you get in Chant.

MC: Explain that to RIG! [who suggested doing the project in additive synthesis rather than in Chant] I mean, it's really important because *he* thinks this works!

The sense of AV compromising his musical needs, of his weighing up the project against other experiences, comes through strongly. In admitting that he had given up searching for a better quality of sound materials and had concentrated on syntax without that, AV admitted defeat on attaining both goals together — syntax and better sound materials. It is arguable, then, that he had compromised on the project's basic aim: developing a syntax out of the improved sound materials, or timbral transitions, themselves. He conveys that the quality of noise, and so the timbres, that he had been given on the 4X were crude, inorganic, and unmusical — totally different from that with Chant. Further, he hints at a psychoacoustic puzzle whereby the scientifically analyzed spectrum did not in this period, when strictly technologically reproduced, have enough high-frequency energy — what he calls "rubbish" — in it: "you cut off above 8K and you *kill* the voice completely. You do a spectral analysis and there's nothing up there."

In recent years, the computer analysis and simulation of complex spectra has improved, so that some of the subtlety of "organic noise" that was missing for AV in 1984 can now be achieved. Nonetheless, these observations are important because they highlight some phenomenological limits of the technology. First, AV was pointing out that against expectations, additive synthesis could not in practice provide the same timbral qualities as Chant, let alone surpass what Chant offered. This contradicts the view that when given enough sheer power, computer music technologies can, through translation between codes, provide absolutely equivalent facilities. This omnipotent view of the technologies as extremely general and infinitely adaptable—of any one technology as transformable into another by sufficient translation—seemed widely held within IRCAM. Indeed it was the technical concept at the basis of the project. Rather, the story suggests that the different technologies had specific, inherent qualities and limits and were not ultimately assimilable: that they were not infinitely malleable, "open" texts.

Second, AV's experience demonstrates how even computer-aided analysis of the spectra of complex timbres at this time could fail to capture some extremely subtle movements of very high frequencies—the "rubbish" or "microevolutions"—that were not then modeled by the software. This points to another important phenomenological insight: the technology's nonequivalence to "real" sound. Again, it was held within IRCAM that computer music technologies, despite their inherent digital approximations of what are complex physical processes, can and do provide aural simulations that are functionally and perceptually equivalent to "real" sound. AV was questioning this view, pointing to the limits of computer analysis and simulation and the problems with computer timbres achieving fully organic timbral qualities. He was raising the nonequivalence of the two domains of aural experience. Such a view should not, of course, be news to IRCAM intellectuals. What was surprising was their willingness to forget that computer generated timbres are simulations, representations of extremely subtle physical and aural phenomena, and are therefore likely to differ from them. But IRCAM ideology, with its implicit evolutionist principle of technologically led aesthetic progress, held to the computer's power to produce absolute equivalence—its ability to "equal" and, on that basis, to surpass ambient music—rather than being interested in the possibilities of difference.

In the end, MC asked AV to tell his criticisms to RIG, whose idea the whole technological configuration had been. Underlying this were the nationalist and ideological tensions mentioned earlier, between the

(French) IRCAM software designers and the proponents of (American) patch languages. Thus, while RIG thought that additive synthesis could do anything that Chant could do, MC, leader of Chant/Formes, believed that Chant had unique properties that patch languages such as additive synthesis — whatever sheer computing power they had driving them — could not achieve, a view that AV had just corroborated.

CHAPTER IX

Aporias

*Technological and Social Problems
around Production*

AV's project raises some general features and problems of IRCAM's research and production that I now want to pursue, issues concerning technological dependence and the instability of the research environment. One of AV's main complaints concerned the lengthy delays and slowness of the system, which was compounded by its constant crashing. These problems can be illustrated by the following diary extract from a particularly crisis-ridden week.

14.5.84: Big problems with the VAX and 4X: the VAX is crashing all the time and was down a lot last week. There is much competition for 4X time: three projects — AV, HY and his assistant WOW, and another composer — are all vying aggressively, tension is high. HY is desperate: he has to finish the computer tape for the premiere of his new piece at the CGP in 4 days.
At midnight, after the *Espace Libre*, there is an argument in the hall over access to the 4X.
AV says: "I've had four days with no time or progress — because the 4X was down most of yesterday and today, there were problems Friday and I was away Saturday! I've got a piece hardly started, which has to be done in twenty days! The program that works worst is Roc, which I'm totally dependent on. It crashes constantly!"
HY replies angrily: "I've got half an unfinished tape, and a first performance on Friday! I've *got* to have more time this week!"
WOW adds: "We just need more time on the 4X. . . ."
Later, over supper, tension drops and HY says half desperately, half jokingly: "Has anyone got a spare piece of tape music I can use for the last half of my piece?!"
16.5.84: There are complaints about the VAX and its programs crashing and

causing big problems from four tutors. They blame the Systems manager, FA, who is away while the major changeover of UNIX from 4.1 to 4.1a is happening: bad planning.

WOW despairs that he has lost half a directory of important files that he is using.

AV says: "I deleted the 'People' directory[1] by mistake last night because of the chaos of disk space on the VAX, and XX deleted all my Roc files! Now I've got to start them all over again!"

AV is furious that they're changing the basic operating system while he's working with the system under pressure. He thinks it's an insult and says he feels like giving up.

NP (squatter-composer) has decided to stay at home to work because it's so frustrating here, with the crashes and overload making the system so slow.

The constant breakdowns of the main computers had several causes, local and more general. Locally, due to the several new programs for AV's project, the new translations of Chant and Formes, and the constant rewriting of them all, there were bugs continually appearing that needed to be corrected. Meanwhile they caused the programs to crash, which in turn sometimes also caused the PDP11 or the VAX to crash. A new piece of software linking two machines, called the "fast link," also caused many crashes; its design was not right. The new Roc program failed to work properly. The link between the PDP11 and 4X was poorly synchronized, which caused the 4X to crash. Then there was a lack of memory and disk space reserved for AV's big files; so that when he ran a big file to compute samples it caused the VAX or PDP11 to crash. Some of this could have been avoided by better resource planning. AV summed up the situation thus: "The VAX was going up and down like a yoyo: it was down for a number of days or came down every hour or two, which meant your job crashes in midstream. If the VAX comes down five or six times a day, the likelihood of finishing one second of sound is small." Thus the scale of new software that it had been decided to create for AV's project made it impossible to stabilize the configuration for productive use within the time available.

But the wider causes of the constant crashes of the VAX and its programs were, first, chronic overloading and congestion, and more importantly, the changeover from UNIX 4.1 to 4.1a. Overloading was exacerbated by the squatters who came in each evening to use the VAX: composers, but also the computer scientists from Vincennes, among them a Professor with high status at IRCAM. In fact, it was unclear who was responsible for managing access to the VAX, as the following illustrates.

Congestion reached extreme proportions in the summer of '84, when the *stage* coincided with another composer's production visit, and there was much crashing of the VAX. This led to the Systems team taking constant measures to "clear space" on the system by deleting various files and programs they judged to be using too much space and to be expendable. Their job was thus, within limits, to coercively manage the system. In this period, typical daily messages from the Systems team to all VAX users were concerned with managing space and resources, as shown by the first two messages in Figure 12. A week later the situation was worsening and more drastic measures were planned, as shown by the third message. The top of this one reveals a telling problem: that the Systems team did not know to whom all the programs on the system belonged, who had authored them.[2] Congestion was at crisis level a week later when Boulez called Systems manager FA in and told him to police the system more fiercely. FA reported him saying: "You're not doing your job properly! You should be removing these unofficial users who are blocking up the system!" FA was amazed, since he considered this a new degree of coercion in his job. Boulez insisted, so that FA sent out the final message shown, which by reference to Boulez's authorization details exactly who were the heaviest users of the VAX and threatens to forcibly remove their excess files. The list makes it clear that IRCAM's in-house researchers were the heaviest users and, against the official view, that squatters did not take up much space. At this point, then, the VAX was overloaded due mainly to official research, and there was much talk of the need to get a second VAX.

The decision to upgrade from UNIX 4.1 to 4.1a was taken partly to link IRCAM up to a major new networking facility. But 4.1a was also needed to support new machines called "Valids" that, in turn, were going to act as workstations for the new 4X units once they were delivered by Sogitec. 4.1a was to be the basis of a network linking these 4Xs via the Valids to the VAX. Thus the drive to upgrade came from the 4X groups and was intended to serve the looming Parisian premiere of *Répons*. Because this changeover involved rewriting the basic coding of all programs in use on the system, it was bound to throw up many bugs, so it would take weeks to debug the system and get back to normal operating. At one level this was simply a poorly timed and badly communicated move. Despite the changeover having been planned for six months, and despite weeks of preparation by the American consultants doing it, a week beforehand many IRCAM tutors and major users of the system apparently knew nothing of the impending chaos. FA decided to go

From: FA   Thu Jun 28 10:13:29 1984
Subject: /people is full
Please start archiving your files onto tape using tar(1).

From FA: Thu Jun 28 14:48:39 1984
Subject: Allotment of sound disk space
The *stage* is going to use the disk /snd.
The removable disk (/snd1 and /snd2) is exclusively reserved for BLr's
production.
The disk /snd3 is reserved for the transfer of files from one disk to
another. Only certain authorized users have the right to use it (notably me, WOW and WUA during BLr's production). ABOVE ALL do not touch the
removable disk without being authorized.

[More Urgent Message Sent a Week Later]

SYSTEM CLEAN UP: the following programs disappear today unless someone identifies the author:
                    loadst queens quiest filt cref disp dx tab trucs

A Poem by the VAX. Understand it and you may avoid Armageddon:
                    Where did all the disk space go,
                    Since last winter in the Paris snow?
                    It was a time when our problem had no Formes,
                    And our ways to analyse it had not been Born.

                    Oh where did all our disk space go?
                    Does someone want to make me slow?
                    One cannot compose without a space,
                    So free some now; get rid of your waste.

[Final Warning]

From: FA   Thu July 12 16:38:12 1984
Pierre Boulez has told me personally to make sure that NO individual
uses more than 2500 blocks of disk space. He said if it is not done by the
end of the week, I am to do it for you, i.e. REMOVE files:

4773	JDK	[Ex Chant/Formes, tutor]
4081	XU	[Chant/Formes computer scientist]
3572	AJ	[4X Signal Processing director]
3470	UO	[postgraduate researcher]
3443	YI	[Systems team]
3246	NGF	[programmer between contracts, so a squatter]
3222	BX	[4X Software team, programmer]
etc....		

12.   Systems messages aimed at managing space on the overloaded VAX, summer 1984. (By permission of the author.)

ahead, ignoring protests from those with urgent production needs, no
doubt himself under some pressure. He was absent from IRCAM during
the crucial week, for which he received an *avertissement* from Boulez.
Within two months he had left IRCAM.

But at a deeper level the need to upgrade and change the operating
system to a new American standard (UNIX 4.1a had been developed at
Berkeley) in order to link to an American-based international network
and American machines derived from IRCAM's dependence upon American technologies, related in turn to America's leading edge in computer
science research and development in this period. We have already seen
another symptom: IRCAM's profound dependence during its first decade on skilled American computer labor. In '84 this was as acute as ever,
and IRCAM searched the United States for its new Systems manager
when FA left.

Similarly, the previous major change in the IRCAM system, the
changeover in mid-1983 from the PDP10 to the VAX, was caused by another recurrent symptom of technological dependence. DEC, the American corporate manufacturers of both machines, gradually raised the service charges on the PDP10 until it became uneconomical to keep it and
better to upgrade and buy their new "standard," the VAX, with its lower
service charges.[3] DEC enjoyed a virtual international monopoly on the
standard minicomputers at this time. Several researchers, as well as the
Systems manager, spoke of the irrationality of the enforced "passing" of
the PDP10, since it was working well for music production and IRCAM's
software was adapted to it. This changeover had also brought a crisis of
rewriting software just as Chant and other programs had been stabilized
for use.

Thus technological dependence and the chronic, cyclical instability of
the computing environment this causes, exacerbated by the retranslation
of all software required each time a basic dimension of the overall system
is changed, were major factors in the apparently "local" technological
problems of instability and unreliability. The extreme instability and
rapid obsolescence were embodied in the many bits of discarded computer technology and peripherals strewn chaotically around IRCAM's
corridors. Some were no more than a couple of years old, yet they lay
around as though suddenly useless. But notably, of all IRCAM's technological problems, although I raised this issue many times, informants
had little to say and were uninterested in the subject. It seems that despite
its profound effects (uncertainty, constant running to keep up, and economic pressure), the phenomenon of technological dependence on the

United States was so self-evident as to be considered banal. There was a determined blindness toward the threat of cumulative technological disadvantage that such dependence brings.

IRCAM's technological dependence was enforced financially, through rising service charges imposed by the American multinationals, but it was equally induced by the seductive desire to keep abreast of the latest, state-of-the-art research environments (such as the latest version of UNIX), without which it was feared that IRCAM research would be outdated. There seemed to be a continuing element of false consciousness in IRCAM's dependency trap: a belief in the need to constantly "keep up with the States" in terms of prestigious hardware and associated software. These were effects, then, of American multinational leadership and control of standardization in this high-technology sector, which in turn brought premature obsolescence to technologies such as the PDP10 that were still entirely functional. This obsolescence was not built-in; it was imposed. Setting the standards and constantly revising them upward gave American corporations in this period the power internationally to force other national research outfits to upgrade and adopt their new standards.[4] IRCAM was, in the mid-1980s, fully caught within this dependency trap.

Ironically, IRCAM's technological dependence and instability were originally stoked by the desire to compete technologically with its rivals in the United States. The initial talks about IRCAM's infrastructure at a "summit meeting" of directors and consultants at Baden-Baden in 1976 resulted in a decision not to buy a copy of the "Samson box," the Stanford CCRMA's machine, which would have provided a tried and tested music hardware and software environment. Instead, management pushed for IRCAM to put its resources behind developing its own new hardware, which became the 4X project, and this in turn meant buying the DEC PDP10 as a research computer.[5] IRCAM's technological dependence thus derived from the politically fueled decision to ignore the ready-made Stanford facilities and develop IRCAM's own prestigious prototype, to which end it was necessary to become linked in to the leading American technologies.

The second general issue illustrated by the chronic congestion and the UNIX 4.1a story is the weakness of IRCAM's resource planning, its lack of scientific and technological management. The problem was commented on by both staff and visitors to IRCAM. It was picked up by Boulez in a Scientific Committee meeting attended by most production staff following AV's departure, at which he berated them for AV's problems and the failure to produce a piece. The meeting began with Boulez announcing the departure of the incumbent Scientific Director, who had held the position for barely a year and had found it increasingly difficult to control the quasi-autonomous subcultures and to balance the other power structures within the institute. As the meeting progressed, Boulez became angry with the lack of coordination between teams and the poor state of equipment. The teams' noncooperation was demonstrated even in the meeting when the 4X designer blamed Formes for being a mess and causing the 4X to crash. Eventually Boulez blew up and began the monologue quoted in chapter 5 in which he threatened to bring in an "autocrat" as Scientific Director. But there was a significant displacement here, since one of the main causes of trouble had been the switch to 4.1a for the requirements of Boulez's own *Répons*. The Systems manager, who received the lion's share of blame, said to me that he had been overridden by these pressures — that the basis of the chaos in the requirements of the 4X and *Répons* was never made explicit in meetings, but that everybody knew. The "irrationality" of technological planning derived also, then, from these implicit pressures, the general sense of chaos no doubt compounded by the culture of silence.

Despite Boulez's view of AV's visit as a debacle, stalwarts of the musicians' vanguard continued to defend it as a risky but productive research project that had explored the possibilities and limits of the technological configuration. From this perspective, no high-level research is without its payoffs. Yet AV did not return to use an improved version of the configuration, and the new programs were not preserved or documented. So it is doubtful whether they were reused in another context, and the visit must go down as one of IRCAM's more expensive and unproductive projects. On the other hand, with the benefit of hindsight AV considers nowadays that all his IRCAM visits, including this one, contributed ideas toward a later piece that has been his most successful yet[6] and that has won an international prize. Thus, AV maintains that from his point of view something very positive eventually came out of the earlier "failure."

TECHNOLOGICAL "IRRATIONALITY": NEGLECT OF THE ANALOG TAPE MEDIUM

A final cause of AV's troubles, deriving from broader problems within IRCAM, was the chaotic state of some of the machinery that he was using. In particular, he found the DACs and the analog tape recording facilities in the 4X studio in very poor condition: they lacked maintenance and were poorly set up for work. AV found that the ways to link up the 4X, the DACs, and the mixing desks were complex and were not generally known, so that, amazed and frustrated, he had to reconstruct this information for himself. Having done this he wrote a step-by-step guide and stuck it onto the mixing console for future visitors. The poor state of the machines was shown by the problem mentioned earlier of mysterious "gremlins" in the mixer that caused the amplitude meters to wave around, as well as by clicks and noises coming from both the mixer and the DACs. At times AV's sounds were full of extraneous clicks, and it was hard to know if they were caused by bugs in the programs, or improper use of them, or the DACs, or the mixer, so they were impossible to trace and remove.

Thus, not all technological problems were due to instability and dependence; they were also due to neglect. For purchased hardware and peripherals, IRCAM had service contracts. But for hard and soft technologies made at IRCAM (the 4X, peripherals such as the ADCs and DACs), and especially for IRCAM's analog audio technologies (tape recorders, mixers), there was no external and little routine internal servicing. In '84 the Hardware maintenance technician left IRCAM and was not replaced for a period, while the one audio maintenance technician was relocated by Boulez to look after 4X Hardware and again was not immediately replaced. The Sound team did not consider maintenance to be their job. Analog audio equipment was therefore particularly neglected, its servicing erratic, which explains its sorry state.

Several further phenomena indicate a striking neglect of and uninterest in the uses of analog tape technology within IRCAM that was deeper than the general technological problems. First, neglect of the recording medium is shown by the fact that so little attention was paid within IRCAM to recording, compared with the quantity of live musical performance. This is suggested by IRCAM's slowness in starting its own record series.[7] It is most glaringly shown by the neglect to record, even for archives, the *Passage du Vingtième Siècle*. The concert series contained many premieres and performances of pieces rarely heard and was thus a unique opportunity to capture the music for posterity.[8] The *Passage*'s exclusive emphasis on live, unrepeatable performance thus highlights the ritual, cultish, prestige-oriented nature of the series.

Further, IRCAM was slow in moving over to digital audio technology in the recording studios and appeared to give it very low economic priority.[9] Even without digitalization, IRCAM lacked basic studio tools, so that AV reported with frustration, "It's due to me making a fuss that there are even tape splicing blocks in the studios!" IRCAM also lacked powerful analog recording facilities, although those available were of high quality. This is conveyed by the following diary note from my first visit, when I was shown around IRCAM with several others by a music director.

> In the recording studios, I was surprised to learn that IRCAM considers 8 or 16 track recording facilities sufficient for their needs; surprised, since in professional popular music production these days less than 16 tracks is considered ridiculous and the norm would be 24, 32 tracks or more. Listening to the director discuss this with another visitor on the tour, a middle-aged, senior American classical music producer who recorded orchestras, their consensus was that the push towards more tracks in recording was an unnecessary commercial conspiracy, fetishizing the technology. Their reasons: the American orchestra producer because he wanted an "ambient," live, room-acoustic sound (common in classical music recording because of the expense, complexity, and fear of single-instrument recording, or of many "takes," where a live recording is hopefully complete in one), the IRCAM director because, he said, with their digital sound synthesizing facilities, more than 8 tracks is unnecessary since so much of the sound processing is done before recording.

The orchestra producer here exhibits an ideology of recording and electronic transformation that was also characteristic of IRCAM's Sound team, who recorded and mastered most IRCAM commissions, and so of IRCAM's dominant aesthetic. This ideology, common among musicians inexperienced or uninterested in recording or electronic media but also propagated by some classical music record producers, holds that the proper approach to recording and amplifying acoustically based or similarly subtle musics is to aim to faithfully reproduce the ambient (live) sound as exactly as possible. The IRCAM sound engineers, for example, when setting up the amplification of my cello for a concert in which I played, talked of "simply keeping the controls flat. We're not doing anything to the sound! It's just as you play it!" The notion here is that by keeping the electronic controls "flat," the acoustic sound remains essentially unaltered by amplification apart from greater volume. In the same way, classical engineers tend to use the controls of the mixing desk minimally in recording, believing this leaves the acoustic sound of instruments relatively "authentic" and undistorted by electronic intervention.

However, this ideology misperceives the nature of these media, since even with the controls "flat," sounds are completely transformed by live amplification or by recording and playback. This occurs simply by virtue of sounds being "captured" by microphones, with their inherent acoustical biases, and by amplification, both of which alter the relationship between the sounds' component frequencies, boosting some and cutting others, and altering the timbre. In fact, amplifying or recording acoustic instruments such as strings without altering their frequency spectra often produces distorted sounds. In short, sounds cannot remain untransformed by recording and amplification: there is no way of retaining the "natural" or "authentic" acoustic sound when using electronic mediation.

The IRCAM/classical music ideology of recording is, then, naively purist and ignores the profound transformation of sound inherent in all electronic or taped reproduction — another naiveté concerning the phenomenology of the technological mediation of sound that is surprising in a culture such as IRCAM. In striking contrast to this purist ideology, popular music producers have since the 1950s embraced the aesthetic possibilities inherent in the electronic and tape-based transformation of sound. Even more than the tradition of *musique concrète*, popular music aesthetics have centered on amplification and "distortion" effects, manipulating the timbre of sounds through recording, and since the mid-1960s, on layering sounds by multitrack recording. IRCAM's absence of awareness of the aesthetic potential of recording techniques and multitracking was remarked upon by AV, who had experience in pop music production and was greatly frustrated by IRCAM's analog facilities. He said, "If there's one thing I'd do if I had the power, it would be to get a top [pop] record producer in here for a year to teach good studio techniques!" Similar comments were made by a junior tutor who had positive experience of pop studio work that he kept hidden from IRCAM.[10]

There are two further observations to be made on this material. First, in the context of high-quality digital sound synthesis, it is irrational to neglect digital recording, since unwanted noise eliminated at great effort during the synthesis stage is likely to be reintroduced by lower-quality analog recording equipment — exactly as happened to AV. Second, the director's view cited above in the diary, and widely articulated within IRCAM, that more powerful recording technology was unnecessary, ignores the fact that whatever the quality and complexity of synthesized sound inputs, multitrack recording yields different aesthetic possibilities through empirical experiment with several such sounds simultaneously in real time, thereby allowing mutual modification. The director's uninterest in the aesthetics of multitracking related to another view expressed by a few individuals from IRCAM's vanguard: a disdain for polyphony, music constructed by the movement of several "voices" against one another. In this perspective polyphony is outdated, since it is irrelevant to the unique aesthetic potential of computer music, such as the ability to explore processes of timbral syntax or the movement of partials within a timbral object.

In the face of all this, we must ask why IRCAM showed such a strong neglect of and uninterest in analog electronic and tape media. These phenomena expressed IRCAM's attempt to define itself through the construction of both technological and aesthetic difference. In this way IRCAM differentiated itself, first, from the "empiricist," tape-based tradition of its close rival, *musique concrète* at the GRM. Less consciously, this character of IRCAM expressed its absolute difference from the techniques and aesthetics of popular music. At the same time, the contempt for analog technologies also embodied IRCAM's rejection of the previous generation of music technology, which was therefore seen as useless to IRCAM compared with digital technology. Hence also IRCAM's purist taboo on mixed analog and digital technologies, which would defy the boundary and confuse the assertion of difference — an issue raised by two of IRCAM's technological dissidents, PL and NI, both of whom in this period saw mixed technologies as yielding greater power and flexibility for fewer resources. IRCAM's music-technological culture was defined, then, by a complex and overlapping set of assertions of difference.

THE CHARACTER OF COLLABORATIVE AUTHORSHIP

We have seen that there was much collaborative work in IRCAM's intellectual culture, and that for the musicians' vanguard collaboration was a utopian principle. However, the tutor-composer collaboration was founded upon differences of status, and we will see that it was experienced by tutors as exploitative and was riddled with patronage and mystification. More generally, the surface spirit of collaboration covered a great deal of competition, secrecy, and rivalry within and between IRCAM research projects.

The tutor-composer division of labor depended on and embodied the classification described earlier whereby tutors were defined as not themselves legitimate composers. This view was acceptable to those tutors who were scientists but was clearly irksome to tutors who did consider themselves composers. Sensitive commissioned composers decried the classification and spoke of their tutors as equals and composers in their own right. Nonetheless, as we saw earlier the classification was promoted by IRCAM management, and tutoring enshrined a status distinc-

tion against which musician-tutors sometimes rebelled.[11] The formal
copyright agreement on musical works produced by visiting composers
at IRCAM with a tutor's assistance specified that rights were to be divided between the composer and IRCAM. The tutor was assumed to be
recompensed by his salary; he was paid as an official for the part of his
time spent on the work. This represents, then, wages for technical labor
rather than a share in the market value of the creative intellectual goods.

However, the actual nature of tutoring labor was often more exploitative, and in a different way. As we have seen, much tutoring work was
done not by the four salaried tutors but, informally, by the exploited and
self-exploiting junior tutors, whose tutoring was entwined with seeking
patronage. They were commonly first invited to IRCAM after having
been spotted on the *stage* and were then asked to work on a commission
or a director's project. During this trial period of establishing patronage,
junior tutors were given recurrent contracts of one, two, or three months
on extremely low pay, or were occasionally unpaid. The process is conveyed by an interview with NR, a foreign junior worker who later became one of the favored "heirs."

NR: After two years studying computer music very hard [in another Euro-
      pean country] I felt prepared enough to come to IRCAM. It turned out I
      was right because I took the *stage* and I was the best one on it — not be-
      cause of gifts but because I'd studied two years more than anybody else!
      I had a very good knowledge of these programs [Music X, Chant], so I
      made examples that were interesting.

GB: And other people found them interesting?

NR: Yes, and then I was asked by AA to work with him on his piece *XYZ*,
      [*mumbled cynically*] like everybody. . . .

GB: So he asked you right after the *stage* to come and work with him on the
      piece?

NR: To keep on working with him, like an assistant [tutor], right. That was
      frustrating because I didn't want [*fades*]. . . . I had a crazy idea: I
      worked, I dunno, eighteen hours a day for him, but I knew that it was
      my only chance to stay here.

GB: How long did you do that?

NR: One and a half months.

GB: What money did you have for that?

NR: Nothing. . . . Oh I was very badly treated at IRCAM from the point of
      view of money. If you do something that you like, sometimes at the be-
      ginning you accept it. And he promised me 5,000 francs for the work of
      one and a half months, because I had to stay here, to live, to pay rent;
      and he couldn't do that.

GB: He couldn't, after he promised you?

NR: No, no. He shared his commission with me. But it was very, very little, something like 1,500 francs. At the same time I had to pay for my [composition] diploma, had to get it. That's a terrible period in which for three months I studied an average of sixteen to eighteen hours a day, including weekends.

GB: So you must have been going mad, working on that and for AA?

NR: Yes, really. That nearly drove me mad.

GB: What money were you living on at the time?

NR: A little from home, a little from teaching that I'd saved. I can live on very little money. . . . Then it was thanks to AA, and I owe him that at least very much: he was the first who had confidence in me, who invited me. We discussed the many problems in his piece, computer problems. . . . It was not. . . . It was very well thought out, but since he doesn't know how to program, all the practical man-machine interface was terrible, terribly bad. So I told him, "You have to do it like that, there must be these improvements." . . . Later I came here permanently. That was a *vacation* for 11 months, very little salary compared to other people. I had 4,400 francs net a month, more or less half as much as others. I was silly, that was also my fault. But for me it was so important to come to IRCAM that I didn't want to negotiate anything. AA promised me a good salary, and I had confidence in him, and I was wrong!

This man was quite aware of his exploitation. But ultimately, as he conveys, there were no hard feelings since the director who had used him became NR's patron, negotiated further short contracts for him, and eventually helped to get him a plum postgraduate position at a prestigious American university.

Some tutoring relationships were more mystified. One example is that between Boulez and BYV, his own long-standing in-house tutor. BYV was officially employed not as Boulez's tutor but as 4X Software director. He spoke of his unpaid work for Boulez as follows. "My main motivation for working with Pierre is not at all because that's what I'm paid to do; as a matter of fact on my contract there's no mention at all of my work with Pierre. That's simply some kind of agreement between him and myself. My main motivation is basically that Pierre is a composer who I believe in very deeply. I feel that he has the key to a lot of problems in contemporary music that no one else has. I find it stimulating to work with him for that reason." BYV's indirect rewards for tutoring Boulez were, however, substantial: his cumulative promotion up to a high directorship.

The attitude of willing and pleasurable labor shown by BYV was expressed whenever tutors worked with composers whom they respected

musically and intellectually. It was, for example, the attitude of tutors
MC, HM, and XH to working with AV. But sadly, the majority of visiting
composers were not so respected, since they were less skilled and could
be quite inept at computer music. Moreover, the tutors sometimes disliked their music. Rather than pleasurable, tutors found working with
these composers frustrating since they needed to be nursed through an
experience that they also found trying, the results of which would inevitably be musically and scientifically disappointing. This kind of "collaboration" with inept composers raises other major issues: first, the question of the authorship of a piece that is the result of collaboration, and
especially of such unequal collaboration. Often, working with unskilled
composers, tutors joked cynically between themselves that the musical
results came out uncannily similar to the tutor's own sounds and music.
Thus, one afternoon in the main corridor several tutors were chatting
together and one said jokingly to WOW, then assisting a visiting composer considered to be untalented and uninterested in the medium: "Hey,
I heard ZZ's piece this morning. Amazing how much it sounds like your
work!" and everyone giggled. WOW was known for his individual, rich,
and expressive use of the medium; he himself considered that pieces that
emerged from his tutoring work often bore signs of his own musical
personality.

On the other hand, tutors were also concerned with possible "guilt by
association." Being employed to help composers who were untalented in
the medium could mean becoming identified with an end result, a piece,
that was far below the tutor's own standards, with the fear of damaging
one's reputation. Perhaps these veiled tensions underlay tutor CX's article criticizing the work of the composer Höller, in which he implied that
Höller had not used the medium successfully and was overly dependent
on his tutor's (CX's) help (chapter 7).

The question of authorship centers ultimately on the fact that whatever the form in which composers gave their input, it was often the tutors
who did much of the actual hands-on work: conceiving and arranging
the technological configuration, writing the dedicated software, writing
the files within the programs that produced the actual computer music
output, controlling the recording process, and so on. Composers' input
came in a variety of forms: from carefully prepared scores and sophisticated technological ideas to extremely vague and unprepared ideas. Two
examples can illustrate. A British composer arrived to do his computer
tape with well-developed ideas, leaving the completion of the full instrumental and vocal score for his mixed ensemble and tape piece until after

leaving IRCAM, whereas a French composer, tutored by WOW, arrived with very loose, fanciful ideas for his piece, conveyed by a few rapidly drawn graphic texts that caused much general amusement. It was to be based on sound materials drawn from recordings of the phrase "I love you" spoken in many languages.

Especially in such cases, but even when composers arrived with fully developed scores, the tutor had to translate the composer's ideas into IRCAM's technological terms, communicate that to the composer, and then enable the ideas to be realized with the available tools. The tutor thus intervened conceptually, technically, and physically in the composer's plans, commonly doing much of the practical realization. The key issue here concerns the weight of the creative contribution of such "technical" realization in musics such as IRCAM computer music that are based essentially on new sound materials as much as on new forms of organization, and in which form may derive from sound materials. Tutors, in conceiving and manipulating the technology, were directly responsible for producing the new sound materials, so that their contribution was central to this music and their part in the overall creative authorship of the piece considerable.

However, certain visiting composers had some knowledge of, at the least, electronic music and recording techniques, and so were less dependent on the tutor's mediation. One visiting composer considered that although he owed a lot to his tutor — for which he was determined that the tutor would always be credited in program notes — the authorship of the piece was, nonetheless, his. This man had substantial experience of electronic music and was therefore not completely reliant on his tutor's help.

The deeper issues raised by the question of authorship of musical works developed through collaboration are aired in the following exchange with Boulez's tutor, BYV. Boulez was known to refrain from hands-on work and to delegate the practical-technological dimension to BYV. Despite this, BYV firmly places ultimate authorship with Boulez and espouses an ideology in which he is the technical aide who realizes Boulez's musical vision.

BYV: During the *Collège de France* [Boulez's seminars] I ran a psycho-acoustical experiment. . . . From then on I was working on Pierre's seminars, at first in a kind of light collaboration, and then more intensely.

GB: Do you actually get on well with Pierre?

BYV: Oh yeah.

GB: Regarding your experimental work with Pierre, do you have an ongoing regular work period with him?

BYV: Yeah. It's a bit difficult with Pierre because he has his commitments outside and so our work is irregular. But it's . . . ongoing, and for a number of things we're on the same wavelength and so we understand each other pretty well.

GB: So you'll discuss things and try things out, and then do you continue working on things while he's away?

BYV: That's right. Sometimes he gives me a small task or a big task, and when he comes back he listens to the result.

GB: Do you feel that your role is translating Pierre's ideas into actual practice, working on the machine? I mean, does Pierre himself have much contact with sitting at the machine and working?

BYV: No, no. When we first started working together I made him work on the machine. But you know, it's like an instrument, you have to keep at it regularly. And Pierre was too irregular so his progress really wasn't that [good]. . . . It's basically out of a positive feeling that I work for him. Otherwise, I would not work with other composers; I would not be a tutor going from one musical universe to another, of varying quality. What I find satisfying in the work with Pierre is the sense of continuity in time. Because on the one hand there's an ongoing project, which is *Répons*, and there are other projects coming over the horizon, and there's working on problems that go beyond particular pieces. The particular pieces are a kind of detail. So it's the ongoing work over time. . . .

But as to whether composers should ultimately work independently, I don't know. That's a little bit idealistic. A lot of people will work by themselves simply because the kids who are growing up nowadays will become familiar with computers. But of course in the last analysis, the computer is just a tool. In the end what is more important is the intelligence of the musician, the composer. So there's a certain going *beyond* the fact that we use the computer or don't use it.

GB: But how about that argument that since you're actually working not just with structure, the conceptual imagination of the composer, but with the production of sound material itself? There's the point about: when you hear people saying here, "Oh that piece, that's all so-and-so's . . ." i.e. the tutor's, because it's got his characteristic sound. I wonder what you feel about the question of how much the other tutors' or your own contribution to the final result is recognized? With Pierre maybe you don't feel that your contribution is terribly high profile in the final result?

BYV: It's hard to say. I've been working with Pierre certainly longer than any tutor here has been working with any other composer, almost five years. What you're raising is, in a collaboration of that kind, the question of authorship. *My* attitude is that the unquestioned author of *Répons* or any piece that I work on with Pierre is Pierre himself, there's no question about that. The solutions that I work on with him will obviously to a certain extent bear parts of my personality. But in the deepest sense of authorship, there's no question that Pierre is by far the main author. And that's not necessarily something that bothers me. The only thing that did for a time . . . when I first started working for him, I didn't always feel that I got enough recognition for the work that I did for him. But that's changed.

GB: For example in publicity, having you clearly on it?

BYV: Yes, things like that. It's a small gesture but it's important.

In this exchange BYV depicts the tutor-composer division of labor as almost a manual-mental one, with "deep" musical authorship firmly Boulez's. Regarding the future of computer music, BYV remained uncertain as to whether the tutor's role will wither away and saw that as "idealistic." Other IRCAM music intellectuals did believe that tutoring was a transient stage in the evolution of the field and that it would become obsolete with the diffusion of computing expertise among the young, a view that helped to numb their ambivalence toward their tutoring roles in the present. But in the interview above BYV evaded the basic issue: that is, if the highest aims of computer music at IRCAM, those centered on the unique musical possibilities of the computer (as with AV's project), involve the unification of sound materials and form, then it becomes problematic to retain the distinction between simple "manual," technical realization of materials (tutor) and higher conceptual and formal work (composer).

Thus, according to the logic of IRCAM's own vanguard we can see that the hierarchical ideology surrounding the tutor-composer division of labor was largely a leftover from earlier forms of music making, a mystification obfuscating and devaluing the creative contribution of the tutor or whoever does the intimate conceptual and hands-on work with the technology. This suggests another antinomy central to IRCAM: on the one hand, a reification of individual authorship replete with the romantic conception of the heroic and individualist artist — a striking romantic survival within a present modernism, and evidence of the continuity between romanticism and modernism; on the other, a practice in which authorship becomes multiple and in which it may be difficult to reconstruct the lines of individuality. IRCAM was therefore a site of absolute if repressed confrontation between the continuing power of the romantic ideology of authorship and its practical and material transcendence. We have seen forces operating in both directions. But overall, the rhetoric of individual authorship remained firmly in place at IRCAM.

The strongest force for its retention was the importance of artistic charisma in the legitimation of institutionalized, nonmarket cultural production: IRCAM's need to legitimize and valorize itself by reference to a series of significant names, if not of significant musical works or technologies. While management, mindful of external legitimation, was constantly engaged in the reproduction of such a rhetoric, within the institute many experienced its contradiction directly in their everyday working lives.

THE "ORAL CULTURE" OF RESEARCH: LIBERTY AND SECRECY

Within the research and production sphere, we have seen that there was an ethos of collaboration, openness, and the cooperative sharing of knowledge linked to IRCAM's image of itself as an oral culture, and together these imbued the culture with a utopian and libertarian spirit. But as well as this, workers were preoccupied with security and secrecy, and the sharing of knowledge was structured by patronage. This relates to IRCAM's chronic problem of lack of documentation of its research and to tensions over intellectual property. As we have seen, the lack of documentation was perceived as a problem both internally and externally, and many IRCAM researchers admitted that there was a failure within IRCAM to develop fully much of the research and programming to the stage where it could be diffused more widely and used by others. Yet at the same time some of those same researchers hotly defended the need for long-term basic research cycles unburdened by calls to stabilize and document. Further factors exacerbated this documentation problem, some of them specific to IRCAM, while others are general phenomena related to the character of the technologies, and in particular, to software as a medium.

The notion of IRCAM as an oral culture, as mentioned earlier, was initially decreed by Berio. The Pedagogy director recalled it thus: "Berio made the famous statement, which became law, that he would have *no documentation* in his studio, because 'music is an oral culture.' This was crazy, but it became the standard here, so that BU [4X Hardware designer], for example, has never bothered to document his work."

We have seen that "openness" and "knowledge sharing" were embodied architecturally and technologically by the glass-walled offices and open-plan lab spaces, the interconnected speaker system and computer networking. They were also enacted in the many formal and informal research meetings at which staff discussed ongoing projects and tried out new ideas. In these meetings, intellectual workers acted as each other's first, internal consumers or critics, so providing a first, experimental completion of the production-consumption cycle (Hennion 1983, 189).

Knowledge sharing also occurred over time. Composers and researchers spoke of a "pool" of accumulated expertise embodied in recorded tapes of sound experiments drawn from previous visits and projects that lay around the institute and were often stored ad hoc and anonymously. Incoming composers could draw ideas from this collective pool of past ideas, unburdened by a sense of original authorial intent. Such a process may have contributed to the gradual sedimentation of an IRCAM aesthetic. The means of producing these sound experiments were likely to be lost in the haze of past, custom-built, undocumented technological configurations if they were not stored in (human) memory by one of IRCAM's permanent staff.

But above all, knowledge sharing occurred in the longer-term collaborations between researchers or with composers, and in the constant informal consultations exchanged between workers trying to understand and use new bits of hardware and, especially, software. Over the working week, as we saw in AV's project, researchers dropped in and visited one another to ask for help with problems that arose or to enquire about possible resources. All of this informal consultation was by word of mouth. It was an oral culture of mutual help largely unaided by documentation, since the technologies in question were usually still work in progress and not yet stabilized or custom-built one-off programming solutions. In either case, documenting the tools was not deemed to be a priority or necessary to the researchers who were knowledgeable about them. Most intellectual staff were amused by the epithet "oral culture" for IRCAM, with its egalitarian and collectivist overtones. These aspects of IRCAM's technological culture appeared to express a healthy disregard for individual authorship in favor of collective endeavor, as well as a disdain for the fixing of research in textual form, which would enable it to become realized as intellectual property. The oral, collaborative ethos appeared also to counter the many rivalrous and ideological divisions within IRCAM's intellectual sphere outlined in previous chapters.

However, things were not so simple. For one thing, visitors did not perceive the culture in this way. An American computer science consultant questioned the collaborative ethos, commenting that "the major contrast for me between Lucasfilm and IRCAM is that there's no cooperation here, no one works together!" Moreover, IRCAM's educational software license legally enjoined the institute to maintain the security of the commercial software, such as UNIX, that it received. This involved protecting the source code, the basic level of the software, from being spied on, copied, or tampered with. Thus commercial interests and legal structures were supposed to prevent all levels of this technology from being openly accessible.

The Systems team said that it was as a condition of obtaining UNIX that they had been obliged to set up IRCAM's first computer security system, a system whereby access to working on the VAX was limited to those who had been allocated a secret individual password that they had to use when they first logged on. Before UNIX came there had been no such security system limiting use of the main system, so in principle anyone could log on. This had been a basic tenet of IRCAM's anarcho-libertarian computer subculture, led by a few internal programmers and the computer science squatters from Vincennes, including the Professor, a leading figure in French AI. The anarchists were proponents of an ideology widespread in international computer cultures and supported by the technical difficulty of protecting computer data, the view that computer technology is inherently democratic and an anathema to notions of private property in knowledge. For example, several of the Chant/Formes group held this perspective, which related to their advocacy of software that evolves through a process of gradual input from users, a process of communal authorship. The Systems manager FA reported that when he had first introduced the password system, several of the computer anarchists refused to comply and would accept no password. They vowed to subvert the security, considering it to be ineffective window dressing in any case. This had set the scene for a half-serious, ongoing game of ideological, pseudoguerilla warfare around the issue of security between the anarchists and FA's Systems team, perceived as the system "police."

Ironically, the members of the Systems team were sympathetic to the anarchist view and ambivalent toward security and their managerial role, so they oscillated between "policing" and themselves subverting the security controls. Central to the password system were "superusers": privileged users of the system who, for management purposes, knew a common "superuser" password that allowed them access to all levels of the system, even its secret code. By contrast, users with ordinary passwords gained access to restricted areas of the system. Only Systems team members were supposed to be superusers and to know the superuser password. During mid-1984, however, it became apparent to me that knowledge of the superuser password was more widespread and that the Systems team would let it be known to those with whom they were friendly or who were pragmatically useful. Thus, several of the senior scientific figures knew it, as well as a few senior programmers; once I had become a friend and intimate with the team I was let in on it, and a visiting computing consultant, BW, a close friend of Systems manager FA, also knew it. FA admitted that even his supposed "ideological opponent," the squatter-Professor from Vincennes, knew the superuser password.

Rather than functioning as a guarantor of security, the password was therefore a currency with restricted access structured by the exercise of patronage, and one that by virtue of its excessive diffusion had currently become debased. Indeed, its content was a meaningful joke. In this period the superuser password was "Men at Work," the name of a then highly successful Australian pop group. The Systems manager FA and his friend BW were Australian, and the password, invented by FA, was a poke in the eye for both IRCAM's high musical pretensions and those of the security system, since it vested the ultimate technological power of IRCAM in a fizzy "Ozzie" pop group.

On the other hand, the anarchic "openness" of access to information at IRCAM also created ambivalence among IRCAM intellectuals; as I showed earlier, it became akin to constant surveillance and denied them privacy for their work in progress. So workers concocted their various informal ways of protecting privacy and retaining secrecy: blocking the glass walls of their studios, working at night to prevent others knowing what they were doing or even whether they were working at all. Two incidents gave me firsthand experience of the fear of surveillance and intrusion.

Several months into fieldwork I was writing an early paper about IRCAM on a word-processing editor on the VAX, being careful to work only at nights and weekends to avoid informants' curiosity. One Sunday the following incident happened, as recorded in my diary.

> I'm sitting typing, almost no one about, when RIG [Pedagogy director] comes in and stumbles about in the office, glancing at what I'm doing. He says, "You're not still using 'vi'? You should use the 'emacs' editor. It's much better, I only use that nowadays." I say, "I don't know emacs, I only know vi because that's what I learned on the *stage*" — which he taught us! . . . He goes next

door. About half an hour later he comes in and says, "Excuse me for looking over your shoulder but . . ." and continues that I should learn some simple formatting rules that will automatically lay out my text. Comment: this "looking over my shoulder" means that RIG had been checking me out, spying on what I was working on at my terminal by getting into my directory and files from his terminal! I must be very careful of what I write, mustn't leave any confidential stuff in my files, because it seems that they can be examined any time. . . . Later, I get scared that RIG will tell HM, HY, and others about my article, that they'll all look and laugh at what I'm doing, turn against me.

My evident paranoia that anyone could look at my work stored on the VAX was misguided less technologically than socially.

Weeks later I asked visiting consultant BW, who had become a friend, for help with making my files more secure, and he wrote me a little program whereby I could cryptically encode my files — scramble them up and make them unreadable except by using a secret decoding device that only I (and he) knew. Later BW enlightened me about another area lacking privacy on the system: a file that stored all the past computer mail that I had sent. BW's telling me was ambiguous because it indicated that he had probably been reading my past mail — another sensitive area, since I had thought my mail confidential. These discoveries gave me a sensation of others having access to my hidden inner thoughts. The ease of access to files and data, even "protected" data, was confirmed by a *stagiaire*, an iconoclast with a flair for programming, who confided to me a few weeks into the course at IRCAM that he had found a way to see inside many confidential institute files on the VAX.

Individuals' desire to keep their work-in-progress private from rivals and critics relates also to tensions over differential access to research. The oral culture of research meant that to understand the technology one was dependent on the oral help of the informed, and as in the case of the security system, this help was socially structured by patronage, since it could be withdrawn or withheld as well as granted. Both main technology groups, 4X and Chant/Formes, were informally notorious for the exercise of patronage, and this caused much ambivalence and frustration. For example, we saw above how the 4X designer took Berio at his word by resisting the documentation of his hardware designs in the name of retaining an oral research culture. RIG described his encounter with this as follows: "I used to work on BU's machines — I did a piece on the 4A, I wrote a lot of the 4A's software. But I gave up and moved over to the PDP10 because it was impossible to work on BU's stuff! You always had to go to him to ask what was wrong, how things worked. There was never any free information. BU has always been totally secretive and not let people in on his stuff. That makes it hell to work with." This view of BU as withholding information was widely held, so that even a 4X Software researcher complained: "An oral culture! There's no documentation for the 4X, so one must go to BU or AJ [BU's assistant] for any knowledge about it." BU was therefore known for bestowing information about his hardware orally on those he wanted to patronize and for withholding it from others.

Similar views of motivated inclusion and exclusion were held about the Chant/Formes group. We saw earlier, for example, how a founding member of the project who left and took another IRCAM post for a salary raise, despite inhabiting the next-door office, found that the group would no longer confide in him. Chant/Formes also engaged in conflicts over secrecy and control with Systems manager FA. FA's job of "disinterested policing" of the main system involved knowing the location and identity of each bit of programming going on in the VAX. But FA had ongoing tussles with members of the Chant/Formes group, who hid parts of their work in the bowels of the computer, refusing to tell him. "They *hide* their source code from me!" he complained. Such an atmosphere bred retaliation. There was an angry system message from Chant/Formes director MC one day demanding to know who had "stolen" some of their essential source code. Thus, despite its advocacy of the libertarian, "open" computer philosophy, Chant/Formes was a highly bounded group. In '84, recruits to the project were limited to MC's own postgraduates.

IRCAM culture thus showed an oscillation or tension between its self-image as a collaborative and open oral culture and a combination of forces — the security imperative, informal rivalries, and researchers' desire to retain privacy for their developing work — that encouraged patronage in the structuring of access to information and that tended toward secrecy and closure. We have seen that IRCAM's utopian principles of openness and collaboration did not simply flow from its technologies, from the supposed inherently democratizing nature of tape media or of the computer. They were equally discursive principles derived from aspects of Boulez's founding vision, as well as from currents widespread in the discourse of new technology.[12] We have also seen how, in addition to official security structures, subjects invented mischievous ways of restricting access to and guarding the secrecy of their work. Ironically IRCAM's "oral culture" and lack of documentation favored secrecy and patronage; while the exercise of patronage, as we saw in earlier chapters, was in itself both a strategy for accruing power and a source of social gratification.[13]

THE UNPRODUCTIVE DRIVE:
HIGH-LEVEL SOFTWARE AS A MEDIUM

The tensions I have outlined contribute to understanding IRCAM's problems of lack of stabilization and lack of documentation of its research, problems that threatened IRCAM's research reputation and that remain significant in the 1990s.[14] The notion of an "oral culture" was in part a utopian rationalization of the chronic lack of documentation, and one that enabled patronage to flower in the realm of research. But underlying this, we can discern two further interrelated forces working against stabilization and documentation, one concerning intellectual property, the other the character of software as a medium.

The material above has shown that tutoring relationships and technological research were imbued with tensions and conflicts over intellectual property, over both the principle of intellectual authorship, itself confused by ideological and moral tensions over the relative merits of individual or collaborative labor, and "real," material interests of ownership and copyright. As well as utopian leanings, the lack of stabilization and documentation expressed subjects' insecurity as to whether their authorship would be respected, which generated ambivalence toward documenting their research. By neglecting documentation, researchers protected their work from others and appeared to retain intellectual, material, and social control over it. Of course, they also failed fully to develop or communicate their work. Further, given IRCAM's problems with industrially and commercially developing its research, and compared with the vanguardist prestige and the social and intellectual stimulation of open-ended research and collaborative bricolage, researchers' incentives for completing a product and communicating their work were very unclear.

Three factors compound this. First, we have seen that IRCAM's software research is extremely unstable due to its being embedded in a series of vertical mediations of hardware and software, all of which are themselves unstable due to technological dependence and the enforced revision of standards and premature obsolescence this entails. Since programs are continually being rewritten for new contexts and are also constantly written and then discarded, the task of documentation appears massive and, ironically, unproductive. Its value becomes debased, since a program documented this month is likely to be transcended or obsolete by next year, if not next month. In this strange symbolic hyper-economy, prestige is not so much gained by stabilized and working products as lost by not being linked in to fashionable wider developments. Hence the pressure on researchers to constantly revise their prototypes and the seduction of responding to every new conceptual and technological trend that appears on the horizon.

Second, we have seen that programs are often developed over time through the collaborative imaginative labor of several authors. Because of this inherent temporal and social mediation, the resultant baroque totality is extremely difficult to decode after the event and is thus opaque to the reconstruction of its total logic — the necessary prerequisite for documenting it. This throws new light on the security battles mentioned earlier, since according to a senior programmer, even with access to a program's full source code this code is often so complex and resistant to intuitive decoding that programmers cannot reconstruct the program's higher meaning or functioning without the help of the writer(s), or someone who already understands it — that is, without the patronage of the knowledgeable. Thus "spying on" or "stealing" the code of complex programs does not in itself allow one to decode or use the program. The hiding of source code was more a game simulating issues of control than the real locus of the issue.

Another implication of the gradual collaborative construction of software is that, even more than for the tutor-composer relation, it renders authorship problematic since it is hard to reconstruct afterward who contributed what to the program. It becomes unclear both who is in principle the intellectual author, creatively responsible (as well as responsible for documentation) and who should gain which material rights in the product if it were to be documented and fully developed — a powerful disincentive. Thus tensions of intellectual property are made particularly acute by the character of software as a medium and weigh against its full development.

A third factor in software research concerns its aesthetic dimensions. There was a conscious polarity among IRCAM researchers between those who conceived of the work in rationalist and mathematical terms and those who saw it as an art, interpretative and inexact, its practice as aesthetically imbued. Programming practice appeared to offer two implicit, unarticulated pleasures for researchers: on the one hand its impermanence, the pleasures of a bricolage that leaves few decipherable traces and so lacks accumulation, consolidation; and on the other what this presentism necessitates — the constant recourse to social mediation and oral communicative exchange, itself a site both of pleasure and, as we have seen, struggle.

In relation to IRCAM's technologies and particularly its advanced software, then, the combination of a discourse centered on the values of vanguard research and utopian collaboration, the lack of prestige, protection or financial incentives for individual authors as well as for the completion of products, the divisive ideological disputes outlined in this and earlier chapters, and all of these compounded by the material and aesthetic qualities described, worked to create a particularly self-absorbed research culture, one that was highly diffident about communicating research internally and to the outside world.

The key problems at issue here are not unique to IRCAM and are found more widely in software research in computer music and AI. Roads (1990) describes the tendency for computer music research to result in a trickle of relatively trivial technological innovations (or "demos") rather than deeper research that is systematically worked through and documented. He traces the problem to researchers' seduction by a series of external institutional and grant pressures — essentially, pressures for short-term legitimation by zappy, hyped-up results that do not so much delay as substitute for more productive and cumulative work. However, my aim in this discussion has been to stress factors internal to a research culture that lead in the same direction.

My observations also recall wider debates within AI concerning the definition of the field, and specifically, the merits of "experimental" programming (Engelmore 1980–85; Bundy 1991). This is a kind of improvisatory, pragmatic, and "empiricist" program building in the search for software that can emulate intelligent behavior, as advocated by pioneers of the field such as Marvin Minsky. Such an approach is criticized by AI "formalists" who take AI research to focus on developing mathematical principles and models that may only later be applied in actual programs. In short, formalists chide experimental methodology for failing to extract and document general principles from what are often ad hoc, messy, and overly complex programs with quite limited applications. AI music research is an area particularly associated with experimental programming, and aspects of IRCAM's research culture fit the description. Moreover the formalist/experimental division is mirrored in the polarized positions taken by IRCAM researchers mentioned earlier. In the wider AI debates, both sides appear to take a voluntarist view of

the issues — as though the question of whether AI should adopt a formalist or experimental method is simply one of competing principles (or
competing aesthetics). I have indicated structural elements of the culture
of advanced software research that resist any such voluntary change,
since they relate to the character of the medium and its technological,
economic, and social environment — elements that foster the lack of "rational" progress in research.

It is notable, finally, that the coexistence within IRCAM of the overproduction of technical codes and texts, discussed in the last chapter,
with the institute's oral culture of mutual help was far from contradictory. Rather, the oral culture was necessitated by the hypercomplexity of
those codes and texts, given the lack or weakness of informative documentation, and by the chronic instability of the environment. Evidence
suggests that some of these dynamics are more generally characteristic of
cultures of advanced software research.

CHAPTER X

Subjectivities

Difference and Fragmentation

In what follows I provide a closer reading of the differentiation of IRCAM intellectuals during 1984 in relation to the institute's two major areas of work, the musical-aesthetic and the technological, and link this to broader cultural and technological developments — that is, to the long-term discourses of modernism and postmodernism. The analysis is summarized by Figure 13, a heuristic chart that I address directly below. IRCAM subjects' positions can be seen both as informed by and yet as particular expressions of those broader discourses. The chart therefore represents an analysis of IRCAM intellectual subjects as interpreted through the lens of the earlier characterizations of modernism and postmodernism, in order to trace and make sense of their differentiation. It will become clear that not just intersubjective differences are at stake, but differences operating within certain subjectivities — various kinds of psychic fragmentation that it seems are necessary for subjects "successfully" to inhabit the wider discourses.

AESTHETICS AND TECHNOLOGY, MODERNISM AND POSTMODERNISM, WITHIN IRCAM CULTURE

At the end of chapter 2 I outlined three ways in which postmodernism is often claimed to effect a radical break with modernism. First, a new recognition of or rapprochement with popular music and culture. However, this recognition still perceives popular music and culture as an "other," to be used as a source or infiltrated. Second, an awareness of

TECHNOLOGICAL →

MUSICAL/AESTHETIC ↓	1) HIGH TECH: high capital, big machines, e.g. VAX, 4X	2) NEUTRAL, inclusive: both big and small machines	3) LOW TECH, commercial: small machines, e.g. Apple Mac, Yamaha DX7
1) MODERNIST: serialist, postserialist canon—high-cultural, elitist	BOULEZ–Director WV–Artistic Dir (Area 1)		
2) POSTMODERNIST: modernism *plus* "best" of popular culture—evaluative, objectivist, discriminatory	*BYV–Boulez's tutor, 4X Soft dir WOW–junior tutor, Chant/ Formes, (Mus Res dir), composer GE–Prof comp sci Chant / Formes team (Area 2)	*HY–Mus Res dir, composer *HM–junior tutor, psychoacoust AV–composer KF–junior tutor and composer HU–junior tutor and composer (Area 3)	*PL–composer, Apple II proj *RIG–Pedagogy dir *WL–composer, previous dir (Area 4)
3) POPULIST: pro popular culture—subjectivist, non-evaluative, consumption-oriented	BU–4X Hard dir (Area 5)	VO–4X Industrialization dir 4X team—e.g.: AJ–Signal Proc dir VR–tech Systems team, FA (Area 6)	*NI–visitor, Casio— bricoleur, composer FL–squatter, junior tutor, composer, DX7 expert (Area 7)

*Americans at IRCAM

13. Differentiation of IRCAM subjects on aesthetics and technology, 1984.

and engagement with the social and political dimensions of music and culture. Both are associated with pluralist leanings and oppose the elitist, formalist, and hierarchical character of modernism. And third, a different attitude toward and use of technology. IRCAM culture exemplifies and yet also modifies these characterizations in important ways. The ethnographic material therefore provides a more complex understanding of modernism and postmodernism as they are inhabited by IRCAM subjects.

In Figure 13 subjects' positions are mapped according to their aesthetic and technological ideologies and practices in the intersecting space between two axes: a technological axis and a musical-aesthetic axis. The analysis is based on observations and interviews from 1984 and makes reference to subjects' broader cultural allegiances — such as their cultural activities and musical tastes beyond work or biographically prior to coming to IRCAM. It does not aim to present a representative sample, but rather it indicates the range and significance of subjects' differences and strategies in this period.

The chart identifies three major and distinct positions along each axis. The technological (horizontal) axis contains three positions ranged between two extremes: proponents of high technology and those of small technology. Position 1, on the left, represents those who favor high technology, who consider large machines such as the 4X and VAX necessary for interesting music and software production, and who denigrate small, commercial machines as inferior. By contrast, position 3 on the right involves a strong advocacy of the creative power and possibilities of low-tech, small, commercial music technologies and computers, and indifference or active hostility to big machines. Position 2, in the middle, is a neutral, pragmatic, inclusive space in which subjects appreciate the possibilities of both. The two poles — advocating big machines and advocating small machines — are thus analogous to the opposition between the high-tech modernist and low-tech postmodernist technological discourses.

The musical-aesthetic (vertical) axis includes the following three positions. At the top, position 1, is the high-modernist and elitist position. In the center, position 2, is IRCAM's postmodern position, a perspective that embraces and appreciates the "best" of both modernism and popular music and culture. Most importantly, this is still an evaluative, discerning, and discriminating perspective (as is the modernist), ambivalent toward commercial interests. At the bottom, position 3, is a populist perspective, favoring popular and commercial culture, subjectivist and less evaluative, and associated with a commitment to the experience of consumption. There are thus two kinds of difference along the aesthetic axis. First, that dividing position 1 from 2 and 3, revolving around a relation or nonrelation to popular music and culture. In position 1, the modernist, popular music is an ignored or denigrated absolute "other," whereas in both positions 2 and 3 there is some kind of positive relationship with and recognition of popular music and culture. The second kind of difference is that dividing positions 1 and 2 from 3, revolving around the presence (in 1 and 2) or absence (in 3) of an evaluative disposition, of investment in objectivizing cultural discrimination.

The analysis represented by Figure 13 thus links IRCAM subjects' technological and aesthetic allegiances to the broader, coexistent technological and musical fields, and beyond them, to the aesthetic and technological differences between modernism and postmodernism. It depends, in particular, on understanding how IRCAM subjects related to those "other" forms of music and technology that in 1984 were absent from IRCAM's official discourse — commercial popular music, and small technologies. We have seen that small technologies did find a place as part of marginal subcultures such as PL's small-system project or the musicians' group vanguard scheme for future research. Yet these gained only very limited support, and IRCAM remained in '84 largely devoted to big-system development. We have therefore already glimpsed a tension between proponents of large and small systems, and in fact the issue was a widespread preoccupation of IRCAM intellectuals, the most highly charged ideological conflict within IRCAM. It may have been inflamed by researchers' unspoken ambivalence about the 4X deal with Dassault/Sogitec and the military-industrial networks in which this high-tech research was embedded. It may, in other words, have been the sublimated form taken by the critique of high technology. More broadly, chapter 2 gave insight into the specifically postmodern ideological connotations of small-system as opposed to large-system development. I have also shown how popular musics made very occasional appearances in dissident IRCAM concert series such as the *Espaces Libres*, and the free jazz events organized by RIG. But we will see below that despite these, the presence or influence of popular musics within IRCAM was quite severely repressed, and covert.

There are seven major areas in which subjects cluster in Figure 13, and in each the subjects' beliefs about small technologies and popular musics tellingly illuminate their relations with the broader cultural fields beyond IRCAM. *Area 1*, at the intersection of aesthetic and technological modernism, is the most elitist position. It contains only Boulez and the Artistic Director, WV. WV programmed the main concert seasons and so defined IRCAM's canon: he was IRCAM's "aesthetic guardian." We saw in chapter 4 the cultural privilege of his earlier life. He had been the manager for several avant-garde composers. Before that he trained as an impresario at Glyndebourne opera and cofounded and managed a major British contemporary music ensemble. His elitism was confirmed in the interview cited earlier in which he reacted against Fleuret's pluralist policies: "all 'les musiques' . . . no, they're not equal, I don't agree. I believe in fine art, I believe in aristocracy, and I believe in elite [culture]." WV left IRCAM in '86 to direct one of the largest British arts organizations, where his concert programming has continued to be perceived by some as pro-modernist and as promoting very difficult music.

Boulez's aesthetic allegiance has clearly been modernist and against the softening of postmodernism. In this interview from 1984, Boulez restated his respect for serialism and disdain for postmodernism, as embodied in the work of American composer George Rochberg. As I have mentioned, Rochberg is well known for turning away from serialism to a neoromantic aesthetic. By analogy, Boulez also criticizes Stravinsky's neoclassicism — a position that echoes Adorno's (1973) classic critique.

> I wouldn't follow, say, George Rochberg's lead in giving up twelve-tone music and composing like Gustav Mahler because I think Mahler has done it much better than Mr. Rochberg will ever do. It seems really stupid to me that in order to avoid a present danger, you adopt the dangers of the previous generation. . . . This was like Stravinsky in the Twenties saying: I want to be "classical," so I will imitate the style of Bach. That was a completely useless reaction. I can already see that our "new" postmodernist buildings are dead . . . even deader than the ones they wanted to replace. (Boulez 1984, 14)

Certain signs from the '80s appeared to indicate a moderation of Boulez's polemical rejection of popular music, shown for example by his conducting the rock musician Frank Zappa's orchestral work in an evening of American music in Paris. But in the same interview, reflecting on the Zappa event, Boulez revealed his modernist distance from even this avant-garde popular music, speaking of worthwhile exchange with "another culture," seen as completely distinct and strange. "When you approach another culture . . . you miss or misspell the laws. But I find that these misunderstandings are often very fruitful, since what you see in another culture is what you want that other culture to reveal about what you *yourself* are doing and searching for. And then suddenly, you find something in common and you take from this culture what you most need" (1984, 14). Nothing expresses better the modernist habit of searching in the "other" for knowledge of the "self." The distance separating Boulez and IRCAM from Zappa was satirized in an article in the CGP monthly magazine publicizing the Zappa concert. It consisted of a "purely imaginary" dialogue between Boulez and Zappa marked by profound mutual respect — Boulez likening Zappa to Wagner — and ended with Zappa asking to come and work at IRCAM: "Frank Zappa moves off. He dreams of his future stay at IRCAM" (CNAC, Jan. 1984, 33). The ending was clearly an ironic comment on the unlikelihood of such a visit.

Regarding technology, not only did Boulez's music use the 4X and VAX, Répons having first call on the 4X, but he actively despised small machines. The key conflict over small technologies during 1984 blew up between Boulez and American Pedagogy director RIG over whether RIG could bring into IRCAM two new, innovative, small commercial digital technologies: Apple Macintosh personal computers and Yamaha DX7 synthesizers (and link to this the MIDI interface). RIG had nurtured relationships with both companies, traveling to Japan in 1983 to contact the major Japanese music technology manufacturers. On his return he reported enthusiastically on the development of the DX7 and MIDI. By summer '84, with the help of a Lucasfilm contact who was a friend of a member of the Mac development team, RIG had set up a deal with Apple in which IRCAM would receive six Macs free in return for Apple retaining some rights over software developed on and for it. RIG reported Boulez saying to him that the Macs would come into IRCAM "over my dead body."[1]

We will see that as well as Boulez, some senior IRCAM scientists were implacably hostile to small machines. But in October the Macs arrived, to be greeted by official cool and caution. With his flair for deals and favors, RIG organized for a young Bell Labs researcher to come over to Paris and work for two weeks unpaid installing the Mac software and linking Macs up to the VAX. The story shows, then, RIG's role as IRCAM's key small system dissident; and how, despite great opposition, he managed "illicitly" in 1984 to bring in small machines on terms very favorable for IRCAM.

Area 2 is the "serious" postmodern position, containing Boulez's tutor BYV and the young junior tutor and composer WOW. WOW's piece Chréode 1 had the effect in '84 of gaining him promotion to the "heir elect," while the following year BYV was promoted to quasi-Scientific Director. Thus, both men rose fast in the IRCAM hierarchy. Both were also involved in the music research meetings of the self-styled intellectual vanguard. And in those meetings both expressed a bias in favor of big machines. BYV worked the 4X for Boulez, and he saw IRCAM's role as developing the Rolls Royces of computer music. WOW had worked in the Chant/Formes group, also in this area on the chart, which at this time programmed on the VAX and advocated big machines as a framework for advanced software research. Similarly, WOW believed that sophisticated music software could be developed only on big machines. He dismissed the work done by composer-bricoleur PL on small Apple II computers because, in his view, their memory was too limited for complex musical results.

In terms of their aesthetic allegiance, both men showed a similar mechanism. BYV, like all IRCAM Americans, was brought up on popular culture and music, and his father was an art director for commercial films. He was heavily involved in jazz as a student and professional wind player, but he said "I also rather quickly came to the conclusion that jazz was too limited . . . that if I was to be really satisfied I should get into serious music. Because of my jazz background I was naturally interested in contemporary music, almost automatically." BYV here spoke a logic common in the postmodern ideology of IRCAM Americans: that interests in jazz and in avant-garde "serious" contemporary music are somehow naturally allied—an attitude that ignores their objective differences. Yet in fact BYV later repudiated his earlier jazz work in favor of "serious" music, as at IRCAM. WOW started out as an autodidact avant-garde rock synthesizer player, and made several records, but he now renounced that past and kept it quite hidden. In discussion of some ambitious avant-garde rock musicians that he and I both knew, WOW invited me to agree that they had lost their way and compromised with a misguided populism. Thus, both men repudiated (and in WOW's case suppressed) a previous involvement in popular music.

However, the ghost of WOW's involvement in rock could be heard in the periodic surfacing of a strong repetitive pulse in his music. In this way, and more than most IRCAM music, WOW's contained a hint of reference to the rhythmic aesthetic of popular music—one of the basic historical aesthetic differences between modernism and popular music, and one that some postmodern composers want to overcome. WOW's music marked him, then, as a key IRCAM postmodern at this time. Confirmation of this view, and of WOW's status as an IRCAM philosopher, came in this teasing sample bibliography entry written by his friend HM in a memo: "WOW (1986)—*Les Présuppositions Spirituelles du*

Symbolisme Musical dans la Post-Modernité, Editions de la Nuit: Paris."
The imaginary publisher here is itself a satirical comment on the leading
avant-garde French publisher, Editions de Minuit.

GE, also in this area, was professor of computer science at a Parisian
university and a leading figure in French AI. GE was one of IRCAM's
persistent squatters, and as we have seen, had an informal arrangement
to bring his students in to use the VAX, since their own computing
resources were scarce. Earlier in life GE had toured playing jazz piano in
a group, and he continued to enjoy good jazz. But he also respected
Boulez's music and had personally taught Boulez the fundamentals of AI.
In our interview, he ridiculed one of the Apple Mac computers that had
just arrived, mocking it as just *"une boîte de bonbons"* (a box of sweets),
revealing his antagonism to small (American) machines.

Area 4, by contrast, contains three American composers who were the
most active ideologues and promoters of small-machine power, including RIG and PL, IRCAM's black American composer. As we saw in
chapter 7, PL was engaged in 1984 on IRCAM's only small-machine
project, working exclusively with Apple IIs and Yamaha synthesizers
linked up by MIDI. We saw that he wrote interactive software allowing a
player to improvise while the computer analyzes that input and "impro-
vises" along. As well as programming in assembler and BASIC, PL had
built his own MIDI units from scratch according to instructions from an
electronics magazine, since they were not yet available in Europe.

PL had no formal training whatsoever in computing, and his abilities
as a small-machine bricoleur were, he said, due to the help of his friend,
the experimental technologist David Behrman (chapter 2). PL was asked
in '84 to submit a project on small, interactive music technologies for a
major exhibition to be held at the CGP, conceived by the philosopher
Jean-François Lyotard, called *Les Immatériaux*. PL put forward a joint
project with Behrman in recognition of his debt to the man. PL's commitment to small technologies therefore had direct and personal links with
the philosophy and practice of the postmodern experimental tradition.
And as in that tradition, his small-machine philosophy was accompanied
by a certain contempt for big systems. Talking one day, PL said cynically:
"What's the 4X? It's the French Flagship, just a big prestige object—
that's how the media treat it, that's what it's really about: a major nationalist cultural prestige project. Sure, the 4X is the biggest real-time
synth at the moment, but it'll be superseded! I'll never be allowed to do a
piece on the 4X because its function is for the big guys, the pecking order

people. 'If you do a piece on the 4X, then it *must* be good!' — *that's* the rationality now."

As we saw earlier, PL was a well-known player working in jazz, improvisation, and avant-garde rock and funk, and he continued that work outside and unrelated to IRCAM. During 1984, among other work he toured intermittently with a French jazz group and went to Japan with a leading American big band. However PL was also a serious composer who had studied philosophy at Yale. He had run a New York avant-garde showcase for some years; and as a player and composer, he was situated mainly in the American and European experimental music scenes. His written composition was far from popular music, while his performance-based improvisations involved both modernist moments and pastiche and parody of popular music genres. PL himself would have rejected these statements, since he was strongly against the classification of musics. Rather, he believed that all musics should be judged, but judged in themselves, and not in terms of rigid genres and predetermined categories. This strategy, combining pluralism with a distrust of naive relativism and a desire to retain judgment and evaluation, was common among IRCAM's postmodern American intellectuals. Nonetheless, PL saw himself as a dissident and a "token black" at IRCAM.

The director of Pedagogy, RIG, as we have seen, was the most powerful "dissident" at IRCAM and a close friend of PL's. RIG was Boulez's bane. He was responsible for encouraging and letting in many squatters. Yet he was also indispensable to IRCAM and Boulez since it was he who negotiated IRCAM's software licenses and the deals for free Apple Macs and Yamaha DX7s. He was thus responsible for some of IRCAM's most important links with the computer companies and with the American computer music scene. In 1984 RIG was smitten with Japanese technology and had a Japanese musician as a girlfriend. He was totally committed to "small is beautiful." As the new Macs settled in, RIG's and PL's infatuation with them spread to others and the machines became invested with a semijoking, fantastic, mythical status. This was concretized in a "fairy-tale" that I found printed out from a Mac and lying around the Systems room soon after the Macs arrived: "La Fabuleuse Histoire d'Apple — Il était une fois deux passionnées de micro-informatique qui vivaient dans la Vallée du Silicium en Californie dite du nord. Ils imagineaient un petit ordinateur destinées aux enthousiastes. . . ."[2]

Like PL's, RIG's technological philosophy linked closely with the experimental tradition, as in his support for live group and improvised performance uses of small machines in his dissident concert series (chapter 6) and in his plans for the musicians' vanguard (chapter 7). Like PL, he had personal contacts with American experimentalists; for example, the composer-technologist Max Neuhaus (chapter 2) visited during '84 and through RIG offered IRCAM a project. The bid was unsuccessful.

Musically, RIG also had close and ongoing ties with popular music and with black American musicians. His first musical memory was hearing his mother's record of Tex Ritter (chapter 4), and as a student he played drums with the Art Ensemble of Chicago—a leading black jazz improvisation group. In the past he had worked with the pop star Stevie Wonder, famous as the major innovator in the use of synthesizers in pop music. Wonder had offered RIG a job, which he declined. Wonder came to Paris one week in '84, and although all his shows were sold out some complementary tickets were specially delivered to IRCAM for RIG. After the concert, RIG told me how he had been taken by Stevie to a wild all-night recording session. The entourage ended up in the early hours, when few are around and subcultures thrive, back at IRCAM, where RIG demonstrated the 4X. Wonder's sound engineer drooled over the machine and asked when they could get to come and use it. RIG confessed that he thought it unlikely they would ever be officially invited to IRCAM. On another occasion, the black free jazz pianist Cecil Taylor passed through IRCAM one evening to see his friends RIG and PL. RIG still occasionally played drums and often lamented not being able to play more. His main training, however, was as a psychoacoustician, and he sometimes composed computer music pieces. These tape pieces were, again, not at all popular music.

Thus, both PL and RIG exemplified a position of advocating small, commercial machines, of being actively involved in popular musics outside IRCAM or in earlier days, but of producing nonpopular and modernist music at IRCAM. This split between different spheres of their production I will identify as another IRCAM postmodern strategy.

Area 3 introduces a different split that is also characteristic of postmodernism: between subjects' production and their consumption. It also illustrates the evaluative or discriminating aesthetic impulse that was a feature of IRCAM's postmodernism. This might be called the "pragmatist" position, that is, the central position on both axes. Technologically, subjects in this area were prepared to use both big and small machines according to context and need.

The composer and director HY was excited by small machines and talked enthusiastically of his visits to Atari and Xerox PARC in the

United States where this technology was being developed; he liked to use his DX7 at home for compositional "sketching." But he was also plugged into big institutions, MIT as well as IRCAM, and worked with their big machines; indeed he had been centrally engaged in testing out musical uses of the 4X during its development. Musically, HY showed in 1984 a split between production and consumption. His own musical aesthetic was nonpopular and modernist. Yet he organized the notorious showing of Michael Jackson's *Thriller* video at an *Espace Libre*, then at the top of the pop charts, and at home he followed popular music enthusiastically as a consumer. Although HY listened to a variety of pop, it was limited to the well-known, whether Michael Jackson (from the chart mainstream) or the avant-garde pop of Laurie Anderson, both high-profile in '84. Discussing *Thriller* with me, he repeatedly stressed how great it was, "really strong," but he couldn't elaborate. When I pushed him to speculate on the way *Thriller* worked, or its politics, he was uncomfortable. He saw no point in thinking that way about it. Thus it was important to HY to make a judgment, but there seemed no language behind the judgment to develop an exegesis. There was an impulse to judgment, but the content was empty. In fact, HY was a hybrid figure who as a youth had contact with both rock music and avant-garde experimentation, but this had been followed by a training at the Juilliard and by becoming a protégé of the leading American East Coast composer, Elliott Carter. While not making obvious his eclectic past, unlike WOW or BYV, HY did not articulate a stand against popular music. However, following his departure from IRCAM in late '84 the balance of musical forces in his compositional aesthetic changed significantly.

Also in this area is AV, the composer whose production visit was detailed in chapter 8. AV worked with the 4X and VAX at IRCAM, but preferred to use his own Yamaha DX and CX equipment at home or the Fairlight based in his British university. He found these small and commercial machines more efficient, productive, and empirically responsive. After the IRCAM debacle he was invited to MIT to produce a piece. But by then he was so skeptical of large institutions and their chaotic high technology that to avoid a similar experience, he prepared most of the computer tape before going on his Yamaha setup at home.

AV was deeply interested in popular music and listened to a broad range. He linked this to his musical roots in Argentinian tango and to his non-"first world" identification. He wanted his composition to successfully unite what he saw as popular music's strengths — its rhythmic power and sophisticated production techniques — with the stronger aspects of the modernist legacy. He saw this as enabling him to learn from popular music, but also to intervene in it. His own "serious" composition remained framed within a modernist aesthetic, although it was more dynamic and rhythmic than much of its kind. AV distinguished that composition, which was for IRCAM, MIT, the world of high institutions, festivals, and prizes, from the film and TV music that he churned out on the Fairlight or Yamaha machines to "sell by the minute"—the music that made his living. This was a mock cynicism: AV greatly admired the skills of producing good commercial music. He had once produced a pop demo tape that he played me late one night at IRCAM. It was credible but overproduced and overpolished rock. Occasionally AV produced a piece that he thought was a successful synthesis of the serious and popular; but he felt nonetheless that such pieces could not be played at highly serious events and operated a careful aesthetic management, playing his different musics in different contexts to "appropriate" audiences.

Yet, crucially, all of this aesthetic planning was not under conscious control. AV described producing pieces that simply followed his own long-term inclinations, being surprised when they found warm responses from the serious festival and prize scene, and then, only post hoc, realizing and being able to calculate—to list quite clearly—which aesthetic components of the piece had elicited such a response. AV produced, then, different kinds of music for different spheres of circulation. His commercial work was quite separate from that produced for the IRCAM circuit; while what he termed his "own" (serious, autonomous, nonfunctional, nonelicited) music derived from internal processes and, according to AV, only after the event seemed to match up to the external expectations of the legitimate cultural world. This part of his internal compositional subjectivity thus appeared to AV as autonomous and yet as fortuitously, prophetically, attuned to the desires of the legitimate sphere. In this way his sense of containing within his own eclectic, even multiple musical subjectivity an autonomous musical core—one independent of both the demands of the market and the (in his eyes) predictable requirements of high musical culture—remained uncompromised.

IRCAM's psychoacoustician, HM, was AV's friend and admired his music. Like AV, he greatly appreciated popular music; he grew up playing in high school bands and, being a West Coast American, identified with the experimental tradition and its oriental leanings. Technologically, HM used big machines for his own research (the 4X, VAX), but also—nonideologically—advocated the uses of small machines.

Two other junior tutors and composers, KF and HU, are also located here. Both were pragmatic, nonideological users of whatever technologies were available. HU, considered one of IRCAM's most promising young composers and theorists, was on poorly paid short contracts in 1984. His music was, once again, strongly embedded in the modernist aesthetic. However, HU had lived in South America for some years and married there, and as a legacy he was known informally as a fine tango pianist. For HU, playing tangos was a form of leisure activity for parties and very rarely, when pressed, for late-night, marginal IRCAM events. HU saw popular music as a mode of leisure and consumption, quite distinct from his serious compositional work; like HY above, HU's musical self was divided between that involved in serious production and that in consumption.

One of the most interesting cases was KF, in 1984 on irregular, short contracts and very anxious to become better established at IRCAM. His musical activities were subject to two competing kinds of self-imposed suppression. Before IRCAM he had produced soundtracks for theater and dance groups and some rock music. But he considered this would be seen by IRCAM as "unserious" and inappropriate, so earnestly, almost moralistically, but with ambivalence, he described making a conscious decision to keep quiet about and drop that work and to change orientation in order to get on at IRCAM. He described the decision in terms of the need to have time to concentrate on doing "only one thing," his IRCAM work, and to overcome his own susceptibility to a sort of loose and lazy musical eclecticism. He dated the decision to the beginning of his work at IRCAM. It obviously related also to having his first small income from noncommercial work.

However KF's suppression of his past was incomplete. Following our first talk on these matters, I walked into a recording studio late one Sunday night—a very dead time at IRCAM—and found KF at work producing an "illicit" soundtrack for some filmmaker friends. The room was booming with a heavy funk rhythm track, revealing KF's expertise in mainstream pop. This was the only time I heard this kind of sound being produced in an IRCAM studio. Like AV, then, KF's strategy embodied a splitting between different spheres of production, and like AV, he kept his commercial and pop musical work hidden from IRCAM, but he also suppressed and hid his musical past. In reality, KF was at this time in a transitional state and remained undecided about whether he was really going to give up the commercial work or was simply going to conceal it from IRCAM. The risk was that if it emerged too much into the light that he still worked in the "other" musical world, this would disqualify him in

IRCAM's terms. KF was, then, calculating the relative gains and losses of both strategies; and he conveyed the strong impression that a factor in the calculation was his continuing desire to exercise his skills for producing funk — perhaps especially this "illicit" and therefore exoticized, eroticized funk — and that this would continue to weigh as an "irrational" and incautious force against the "rational" decision to abide by IRCAM's classificatory doxa. When we talked, KF conveyed his ambivalence about the situation and the internal conflicts involved in integrating his different musical selves while at the same time trying to adapt to the classificatory laws embodied in the institution of IRCAM. Indeed he expressed admiration for the rare composers such as AV whom he felt managed to achieve some kind of integration of different musics in their work: "In the case of AV, it's pretty obvious that the rock style is in his music. The quality of sound comes from that; it's clear, clean, wonderfully made. He does really good stuff. He's one of the only ones who has the intelligence to connect different [musical] worlds." Nonetheless, his own strategy was, in relation to IRCAM and his serious work, to maintain a strict separation: in his eyes, a less high-risk path.

Area 5 contains BU, the 4X Hardware designer, who was committed to large machines and who, beneath a veneer of indifference to small machines, was in fact rivalrous and antagonistic. In an interview he said of the DX7: "It's a good instrument, but it's so limited! Once you've played it a few times, you know it all." The following incident between BU and visiting American technological entrepreneur NI (Area 7 on the chart) betrayed his hostility to small machines. NI brought to IRCAM a souped-up small machine, his modified Casio VL Tone — then one of the cheapest, consumer-oriented synthesizers. NI belonged to what he called the "Casio Underground," fanatic Casio owners who got inside the machines and altered them with analog devices to achieve far better effects. This knowledge was circulated internationally by an underground magazine. NI had modified his VL Tone so that it had eight octaves, could bend notes, and produced sounds ranging from the Albert Hall organ, to a harpsichord, to Jimi Hendrix's guitar. On the afternoon in question, NI sat playing his VL Tone to PL in the reception area just as BU, the Scientific Director FOL, and others were going in to a 4X seminar. NI showed it proudly to BU, expecting interest from a fellow designer. But BU's reaction was disdain. As NI recalled, BU shot him a withering look, as if to say "get this guy out of here," while FOL said sarcastically to PL, "This is *your* department, isn't it?" — implying it was for small-machine enthusiasts only. Thus BU (and FOL) revealed their contempt for small-system bricolage. We saw earlier (chapter 7) that BU was actively hostile to IRCAM and avant-garde music, but that he enjoyed classical and popular musics. Hence his desire to emulate the earlier success of Wendy Carlos's *Switched On Bach* in order to demonstrate with "good" music the resources of the 4X.

Area 6 contains computer technicians and service staff and the 4X Industrialization director, VO. These people were keen on and professionally involved with both big and small machines. They were computer enthusiasts and populists, and nonideological in their attitudes toward the technology. VO, however, was more ideological. He finally left IRCAM over the issue of developing a small, commercial version of the 4X for the broader market of musicians, including those from popular music, and intended to set up his own company to do so. VO was firmly committed to the view that small machines open up potentially different musical markets than the big systems supported by elite institutions such as IRCAM, which give access only to "serious" or avant-garde composers. Like BU, VO was scathing about most IRCAM music, and in his philosophy small-machine development related logically to his dislike of avant-garde music.

FA, the Systems manager, was more even in his support for small and big systems. He installed computer graphics software on both the VAX and the Macs and encouraged people to play with both. The Systems team and their technician friends were the most visibly active and enthusiastic consumers of popular music within IRCAM. They often went to low-brow MOR and rock concerts, followed these scenes closely, and were loose with their praise and not concerned with serious judgments. The Systems manager confessed to being a blues fanatic and had a big record collection. These workers were, then, keenly interested consumers of popular music who perceived IRCAM music as simply another sound and nothing special. The Systems team's use of the name of the Australian pop group Men at Work as the superuser password betrayed their teasing, "unserious" iconoclasm toward IRCAM's dominant aesthetic.

Unknown to most, VR, employed as a 4X technician, was a professional sound engineer outside IRCAM. He had built and currently ran his own professional recording studio working in *variété* — French MOR pop. One of his singles had gone high up the French charts. Thus, the most experienced pop recording engineer within IRCAM was known officially only as a lowly technician. Our interview was stilted and VR was not articulate. But after the tape was off, hearing that I play bass guitar, he sprang up and took a Lynn Drum synthesizer (then much used in pop recordings) from a locked cupboard. He plugged it enthusiastically into a studio console and started to play with rhythms, inviting me to bring my bass to play along: a moment of telling desublimation. I learned about VR's "other life" from other technicians some months into my stay, and I was confided in only as word began to spread among them that I played rock bass guitar. Soon after this, another interview, with the 4X Signal Processing director AJ, ended with him keenly inviting me to bring my bass in one day so as to put its sound into the 4X. On the quiet, for their own use and amusement, these 4X engineers were recording a range of sounds drawn from rock and pop into the 4X's database. For them, these sounds were more interesting than the official musical uses of the 4X, and they were sure that no IRCAM musician would create such a database.

Area 7, finally, contains two people marginal to IRCAM who were strong proponents of a populist and pluralist approach to both technology and music. Both men were humored, treated as a bit of a joke, during 1984. FL, son of a highly regarded eastern European composer, worked sporadically for IRCAM as a junior tutor and studio technician. In '84 he was either without a contract — a squatter — or on intermittent, short, low-paid ones. Since he was treated as a part-time technician, it took months for me to realize that he was himself a composer. FL was unabashed about his involvement in popular music, jazz, and experimental performance. He was also at this time more deeply immersed and expert in the new Yamaha DX7s than any other IRCAM worker. The DX7s arrived in Paris from Japan with notoriously poor documentation, so musicians found them extremely difficult to understand and use. With friends from the pop scene, FL set up some commercial courses on how to use the DX7 that they ran for Parisian pop musicians. This sphere of his activities was completely outside and unacknowledged by IRCAM.

American computer musician NI, whose encounter with 4X designer BU over his Casio VL Tone I described before, was ex-Bell Labs and a technological bricoleur. He had modified his VL Tone by putting a few simple analog devices in with the digital ones. NI talked at length about the enormous potential of such mixed digital/analog technologies, which could at low cost massively enhance even the cheapest commercial system.[3] He derided what he saw as the irrational purism within the dominant discourse of computer music toward the uses of analog technologies. Although not in principle against big systems, NI was hostile to the militarist links of machines such as the 4X (chapter 5). NI's own music, composed for films and advertising, was New Age: tonal, mesmeric, based on endless repetitive sequences of phrases. He was not keen on IRCAM music, which he found alienating and hard. NI had a slightly paranoid air, and his exclusion from IRCAM's scientific and musical company was unsurprising to him. His VL Tone innovations had been shunned by the Japanese Casio company. He had taken the modified synthesizer to Casio's U.S. headquarters in New Jersey, and had finally been allowed to play it for a senior Japanese manager. But the man backed up against a wall in horror and as much as offered to pay NI to take the machine away and bury it. NI's explanation was that Casio made careful distinctions between each synthesizer in their range, and that his machine threatened to destroy this marketing structure by usurping the aesthetic power of higher-cost machines. Hence, "They hated the aesthetic: the raunchy and stronger sounds coming out of it." Other potential manufacturing deals had also fallen through; so that NI came across as a broken and disillusioned idealist. No one, it seems, wanted to know about his tiny, cheap machine that could sound so powerful that it might put larger digital synthesizers to shame.

MECHANISMS IN THE CONSTRUCTION OF AESTHETICS AND TECHNOLOGY AT IRCAM

The material above suggests some common mechanisms at work in the construction of aesthetics and technology in IRCAM culture. They are of three kinds: sociological, such as generation and professional interest; discursive, linking subjects' positions to the broader characterization of modernism and postmodernism; and intrapsychic. As I have argued, they are interrelated: certain intrapsychic forces "suit well" the aesthetic dispositions appropriate to modernist or postmodernist discourse. In conjunction, these mechanisms structured the differences between subjects but also differences within individual subjectivities — that is, they structured both social and intrasubjective differentiation, in particular the fragmentation of composers' musical-aesthetic identities.

In terms of intrapsychic forces, we saw three forms of fragmentation. The first was the splitting by subjects of one sphere of their musical production from another, as in the examples of PL and RIG from Area 4 and AV and KF from Area 3. The second involved subjects splitting their production from their consumption, as in HY and HU from Area 3. These splits managed to retain a modernist aesthetic orientation in the subjects' musical production, especially the part of their production that took place at IRCAM. At the same time these composers enjoyed and had sympathy for popular music and culture as consumers, or they may have consumed popular culture because it was de rigeur without having much understanding. Or again, they may have been active producers of popular music in other spheres, outside IRCAM (or at night within IRCAM), and so accepted the split pragmatically.

These two kinds of splitting have very different statuses. While the first was in a sense the most realistic adaption to objective discursive and institutional forces, the second relegated popular music to a completely different order and so involved its implicit denigration, indeed its denial, as music that might legitimately be addressed by a composer. Beneath a veneer of "neutral" recognition of difference and consumer respect, then, the production/consumption split was highly problematic, designating popular music by sleight of hand as the absolutely "other."

The third mechanism at issue was a splitting between aesthetic past and present, involving the repudiation or suppression of a past musical self and thus another tendency to denial. We saw this in the examples of BYV and WOW from Area 2. This was a more verbally articulated and explicitly ideological position than the largely tacit splitting mechanisms above. BYV and WOW had arguments as to why popular music had not been sufficient to hold them, rather than just assuming it as self-evident. This articulated aesthetic certainty and the inclining toward modernism may link with their promotion within IRCAM and indeed their closeness to Boulez. WOW continued to rise within IRCAM, becoming eventually the director of Pedagogy, and by the '90s he was IRCAM's leading public critic of a populist, market-led version of postmodernism. Yet contradictorily, in practice he was one of very few IRCAM composers to draw subtly on the rhythmic aesthetic of popular musics.

The most revealing case was that of junior tutor and composer KF, since in 1984 his aesthetic disposition was in transition just as he was attempting to gain greater credibility within IRCAM. When KF spoke of his musical reorientation and his adaption to IRCAM's classificatory system, he had the air of an apprentice ambivalently learning or trying out a new discursive position and its appropriate psychic forms. Yet unlike BYV and WOW, he had not yet fully repudiated his musical past, although aware that this was a task. He was, then, rehearsing this configuration, perhaps too consciously for its effective introjection. There were telling contradictions, blind spots, an "unseriousness" in some of his words; and it was unclear how successful he would be at adapting. At the same time he toyed with a different intrasubjective strategy — splitting different spheres of his production; hence his "illicit" pop soundtracking at night. As yet, KF remained very junior within IRCAM. By the early '90s he was a successful figure.

The examination of different forms of splitting in IRCAM composers' aesthetic subjectivities, then, makes sense of several kinds of fragmentation of their musical and authorial selves. For subjects such as AV, PL, RIG, or KF, when they were identifying with IRCAM they considered certain areas of their musical practice legitimate, "good" in IRCAM's terms, while other areas were deemed illegitimate, certainly not for IRCAM (although they continued to produce these "other" musics for "other" domains). Whereas for WOW, a past musical self was apparently denied, obliterated as relevant to the present — again in line, fortuitously, with the requirements of IRCAM aesthetic discourse. Crucially, the splitting involved an introjection of and an accommodation to the values of the institution, which were in various ways in conflict with other areas of the self.

A sympathetic view is to see these cultural defense mechanisms — subjects' splitting between areas or periods of their practice, or between their production and consumption — as characteristic of the anomalous position of postmodern intellectuals, and as a way of dealing with the contradictions that arise in trying to integrate two worlds of discourse or cosmologies — modernism and the popular — defined by absolute aesthetic and socioeconomic differences. A skeptical view is to see them as pragmatic strategies derived from the need to gain aesthetic legitimation as composers within the world of serious contemporary music, which still meant retaining a distance from popular music, thereby guarding the "high seriousness" and introverted "autonomy" of the avant-garde. The splitting shows the continuing illegitimacy of popular music, a judgment that IRCAM subjects had consciously, as with AV and KF, or unconsciously internalized. In different ways, then, IRCAM's young composers had introjected the aesthetic precepts of modernism and its attendant psychic forms. In KF we have seen the introjection in progress at the time that he was trying to gain kudos at IRCAM. The opposite — a lessening of these forms, a refusal of introjection — sometimes occurred in composers who arranged to leave. Thus, PL had set up a pragmatic arrangement for a year or two but never intended to stay, while HY found it increasingly difficult to inhabit IRCAM and left late in '84 for an American job. Within a short time after his departure, HY's music had perceptibly changed: his aesthetic became clearly postmodern, perhaps influenced by the rock music that he had played as a youth and had continued to consume, and including moments of lush tonality and pulsing rhythm.

A fourth intrapsychic mechanism concerns the basic distinction drawn between positions 1 and 2 as against position 3 on the aesthetic axis: the existence of an evaluative and objectivizing aesthetic disposition, shared by IRCAM modernists and postmodernists and applied by the latter to both serious and popular musics. This contrasts with the subjectivist, less evaluative and nongeneralizing aesthetic disposition of IRCAM populists. The evaluative disposition is a thought habit embedded in the pedagogic and prescriptive character of modernism; and its existence in IRCAM postmodernists indicates a basic continuity in the form of aesthetic discourse between modernism and postmodernism at IRCAM. Postmodern IRCAM subjects seemed caught up in the necessity for "serious judgment." The nakedness and fragility of the habit were revealed above in one individual's judgment about Michael Jackson, which he could not, however, develop — an impulse to judgment without a language of exegesis. Psychically, the recourse to objectifying judgment suggests a susceptibility to a controlling omnipotence in IRCAM modernists and postmodernists alike. This is not to say that IRCAM populists and popular culture consumers did not evaluate and did not choose between alternative experiences. The distinction has rather to do with the weight attached to this process and the need for subjects to objectify their cultural judgment.

In terms of discursive negation, the aesthetic disposition of IRCAM postmodernists confirms the historical hypothesis proposed in chapter 2 by showing a negation of the modernist negation of popular music and culture through subjects recognizing and in some ways engaging with those forms. However, the evaluative attitude helped to retain distance and ambivalence so that, as we have seen, popular culture was still considered "other": a form of leisure, a source of influence, or "another" (hidden) sphere of production to be infiltrated.

The shift from aesthetic position 1 to 2, from modernist to postmodernist, was also a generational shift: from Boulez's generation, the elder avant-garde, to the younger IRCAM composers of the '80s, almost all of whom were under thirty-five. It seems that none of this younger generation could take an unabashed elitist, modernist position, but they could take forward the evaluative disposition and bring that to bear, as though meritocratically, on the broader musical field, and thus discriminate between different musics — including popular musics.

The populist aesthetic position, beyond the modernist/postmodernist oscillation, appeared a more naive cultural position, simpler, less intellectually mediated; hence the inarticulacy of VR and AJ. This position was typically held by those with no professional interest in music. Conversely, whereas there were no official IRCAM musicians in the populist position (3), they were all (except Boulez) in the postmodern position (2), the respectable place for a serious composer of the younger generation. The power of this positioning was revealed by the fate of those IRCAM-associated musicians who asserted a more populist than postmodern view — who had therefore failed to introject the correct psychic-aesthetic disposition. These people, such as FL, remained in marginal employment and were never officially defined as musicians within IRCAM.

Regarding technological positions, there are two basic mechanisms at issue: discursive negation and professional interest. In position 1, favoring high tech, were those — almost exclusively European — individuals most professionally involved in big machines, individuals who also showed an ideological commitment to them. In position 3, favoring low tech, were those — almost exclusively American — composers who promoted an ideology of progressive decentralization and miniaturization of computer power, small as beautiful and portable, and who believed that big systems involved unacceptable and irksome centralizations of power. The positions therefore involved mutual negation and rehearsed the opposition described in chapter 2 between the technological philosophies of musical modernism and postmodernism at large. The big system–small system tension was also in the mid-1980s a feature of the wider computer music community,[4] just as it resonated with the polarization in broader debates on the "information society" between a utopian view of progressive decentralization and a dystopian fear of increasing elite and multinational centralization and control.[5]

Position 2 — pragmatic, inclusive, less ideological — was held by those with a professional interest in both kinds of machine, both composers and lower-level, younger computer workers. Again, generational difference structured the pragmatic interest of younger staff in the new small systems. However, all of the professional computer scientists and technicians occupied positions 1 or 2 on the technology axis: that is, advocating large systems or neutral regarding the scale of technology. Only technological bricoleurs and autodidacts — IRCAM's marginal, dissident, and ideological technological postmodernists — occupied position 3. Overall, it was the people with the strongest professional and highest career interests in either music or technology who felt compelled to hold a more articulated and evaluative ideological disposition — the postmodern aesthetic or the position favoring high tech. The lower-status computer workers were less compelled to take a polemical position and could be laid back about both machines and music.

We have seen, then, some simple motivations — generational difference, professional prestige and interest — at work in subjects' allegiances, but also strong discursive negation, aesthetic and technological, in accord with the earlier analyses of modernism and postmodernism. While technological dissent was overt and explicitly ideological within IRCAM, aesthetic dissent was repressed and did not surface. As I have shown in previous chapters, there was an absence of open aesthetic debate, so that any aesthetic disagreements or uncertainties that arose were experienced fragmentedly, as individualized and private doubts. Most importantly, this analysis has suggested a deeper level at which aesthetic conflict was "managed" and difference averted: through intrasubjective aesthetic fragmentation — intrapsychic mechanisms of splitting and denial — that had the effect of censoring areas of music that were not deemed legitimate within IRCAM.

IRCAM "POSTMODERNISM": EXPERIMENTAL MUSIC AS MARGINAL SUBCULTURE AND THE EXCLUSION OF POPULAR MUSIC

I have argued that we can make sense of IRCAM intellectuals' aesthetic and technological allegiances by reference to characteristic differences between modernism and postmodernism, and, aesthetically, between them and popular music. In 1984 there were in fact few explicit references to postmodernism around IRCAM. Two were mentioned earlier: one the joke reference to junior tutor and "heir elect" WOW as a postmodern philosopher; the other the editorial in the first issue of a new music journal in '84 devoted to "Musical Thought at IRCAM" by its editor, the British composer Nigel Osborne, himself an IRCAM-commissioned composer (chapter 2). Osborne writes of "our postmodern pluralism" in the serious musical world of the 1970s and 1980s, a period of "fragmentation and diversity . . . [of] the demise of the composer-scribe." He continues by celebrating the "spontaneity, immediacy" of contemporary music, which is "a far cry from the rigorous intellectual control and pompous strictures of the 1950s." The recent period, says Osborne, has witnessed a "massive and exhilarating expansion of the musical world view, from a questioning of the very bases of human musical experience, through a weakening of ethnocentricity, and an accommodation with popular culture" (Osborne 1984, i–ii).

Thus, Osborne's utopian espousal of postmodernism emphasizes cultural diversity, which is equated with a new receptivity to nonwestern and popular music and culture. In the articles that follow this editorial, introductory pieces on IRCAM by young intellectuals and directors, this broad pluralism is moderated. One summarizing piece, addressing the question of whether IRCAM has developed a house style, finds that there has been little standardization and that musical diversity is common in the institute. This reflects the fact, the author says, that contemporary serious music is no longer dominated by one overriding ideology. Instead, he insists that "talent" and "message" are the most important issues at stake. We see, between the two articles, a telling semantic shift away from positive reference to anti-ethnocentrism and popular culture to a view of IRCAM's postmodernism as to do with narrower concepts of "talent" and "message."

However, we have also seen that the substance of aesthetic postmodernism had a presence within IRCAM in the attitudes of composers such as AV, PL, or RIG, who asserted that their music was beyond modernism and had transcended any antagonism to popular music. I have implied, then, that even if relatively unarticulated, IRCAM had an incipient postmodernism that is revealed by elements shared between IRCAM subjects and postmodernism at large: some positive relation with popular culture and a technological discourse of small-machine power that resonated with that of experimental music. Yet the music produced for IRCAM, even by those such as AV, PL, KF, and RIG who produced a variety of popular musics elsewhere, remained in this period primarily modernist in character: it was less influenced by the aesthetics of popular music than other, non-IRCAM postmodern musics. I want to substantiate this point by delineating some basic aesthetic distinctions.

There are, I suggest, four basic dimensions of aesthetic difference between musical modernism and popular music. They are: popular music's basis in tonal or modal harmony or melody; its regular, repetitive, pulse-based and pattern-based rhythmic character; its wider use of repetition at various levels of the whole—in rhythm, melody, harmony, or form; and its range of uses of improvisation—from micro improvisations, as with instrumental and vocal expressive inflections, to macro, extended improvisations, whether in solos or completely improvised pieces (Keil 1966b, Chester 1970, Middleton 1983, 1990). Any one or combination of these elements can suffice to identify the broad aesthetic character of popular music. (For example avant-garde jazz, sometimes considered modernist, employs the free improvisational component of popular music in a way very different from the restricted modernist use of improvisation.) By contrast, the modernist aesthetic eschews tonal or modal bases; it is arhythmic or rhythmically irregular and avoids pulse and sustained pattern in favor of calculated durations and complex, irregular temporalities; it avoids perceptible or simple repetition; and improvisation, if brought in, is highly constrained and determined by score-based compositional directives.

When we scrutinize aurally the IRCAM music of IRCAM's young postmodernists from this period it becomes clear, above all, how dissimilar it is not only to mainstream popular music but also to the non-IRCAM postmodern experimental tradition: composers such as Glass, Reich, Nyman, Rzewski whose works are in different ways aesthetically closer to popular music, with greater tonal or modal reference, pulse, repetition, and so on. Figure 14 depicts the basic aesthetic distinctions that I am suggesting existed in this period between IRCAM modernism (Boulez), IRCAM postmodernism (the IRCAM music of HY, WOW, HU, AV), non-IRCAM postmodernism (Glass, Reich, Rzewski, Nyman) and (non-IRCAM) popular music (Stevie Wonder, Michael Jackson). At this time, then, IRCAM's "postmodernism" remained closer to the modernist aesthetic; there was little audible evidence of a rapprochement with popular, nonwestern, or indeed classical or romantic musics.

This is demonstrated equally by other levels of mediation that were commonly sought by young IRCAM composers in the mid-1980s and that are more characteristic of postserialism than experimental or popular musics: the very large scale of resources and hypercomplex physical and technological forms employed (typically, combinations of orchestra or ensemble, soloists, electronic amplification, computer tape, real-time computer transformation); the traditional hierarchical division of labor embodied in the work (composer-theorist, constrained interpreter, passive audience); and the highly (scientifically and technologically) theorized conceptual basis of the music. In short, the rhetoric of postmodernism was superficial within IRCAM. It was not matched by marked changes in practice; so that, aided by splitting mechanisms, IRCAM's "postmodernism" stayed modernist, both musically and in terms of its multiple mediations, while popular music remained an "other" kept absent from IRCAM.

Other signs confirm the near total exclusion of popular music from

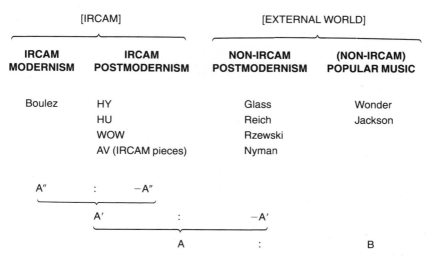

14. Guide to aesthetic differentiation between IRCAM and non-IRCAM musics.

IRCAM. Thus, although IRCAM had one small temporary research project in 1984 related to jazz, its status was very low and its legitimacy continually in question. Moreover we have seen how even world-famous American pop and avant-garde jazz and rock musicians — Stevie Wonder, Cecil Taylor, Frank Zappa — were made aware by "dissidents" such as RIG that it was not appropriate that they should work at IRCAM. It cannot be assumed this situation was accepted as "self-evident" by these musicians. For example Anthony Braxton, the leading black American avant-garde jazz musician, in a general interview given in 1988 specifically mentioned his resentment at his certain exclusion from IRCAM.[6] In fact the question of popular music's access to or exclusion from IRCAM is also an occasional theme of middle-brow popular music journalism, and one that rather than unconscious envy reveals a mixture of quite conscious, if at times gauche, admiration and fascination or occasional cynicism.[7]

By contrast, the experimental tradition had a presence within IRCAM as a marginal, dissident subculture, aided by its representatives RIG and PL — IRCAM's key American postmodernists and small-system devotees. As we saw, RIG and PL had personal links with two well-known composers cum technological bricoleurs from the experimental tradition, Behrman and Neuhaus. Both were to be part of proposed IRCAM projects, but neither took place, which suggests that experimental music remained at this time antithetical to the dominant discourse of IRCAM. That the experimental tradition has at least been acknowledged by IRCAM is shown by the fact that three other major experimental composers have worked at the institute: Cage himself (1981), Rzewski (1977), and Terry Riley (1986) — a modest showing.

Finally, all of this throws light on the technological "irrationalities" discussed in chapter 9: IRCAM's neglect in this period of the analog tape medium and of recording techniques, as well as the purist aversion to mixed analog and digital technologies mentioned by NI above. It is now clear that these technological characteristics were overdetermined by IRCAM's broader assertion of difference from popular music and from the postmodern, experimental tradition, both of which were associated with empirical use of the tape medium and with analog studio production. While IRCAM completely disdained the techniques of popular music production, it also attempted to transcend the mixed technologies and analog bricolage of the experimentalists and of *musique concrète*. So the disdain within IRCAM for these processes expressed the exclusion of these other musical discourses, and IRCAM's technological culture itself embodied the broader discursive differentiation.

How does this account of IRCAM culture compare with the hypothesis in chapter 2 of the historical relationship between modernism, postmodernism, and popular culture? The analysis summarized in Figures 13 and 14 confirms aspects of that hypothesis, and yet modifies it in relation to IRCAM. Postmodernism at IRCAM appears to involve a negation of the modernist negation of popular culture. But aesthetically, despite the signs of rapprochement, the music produced at IRCAM during the mid-1980s was primarily modernist, different from other extant postmodern musics, and without aesthetic reference to popular music; thus popular music remained a distanced "other," kept largely beyond IRCAM. However the technological discourse of experimental music did infiltrate IRCAM as a dissident ideology, its proponents IRCAM's American intellectuals. The analysis shows further how, without the need for overt aesthetic censorship, these discursive interrelations were "managed" through fragmented aesthetic subjectivities: through the mechanisms of splitting production from consumption, splitting production in one sphere from that in another, and repudiation or denial of another (past) cultural self. These mechanisms achieved the externalization of commercial popular culture from IRCAM — particularly the music, less so the technology. They also therefore maintained a conflictual balance within IRCAM of a dominant modernism under attack by a dissident, youthful and "vanguard" postmodern culture, the conflict expressed in both generational and European-American rivalries. But this was largely a negotiation between charismatic leader and would-be heirs, a pseudoconflict amounting to aesthetic stasis. I suggest in the next chapter that while the technologies have been allowed to change, IRCAM's dominant aesthetic has not.

At another level the analysis emphasizes the role that Americans play in spreading the postmodern message. It is striking that Americans were the most sincerely optimistic, active, and populist proponents of postmodernism within IRCAM, as is shown by their advocacy of low tech and by their populist consumption behavior. They cluster to the right and bottom of Figure 13, that is, toward low tech and toward the populist aesthetic.[8] From qualitative interview data, it is possible to speculate that postmodernism derives its subjective origination and power from a specifically American experience of cultural pluralism: in simple terms, nearly all the Americans at IRCAM had been brought up with black and white popular musical forms as well as with "serious" music, and saw both as deep in their own cultural heritage. This cultural pluralism — its subjective traces deeply etched in individual cultural experience — becomes easily linked to the pervasive American myth of the achievement of a classless society and of the progressive potential of competitive capitalism. It becomes "natural" both to ignore the objective institutional differences, and differences of status and legitimacy, of different musics and to view culture and music as themselves autonomous and effective forces for overcoming socioeconomic difference. Thus, aesthetic difference is divorced from extant socioeconomic arrangements and comes to be read as itself a progressive social force. This perspective is lived out in the American cultural condition, and it has much emotion and nostalgia invested in it precisely because of the weight of social and economic contradiction, and the hopes, that it bears. Hence its subjective power and apparent truth for my American IRCAM informants; hence also the nostalgic air of American writers such as Jameson (1984a) and Berman (1984). Yet as we have seen, none of this prevented IRCAM Americans from also submitting to IRCAM's musical discourse — by fragmenting their production and consumption, and by implicitly agreeing to censor certain musics from IRCAM.

This may give insight into further subjective dimensions of the phenomenon of postmodernism, which would complement macro socioeconomic analyses such as Jameson's (1984a). In his periodization (ibid., 78), modernism and postmodernism correspond to the eras of monopoly

and multinational capital, so that postmodernism is the cultural manifestation corresponding to the postwar establishment of American multinational dominance. Postmodernism is precisely, then, the form of
American cultural hegemony. But such an analysis, as it stands, fails to
account for why postmodernism has been so appealing to Left and liberal American intellectuals. In brief, the material here begins to hint at
how American intellectuals may experience postmodernism imagina-
tively as progressive, as though the aesthetic portends social change, as
though it had the power to level social differences and to unite social
groups, while they continue, impotently, to conform to extant cultural-
institutional arrangements.

Finally, it must be noted that the element of antiformalist social and
political critique that is supposed to inhere in "vanguard" postmodernism was more or less absent from IRCAM's postmodernism, even — despite their utopian reflections on certain social dimensions of IRCAM's
work — from the discourse of the musicians' group vanguard. The only
elements of sociomusical critique within IRCAM were the musicians'
group's focus on the social relations of research and their technologically
mediated concern with the progressive decentralizing potential of small
systems — a perspective influenced by the experimental tradition, per-
vaded by commercial interests and, as I show in the next chapter, soon to
become hegemonic in computer music. The analysis of IRCAM postmodernism thus also confounds this wider vision of the potentially critical character of postmodernism proposed by writers such as Bürger
(1984), Foster (1985a), and his contributors (Foster 1985b). As we saw
in chapter 2, the loss of this dimension of modernism — itself always
historically unstable — long predates IRCAM and was largely accomplished with the rise of the various mid-century formalist avant-gardes in
both music and the visual arts.

The implications of this analysis are to throw profound doubt on
IRCAM's postmodern tendencies. Rather, the character of IRCAM's
musical discourse, even that produced by the younger "dissidents," situ-
ates the institution firmly as a moment or mutation within modernism.
The material shows also how even those composers uncomfortable with
IRCAM discourse allowed themselves ultimately to be constrained in
their IRCAM practice, and how very subtly and unconsciously this was
achieved — essentially, through the psychic fragmentation of the com-
poser/author as subject. Notions of "self-censorship" are quite inadequate to convey the often unconscious character of these processes and

how authentically they are experienced by the subject. Finally, the analysis — both historical and in relation to the present — points to the wider conclusion that postmodernism in music writ large, in its basic self-definition by the negation of modernism and by maintaining its distance from the absolute "other," is also best conceived as a variation within modernism.

CHAPTER XI

Conclusions

IRCAM, Cultural Power, and the
Reproduction of Aesthetic Modernism

The overriding impression of IRCAM in the early 1990s is that it has become, in its own terms, an efficient ship. The institute has managed to smooth out some of the practical and ideological obstacles to its functioning, just as some of its stranger irrationalities have been mitigated. There are thus marked changes from the state of affairs described in earlier chapters, changes with both positive and negative dimensions. But there are also significant continuities.

CHANGES

IRCAM has undergone a developmental cycle in regard to both its functioning and its personnel. At the start, in the 1970s, the institute revolved around the several codirectors with international reputations who were hired to complement Boulez in order to establish the project in the public mind, and who in turn were dependent on American scientific staff. By the turn of the '80s younger and less-established staff, including more Americans, were brought in to consolidate IRCAM's technological and computer music expertise, and these staff also posed less competition to Boulez's rule. It is the end of this phase that has been the focus of this book. But from the middle to late '80s, soon after this period, the American presence began to decline as local talent was found to be capable in the field. By the '90s the population of IRCAM — staff, researchers, and commissioned composers — has become largely European and predominantly French. In January 1992 Boulez stood down as the active Director of IRCAM, becoming Honorary Director, and Laurent Bayle, a French music administrator who had been IRCAM Artistic Director since 1986, took over as Director.

The shift away from American influence in the later '80s was the result of several factors. It was partly the result of the vast French investment in music research over the decades, as well as the maturation of a generation of young researchers who had come through IRCAM's own haphazard training processes. It was also no doubt due to an intensified resistance to hiring Americans that had been clear in the earlier '80s. But it was enabled above all by changes in the international distribution of technological expertise following the quiet revolution in small computer music systems from the mid-1980s on, which moderated American technological hegemony and established a common basis from which a far wider international community of researchers could find points of entry. Still, it is striking that the directors of IRCAM's two most high-profile technology projects in the late '80s and '90s have been American[1] and that IRCAM's recent partners in putting its technologies into industrial production have been successful American firms.

The declining American presence that began in the late '80s was accompanied by two highly significant and yet contradictory outcomes. First, proponents of a more populist postmodernism all but disappeared from among the higher music staff. Hence the representation of this discourse within IRCAM in the earlier '80s depended on a dissenting American presence which, in retrospect, was passing. Second, a major change occurred in IRCAM's technological orientation. Already by 1985, the hostility from the IRCAM establishment toward small and commercial systems had rapidly declined; so again, the period described in the ethnography was transitional — as it were, the peak tension before the bursting of the dike by a flood of commercial computer music innovation. On the one hand this involved the exponential growth during the later '80s of increasingly sophisticated, dedicated computer music technologies — synthesizers, samplers, software packages for analysis, notation, and so on. On the other hand it reflected the arrival of increasingly powerful general microcomputers; thus, within a couple of years new Apple Macintosh personal computers appeared (Mac IIs) that were equal in power to the old DEC VAXs — IRCAM's main research system in '84. Both kinds of small technology could be linked into a network via MIDI.

The period of greatest change in IRCAM's technological discourse was 1985–86. It saw a sudden decline in objections to and a rapid

increase in work with commercial microcomputers. The main developments related to the more powerful Macs and the Yamaha range of DX,
CX, and KX synthesizers. The change was shown by several other phenomena, for example by the inclusion of "*petits systèmes*" as an item in a
paper by the new Technical Director discussing how IRCAM could valorize its research, with a commentary that the aim should be, through this
technology, to disseminate IRCAM's knowledge as widely as possible.
Interestingly, the aim of this paper was both to define how IRCAM's
research should be valorized and to summarize the progress of various
areas of research that it was assumed would legitimize the institute's
scientific activities. We see again here a combined emphasis on the legitimation, and on formulating the terms of legitimation, of research. Signaling the new legitimacy of small systems, RIG, previously Pedagogy
director and IRCAM's key small-machine ideologue, set himself up as
director of a new (one-person) department: *Microinformatique*. And a
course of public lectures on "*Musique et Microinformatique*" took place
in early '86.

The Chant/Formes group worked enthusiastically throughout '85 on
rewriting their software for the new Macs (as well as for the 4X). The
team's objections to small systems were overcome, they explained, because of their much-increased power. IRCAM's ex-Systems manager,
FA, returned to develop a program called Macmix that linked up many
of IRCAM's technologies with the Macs. They were interfaced to both
the VAXs and the 4Xs, and all of these in turn could be linked via MIDI
connections to a virtually unlimited range of other peripherals — small
synthesizers, digital effects, and so on.

During '85 the Yamaha corporation negotiated through RIG to equip
IRCAM, for free, with a studio containing exclusively Yamaha technologies. By '86 there was an operational "Yamaha Studio" at the top
of the old building, the first outpost of commerce within the body of
IRCAM. It was manned by the (British) Yamaha representative WI, well
known in the computer music community as the man who "voiced"
(designed the timbres of) the innovative DX7 synthesizer. However, WI's
relations with the institute were uneasy, and he felt especially distant
from IRCAM musically.[2] WI expressed his technological disdain for
IRCAM's supposedly unique computer music tools by boasting to me
that in five minutes and using a network of several Yamaha machines he
could make an imitation of the timbral transitions possible with Chant.
Indeed, he rapidly produced a passable bell-to-voice timbral transition,
and unlike Chant's, one that he could then use polyphonically — that is,

use in real time to drive a keyboard and so build up into several voices or chords. In his view, anything Chant could do he could also do, faster and with more versatility, with the Yamahas. Thus, continuing rivalries nested within the closer relations between IRCAM and industry.

These developments were a delayed vindication of the small-system ideas of the musicians' group and a kind of victory for the small-machine ideologues, just at the point that several of the most vocal were leaving. However it should not be assumed that, then or now, they signaled an embrace of small-machine empiricism or utopianism or too great a change in IRCAM culture. The lecture course on musical microcomputing attended by external musicians keen to understand the latest developments, for example, remained highly theoretical and technical and had no practical work and no sound examples at all. Yet undeniably, IRCAM's technological culture has been transformed, as much as anything by a new awareness of the benefits of working on and with technologies (unlike the 4X) that will reach into and feed the common pool of development—a consciousness that has on occasion, if not sustainedly, been put into practice.

There have been two main successes of this policy in the last few years. One is a software package called Max, built to run on the Mac and other systems, that offers a Mac-type graphical interface—icon-driven, supposedly simple and clear, and now a classic in the field—enabling control of a range of sound synthesis and processing techniques. The other notable success is the IRCAM Musical Workstation (*Station d'Informatique Musicale* or SIM), which allows a series of real-time and near real-time sound synthesis, transformation, and control procedures for both live concert and compositional use. The SIM is, in a sense, the followup to the 4X and offers similar possibilities, yet pragmatically, it was designed for specific use with the commercial Next microcomputer, itself conceived as the next generation of microcomputer and a more powerful replacement for the Mac. Both Max and the SIM have been put into production by American companies, and both appear to be selling quite well.

These technologies illustrate further interrelated changes in IRCAM culture. First, a capacity to sustain research projects through stabilization and full development so as to bring them to fruition as finished products. Second, as indicated earlier, a new drive to valorize IRCAM's scientific and technological research. Third, the commercial production of the technologies, so that they are valorized by finding an external market. All of these were implied in the move toward working with commercial technologies and more closely with industry than before, yet it must be stressed that they characterize some but not all of IRCAM's current research projects. They followed close on the period of the ethnography, perhaps made acute by the failure effectively to put the 4X into production and by its bizarre nonmusical fate, and they are no doubt due also to external pressures on IRCAM for evidence of productive research. So the prestige attendant on exclusive technologies (the 4X) has been eclipsed by the potential for wider validation by industry and the market.

Finally, there is a new concern with the user interface, with attempting to produce technologies amenable to musician users who are without vast technical and scientific expertise. But while there are notable improvements in this direction with software such as Max, its adequate use still depends on a mastery of the interdisciplinary technical and scientific knowledge outlined in chapter 8. It is just that the inscription of this knowledge in the new programs has been streamlined — made more coherent and productive — by being subordinated to the logical and visual structures of the Mac graphical interface.

Even what were previously pure scientific departments — such as Acoustics — have been transformed by the new performative ethos. Following a decade of desultory IRCAM research on room acoustics, a series of breakthroughs by one researcher in the late '80s made it possible to plot the covariance of a room's physical properties with significant changes in subjects' perception of sound. This represented important progress in the scientific understanding of room acoustics. It was followed by a great increase in staffing and prestige, and by the early '90s the project had become one of the largest in IRCAM, while one of its researchers was promoted to Scientific Director. At the same time, this research became tied to several areas of industrial applications. These include consultancy to architects on the aural design of public spaces and concert halls and appraisal of existing halls, but also aspirations to make a significant splash in the currently most fashionable field of high-level computing — virtual reality. IRCAM proposes that its room acoustical research will lead to technologies that perfectly simulate the spatialization of sound — that is, to aural virtual reality. With the enormous commercial and military interests in this area (Sherman and Judkins 1992), such a development would bring great kudos and revenue; but as yet it is far from achieved, and its musical uses remain obscure. Given this new success, it may become increasingly unclear how IRCAM's work differs from sophisticated commercial research and development in this field. Hence, a certain haunting ambiguity surrounds the performative ethos, challenging as it does Boulez's original principles, IRCAM's founding charter, and the former official conception of IRCAM's role in the field.

The other main axis of change within IRCAM concerns links to the outside world through marketing and education. Under Bayle's influence, IRCAM has shown in recent years an increasing emphasis on active marketing. The Public Relations (previously Diffusion) department has grown; new personnel have been brought in specifically to market IRCAM's scientific and technology projects as well as music. The push on external and internal communication is evidenced by a profusion of journals and magazines directed at every level of public interest: from IRCAM's high-brow music theory journal, *Inharmoniques*, to a middleweight publication directed at the ordinary public, *Résonance*, to an internal house magazine — lightweight, friendly, fun — called *Opus*. This is a sophisticated and determined onslaught aimed at converting each category of public opinion — professionals in music and science, the media, the interested public, workers — to a sympathetic and appropriately "informed" view. Compared with IRCAM's erstwhile gestures, it is scientific marketing.

The same thoroughness of vision and concern with meeting different demands characterizes the now transformed educational structure. It includes a doctoral program in musicology, a one-year *stage* in computer music for select international students and graduates of the *conservatoires*, and there are plans for a similar *stage* for science graduates wanting to enter computer music research. This is light-years away from the inadequacies of the six-week *stages* of '84, although *stagiaires* still go on to be exploited as junior tutors (and thus to gamble on higher promotion). Through these initiatives the widely held impression of IRCAM as uninterested in training unknown locals and as unconcerned with making links to other training bodies — the music schools, the universities, the CNRS — is being overturned.

At the same time, the developments in education and marketing ensure the wider and deeper diffusion of IRCAM's ideology and genealogy of modern music, its multiple penetration into various diverse publics. They represent, in other words, an attempt to stimulate a constantly expanding reproduction of cultural capital.

While the net result of the changes described is that IRCAM has become a dependable machinery for music and technology production, the new performative and pragmatic ethos has not been incurred without losses. Soon after the period described in the ethnography there was a change of atmosphere in the institute, and especially its research culture, toward what is seen as a "dark age" or spoken of simply in terms of profound closure. Thus ended the culture of collective debate and utopian speculation of the musicians' group vanguard in '84, as did the more mundane habit of cross-project collaboration. Projects became discrete affairs with little mutual dialogue. Researchers and composers just got on with the job. There were no general, open research meetings to discuss work in progress and float future ideas. (In 1992 I happened to be present at the first such meeting in years. Significantly, few in the room knew of the earlier precedents.) The change was symbolized in the new custom of locking all offices, studios, and labs. Practical and imaginative mobility were reduced; knowledge became increasingly private and individualized. Informants mourned the passing of the earlier spirit of IRCAM, which existed partly through the influence of certain key figures — among them several American directors who left in the middle to late '80s — and which vanished as IRCAM's young adulthood turned into the settled and "stabilized" maturity of the present.

CONTINUITIES

Despite these developments, the basic social, theoretical, and aesthetic dimensions of IRCAM appear largely to be continuous with the past, as do some of the central problems and contradictions of music research and production. As an organization, IRCAM remains as it has always been: a hierarchical, now increasingly efficient bureaucratic institution. The direction and control of IRCAM remain strongly centralized in the hands of the new Director. However, staff speak nearly unanimously of his more humane and pleasant regime, and it seems that many of the Machiavellian excesses characteristic of internal politics in earlier eras have gone.

The division of labor at the heart of music production remains the same. Tutors are still employed as technical assistants, despite the creative nature of their work and its centrality to IRCAM's production. Tutors also remain key repositories of knowledge about IRCAM technologies and their musical potential in the still largely oral culture of research and production. Officially, they are denied the status of composers. Yet as one tutor told me, when he complained of the level of his wages an official retorted off the record that the tutor also had "secret"

time for his music, didn't he? — thus making plain the tacit and contradictory agenda of the contract. While resting on a complex and collaborative labor, then, IRCAM music continues to be officially conceived in
terms of the reified individual author.

One of Bayle's main strategies in the present is to cultivate IRCAM's
relations with a new, younger generation of primarily European "star"
composers[3] — indeed, to bring them into being as "stars." This is no
altruistic mission, since with the waning of the older generation and
specifically of Boulez it is imperative for IRCAM to bring on talent that
in its turn will serve as the basis of IRCAM's legitimation. Given the
urgency of this need, given the weighty apparatus of marketing, and
given that the relationship is two-way — IRCAM legitimizing its composers while at the same time depending on them for validation — there
may well be a temptation for IRCAM to confuse roles and behave increasingly like a promotional agency. Central to these processes of legitimation and marketing, again, is the romantic reification of authorship.[4]
In its official ideology IRCAM therefore continues to reproduce a fundamental tension by ignoring the objective dispersal of authorship and so
the radically transformed nature of its own practices.

My intention here is not to suggest that we dissolve the category of the
author into the division of labor as a whole; or to make a utopian celebration of the computer's "subversive" potential for indeterminate authorship (as, for example, in Poster 1990, 114–15). My point is not that
authorship becomes in principle shared equally among all parties contributing to the final result; it is simply that an attempt should be made
to take precise stock of different contributions and of the social relations within which collaboration occurs, an assessment that is currently
avoided. We have seen in earlier chapters that IRCAM contains within
itself the two extreme tendencies of this avoidance, each with its own
problems: in music production, an excessive preciosity of the heroic
individual author; in software development, an excessive disregard for
the protection and reward of individual intellectual property.

Bayle has proposed that a key priority is for IRCAM to cultivate
regular, longer-term relations with a number of composers (Bayle 1992,
29). Creating a group of more self-sufficient and technologically literate
composers may weigh against the continuing need for tutoring. But as
long as composers only visit, they will remain in need of help from those
continuous residents with up-to-the-minute (orally bequeathed, socially
mediated) knowledge of IRCAM tools and research — a key function of

the tutors. Moreover a caste of semipermanent composers will invite accusations of closure and of excessive privilege.

Some of IRCAM's software-based research and production projects continue to be marred by problems of lack of stabilization and documentation: by an overproduction of software "waste products" that absorb a great deal of energy but that are not made available for wider or repeated use. There is thus a continuing tendency for unproductive and introverted research. While most of the forces analyzed earlier continue to be relevant, with the new possibilities for commercial production the authors of a working program may now gain some recompense for their work. So there are stronger incentives to stabilize and document, as well as to assert intellectual property rights. Yet these still seem in certain cases to be outweighed by the unstable and ever-changing environment, the tendency for an oral culture, and the seductions of a medium encouraging a constant open-ended process of creative bricolage.

IRCAM continues to develop more ambitious, high-level software for music conceptualization and control. As before with Formes, this has the air of an advanced area of research but one that is fragile and speculative — a fragility that threatens to deepen in the new performative context. Two projects of this kind existed in the early '90s, and both were very small. They focused on rival French composers brought in to represent two opposing compositional ideologies: one a Boulezian postserialist, the other in the tradition of "spectral" composition, concerned with deriving musical structure and process from timbre, and particularly timbral transitions. This was, then, the latest attempt to create an experimental nexus of ideological conflict within the institute — to stage a battle between the two tendencies. The meeting referred to earlier — the first open research discussion in years — was called in '92 to debate the merits and fate of the "spectral" project, which vied with its rival in front of an internal audience of directors and researchers. The "spectral" composer had developed a program called Patchwork that offers an elegant (Maclike) graphical interface through which spectral analysis, synthesis, and music-structural processes can be pursued, and this had become the centerpiece of IRCAM's new push in an area designated "Computer Aided Composition." Differently conceived, but in the same tradition as Formes (and similarly written in the AI language LISP), Patchwork raises the continuing questions of what status these advanced programs have vis à vis composition, and given their ethereal, noncommercial status, their role in IRCAM's legitimation. I want now to look at these questions in detail.

REPRODUCTION: LEGITIMATION, DISPLACEMENT, AND DENIAL

We have seen that the theoreticism, concern with technology, and scientism of IRCAM's musical discourse are no spontaneous conjuncture but are legacies of the continuous character of modernism through the century. At IRCAM and within high-level computer music these elements are reinvigorated and obtain new force. It is proposed that music research, psychoacoustics, and cognitive science in music, and their application in AI-influenced software such as Formes, PL's interactive system, the musical expert system, or Patchwork, will provide new constructive or generative bases for composition through their capacity to analyze and then model the fundamental structures and "rules" of musical process.

A classic article on AI and music by Roads (1980) provides an overview of these developments and epitomizes the rhetorical flavor of the argument:

> The germ idea of organizing musical compositions around a set of systematic procedures contains within it the implication that these procedures could be made automatic. The inverse notion, gaining ever more significance, is that these procedures and syntactic structures can be *recognized* automatically. Indeed, one of the fundamental notions of any AI application is that it can be characterized as rule-structured. Certainly one of the major tasks of composition is creating a rule system . . . for a piece.
>
> (Roads 1980, 14)

Roads adds a rhetorical device symptomatic of this discourse: "Clearly, creative composers do not simply execute a fixed set of instructions. . . . Of course music is not just rules; but rule specification is one component of composition" (ibid.).

This qualification appears to make the prior claims quite reasonable, and yet throughout the rest of the discussion its implication — that there is more to creative composition and aesthetic innovation than the following or executing of formal musical structures — is never developed. Roads's piece discusses various formalist AI approaches and concludes with a list of applications of AI techniques in computer music, including: "intelligent instruments . . . intelligent musical data bases . . . a better understanding of human musical cognition and musical universals." It ends by returning to composition: "and new and interesting compositional rule structures" (ibid., 23).

Similar rhetoric is also characteristic of IRCAM. A 1985 paper by the then director of Music Research begins with the assertion that the main issues confronting contemporary music research are cognitive and not technological. With reference to AI, he calls for work that makes explicit and formalizes musical knowledge in the search for improved means of control of musical processes.

This is therefore a new, currently dominant discourse aimed at transcending the negational character of musical modernism. At one level these areas of research are continuous with the earlier attempts to make sciences (previously maths, information theory, acoustics) the basis for musical composition. But at another level, by attempting to derive scientific models specifically from music, they appear closer to music and less arbitrary in their relation to it. Despite this concern to develop metalanguages for music that derive from the "nature" of music itself, the same logic is at work: the view that domains of knowledge purportedly analogous to or derived from the analysis of music can become the basis of new music. Thus, in texts written from this perspective one finds a constant elision or movement between computer-aided music analysis and computer-aided composition, based on the assumption that refined analysis can be used to generate compositional ideas. Or, continuous with modernism in general, there is simply the assumption that the "aesthetics" of science will also translate into, and provide, an aesthetics for music — the notion underlying the many instances that we saw within IRCAM of more arbitrary conceptual foraging from science (genetic biology, fractal geometry) as a basis for composition.

While apparently providing more "appropriate" metalanguages for music, there are several problems with the AI approaches. They derive either from very general physical, perceptual, or structural characteristics of musical sound (as in acoustic and psychoacoustic research), or from very particular aesthetic characteristics (as with computer analysis of the aesthetic patterns or "rules" of specific, extant musical forms).[5] In the first case, it is questionable to assume that an aesthetic can be deduced from such general laws, which may be necessary for composition but, crucially, are not sufficient. A good example of this kind of strategy — the move from the general and scientific to the aesthetically particular — is an article by Lerdahl (1988), an American composer-researcher who has made several visits to IRCAM. He begins by proposing various cognitive constraints on musical comprehensibility, moves from this through a critique of the "cognitive opacity" (251) of serialism, and ends by putting forward two aesthetic principles for good music that accommodate the cognitive constraints, with the clear implication that these can help to prescribe compositional guidelines. Lerdahl thus moves from cognitive "rules" to aesthetic critique, and from this to "aesthetic claims" (255–57) or propositions framed, still, in very general cognitive terms.

As regards the second case above, it is problematic to depict the "rules" derived from analysis of one musical aesthetic as either musically universal or generative of new aesthetic forms. In fact, the likely effect of applying "rules" derived from one musical genre to composition is to inhibit any possibility of profound aesthetic innovation and to encourage just variants of the extant genre. In this sense, AI-influenced composition represents its ultimate rationalization, the scientistic, high-cultural version of what Adorno (1978a, 1990) accused the cultural industries of bringing about: the standardization of music.

Yet within IRCAM such areas of research are applied in technologies that it is claimed or implied are both universal and aesthetically valuable in a general sense. We saw this in PL's reluctance in the mid-1980s to discuss the aesthetic specificity of his improvising software. But the strongest example was the Formes program, which, based on LISP, provided a set of hierarchical and recursive principles for structuring musical "objects" into compositions. The program was proposed as a general or universal compositional environment; its basis was a deductive hypothesis of musical structure or grammar. It was seen as an aid to composition—implying that its syntactic character could be transformed into specific compositional or aesthetic semantics. Yet at the same time as the designers encouraged this move from the general to the musically particular, they were also tempted in the opposite direction, beyond music, toward even broader and more universal uses of the program: they proposed that Formes could find equally valid applications in computer graphics, video, and robotics.[6] There is, then, a constant desire to universalize, either by moving from the scientifically (for example cognitively or perceptually) "universal" to the aesthetic (and therefore particular), or to universalize what are specific aesthetic characteristics. This universalizing tendency, and the claims that the models derive from the underlying "nature" of musical processes, are legitimizing strategies, and ideological. They are ideological in attempting to evade and cover up what is most difficult and appears to be most missing: particular, innovative aesthetic developments—interesting new musical directions. No less than with the other arbitrary, scientistic intertextual references in musical modernism, the discourse of AI in computer music is used to overdetermine the music rather than, as it presents itself, to "reflect" (or "explicitly model") the "nature" of music.[7] It is an attempt to provide an ahistorical, acultural and, paradoxically, nonaesthetic basis for musical aesthetics.

Something of the fragility of this evasion of the modernist aesthetic impasse through the elaboration of a vast superstructure of scientistic theory can be glimpsed through a few significant doubts expressed privately by key IRCAM subjects. Thus, we saw in chapter 7 how both Boulez and a composer centrally involved in the musicians' group vanguard expressed skepticism about the theoretical project of music research and its usefulness for composing. And one of IRCAM's psychoacousticians, whose research was often cited by IRCAM composers as the basis of their pieces, said with frustration and doubt that he really could not see how his work was applied in their music. He dismissed the supposed psychoacoustic bases of the music of four well-known IRCAM composers as pure rhetoric. Perhaps these private doubts, focused on the contradiction between public rhetoric and actual musical practice, signaled these individuals' own sense of the arbitrary and mystifying relation between theory and practice.

Finally and more simply, we have seen phenomena that question the rational, scientific basis of computer music even at the level of synthesis and analysis of sound materials. We saw this in the lack of predictability of digital synthesis of rich and complex sounds, despite the apparent rational control of all variables (chapter 7), and in AV's dissatisfaction with the digital simulation of organic timbres based on thorough computer analysis of their components — his sense that there was nonetheless something missing (chapter 8). These small but significant moments undermine the omnipotent rhetoric that surrounds computer music synthesis. Whatever the limitations of the technologies in 1984, and despite individuals' assurances that problems such as these have since been superseded due to technological progress, there remain certain subtle but significant qualities of ambient sound production that continue to elude computer simulation.[8]

By the '90s, IRCAM subjects seem more aware of these issues and more prepared to air them. Yet in doing so they reveal the contradictions of the cognitivist tactic. In the open meeting in '92 to debate Patchwork, researchers were tentatively prepared to admit the aesthetically imbued nature of the program, and that its musical character was in some ways overdetermined not only by the "spectral" aesthetic of the designer-composer but also by the conceptual character of LISP. But it was noticeable that in this meeting, concerned with formulating the program's proper terms of legitimation, no one thought to defend it on the basis of the specific and therefore limited aesthetic that it does favor. The program's particular aesthetic character, then, did not serve as sufficient justification. Indeed, because the program's aesthetic "partiality" was now nakedly revealed rather than obscured by a cloud of grandiose universalizing claims, it was used as a basis for launching an attack by the designer-composer's ideological rival, who relished the opportunity to chide the program for being aesthetically biased — as though this was a fault that could be avoided. Symptomatically, another commentator, a tutor, in criticizing the musical limits of Patchwork (he said it was "not very musical," meaning not to his own aesthetic tastes), sought to mitigate his critique by a return to universalizing rhetoric: he added that the program was useful nonetheless as a "metalanguage."

The whole discussion centered on the extent to which any program can be expected to be polysemic, multivocal, and so allow different uses — and in this sense be "structural" or "universal." Yet, with the exception of the rival composer driven by polemical intent, the meeting was evasive about the logical corollary — that is, that any program will also be closed and offer only a limited range of possible expressions; so that the important question is, what range, for which aesthetic, and which composer-users? Despite the signs of greater awareness of these issues, the events described therefore show the continuing inhibition within IRCAM about facing specifically aesthetic issues, the tendency to back off from articulating, making, and defending particular aesthetic choices — all of which reproduces an internal culture of implicit aesthetic uncertainty, as before.

But this is not the public face of IRCAM in the 1990s. Bayle has argued in no uncertain terms that IRCAM will continue in the tradition of Boulez — that the task is to reinvigorate the original, by implication modernist, goals. And this task is now articulated by Bayle and his colleagues in explicit and scathing opposition to postmodernism. Thus, the departure of the Americans in the late '80s has been timely for what amounts to IRCAM's current ideological reconstruction.

It is interesting to trace the roots of this process in Bayle's approach when he first arrived as Artistic Director in 1986. He came from being the founder and director of the innovative Strasbourg *Musica* festival, centered on contemporary music but with an eclectic program including elements of "advanced" jazz, mixed-media events, and concerts sited in factories. Bayle was able to build up a sufficiently large audience that the festival became renowned as the first in France to obtain a substantial proportion of funds from ticket sales. Newly arrived, Bayle spoke of bringing fresh perspectives to IRCAM, despite resistance, and of increased pressure from the Ministry for evidence of greater public interest in IRCAM. However, despite the wider musical perspective of *Musica*, Bayle was firm that these pressures required no change of artistic policy. IRCAM should continue to invite the same kind of composers as previously — he called them *"les IRCAMiens,"* implying this was now a well-recognized category — since the character of the institute was already fixed and its parameters set. The task, then, was to do well what IRCAM had set out to achieve.

> To continue to exist, it's imperative that what IRCAM has defined as its project must succeed strongly. . . . Because if I now bring in Joachim Kuhn, Frank Zappa — all these names that I hear around [fades out] . . . the more people here are weak, sectarian, the weaker they'll get. I think we must first prove that the research here is important, can find a public, can make commercial and industrial links, can have a strong image. . . . First we must establish all this; and after the public perceives IRCAM differently, we can discuss again.

Bayle mentions Kuhn, a modern jazz pianist, and Zappa, the avant-garde rock musician, implying that names such as these were being suggested by some people as candidates for invitation. But Bayle was adamant that although Kuhn may have played in one of his festivals, this was far from appropriate for IRCAM. He expressed his conviction that IRCAM must stick to its founding musical identity in a political metaphor: he said that if the Socialists were to come too close to the Communists, they would inevitably lose their identity, cease to exist, disappear.

Instead of a changed musical policy to revivify IRCAM's flagging public image, Bayle proposed devoting increased attention and resources to the marketing of IRCAM and its music. This was the origin of the developments mentioned earlier. He said that his purpose with *Musica* had been to answer a fundamental question: whether the lack of a public for contemporary music was due to the "problem of [musical] language," the aesthetic crisis of modernism, or due to a problem with how the music is presented to the public — which he called its *"insertion sociale"* (social integration). While conceding that there may perhaps be a problem of language, Bayle stressed that his festival had obtained good results by new strategies of presentation: "[It] had an image, color, vivacity . . . the aim of marketing is to project contemporary music with these qualities"; and he proposed to take the same approach with IRCAM. Bayle soon also began his policy of shifting public attention and IRCAM resources systematically toward a group of younger, less-known, and primarily European IRCAM composers, as shown by the selection of composers to represent IRCAM in the important tenth anniversary concerts at the CGP in 1987.

The imagination and energy that Bayle and his colleagues have put into revolutionizing the *insertion sociale* of IRCAM music are astounding: the improved marketing and education program; the greater links with the outside world evidenced by launching journals, public open days, conferences; the planning of a new annual IRCAM festival; a stress on the need for concerts and performances to work as "spectacle," as "event." The message is that a continuation of IRCAM's Boulezian charter need not mean social closure. In conversation, Bayle made a teasing analogy with *perestroika*, arguing that like the former Soviet Union after Stalinism, IRCAM after Boulez must open up to the outside but still hold strong to its unique history and identity, the implication being that the key issue at stake is how to accommodate market forces without losing the strengths of "autonomous" (statist) social and cultural planning.[9]

Bayle has made two other canny innovations in the insertion of IRCAM composers into broader cultural life. First, he is encouraging his composers to go further afield, to be played internationally, so that they come to be perceived not strictly as "*IRCAMiens*" but as autonomous talents validated by the wider musical world who also have a presence at IRCAM. Second, he is urging IRCAM composers to work beyond the concert hall — not quite in factories, but in opera, in collaboration with dance, in film, and so on, sometimes on a grand scale. (One of the cohort, Philippe Manoury, has a commission from the *Opéra de la Bastille*.) This opening up of the forms of IRCAM music and the creation of alliances with other cultural domains is in some ways a long-overdue step in the direction of closer links between IRCAM and the other high arts, and between it and the media — a task that the present director of Pedagogy has commented upon (Barrière 1990, 154). Thus, it may be that a new era has arrived that will effect a greater popularization of IRCAM music and a broadening of its audience.

However, despite the diversity of forms and improved *insertion sociale*, in the early '90s the basic aesthetic of IRCAM music remained similar to that in the '80s, as did its theoretical mediations. Bayle's ambitious strategy may therefore also be to some extent a displacement that evades the core problem of his own designated task for IRCAM: the renewal of the modernist aesthetic. Thus, a plurality of forms and of alliances with the other arts risks substituting for a real diversity of aesthetic or for specifically musical innovation; while activities in the domains of diffusion, reproduction, and reception risk displacing attention from the problems and particularities of production.

It is useful here to examine briefly how IRCAM's leading figures of the present construe postmodernism. On the one hand, Bayle suggested with humor in an interview that the majority of IRCAM musical works these days *are* postmodern in the sense that they are capable of "seducing" the listener musically and dramatically, implying that they are no longer austerely modernist and can draw a public. Yet in an article from 1990 Bayle takes the Boulezian stance, criticizing the postmodernism that rummages among past forms as regressive, and writing scornfully of the '80s as privileging "immediate seduction" and as an era of impoverishment and standardization dominated by the dubious legitimacy of the "majority" (Bayle 1990, 11, 14). The director of Pedagogy, in another polemical essay, attacks postmodernism in many guises: in terms of the nostalgic cult of the past; in terms of the neoliberalist advocacy of market forces in culture; in terms of the equation of market value with artistic value; in terms of the omnipresence and dominance of publicity as a cultural form (Barrière 1990). What these positions have in common is a renewed Adornian cultural critique. They are notably ambivalent on the question of the progressive aspects of "seductive" aesthetic appeal.

This ambivalence is quietly echoed in IRCAM music. Overall, the music is still characterized by the willful and rebarbative complexity and dissonance of the modernist aesthetic. A few current IRCAM works do have the shadow of postmodern aesthetic influence — although not, it is true, of the "retro" kind of which Boulez, Bayle, and others are so dismissive. There are gestures at both greater "simplicity" (within the modernist framework) and at lush orchestration (characteristic of *Répons*), but these are really dilutions rather than transformations of modernism. More interestingly, certain pieces include hints of ethnic and modal reference, of rhythmic pulsation or repetition. Is this a sleight of hand — the introduction of elements of nonwestern or popular music aesthetics in practice while the rhetoric remains aloof, and so a subtle (and disavowed) shift toward postmodern aesthetic terrain?

Yet despite a certain destabilization of the terms, the dominant mode of address of IRCAM discourse — music and theory — is telling and remains continuous with the analyses given in chapters 2 and 10: that is, postmodern art music is addressed, if scorned, or if ambivalently; the cultural market at large is addressed and berated; whereas popular music itself remains significantly unaddressed, or only fleetingly addressed, and so absolutely "other."

We have seen, then, that while change in IRCAM's technological culture has been possible in response to changing external conditions (the rising importance and power of small systems), aesthetic-musical change has not. Of the two key arenas of discursive struggle within IRCAM in the mid-1980s, technological conflict, which was explicit and overtly ideological, in conjunction with external pressures could produce cultural change, while aesthetic dissent, which was largely hidden, fragmented, and dealt with by intrasubjective mechanisms, could not. It seems therefore that IRCAM's aesthetic character has been central to the definition and maintenance of its identity and must appear, at least, to be unchanging.

Two discursive mechanisms seem to be dominant in the continuing historical reproduction of musical modernism. One is its carefully maintained avoidance of the components of popular-music aesthetics. Meanwhile the "enemy" explicitly addressed is regressive postmodern art music. So the aesthetic denial of popular music remains (nearly) complete. The second is the creation of a sense of aesthetic change or "progress" through various sublimations or displacements: on the one hand, the alliance with technological change and scientific advance; on the other, the sense of movement generated by making bridges to or analogies with the other arts. As I have argued, both of these sublimations have characterized modernism throughout the century. Both involve a turning outward to other highly legitimate fields for inspiration, as though this in itself would solve the essentially internal aesthetic problems of modernism.[10] The displacements also act as a kind of alibi masking the deeper mechanism: denial of that closer kin, popular musics. In adopting only sublimated solutions to its musical problems, the antidiscourse that is musical modernism acts as a brutal machinery not only for the denial of the utopian moments of popular music and culture, but also for the suppression of its own real transformation — a stasis that is no doubt encouraged by the desire to hold on to the hegemony that it has enjoyed in past decades.

The production of IRCAM music has both been "transformed" — or at least certain of its mediations have been changed (its technologies, to some extent its economic and ideological forms given the increasing emphasis on scientific and technological performativity and their cohabitation with commerce), but there has also been an underlying continuity of the aesthetic, theoretical, institutional, and social forms of production. As yet, the combination of a statist institution founded basically, still, on cultural capital and the modernist aesthetic imperative has served to contain other potential sources of change and to maintain the mobile stasis of a hegemonic cultural system. As a long-term cultural system, musical modernism thus reproduces itself.

I do not intend to imply here that all cultural systems are essentially stable and tend toward simple reproduction. Rather, I would suggest that certain dominant cultural systems — as revealed by Foucault's analyses, and as disclosed here for musical modernism — do tend toward continuity and the absorption or suppression of difference because of the cumulative momentum of historical authority and power that they bear, and because of their capacity for subjectification — for forming subjectivities in the image of their own cultural unconscious. We have seen some of the means by which these are accomplished: the construction of genealogies, the control of reproduction and the linking of it to production so as to legitimize present work by reference to the past, and thus the cumulative legitimacy of powerful cultural systems (a strategy central to Boulez's personal history, to the history of modernism, and to IRCAM); and at another level, the molding of subjectivity shown by the processes of intrasubjective fragmentation and repression that prevent different aesthetics from entering IRCAM. The result of these intrapsychic forces is to evade any challenge to the legitimacy of IRCAM's dominant aesthetic and to produce compliant subjectivities within IRCAM. However, in principle not all cultural systems will be equally powerful or so able to evade transformation. And despite this analysis, there is always an element of indeterminacy: there may be factors, whether internal or external, beyond IRCAM's control that may still produce pressure for change within the institute.

While the commercial production of its technologies appears increasingly successful, IRCAM does not gain external legitimacy by finding a substantial public for its music. However, we have seen that the institute touches on a number of overlapping specialist domains — scientific, technological, artistic — so that rather than great success in one or two domains, it relates to and exchanges with several disparate constituencies. Added up, this composite public for its work is not so small and is international, highly legitimate, and powerful.

We have also seen throughout this study an emphasis on internal legitimation within the institute. Indeed, despite their criticisms, officials from the Ministry of Culture in 1986 acceded to this as an appropriate state of affairs for such a highly privileged and unique institution: that IRCAM should be subject to a process of self-monitoring and self-assessment. Thus IRCAM has to legitimize its work, but it does so through a constant reflexive search to formulate the terms of its own legitimation. Where Lyotard (1984, 38) depicts this as characteristic of scientific discourse, we have seen — in both the historical analysis, including Boulez's career, and the ethnography — that it is equally characteristic of artistic discourse, in which production is linked to and legitimized by reproduction, while the latter is itself accomplished through the production of a discursive genealogy — a canon.

We can see, finally, that IRCAM's legitimation is accomplished by the subtle interplay between two dimensions of modernist discourse. First, by the explicit, substantive ideological content of the discourse, with its utopian stress on innovation and progress, its orientation to the future. And second, by its implicit structuration: the long-term historical continuity of modernism and so the cumulative authority and legitimacy that it has accrued. The two dimensions are, logically, in contradiction, and there is a profound tension between them — the apparent leaning toward the future and the careful, deep-structural conformity to tradition. Yet when this is overlooked and the two are unconsciously experienced as complementary, they create together a formidable legitimacy, satisfying the desire for both rupture, newness, change, and for historical continuity and consolidation.

In a summarizing statement on postmodernism, Lyotard writes: "The artist and the writer, then, are working without rules in order to formulate the rules of what *will have been done.* . . . *Post modern* would have to be understood according to the paradox of the future (*post*) anterior (*modo*)" (1984, 81; emphases in original). But this idealization describes not so much the practice as the ideology of the avant-garde, since, as I have tried to show, once the long-term aesthetic and discursive continuity of modernism is traced, this undermines the avant-garde rhetoric of constant innovation and change. It becomes possible to discern the implicit discursive "rules" being followed within IRCAM and elsewhere that continue to construct and constrain the "innovations" of avant-garde musical practice.

WHAT IS TO BE DONE?
THE VIEW FROM THE TOWER

In 1990, the latest of IRCAM's architectural expansions occurred with the opening of the "tower": a tall, glass-walled and red-brick construction rising from the Place Stravinsky that now houses the administrative departments and the offices of the Director. With bullish confidence this was announced as just the first phase of planned extensions. What does the political landscape look like from the heights of the tower? What does this bode for IRCAM's future?

IRCAM suffered particularly bad press in the early 1990s. The low point was a vitriolic exchange conducted in the pages of the quality French papers between Boulez and Michel Schneider, then director of music at the Ministry of Culture and supposedly in charge of French musical life. Schneider was known for his "democratizing" plans, and had also come into conflict with those directing changes in the French Opera houses. Schneider argued that even IRCAM, along with all state beneficiaries, should undergo an evaluation of its use of public funding. This was no covert neoliberal attack on state money for the arts but part of a program to set up an apparatus to judge, coolly, the current state of music policy. Boulez resisted, and in 1991 Schneider resigned — an outcome that many took to confirm the extraordinary political power wielded by Boulez[11] and the continuing draw in high places of his determinedly modernist and centralist rhetoric.

But these events also point to the ambiguity of Boulez's current role vis à vis IRCAM. On the one hand he has appeared as IRCAM's guardian angel, affording the institute absolute protection. On the other, for postmodernists, Leftist populists and Rightist neoliberals alike, he has come to symbolize the worst excesses of the modernist and statist cultural project and he has become an obvious whipping boy. In this sense he may equally be a liability for IRCAM.

Recent years have also seen shifts in the music research policies of the *Direction de la Musique*. For decades its funding category of music research has been synonymous with the pursuit of technology and "hard" experimental science around music. Now, the grosser technicism of the concept is being questioned and it is gradually being understood to include the "softer" human sciences of music — musicology, ethnomusicology, sociology of music. But IRCAM — in any case not dependent on the *Direction* for funding — seems as yet to have been relatively immune to these wider discursive shifts. Ironically, they have reinforced its dominance of the French field, since a number of smaller music technology centers have closed.

Fortuitously, the composition of Bayle's cohort of promising composers, coinciding with the rise and rise of Europe as a political entity, is in accord with wider interests in providing European rivals to American cultural postmodernism. At the same time, and in line with the deepening recession, there are also hints of a nationalist retrenchment in French cultural policy.[12] The paradox is that adopting a "localist" strategy at IRCAM, while promoting European and French composers, is also likely to lower its international prestige, so weighing against the institute's survival in its present form. From the composer's point of view, according to an American informant, IRCAM's international profile has lessened, and given the technological changes that mean composers can work with technologies almost as sophisticated as those on offer at IRCAM in their own home, there is now little inducement to go to IRCAM. A British composer agreed, arguing that it was the possibility of a first-rate performance of one's composition by the EIC and the still-great prestige of a Parisian premiere that drew composers enthusiastically back.[13]

On the domestic front, the landslide success of the French Right in the parliamentary elections of 1993, the subterranean shifts in public opinion this reflected, and the new climate of austerity arising from the government's huge budget deficits are felt by some to bode ill for IRCAM by weakening the institute's political support. As I have shown, despite certain differences in cultural policy and despite unending public cultural debate and polemic, there has nonetheless been a remarkable continuity and consensus between governments of the Right and Left in recent decades concerning the dominant French cultural institutions. This is, of course, what has allowed many significant new developments to occur and to flourish. In the volatile context of fin de siècle Europe, in which all previous certainties, including those of cultural modernity, are being undermined, the coming period may see the end of this cumulative cultural-political trajectory and a profound questioning of the place of an institution such as IRCAM. On the other hand, the major cultural institutions appear to be so definitive of French cultural and intellectual identity that such an apocalyptic scenario may be quite misjudged. Certainly, IRCAM's status as an institute of creation and production as well as reproduction endows it not only with greater privilege but also with greater vulnerability and risk than its sister institutions — the museums, opera houses, conservatoires that deal primarily with the art of the past, with exhibition, performance, and education.

Given the uncertainties of the wider political arena, we may still speculate: will IRCAM be able to hold together its mixed economy of performative criteria in one domain (technology) and "autonomy" in the other (music)? Will there be a transformation also of the criteria for the music and an invasion of market forces? Or will the centrifugal structuration produced by the two forces lead in the opposite direction: to a logical completion of the modernist project of increasing autonomization of composition and musical creativity, now realized socially, to match the autonomization of the aesthetic? Will there come a time when IRCAM composers are liberated not only from the "seductions of the market" (the pleasing of the broader public) but from institutional dependence and the equally powerful injunctions this brings? Perhaps by being individually salaried by the state (Barrière 1990, 157–58), so that they and other artists and intellectuals come to constitute a kind of social caste, judging and managing their own affairs and becoming, even more than today, the legitimate audience for their own work.[14] But is this to be desired?

Appendix

*IRCAM Workers and Visitors as
Introduced in the Text, by Acronym*

CHAPTER 4

BU	4X Hardware director, also 4X designer
KR	Low-status service/administrative worker
TY	Director in the Administration
VO	4X Industrialization director
WOW	Junior tutor, ex–Chant/Formes, composer, later Music Research director
WS	Director in the Administration

CHAPTER 5

AV	Visiting composer on commission in 1984
HM	Junior tutor, psychoacoustician, later Pedagogy director
HY	Music Research director, composer
ID	Visiting American music software researcher
LK	Administrative assistant
MC	Chant/Formes project director
NI	Visiting American commercial music technology entrepreneur, composer
NR	Junior tutor, composer, later Music Research director

RIG   Pedagogy director

WL   Past departmental director, composer

CHAPTER 6

PL   Commissioned American composer, small systems (Apple II) project

CHAPTER 7

BYV   4X Software director, Boulez's unofficial tutor

CX   Past tutor, composer

FOL   Scientific Director

HU   Junior tutor, composer

JDK   Tutor, computer scientist, ex-Chant/Formes

WR   Tutor for Stockhausen visit, composer

XU   Chant/Formes computer scientist

CHAPTER 8

NP   Composer-squatter, later commissioned

XH   Temporary tutor, American researcher and composer

CHAPTER 9

BW   Visiting consultant with Systems team

FA   Systems manager, Systems team director

CHAPTER 10

AJ   4X Signal Processing director

FL   Squatter, sometime junior tutor and technician, composer

GE   Squatter, professor of computer science

KF   Junior tutor, composer

VR   4X technician

WV   Artistic Director

CHAPTER 11

WI   Yamaha corporation representative at IRCAM

Glossary of Terms and Acronyms in the Text

ACOUSTICS: The scientific study of sound, especially its physical properties.

ADC/ANALOG-DIGITAL CONVERTER: A *peripheral* that translates *analog* electronic signals (such as sounds received from a microphone or audio tape) into *digital* coding, which is then passed on for computer processing. (See also *DAC*.)

AI/ARTIFICIAL INTELLIGENCE: A field concerned with developing the use of computers to perform operations analogous to human capacities for learning, or accumulating knowledge and experience, and decision making. Often used to embrace *expert systems* and knowledge-based systems. Incorporates both the cognitive analysis of human reasoning in different areas, in order to model it, and the development of computer programs that simulate "intelligent behavior" and so are presumed to emulate such cognitive processes. Thus, AI exists at the juncture of cognitive science and computer science.

AMPLITUDE: The loudness of a sound, corresponding to the maximum value attained by a sound wave at a given time.

ANALOG: A technology, such as electronic musical instruments and sound processors, based on the operations of continuous electronic signals. (Contrasts with *digital*.)

ASSEMBLER/ASSEMBLER CODE: A program that operates on a higher-level symbolic language or program to produce *machine code*.

CARL: Computer Audio Research Laboratory, University of California at San Diego, USA.

CCRMA: Center for Computer Research in Music and Acoustics, Stanford University, California, USA.

CGP: Centre Georges Pompidou.

CHANT: A computer program for sound synthesis developed at IRCAM, based on simulating *formants*.

CNRS: Centre National de la Recherche Scientifique.

CNSM: Conservatoire National Supérieur de Musique.

CRASH: A failure of the computer system, caused by errors (or bugs) in either hardware or software.

DAC/DIGITAL-ANALOG CONVERTER: A *peripheral* that translates *digital* symbolic representations, for example those of sound waves, into *analog* electronic signals, which in turn drive a transducer such as a loudspeaker, so producing actual sounds. (See also *ADC*.)

DEBUGGING: The process of tracing, and then correcting, bugs (mistakes or logical errors) in a computer program, piece of software, or computer system.

DEC: Digital Equipment Corporation, one of the major multinational computer manufacturers, based in the United States.

DIGITAL: A technology, such as the computer, involving the manipulation of numeric representations based ultimately upon combinations of binary digits, hence upon discrete entities. (Contrasts with *analog*.)

EIC: Ensemble Intercontemporain, IRCAM's principal collaborating orchestra or performing ensemble: a separate organization with the same founder (Boulez) as IRCAM.

ENVELOPE: The overall shape of temporal development of the *amplitude* of a tone, involving phases of attack, sustain, decay, and release.

ESP PRO: Espace de Projection, IRCAM's main concert space, which has a physically modifiable acoustic.

EXPERT SYSTEM: A computer program that encodes a data base of expert knowledge, making it available as an aid. (See also *AI*.)

FILTER: A device that removes or subtracts some specified *frequency* or frequency region of a sound wave or its representation, so allowing only certain frequencies to pass and altering the timbre of the original sound.

FORMANT: A peak *amplitude* in the *frequency spectrum* of a musical tone or sound that corresponds to a peak resonance in the sound source. A characteristic of *timbre*.

FORMES: A high-level computer program for control of musical structure and materials, developed at IRCAM.

4X: A powerful *digital signal processor* developed at IRCAM during the early 1980's, used as the hardware basis for a variety of real-time digital sound synthesis, processing, and analysis techniques.

FREQUENCY: The rate at which the vibrations of a sounding body complete a full cycle, measured in cycles per second (or hertz).

GESTURAL CONTROL: Concern with developing appropriate and enhancing means of human physical, usually manual, control of a technology, whether forming part of a computer terminal or other peripheral, a sound synthesizer (*analog* or *digital*), or an orthodox musical instrument.

GRM: Groupe de Recherches Musicales, based at Radio France (RTF), and part of INA (Institut National de l'Audiovisuel).

HARMONICS/HARMONIC TONES: Complex tones composed of *partials* whose *frequencies* are integral multiples (i.e. multiples of 1, 2, 3, 4 . . . etc.) of the frequency of the fundamental (i.e. the lowest-frequency partial of the tone). (Contrasts with *inharmonics/inharmonic tones*.)

ICMC: International Computer Music Conference.

INHARMONICS/INHARMONIC TONES: Complex tones composed of *partials* whose *frequencies* are *not* integral multiples of each other. (Contrasts with *harmonics/harmonic tones*.)

INTENSITY: The physical property of sound energy.

INTERACTIVE: A computer system or program that is designed to elicit information from, and then "respond" to, the particular attributes or requirements of the human user of the system.

IRCAM: Institut de Recherche et de Coordination Acoustique/Musique.

LAUNCH (A PROGRAM): To set a computer program going to compute samples or perform its functions.

LISP: A programming language designed to manipulate symbolic rather than numerical data, with primary use in *AI* applications.

MACHINE CODE: The coded system adopted in the design of computer hardware to represent the repertoire of possible operations. Hence, instructions written in machine code can immediately be executed, and all higher order languages and programs have ultimately to be translated into machine code in order to control the hardware.

MICROTONALITY: Musical systems based on *pitch* scales of less than a semitone.

MUSIC RESEARCH: General term encompassing *acoustic* and *psychoacoustic* research and research on technological developments around music.

MUSIQUE CONCRÈTE: A composition technique invented by Pierre Schaeffer in 1948 that became the basis of his group, the *GRM*. Originally based on the physical manipulation of recorded natural sounds by techniques of editing, reversal, speed-changing, etc.

OPERATING SYSTEM: General software environment that oversees all other resources within a computer system — hardware, programs, data, and so on. A program that supervises the running of all other programs within a system.

OSCILLATOR: An electronic device that produces a sound waveform: the basis of electronic sound synthesis and so of electronic musical instruments. (In computer music synthesis, oscillators may be simulated by computer.)

PARTIAL: Any component *frequency* of a complex tone.

PASSWORD (COMPUTER): A confidential, usually personal code or group of characters that on input from a terminal allows a user access to use a computer system. Standard form of computer security.

PATCH: In electronic music, the specification and control of a task to be accomplished, for example the production and manipulation of a synthesized sound, using variables such as *frequency, amplitude*, and duration.

PATCHBOARD: A physical device — a board with various means of *gestural control* — that allows key variables to be specified, linked up, and varied in real time, so producing a *patch* for electronic sound and music synthesis. (In computer music synthesis, patches and patchboards may be simulated by computer.)

PDP10, PDP11: Minicomputers manufactured by *DEC* during the late 1970's and early 1980's. IRCAM's main research and production computers during this period.

PERIPHERAL: Machine or physical device that can be operated under the control of, or that acts as an extension to, a main computer system.

PITCH: The perceptual quality of tone height or register.

PSYCHOACOUSTICS: The scientific study of the perception and cognition of sound and music.

REAL-TIME COMPUTING: A computer system in which virtually no apparent time lapses between data input and the result of its processing. Hence, the process appears instantaneous and the results of computer processing are available as immediate feedback to the user.

SERIALISM: A technique of composing in which the material for a piece is derived from a fixed sequence, series, or row of the twelve chromatic notes of the scale, and from various structural permutations and transformations of that series.

SIGNAL: An *analog* or *digital* electrical value that represents some physical phenomenon such as sound.

SIGNAL PROCESSOR: An electronic or computer system designed to operate on *signals* so as to transform their characteristics (as, for example, a *filter* does to the *envelope* of a synthesized sound) or to generate *signals*.

SOURCE CODE: The symbolic code in which the operations of a higher computer program or language are written, but which itself requires translation into "object code," which may in turn need translating into *machine code*, in order to be understood by the computer.

SPECTRUM: The physical ingredients of a complex tone: a combination of *partials*, each with a different *frequency, amplitude envelope*, and phase.

STAGE: IRCAM's educational course in computer music for visiting musicians, which lasted six weeks in 1984. (By the 1990's there were several stages of variable length and intensity.)

STAGIAIRE: Student attending a *stage*; postgraduate student.

TERMINAL: A combination of a VDU (screen), keyboard, and perhaps a mouse or other gestural control device, used to receive and input information into a computer system and to write or run programs.

TIMBRAL SYNTAX: The notion of developing principles of musical structure or form from an analysis of the timbral properties of the sound materials in use.

TIMBRAL TRANSITION OR TRANSFORMATION: The notion of creating a process of perceptible change between two or more distinct, identifiable *timbres*.

TIMBRE: Sound color or quality: the attribute of a sound that enables a listener to discriminate between two sounds that are identical in *pitch* and *amplitude*.

TOOL: Slang term used metaphorically by IRCAM researchers to designate any operative combination of software and hardware built to achieve a specific task.

TOTAL SERIALISM: The extension of serialist principles from the organization of *pitch* to all other musical parameters, such as rhythm or duration, dynamic, *timbre*, or attack. (See also *serialism*.)

TURNAROUND TIME: The time that elapses between the input into a program of key variables for sound synthesis or processing and the result being available — or hearing the resultant sound.

UNIX: A well-known computer *operating system* originally developed by Bell Telephone Laboratories in the United States and widely adopted by many manufacturers. Originally linked especially with the *DEC VAX* computers.

VAX: A well-known model of computer made by *DEC* starting in the early 1980's and still in widespread use. IRCAM's main research computer in the mid-1980's.

VDU: Visual Display Unit or televisual screen on which users receive information on computer processes and on their own input of data. Usually linked to a keyboard or similar input device, so making a computer *terminal*.

WORKSTATION: A fully developed, individual computer "environment" where a user can deploy the potentials of a computer system. Usually also incorporating "intelligent" programs, thus giving the user access to a range of high-level operations and controls.

Notes

INTRODUCTION

1. For a fuller discussion of serialism see chapter 2. In brief, serialism is an abstract method of composition developed by Schoenberg and others during the 1920s, following the demise of tonality. It rests on various structural transformations of a basic series or row, itself consisting of an arrangement of all twelve chromatic notes of the scale.

2. On the modern art market see Myers (1983), Hughes (1984), and Crane (1987). On the influence of modernism and the avant-garde on popular culture and commercial art see Walker (1987), and Frith and Horne (1987). The contrast between the fates of modernism in the visual arts and in music emerges by comparing the analyses in Crane (1987) and Menger (1983).

To qualify my point, musical modernism has influenced certain avant-garde experiments in jazz, rock, and pop music; and some film scores owe a debt to the dissonant musical idioms of modernism. But in the first case, the experiments remain marginal and have never gained widespread popularity; and in film music, the modernist element remains a relatively "unconscious," and arguably subordinate, component of the filmic experience (Gorbman 1991). In neither case have modernist experiments fed back into greater public interest in modernist concert music itself — unlike analogous developments in the visual arts.

3. See the work of the American music critics John Rockwell (for example, Rockwell 1984) and Gregory Sandow, who have written for the *New York Times* and the *Village Voice* respectively. Their mediating influences on American composition are discussed in McClary (1985, 1989). It is significant that a recent American visit by Boulez and the Ensemble Intercontemporain, the orchestra closely associated with Boulez, received a scathing review from one of the main music critics of the *New York Times*, Donal Henahan. *New York Times*, 23 February 1991, section 1, 17.

4. This kind of attitude is associated in Britain with composers such as Nicholas Maw and Robin Holloway and in the United States with composers George Crumb, George Rochberg, David Del Tredici, and John Corigliano. In a recent interview, Maw addressed the problem thus. He posed "some pretty hard questions" arising from the absence of recent serious composition in the standard concert repertoire: "Does anyone need my music? Who is the audience, if indeed there is one? What responsibility does the composer, or the audience, have?" (Maw, interview with Fiona Maddocks, *The Independent*, 20 October 1988, 14). Del Tredici has discussed the issues as follows: "Composers now are beginning to realize that if a piece excites an audience, *that doesn't mean it's terrible.* For my generation, it is considered vulgar to have an audience really, *really* like a piece on a first hearing. But why are we writing music except to move people and to be expressive?" (Quoted in Rockwell 1984, 83).

5. I use the term *discourse* in this book in two related, more and less inclusive senses as it was developed in the work of Foucault (1972, 1977, 1980). (See also Laclau 1980 and Cousins and Hussain 1984, 77–97). The restricted sense refers to a system of meaning produced in linguistic practices. The inclusive sense refers to Foucault's theory of "discursive formations" in which, by historical analysis, he traces the close interrelations between power and dominant systems of knowledge as they are embodied in, or produced by, specific practices, institutions, and technologies. In this wider sense discourse thus includes the practices, technologies, and institutions enjoined by a particular form of knowledge — its material and social embodiment.

6. The main example I have in mind is the now classic collection edited by Clifford and Marcus (1986) in which the primary orientation is textual, a critical exploration of the forms of ethnographic practice and writing. The reflexive question in anthropology thus comes to be understood in terms of literary and representational practices alone, as they relate to ethnographic experience. This tends to neglect questions about the social relations, politics, and institutions that underlie the production of anthropological and other knowledges. The only papers in Clifford and Marcus that substantially address these issues are those by Asad and Rabinow.

7. The strongest statement in support of this kind of work comes from Rabinow (1986, 1989), who draws explicitly on Foucault in calling for anthropology to engage with analysis of the power relations inherent in modern forms of representation and knowledge.

Another area in which the need for analysis of the relations between representation and power has been raised is that of debates around Said's *Orientalism* 1978. See, for example, Mani and Frankenberg's (1985) lucid "review of reviews" in which they criticize the tendency to dissociate questions of representation, knowledge, and power from their specific historical and institutional settings.

8. Of the original quotes from interviews, dialogues, and meetings given throughout the book, some have been transcribed directly in English while others have been translated from French. This also helps preserve the anonymity of informants.

CHAPTER 1

1. This state of affairs is noted by Hannerz (1986). Important exceptions are Latour and Woolgar (1979) and Bourdieu (1988).

2. But see Dimaggio (1986), several works of Bourdieu discussed later, and the recent growth of museum studies (e.g. Lumley 1988; Bennett 1988, 1990a; Karp and Lavine 1991; Karp, Kreamer, and Lavine 1992, MacDonald 1992, 1994).

3. The key exception is the tradition of research on production in media studies. See, for example, Glasgow University Media Group (1976), Schlesinger (1978), Silverstone (1985). See also note 5 below.

4. Exceptions are Faulkner (1971, 1973a, 1973b), Kingsbury (1988), Hennion et al. (1983), Hennion (1988), and Menger (1980) and (1983).

5. This is the kind of approach taken in Becker's studies of artistic and cultural production (e.g. 1974, 1978, 1982) and in the work on music of several of his students. See H. S. Bennett (1980), Faulkner (1971, 1973a, 1973b), and Kealy (1974, 1979).

6. These limitations are acknowledged in the editor's preface to Caughie (1981), the standard introduction to poststructuralist debates on authorship, mainly in relation to film theory.

7. For evolutionist perspectives see Cutler (1984, 1985), and Shepherd et al. (1977), the former a Marxist approach, the latter referring to McLuhan's media theory. Instrumentalist views are common in postmodern cultural studies and popular music theory, in which new music technologies are seen as heralding new progressive forms of popular music: punk, rap, hip hop and so on (e.g. Hebdige 1987). Evolutionist views are also prevalent in the fields of art and popular music themselves. Théberge (1991) shows the centrality of evolutionist discourse for popular music in his analysis of commercial magazines explicating the new digital technologies during the 1980s.

8. See Mowitt (1987), Théberge (1989), and Goodwin (1990).

9. See, for example, Turkle (1984), and Suchman (1987).

10. None of the extant disciplines for the social and historical study of music provide a satisfactory basis for this book. With few exceptions (e.g. Kingsbury 1988; Finnegan 1989; Cohen 1991), ethnomusicology has not focused on the musics of western societies. There has also been a tendency to analyze musical cultures internally and locally, with little reference to the broader social and historical context. Musicology has studied the history of western art music using primarily formalist and positivist approaches, while the most dynamic developments in the sociocultural study of western music have been in popular music studies. This split — art music studied as music, popular music studied as social form — is now being questioned (e.g. Leppert and McClary 1987; Wolff 1987; Norris 1989). Kerman (1985) has envisaged a musicology that would address the wider social and cultural dimensions of art music, and certain musicologists are moving this way: see the work of McClary, Subotnik, Pasler, Taruskin, Kramer, as well as Tomlinson (1984) and Treitler (1989), who call for an anthropologically informed musicology. At the same time, popular music scholars are now

attending to musical and aesthetic issues (Frith 1987; Middleton 1990, chap. 7; Wicke 1990).

11. By this I mean to distinguish the work that I discuss from the formalist semiotics of music associated with musicologists Nattiez, Ruwet, and others.

12. I will clarify here my use of classificatory terms for music. I use terms such as "serious," "art," "classical," "modern," "avant-garde" as "emic" concepts drawn from the discourse of high music culture and of my informants; but when freed of excess ideological baggage they also delineate and help to periodize distinct musical cultures. "Serious," "art," and "classical" refer interchangeably to the whole historical body of high-cultural and professional musics of church, court, and concert. As "emic" concepts the terms are used both descriptively and evaluatively: these musics are given high value, often by implicit contrast with the "other" of "low" musical cultures — folk, popular, and mass commercial musics. See Durant (1984) for a deconstruction of "classical" music.

I use "popular music" to delineate *en gros* the "other" macrosociological sphere of modern and contemporary musics, a sphere subsuming all those musics that exist largely separate from the institutions of cultural subsidy. This knowingly elides commercial popular musics with those that are self-produced and marginal or external to commercial circuits. In chapter 2, I sketch out how both have been, in different ways, "other" to musical modernism and postmodernism. In its nondifferentiation, then, "popular music" is a category constructed by the discourses of legitimate music, and it threatens to occlude the enormous variety of musical cultures it subsumes. However there are also undeniable socioeconomic differences between the two macrospheres. (See the discussion of Bourdieu's sociology of culture later this chapter).

13. See Born (1991, 1993a) for a sketch of a social semiotics of music. I draw on these articles in this section.

14. My reading of these shifts in sociocultural studies of music parallels recent moves in media (especially television) studies beyond a limited conception of the text (e.g. Morley 1989).

15. The "authentic performance" movement, with its desire to reinstate "original" instruments, is an extreme expression of this. For a discussion, see Kenyon (1988).

16. The classic example of such an analysis is Turner's (1962, 125) distinction between exegetical and operational meaning in the analysis of ritual symbolism.

17. For a lucid inquiry into the relation between musical notation, music theory, and composition see Cook (1990), although I differ significantly in advocating a more critical exploration of the status accorded to representations and theoretical systems around different musics, and their autonomous ideological and legitimizing effects.

18. I do not intend here to review the centuries of debate on the relation between music and language, and I would concede that, as Lévi-Strauss (1986, 14–30) has argued with implicit reference to Saussure, music shares with language a basic propensity for syntagmatic and paradigmatic organization. My point, however, is to express a fundamental skepticism toward both those theories of music that assert in various ways a natural affinity or analogy between

music and language, as well as those asserting the obverse — that (good) music should have no such relation. In their aesthetic partiality, both approaches fail to interrogate the relations established historically between certain kinds of music and certain forms of language and discourse — which is what I mean to do for IRCAM.

19. Wolff (1987, 11), discussing music's abstraction, argues that this is not unique because abstract painting is also nonrepresentational. In this she confuses an ontological core (music's immanent abstraction) with a formal strategy (abstract painting as a historical style).

20. This is Tagg's (1982) justification for initially using music as a metalanguage for itself. I have evaded here the issue of program music, which is sometimes claimed to have denotative functions. I would argue, however, that this kind of "denotation" is very far from that envisaged by Barthes when he characterized it by reference to the literalness of certain kinds of visual and linguistic representation (Barthes 1977a, 42–46). Thus, I would dispute the view that program music is denotative. We might say, rather, that it aims to be more "literally connotative" than other musics.

21. Feld (1982, 1984a, 1984b) and Roseman (1984, 1991) stress the importance of metaphors in the discourse around music, which are taken as real, and which exist both to express the experience of musical sound and to construct both that experience and composition.

22. My stress on the naturalization of metaphors and discourses around music as a pointer to ideology extends the approach of Becker and Becker (1981), who depict naturalized metaphors as "iconic" and aesthetically powerful without raising their potential ideological effects.

23. For example, the work on music of Dilthey, Simmel, Weber, and Schutz. All treat it as the epitome of their particular theoretical orientation: thus for Weber (1958), the evolution of musical systems exemplifies increasing rationalization, and so on. (See also Bradley 1981).

24. For a well-known theory of music as akin to a "language" of the emotions, see Cooke (1959). On the many historical recurrences, from Pythagoras to Rameau and onward, of theories of music in relation to mathematics, astronomy, and science, see Weiss and Taruskin (1984).

25. It is not my purpose at this point to justify my skepticism toward theories of the mathematical foundations of music. However, for an eloquent critique of this tendency, directed at serialism, the main technique of musical modernism, see Bloch (1985), discussed also by Norris (1988).

26. Adorno's essay "Culture and administration" (1978b) indicates the limits of his approach to subsidized high culture. Rather than critical analysis, the essay depicts it as a refuge from consumer society — a space in which "spontaneous consciousness" might still be able to "create centers of [cultural] freedom" (111).

27. It is important to note that these difficulties are also posed for orthodox music analysis by popular and nonwestern musics, in which the role of heightened timbral inflection and change, microtonal slides, very subtle rhythmic shifts within a simple and repetitive basic meter, and other qualities characteristic of improvisational and nonnotated musics are central. This points to a deeper problem: the inherent bias of visual and text-based forms of analysis toward visually

notated, score-centered musics because of the mutual tendency to focus primarily on pitch—the only dimension of music that seems easily reducible to visual representation; hence the potential for evaluative collusion between these forms of music and music analysis. For a discussion that touches on some of these issues see Cook (1990), esp. chap. 4.

28. It is disappointing that recent work does not implement Wolff's program. For example, three texts by influential theorists in the sociology of culture and cultural studies, despite quite different perspectives, share a seeming indifference toward understanding the institutions of high culture (Eagleton 1990, Thompson 1990, Zolberg 1990).

29. In generalizing aspects of my analysis in chapters 4 and 5 so as to protect informants' confidences, a couple of key instances of the place of gender in articulating IRCAM's internal politics have had to be disguised. Suffice it to say that significantly, given the relation of gender to status and stratification that I outline in those chapters, some of IRCAM's most vocal, if private, internal critics were women employees with little investment in the institute's higher economy of artistic prestige and charisma.

30. Benjamin writes, "[Brecht] was the first to make of intellectuals the far-reaching demand: not to supply the apparatus of production without, to the utmost extent possible, changing it in accordance with socialism. 'The publication of the *Versuche*,' [Brecht] writes in introducing the series of writings bearing this title, 'occurred at a time when certain works ought no longer to . . . [have the character of works], but should rather concern the use of certain institutes and institutions.' . . . I should like to content myself here with a reference to the decisive difference between the mere supplying of a productive apparatus, and its transformation" (1978, 261).

31. For formulations of the turn to Gramsci in cultural studies, see Bennett et al. (1981) esp. section 4, and Hall (1981, 1982).

32. Robbins (1991, 140–41) suggests that this essay also represents an analytical reflection by Bourdieu on his own position within the intellectual field, on the "situation of his own products within the market of symbolic goods" (140).

33. Bourdieu's distinction is equivalent to Laclau's (1980) elucidation, after Kant, of the two classical forms of antagonism, which Laclau then defines as fundamental structures of discourse.

34. For an extended discussion, see Bourdieu (1987, 126–35).

35. For a comparison, see Théberge (1989) on rationalization in the technologies and social organization of popular music recording.

36. Exceptions include Schorske (1961) and Franklin (1985).

37. There is a certain irony in using Foucault for the analysis of IRCAM, since Foucault and Boulez knew each other (Eribon 1991) and were interviewed together (Boulez and Foucault 1985). It was Foucault who in 1975 initiated Boulez's election to a chair at the Collège de France (Eribon 1991, 65), while Boulez is on the governing council of the Center established after Foucault's death to continue his work (Armstrong 1992, 347). The day that Foucault died in 1984, IRCAM secretaries were saddened and spoke fondly of his visits to the institute.

38. For an illuminating account of Foucault's historiography, see Cousins and Hussain (1984), chap. 4.

39. See Dews (1987), chap. 6 for a lucid discussion of these criticisms.

40. See Foucault (1980, 81–85) on the hierarchization of knowledges.

41. I refer to questions of the cultural specificity of certain psychopathologies or classical Freudian structures, or the anthropological speculations in Freud's own work. I make no reference to Lacanian theory in this book.

42. See Spillius (1988, 221–25) for an overview of both areas.

43. For definitions and discussions of these terms, see Laplanche and Pontalis (1973), Rycroft (1972), and in relation to Kleinian psychoanalysis, Segal (1979, 1982) and Hinshelwood (1989).

44. On introjection as a psychological mechanism of groups, see Hinshelwood (1987, 71–72). On "social defense systems," see Hinshelwood (1987), chap. 13, and Menzies Lyth (1988a, 63–81).

45. This idea has obvious parallels with Althusser's (1971) concept of the role of social institutions in the interpellation of subjects in ideology.

46. On Klein's analysis of primitive defenses, in particular those associated with the paranoid-schizoid position such as splitting, omnipotence, and denial (which I discuss further shortly), see Segal (1979), chap. 9, Segal (1982), chaps. 3 to 5, and Hinshelwood (1989).

47. Spillius (1988, 223–24) understands this criticism when she writes, "It is hardly surprising that other disciplines react badly to those psychoanalysts, Kleinian and others, who invade their territory without having learned about the field from the discipline's own point of view."

48. I am following a convention in which "phantasy" implies unconscious phantasy, while "fantasy" implies conscious fantasy.

49. On the relation between classification and ideology, see Hall (1982), esp. 70–74.

50. Klein placed great emphasis on envy as the unconscious wish to devalue, destroy, or obliterate the creativity of the (m)other (Klein 1977a). See also Segal (1979), chap. 11, and Segal (1982), chap. 4.

It is easy to see how the language of Kleinian psychoanalysis ("envy," "idealization") can lead to accusations of moralizing. This mistakes the register of what is, essentially, a clinical language aimed at understanding suffering. There is, however, no question that splitting, fragmentation, and so on are considered, psychoanalytically, to be distorted forms of thought. So in making links between these concepts and the theorizing of ideology I am raising the long-standing problem of to what extent ideology also involves distortions. In short, and in contrast with Thompson (1990, 56–57), I think that distortion or delusion — understood not so much as "error" in the rationalist terms of epistemology, but in the psychoanalytic sense outlined here, as well as in terms of the categorial conflations discussed earlier this chapter — are constitutive of ideology. I am convinced, as much as anything, by the arguments advanced here about splitting as a key mechanism by which the cultural unconscious is implicated in the production of ideology.

51. This formulation is close to Foucault (1989, 183–84).

CHAPTER 2

1. My emphasis on the strong and enduring regularities of modernist dis-
course echoes the (varying) approaches of many writers including Bradbury and
McFarlane (1976), Poggioli (1982), Anderson (1984), Calinescu (1987) and
Wollen (1987, 1989a). As well as these, I draw on the following sources for my
discussion of modernism and the avant-garde: Richter (1965), Gombrich (1966),
Gay (1968), Apollonio (1973), Shapiro (1976), Laing (1978), Willett (1978),
Bloch (1980), Hughes (1980), Frascina and Harrison (1982), Buchloch et al.
(1983), Crow (1983), Greenberg (1983, 1985a, 1985b), Guilbaut (1983), Haskell (1983), Huxtable (1983), Bürger (1984), Vitz and Glimcher (1984), Whitford (1984), Frascina (1985), Debord (1987), Williams (1988, 1989), Timms
and Collier (1988), Wollen (1989b), and Varnedoe and Gopnik (1990).

On postmodernism: Jencks (1977), Jameson (1984a, 1984b, 1985), Lyotard
(1984), *New German Critique* 33 (1984), Foster (1985a, 1985b), Huyssen
(1986), Institute of Contemporary Arts (1986), *Cultural Critique* 5 (1986–87),
Hebdige (1988), *Theory, Culture and Society* 5, no. 2–3 (1988), Harvey (1989),
October 56 (1991).

2. Anderson has warned against the tendency to treat modernism as unitary,
when in fact it spans a variety of aesthetic currents and was unevenly distributed
both temporally and geographically (Anderson 1984, 102–3). Despite this I
argue, as does Anderson himself, that there are certain defining attributes or
"coordinates" of modernism.

3. Wollen summarizes these developments as follows:

The first wave of historic modernism developed an aesthetic of the engineer, obsessed
by machine forms. . . . An art of the leisure class, dedicated to conspicuous waste and
display, gave way to an art of the engineer, precise, workmanlike and production-
oriented. This trend, which grew alongside and out of an interpretation of cubism,
culminated in a wave that swept across Europe: Soviet constructivism, the Bauhaus, De
Stijl, purism, Esprit Nouveau. All . . . saw artistic form as analogous to . . . machine
form, governed by the same functional rationality.

(Wollen 1987, 5)

Wollen sees the machine aesthetic as closely linked with functionalism; I would
argue that modernist fascination with technology and science was an autonomous force, separate from functionalism.

4. Seurat, for example, related his development of pointillism to scientific
theories of color vision. The general appearance of a close interest in modern
science by modernist artists is the theme of Vitz and Glimcher (1984).

5. The leftist Soviet art groups argued that postrevolutionary art must seize
on the new mass art forms: film, photography, the new graphic arts (posters,
magazines), murals. In a 1920s text, Soviet poet Mayakovsky wrote of the process of writing poetry as a "manufacture" (Laing 1978, 32).

6. This view is supported by Poggioli (1982, 131–47) and Anderson (1984,
105). Poggioli stresses the avant-garde's rhetorical borrowing of terms from
scientific discourse ("experimentalism," "research," the art "laboratory"); and
the use of quasi-technical names for artistic styles ("pointillism," "cubism," "vor-
ticism"). "Avant-garde scientificism remains a significant phenomenon even

when one realizes that a purely allegorical and emblematic use of the expression 'scientific' is involved" (Poggioli 1982, 139).

7. These origins account for the double political and artistic meanings of the term "avant-garde" and the association, beginning in the mid-nineteenth century, of artistic "radicalism" with radical politics (Manuel 1956; Shapiro 1976; Poggioli 1982). Poggioli charts a gradual shift in the French avant-garde over the nineteenth century such that, by the 1890s, avant-garde artists had turned to anarchism and libertarianism, ending their uneasy alliance with socialism. Instead, they identified with Parisian bohemia, calling themselves "decadents"—a term of abuse by socialists. Thus, by the 1890s the two avant-gardes had become divorced, and the secondary, artistic-cultural meaning became primary, retaining powerful connotations of political radicalism (Poggioli 1982, 8–12).

8. Discussing the climate of social revolution and the effects of the Russian Revolution on early modernism, Anderson notes cautiously that "the possible revolutionary outcomes of a downfall of the old order were . . . still profoundly ambiguous" (Anderson 1984, 104–5), so that modernism's political affiliations were labile and unfixed. He pursues this point with regard to the modernist fascination with technology. "It was not obvious where the new devices and inventions were going to lead. Hence the—so to speak—ambidextrous celebration of them from Right and Left alike—Marinetti or Mayakovsky" (ibid., 105), i.e. Italian futurism (which became aligned with Italian fascism) or leftist Soviet constructivism. Thus modernism, like romanticism before it, had no inherent Left bias; indeed it was subject to Left critique, for example from Lukács (Bloch 1980).

9. Under both the Nazi and Stalinist regimes modernist art, including serialist music, was banned as decadent. In the Nazi case, modernist music was seen as exemplary of "cultural bolshevism" and of a "dangerous internationalism" (Levi 1990, 172, 175). This censorship, and its identification with totalitarianism and fascism, became the basis of the postwar championing of modernism in the West and of its reading as an expression of progressive rejection of totalitarian domination. This is nowhere better argued than in Greenberg's classic paper "Avant-garde and kitsch" (1985a). The process is analyzed by Guilbaut (1983), who charts the postwar promotion of American abstract expressionism, despite its political neutrality, as embodying a critique of Stalinism (see chap. 3).

10. Similarly, Haskell (1983) points to the rise of a new relation between artists and the public in early modernism, based on an unprecedented degree of institutionalized hostility and incomprehension toward a number of innovative painters. This codified a now familiar cycle of public hostility to modern art, followed later by reappraisal and rapprochement—with the art critic as mediator.

Central to the construction of that hostility was artists' self-definition around a double antagonism, toward commerce and the bourgeois market, and toward academicism and the canons of official art (Williams 1988; Anderson 1984; Poggioli 1982; Shapiro 1976). Hence their uncompromising ethos of progress and subversion of the status quo, their embrace of the notion that there is "some specific kind of art that is 'ahead' of others, an art that by definition would not run the risk of being contaminated by too early a welcome" (Haskell 1983, 24).

There was nothing natural about the transition to this view, which was only gradually internalized by artists, as shown, Haskell says, by "looking at the frenzied attempts made by artists on the one hand not to be liked too soon . . . and on the other to have anticipated the future" (ibid., 25).

11. Crow (1983), discussing the influence of mass popular culture, shows how the impressionists and postimpressionists, in their search for taboo subject matter to shock the bourgeoisie, made reference to urban popular culture. Hence the centrality in their work of representations of the "other": the lives and leisure of the urban working class, the paraphernalia of mass culture. Crow describes a trade-off between this new subject matter and modernist formal experiment. Both were equated, for some painters at some times, with radical political allegiances. But he shows how, eventually, subject matter became subordinate, simply a carrier of formal play, as with cubist collages incorporating the debris of cafe life. Thus, reference to popular culture and its critical meanings gave way to a formalist modernism characterized by self-referential abstraction. Coutts-Smith (1991) argues that a similar process of formal subsumption, in the service of the "elevation of style to an absolute principle" (29), occurred in modernist artists' appropriation of nonwestern art.

12. Huyssen writes: "Ever since the mid-19th century, the culture of modernity has been characterized by a volatile relationship between high art and mass culture. . . . Modernism constituted itself through a conscious strategy of exclusion, an anxiety of contamination by its other: an increasingly consuming and engulfing mass culture. . . . The opposition between modernism and mass culture has remained amazingly resilient over the decades" (Huyssen 1986, vii). Like Bürger (1984), Huyssen makes a distinction between modernism and the avant-garde, suggesting that while modernism was founded on a hostility to mass culture, avant-garde movements (and he cites the same ones as Bürger) tried to transcend it by effecting a new relationship with mass culture.

13. See for example Greenberg (1985a) and Adorno (1978a, 1990).

14. Modernism was continuous with nineteenth-century romantic and nationalist discourse in making a split between a denigrated urban "mass" and an idealized, "authentic" rural or "primitive" (nonwestern) people (Burke 1981). Early and later modernists, like the romantics, have thus found it easier to idealize an exotic "other" than the nearer urban "mass."

15. In Jameson's well-known essay on postmodernism, which is generally quite pessimistic, one significantly optimistic passage hinges on a reference to "the synthesis of classical and 'popular' styles found in composers like Phil Glass and Terry Riley, and also in punk and new wave rock" (1984a, 54). In this Jameson asserts that in musical postmodernism, modernism and the popular are finally reconciled. Another common position (e.g. Ulmer 1985) is to cite John Cage, musical forefather of composers such as Glass and Riley, as exemplifying the postmodern synthesis through his reference to nonwestern musics and cosmologies (discussed later this chapter).

16. I draw on the following main sources for my account of modernism and the avant-garde in music: Schorske (1961), Boulez (1971, 1976, 1986), Adorno (1973), Cott (1974), Rosen (1976), Griffiths (1978, 1979, 1981, 1986), Hamm (1983), Neighbour et al. (1983), Weiss and Taruskin (1984), Franklin (1985),

Kerman (1985), Glock (1986), Smith Brindle (1987), Whittall (1988), McClary (1989), and Nicholls (1990). On postmodernism and music: many of the above and Cage (1969), Nyman (1974), Mertens (1983), Rockwell (1984), Griffiths (1985), Manning (1985), McClary (1985, 1991), Emmerson (1986), and Goodwin (1991). My discussion of experimental music is particularly indebted to Nyman's detailed and insightful account (Nyman 1974).

17. According to this principle, each pitch in the series has equal importance and is dependent upon its position relative to the other eleven notes.

18. Adorno advocates the negation in Schoenberg's serialism in these terms. "Advanced music has no recourse but to insist upon its own ossification without concession to that would-be humanitarianism which it sees through . . . as the mask of inhumanity. Its truth appears guaranteed more by its denial of any meaning in organized society . . . than by any capability of positive meaning within itself. Under the present circumstances it is restricted to definitive negation" (Adorno 1973, 20).

19. I refer here to the phenomenon of a strict separation between composers' serious, professional musical work and their unserious work or leisure pastimes — a separation that we will see is also characteristic of some IRCAM intellectuals. Thus, Schoenberg is known to have written cabaret music in "other" settings (Stuckenschmidt 1977, 47–60), whereas Babbitt briefly attempted a career in American popular music in the immediate postwar years and wrote an unsuccessful musical comedy. Right after, he joined the Princeton music faculty and became, eventually, the leading figure in American total serialism (Rockwell 1984, 35). At no time, however, is the interest in popular music allowed to affect modernist composers' serious compositional work.

20. The rhetorical nature of Varèse's views on the kinship between science and music is conveyed by this quote from a 1936 lecture: "The emotional impulse that moves a composer to write his scores contains the same element of poetry that incites the scientist to his discoveries. There is a solidarity between scientific development and the progress of music" (Middleton 1978, 68).

21. All of the dominant developments described may be contrasted to the one significant expression within prewar musical modernism of nonformalist critique: the work of composers Eisler and Weill. Their collaborations with Brecht in Weimar Germany during the late 1920s and 1930s engaged with the social and political functions of culture and were informed by Marxist cultural political debate, including the conflict between Adorno and Brecht over the limits of a purely formal cultural politics. With Brecht, Weill and Eisler advocated reworking the aesthetics of popular music in order to reach and influence the popular audience. As we have seen, although aesthetic borrowing of this kind occurred among other early modernists, it was not linked to a wider cultural politics, while such aesthetic strategies were altogether absent from mainstream midcentury modernism. Their experiments in critical musical populism, and Weill's work in particular, remain an extraordinary example of a politicized modernist intervention in popular music, an intervention so heartfelt that when Weill later arrived in the United States, alone of all modernists he "crossed over" completely and became a composer of the popular song that he had been parodying (Sanders 1980). It was not until the 1960s that any nonformalist cultural politics re-

emerged in the work of some experimental composers, and of a few Europeans. Notably, given the hegemony of serialism, until recently the work of Weill and Eisler remained relatively marginal.

22. Nicholls (1990) traces the American experimental music movement back to the decades around the turn of the twentieth century. He argues that profound tensions were already apparent within American composition during the 1920s between the "radicals," such as Ives, Cowell, and at times Ruggles, Varèse, Slonimsky, and others, and the "acceptable Europeanised modernists" (1990, 2) such as Copland, Piston, Sessions, and Virgil Thomson. These two groupings were quite self-conscious and carried strong ideological overtones. The "radicals" saw themselves in this period as pioneering an American national music: as Cowell put it, a music produced by "men who have studied in America, and who, although often cruder in technique than [those with a French training], are building up a style distinctly rooted in the feelings and traditions of the country" (quoted in Nicholls 1990, 4). At the same time, they were concerned to shed the legacy of European, and particularly French, teachings with which the other group were identified. Thus nationalist rivalry was apparent even in this earlier period among the "radical" American modernists toward European influences.

23. According to Cage, "The opposite and necessary co-existent of sound is silence. . . . Therefore a structure based on durations . . . is correct (corresponds with the nature of the material), whereas harmonic structure is incorrect (derived from pitch, which has no being in silence)" (quoted in Nyman 1974, 28). Nyman notes that in this Cage was disdaining the "pseudo-logics" and methodological strictures of serialism and advocating a new, radical materialism based on the nature of sound itself, a direction also taken by followers such as Feldman. Cage's disparaging remarks on the primacy of pitch thus represent a direct attack on serialism, derived as it was from a logic of pitch.

24. Rather than for music to deliver a perfect experience to the audience, experimental composers called for interactive performance, for audiences to be active and participatory, for fluidity between the roles of composer/performer/ listener. Experimental scores typically set up series of tasks, actions, or games and described performance situations and strategies rather than predetermined sonic outcomes. Performers were expected to bring initiative, audiences would be thrust into the role of performer, and both were enjoined to explore their active subjectivities. Thus, in Cage's infamous piece 4'33" nothing at all happens for the duration of the piece apart from the pianist sitting at the piano, highlighting in this way the minimal and ritual requirements of performance and the audience's role in the production of meaning.

25. Greenberg articulates this view as follows: "Because of its 'absolute' nature, its remoteness from imitation, its almost complete absorption in the very physical quality of its medium, as well as because of its resources of suggestion, music had come to replace poetry as the paragon art. It was the art which the other avant-garde arts envied most, and whose effects they tried hardest to imitate . . . the advantage of music lay chiefly in the fact that it was an 'abstract' art, an art of 'pure form' " (Greenberg 1985b, 41).

26. This ranged from Rzewski's treatment of the Chilean revolutionary song

"The People United Will Never Be Defeated" as the basis for a set of complex, quasi-serialist piano variations, to Cardew's founding of a Maoist pop group, called People's Liberation Music, that set didactic lyrics to wooden imitations of current pop. The results were often uncomfortable and cerebral aesthetic compromises.

27. The most extreme example was the Maoist Scratch Orchestra started by Cardew in 1969, in which the performer's role was democratized and "demystified" to the extent that anyone motivated to come together, whatever their skills, could play in symphonic works. Concerts took place anywhere: in town halls, pubs, playgrounds, weddings. The Scratch Orchestra constitution cited the "Research Project" — learning through direct experience — as an obligatory activity for all members, to ensure cultural expansion. For Cardew the orchestra was "the embodiment of certain educational, musical, social and ethical ideals" (Nyman 1974, 113). It became the model for a number of similar groups.

28. To clarify, influenced by close encounters with jazz and rock, these composers have tried to cross over into popular music and to market their music commercially. This has been seen as a final postmodern turn away from modernism and toward overcoming the "otherness" of and separation from commercial popular culture. However, this trend has been exaggerated by commentators (e.g. Rockwell 1984; Jameson 1984a). To expand on my point in chapter 1, there remain significant aesthetic and socioeconomic differences between the postmodern and pop. Composers such as Glass and Nyman are not fully or successfully integrated into popular music, nor is that their aim. They want to infiltrate that market while retaining their "serious" status, their high-cultural bases and sources of legitimation. Glass's operas are produced at the Metropolitan Opera in New York and at the British English National Opera, Nyman's at the Institute of Contemporary Arts in London. So this postmodern strategy is more accurately one of diversification based on antagonism to but inclusion within the spheres of legitimate culture.

29. Some of the main elements of experimental music practice — improvisation, live group work, the empirical use of small, commercial electronics in performance — were pioneered in the jazz and rock of the 1950s and 1960s. Moreover, the politics of experimental music are similar to those of the advanced black jazz of the '60s. Its musical collectivism, for example, was prefigured by the Chicago black musicians' cooperative, the Association for the Advancement of Creative Musicians (AACM), which became a model for later progressive, cooperative music organizations. The fact that these influences often remain unacknowledged and subterranean, even within experimental music, signals their status as deriving from an "other" culture and the reluctance of the postmodern sphere of legitimate music to admit its indebtedness to the "other."

30. Cage comments on the state of the avant-garde: "The vitality that characterizes the current European musical scene follows from the activities of Boulez, Stockhausen, Nono, Maderna, Pousseur, Berio, etc. There is in all of this activity an element of tradition, continuity with the past . . . whether in terms of discourse or organization. . . . However, this scene will change. The silences of American experimental music and even its technical involvements with chance operations

are being introduced into new European music. It will not be easy, however, for Europe to give up being Europe. It will, nevertheless, and must: for the world is one world now" (Cage 1969, 74–75).

CHAPTER 3

1. Much high-level American computer research, including the field of artificial intelligence (AI), has originated in Pentagon-funded defense projects. On this, see Marbach et al. (1985), and Athanasiou (1985, 31).

2. Mathews's seniority in the telecommunications research world is signaled by the fact that he was given the task of decoding the Watergate tapes.

3. Chowning and the CCRMA were glad of the freedom granted by the substantial FM royalties. For political reasons, Chowning had earlier divorced CCRMA from its parent institution, SAIL, the Stanford Artificial Intelligence Laboratory, since his group objected to SAIL's heavy defense funding; so for a period before the Yamaha deal, the computer music studio had been poorly funded. This indicates how commercial links may sometimes allow the academic community to achieve autonomy from compromised industrial links such as defense applications.

4. This phenomenon is analyzed by Reader (1987), who points out the related, yet contradictory, strong traditional links between intellectuals and the political Left—contradictory because the Left has not often been in power. Reader notes the influence of two key historical events on these relations—the 1789 Revolution and the Dreyfus Affair of the late nineteenth century—both of which brought alliances of intellectuals into the forefront of public and political life, on both occasions in association with the Left. However, Reader's main purpose is to analyze the unprecedented decline of that association in the post-'68 restructuring of French politics. Reader discusses "the silence of the left-wing intellectuals" (136) following Mitterrand's 1981 election, and the refusal of certain erstwhile sympathizers (notably Foucault) to take up posts offered to them by his government. Reader links this to a broad shift over the last twenty years among French intellectuals towards a "non-étatiste" view of politics involving a critique of traditional political forms, an intensifying distrust of socialism, and a rejection of grand theory, Marxist or structuralist.

5. See Guilbaut (1983), esp. chap. 4, for an analysis of these processes and Greenberg's role in them.

6. This was also true of the American mass-culture industries—film, popular music, and later, television—which gained increasing international reach. See Guilbaut (1983, 133–38) on the postwar American threat to the French film industry.

7. Williams (1981, 83–84) portrays the historical avant-garde as the first truly internationalist position within culture. In this, despite mention of the shift in art dominance from Paris (1890–1930) to New York (1940–1970), he surely underplays the nationalist base of bids for cultural hegemony—the necessity of a stage of marginality or localism in the development of an avant-garde.

8. I draw on Manning (1985) and Griffiths (1978, 1979, 1981, 1986) in this section. Throughout this and the following sections I have also drawn exten-

sively on Menger's invaluable work (1980, 1983) on the recent cultural politics and economics of French contemporary music.

9. For example, subscribers for the 1962–63 season included the relations of many leading intellectuals, among them Ionesco, Kandinsky, Ernst, Lacan, Robbe-Grillet, Boulanger, Poulenc, and Eloy, while those from the haute bourgeoisie included several wives of Rothschilds (Menger 1983, 375). Visual artists, Menger notes, had a pronounced place in the *Domaine* salons (1983, 374), signaling a strong alliance in France between serial music and abstract painting. Cross-media support was therefore as strong in French avant-garde circles as in the United States.

10. The main biographical sources on Boulez used in the remainder of the chapter are Heyworth (1973a and 1973b), republished as Heyworth (1986). I also draw on Jameux (1991).

11. Boulez himself is not unaware of these issues, and has discussed how the IRCAM project was indeed conceived to help overcome certain "fundamental obstacles" in his compositional work — obstacles, however, that he sees as characteristic of contemporary composition as a whole. See Boulez quoted in Jameux (1991, 169). As well as *Répons*, "... *explosante-fixe* ..." — another piece involving live computer transformation of soloists and ensemble, in the early 1990's still being revised and developed by Boulez — may come to merit the status of a major work.

12. If we compare the 1978 budgets of some major Parisian music institutions, IRCAM received twelve million francs (3.5 percent of the total state music budget); the Paris Opera, the highest publicly funded music institution, received approximately one hundred and fifty million francs (43.5 percent); and the Conservatoire National Supérieur de Musique (CNSM), the second-best funded institution, received approximately twenty-three million francs (6.7 percent) (Menger 1980, 14). All three figures illustrate the centralization of musical life around the dominant Parisian institutions.

13. After (Schaeffer's and Henry's) GRM, the earliest state-funded music research center was Xenakis's Centre d'Études de Mathématiques et d'Automatiques Musicales (Jameux 1991, 187). Yet it is striking that given Xenakis's pioneering work in computer music, his studio has remained a small affair compared with Boulez's IRCAM.

14. My interviews with officials were carried out in 1986, and so relate to the mid-1980's: the ethnographic present in the study. In the final chapter I describe changes that occurred by the early '90's both in the music research field and in the attitudes of the *Direction de la Musique*.

15. The musicologist Nattiez, for example, makes a favorable comparison between Boulez and Wagner, arguing that their kinship stems from a shared concern with changing the conditions of musical experience as a whole (Nattiez 1986, 25).

16. This kind of tribute may be found quoted in Heyworth's biographical essays (for example Heyworth 1973a, 45).

17. For example, Boulez sums up his mentor Wagner in the following way: "The revolutions that ... have the profoundest and most far-reaching results are revolutions in our mental categories, and Wagner initiated ... the irreversible

processes of such a revolution" (Boulez 1986, 277). Heyworth quotes Boulez saying, "You cannot make a revolution with anarchists. . . . There I am three hundred per cent Leninist" (Heyworth 1973b, 64). Nattiez writes of Boulez's self-professed "desire for immortality" (Nattiez 1986, 20). He also discusses Boulez's idea of history, quoting him thus: "Any vision of history . . . implies . . . a sharpness of perception in judging the moment. . . . It is the gift . . . to grasp the totality of a situation . . . and to apprehend its structure on a cosmic scale — that is what is demanded of any candidate who aspires to the title of 'seer' " (ibid., 20).

18. Two such texts, of very different kinds, are Peyser (1976) and Glock (1986): the first a biography by an American journalist that was considered by some at IRCAM to be rather scandalous, the second a tribute by senior figures such as Sir William Glock, Boulez's patron in his work with the BBC Symphony Orchestra, on the occasion of Boulez's sixtieth birthday. It is interesting to note that in the republication of Heyworth's (1973a and 1973b) biographical essays in this volume thirteen years later, certain critical passages were excised, thereby making them more adulatory than before. The reason, apparently, was Boulez's successes with both IRCAM and *Répons*.

19. Nattiez summarizes the phenomenon thus: "[Boulez] chose his own ancestors who, leaving the composers aside, include a number of painters (Cézanne, Klee, Kandinsky, Mondrian), and a great many writers (Baudelaire, Mallarmé, Proust, Joyce, Kafka, Musil, Genet, Char, Michaux)" (Nattiez 1986, 21). References to modernist greats from the various arts are sprinkled liberally through Boulez's writings.

20. This should not be confused with a crude popularizing strategy. One of Boulez's recent involvements in the French media has been as a cofounder of *La Sept*, the French television channel devoted to cultural issues, which is known for its thoroughly high-brow tone.

21. In "From work to text" (1977c), Barthes portrays postserial music as the epitome of an open, "collaborative" text. "We know today that post-serial music has radically altered the role of the 'interpreter,' who is called on to be in some sort the co-author of the score. . . . The Text is very much a score of this new kind: it asks of the reader a practical collaboration" (Barthes 1977c, 163). Barthes contrasts this with "the reduction of reading to a consumption" that produces the boredom commonly experienced by the audience when faced with "the modern ('unreadable') text, the avant-garde film or painting" (ibid.). Somehow, then, for Barthes as by implication for Boulez, the problem of meaning resides not in the character of the text, since avant-garde music, film, or painting can be experienced either way, but in the unanalyzed difference between reading as active, "practical collaboration" or as "consumption."

22. For a very different reworking of Barthes on music, see Attali (1985), especially the contrast between chap. 4, an indictment of postserialism as an elite and technocratic music, and chap. 5, a utopian reverie that echoes Barthes's theory of "*musica practica*" (Barthes 1977b).

23. Behind the rhetoric, Boulez's politics are complex. It is clear only that he has been in no simple way aligned. According to Heyworth (1973b, 58), Boulez was briefly a Communist in his youth and left the party, with many others,

through disillusion with Stalinism. He signed a manifesto in 1960 against the Algerian war; and took a contradictory position on the events of May '68. He was skeptical of the students' chaotic anarchism, yet he resigned from his presidency of the Musicians' Union when its parent organization, the Communist CGT, failed to support the events. After the government had regained order, Boulez signed the now infamous Left manifesto published in the journal *Tel Quel* that, as Heyworth reports, "[deplored] the notion of 'spontaneous' revolution and [saluted] Marxist-Leninism as 'the only valid revolutionary theory of our time'" (ibid., 58). Boulez has rejected the notion of politically "engaged" art. Rather, he has argued, aptly for the IRCAM project, that "to be an effective revolutionary, you have to enter organizations and change them" (ibid, 72).

CHAPTER 4

1. For greater detail on the two early periods of IRCAM, and on the reorganization of 1980, see Jameux (1991), chap. 11.

2. I have distinguished throughout the study between the many functional heads of IRCAM departments, some of which consisted of only one or two people, who are referred to as "directors," and IRCAM's three senior executive officers, who are referred to as "Directors" — the Director of IRCAM (Boulez), and the Artistic and Scientific Directors.

3. The relative funding of IRCAM and the CGP can be gauged by figures from 1981, when IRCAM's budget (approximately nineteen million francs) was around 10 percent of the CGP's total budget, while IRCAM's employment base was just 5 percent (fifty-four full-time salaried positions) of the CGP's (about one thousand). IRCAM thus received twice the funds equivalent to its employment base. IRCAM officials justified this by reference to the institute's technological infrastructure and production needs.

4. The average attendance at IRCAM concerts in 1983 was 55 percent. The IRCAM Esp Pro concert space held between 220 and 360 people so that even if it consistently drew full houses, it did not earn much in ticket receipts. IRCAM's prestigious concert tours abroad may also appear to be potential earners. But they are extremely expensive and so generally lose money and require substantial sponsorship. The US tour of *Répons* in 1985, for example, which took in five major cities and fourteen concerts, cost around $40,000 per concert. It was totally subsidized by the cities concerned and by corporate sponsors, including the computer giant IBM.

5. In 1990, IRCAM's yearly income was approximately thirty-nine million francs, of which about 70 percent (twenty-seven million francs) still came from the Ministry of Culture — the same percentage as during the early and middle 1980s. But by the '90s IRCAM was earning more from its own activities, sales, and licensing agreements.

6. The Music Research director had studied at the Juilliard School, the prime East Coast conservatory, and later with Elliott Carter, one of the most senior figures of American composition, who remained a friend. He returned regularly to the United States for concerts and research, and after 1984 gained a job at a prestigious East Coast college.

7. Fees for commissioned composers due to come to IRCAM in 1985–86, for example, ranged between 20,000 francs for young unknowns and 30,000 francs for a well-known British postserialist composer, to 35,000 francs for a senior Italian composer. Given that a commission is likely to represent more than six months' work, payment is not high, despite additional living expenses. The different treatment given to "star" composers may be illustrated by developments prior to Stockhausen's 1984 visit. In advance of his arrival, secretaries reported being issued with extraordinary, mythic instructions for his hotel accommodation, redolent with sexual innuendo: to find a bed big enough for three, and a bedroom with an antechamber just off it to which Stockhausen could retire to compose. Collective fantasy or not, much awe and hilarity passed between the secretaries. Ordinary visiting composers are simply given a list of recommended hotels and CGP flats.

8. By IRCAM's own account, up to 1987 there had been thirty-six completed French commissions, twenty-four American, ten German, ten British, seven Italian, and six Finnish.

9. In writing of "exploitation" I refer to the looser meaning of the term rather than the classic Marxist definition.

10. Of the technicians, the Esp Pro team ran a small professional theater group beyond IRCAM. The Sound team director was himself a composer outside IRCAM, and the team hired out the IRCAM recording facilities to outside classical performers. Three of the four Systems technicians had "secret" artistic lives: one was a composer, one a sculptor, one a graphic designer. Of the women directors, the Diffusion director previously had a career in publishing and was from a sophisticated cultural milieu, while the Production Office director had earlier worked for the major Parisian cultural festival, the *Festival d'Automne*.

11. One low-status service worker spoke thus of Boulez and IRCAM music:

I don't go to concerts, it's too expensive. But . . . I've listened to one record by Monsieur Boulez, but the music is difficult to register, to take in. . . . [Of IRCAM music:] It's not that it's not for me; it's that my ears aren't used to that music! I can't explain . . . it's not easy to say. I've helped with a rehearsal—I can't remember which music, directed by Monsieur Boulez in the Esp Pro. I don't know what it was! I watched it: an enormous number of instruments. [*Reverently*] I saw Monsieur Boulez who conducted. . . .

12. Pay differences for computer scientists between France and the United States were great. One young programmer reported that he would treble his income by moving from IRCAM to a position at Bell Labs; while a consultant, told that his pay would be—for the short duration of his consultancy—in the region of Boulez's, said that it was equivalent to the lowest consultancy rate that he charged in the States, at Lucasfilm. Thus for Americans, coming to IRCAM often involved a substantial drop in pay. French computer scientists who left IRCAM went to leading computer research centers such as INRIA (Institut National de Recherche en Informatique et Automatique).

13. This is shown nowhere better than by the advice given to me by several IRCAM musicians that if I used my time at IRCAM to produce some interesting music research it would do wonders for my career, while simply to have made a visit was prestigious for my c.v. It was as though, momentarily, they projected on to me their excitement at the potential accumulation of prestige.

CHAPTER 5

1. The nationalist pomposity of the memos from the Ministry occasioned some mirth among technicians and researchers when they read that henceforth "bugs" were to be known as "*bogues*," "spool" as "*spoule*," and "restart" as "*relancer*."

2. Weber describes four ideal typical forms of succession to charismatic leadership, of which one comes close to this process: "Designation on the part of the original charismatic leader of his own successor and his recognition on the part of the followers. . . . In this case legitimacy is acquired through the act of designation" (Weber 1968, 247).

3. Boulez was quite aware of the problem of succession, as shown by this press interview. He reveals a humorous self-awareness, playing on the analogy between himself and absolute monarchs, thus acknowledging the elements of charismatic and autocratic leadership in his position. But he also displays, disarmingly, a certain humility about how he will be judged by history.

> Q: Do you think about organizing your successor [to direct IRCAM]?
>
> Boulez: Ah! So! I am not Tito, but. . . . It's a problem that I must reflect on. But I don't believe in institutions nor in wills. Sometimes, I reread the passage from Saint-Simon on Louis XIV's will. It's a marvelous text! From the morning after the death of the Sun King, the absolute monarch, his will—nobody gave a damn! I tell myself that if it was like that for Louis XIV, what's it going to be like for the little Director of IRCAM! So, it's useless to plan a succession. The organism [IRCAM] is in place. Tomorrow, if I had a car accident, it would function for several months, perhaps a year. . . . Who would replace me? I don't know. It needs someone with energy, ideas, altruism, organization, and someone who keeps everyone in mind. You don't find that under a horse's hoof!
>
> Q: IRCAM is therefore your instrument?
>
> Boulez: Yes, temporarily. But at the same time, no one is indispensable. When I read the obituaries—"What an emptiness has been left by [the death of] Mr. X or Y!"—I always think: one tree falls, 46,000 shoot up!
>
> (*Le Monde de la Musique* no. 24, June 1980, my translation)

4. Fear of the Administration was apparent in another secretary's reaction to my interviewing her. For the first hour, in contrast to her earlier friendliness, she was reticent and barely spoke. I suggested we take a break and asked her what was wrong. She then revealed that she was under the impression—despite my repeated assurances to the contrary, and my having been around as an independent presence for some months—that my research was for the Administration, implying that it could be used to check up on her and others. This secretary had previously experienced problems in her work relations with a difficult director. Her reactions speak of a strong sense (or phantasy?) of persecution by management among lower-status workers. Certainly, hostility toward the Administration appeared widespread among them.

5. The secretary described Boulez's role in the situation thus:

> Pierre Boulez was very nice. . . . [He] said: "Move across into the scientific sector and all will be well." He was very understanding, he kept his word. Pierre is very charming, very good. . . . It wasn't *regular* to do that, take off the *avertissements*. But I'd negotiated it with Pierre, you know. It shows where the real power is. Then the funny thing is,

the same summer, when Mitterrand came to power, he decided to amnesty all the *avertissements* in the whole of the country! So I was amnestied along with how many thousands of others! [*laughs*] — a gesture of expansion, humanism.

Boulez's help is here equated metonymically with the greater humanitarian largesse of the nation's leader, Mitterrand. The secretary spoke finally with emphatic realism of the resolution of the situation: "And I realized that if Boulez told me to go down, I had to go down. If Boulez says that, you must go."

6. RIG provoked the Administration by bringing in squatters, by his below-board and unofficial technological deals, by resisting bureaucratic paperwork, and by spending a lot of IRCAM money on phoning America and Japan.

7. ID was a software director from CARL (Computer Audio Research Lab) at UCSD (University of California at San Diego) — which, with Stanford's CCRMA, was the second major West Coast American computer music center at the time. CARL had produced some of the most widely used computer music software, taught, for example, on the IRCAM *stage*. ID is a Stanford graduate and was a regular visitor to IRCAM. NI is an ex-Bell Labs researcher who was trying to make his way as an independent, low-tech computer music entrepreneur, both as a producer of technologies and as a commercial film music composer.

8. ARPA is the Advanced Research Projects Agency, the declassified section of the U.S. military technology research apparatus.

9. NI continued to elaborate his fundamental philosophical and aesthetic differences with IRCAM in down-to-earth language:

> What kind of offense is [the 4X militarist deal]? It's a blindness. It's the kind of engineering politics that put fluorescent lights in here [*gesturing around*]. I mean, you can't think creatively with fluorescent lights! They're sterile. It's this building too: a cathedral to mind, without heart or ... [*flirting*] all the other parts of the body too. It's no accident they get the music they get here! That's why I was able to do things at the [Bell] Labs: I brought in my own incandescent lamp [and] turned off all the fluorescents. [*Exasperated*] These engineers: they put fans into everything that are so loud you can hardly hear the music! So I put a convection cooler into my synthesizers, modified them [to avoid] that. Truly, it takes a *musician* to design a musical instrument — period.

CHAPTER 6

1. On organicism in German romantic thought and its influence on both early scientific work and nineteenth-century music, see Montgomery (1992). For a critical analysis of organicism in writings on music, see Levy (1987).

2. Figure 7 is a crude measure, ignoring the scale of pieces played (from large orchestral works to chamber music to tape pieces), their length, and the size and prestige of the performance venue.

3. An apocryphal IRCAM story told of efforts by Boulez and the Artistic Director in 1983 to persuade Ligeti — from Figure 7 the highest-status living composer who had not yet worked at IRCAM — to come and produce a tape at IRCAM for his new opera. They took Ligeti to dine in Stuttgart. At the outset, Ligeti is said to have believed that the composer had to know everything about the computer before being able to work at IRCAM. By the end of the meal, his hosts had convinced him that this was not the case, and so he agreed to come. The story marks a controversy since, although the reassurance given to Ligeti

may have been pragmatic, it contradicted the tutors' belief that to make the most of the technologies visiting composers did need some prior technological experience to prevent them being entirely reliant on tutors' help. In fact, the Ligeti visit did not occur due to administrative oversights — which caused much embarrassment.

4. The flavor of the preface, which takes a poetic form, is conveyed by the following excerpts:

> A permanent feature of our [IRCAM's] activity will be . . .
> constant contact with diverse publics,
> the investigation, also, of the different forms that this
> contact can, and must, take.
>
> At the threshold of [IRCAM's] existence, then: *Passage du XXe Siècle*
>
> What must not be done:
>   a statistical balance-sheet
>   straight lines
>   decided choices
>   fixed ideas
>   . . .
> Let us consider together
> Let us traverse this century
>   with the certainties that it has abundantly provided,
>   with the uncertainties with which it is no less
>   prodigiously provided.
>   (Pierre Boulez, from preface to *Passage du Vingtième Siècle*
>   program book, 1977, 9, my translation)

5. This "open" *Espace Libre* was held, significantly, on an annual June holiday set up by the Socialists called "*Fête de la Musique*" that was intended to celebrate musicmaking in all its forms, and in which people all over Paris took the day off and played music on the streets.

6. It is fascinating that the "openness" of the *Espaces Libres* accompanied a profound ambivalence in HY. Despite including the music of amateurs and of IRCAM's "illegitimate" composers in his events, at other times he conveyed the impression that he considered Boulez and himself to be the only "real composers" at IRCAM.

CHAPTER 7

1. The unpredictability of the synthesis outcome might well have had to do with the effects of "foldover" on analog aspects of the system — such as aspects of the DACs — rather than the software. Nonetheless, the sonic outcome was unpredictable.

2. The Yamaha DX7, for example, was renowned for innovative gestural control. It was the first widely available, medium-cost digital synthesizer to provide a pianolike touch-sensitive keyboard that could be programmed to control various parameters of the sound (e.g. attack, intensity, vibrato). It was much lauded by IRCAM's small-machine enthusiasts in 1984.

3. This attitude was revealed, for example, in the incident described in chapter 5 when a major commercial firm came to demonstrate their latest high-cost

system, only to be humiliated by the failure of their music transcription program, spotted by Boulez himself, which made the firm appear musically inept.

4. Interestingly, this was later modified. A friend reported of HM in 1987, "He's given up on the idea of becoming a composer. He accepts that he's a good psychoacoustician, but that doesn't mean he's a good composer or can become one."

5. The project, on computer analysis of the "rules" of jazz improvisation, involved two outsiders unpaid by IRCAM: a postgraduate who knew nothing of music and a French musicologist who had written on jazz phrasing. In May the project came before a Music Research meeting for assessment where, despite the backing of RIG, its legitimacy was continually questioned. Another director asked dubiously, "Is this *really* a music research project? How do you see it being generalized here?"

6. For the overriding purpose of maintaining the anonymity of my informants, in this section, with permission, I have not divulged the journal's name or given full references for the short quotes taken from articles.

7. MC meant here that the speakers in his room linked to the interconnected speaker system were always turned on, in order that he could overhear *stagiaires'* sounds and so judge their talent.

8. Lyotard argues that the self-legitimation by the quest for truth characteristic of science until the late nineteenth century has been "delegitimized": "a process of delegitimation fueled by the demand for legitimation itself . . . an internal erosion of the legitimacy principle of knowledge" (Lyotard 1984, 39). He summarizes: "The goal is no longer truth, but performativity. . . . The State and/or company must abandon the idealist and humanist narratives of legitimation. . . . Scientists, technicians, and instruments are purchased not to find truth, but to augment power" (ibid., 46).

CHAPTER 8

1. The Music Research director and Boulez were both at times lucid concerning the metaphorical status of these discourses around music.

2. On the other hand, the same visiting composer, YY, recalled how the director of his conservatory, hostile to YY's music and disbelieving that YY could really imagine aurally the sound of his own scores, had tried to catch him out by playing a piece of YY's at the piano and inserting deliberate mistakes. YY had recognized them, and so proved that he could in fact "hear" the music in his scores.

3. At base, this involves only the use of an operating system such as UNIX and an editor, but preferably more advanced programming skills in relevant languages.

4. Interesting, too, is the content of some mnemonics: for example, the Formes program initially used "God," "Father," and "Son" to describe hierarchical classes of objects. By the 1985 version, this patriarchal terminology had been modified to terms such as "Parent" and "Child."

5. The Array Processor was a new piece of hardware — a parallel processor — providing greater "number-crunching" or calculating power, that had been bought in order to try and make demanding synthesis faster.

6. The following two quotes convey this:

AV: There was a month of soft writing before I could work at all with the first "real thing": full of bugs, but it was there. That took about three man months: MC, XH and HM all worked on it. . . ."

GB: How much time did you put into tool design?

HM: In 1982 about two or three weeks full time just to build the instruments. MC did the equivalent on Chant, setting up the user routines. . . . This time I did the additive synthesis instrument for the 4X: that was a good solid week, because we went through many different versions before we found what we wanted.

7. This is a private joke of mine referring to the fact that tritones are dissonant, unresolved chords commonly associated with atonal and avant-garde music. That the technology should automatically produce a tritone as an error seemed highly aesthetically appropriate to IRCAM, and a bizarre coincidence!

8. AV based the form of this "race" message on a mathematical puzzle known as the Paradox of Zeno — a phenomenon to which Borges, one of AV's favorite writers, has alluded.

CHAPTER 9

1. The "People" directory was the main working directory employed constantly by all users of the VAX.

2. The satirical poem in this message illustrates the teasing relations between the Systems team and researchers. It refers to "Formes" — the software group considered by FA to be the heaviest users of the VAX — and to "Born" (myself) as the means of analyzing IRCAM's problems.

3. The servicing of high technologies can be done by independent firms, but the equipment is so specialized and secret that manufacturers and their agents have virtual monopolies. Service charges are therefore enormous: they start at about 10 percent of the purchase price and rise steeply thereafter. In this way the companies control the market and force customers to upgrade to the next machine. Thus, by '83 DEC was demanding such high service charges for the PDP10 (87,000 francs for a three-month service) that it was judged economical to close it down and buy the new VAX. DEC's stranglehold was confirmed by the fact that despite IRCAM's offer to give the PDP10 to any institution, none took up the offer: the service charges were too high.

4. This is one cause of the segmentation of technology manufacture, illustrated by the Japanese move into small systems: a way to evade the dependency stranglehold and to take the lead in a different technological sector.

5. Pedagogy director RIG, who was against this decision, described it thus: "They decided to go with the PDP10 and pour everything into the hardware prototype. That was a crazy decision! If we'd got the Samson box, as I wanted, we'd have immediately had a working environment set up for music production. Also, it would have set up alternative criteria by which to weigh up the 4X project. But it didn't happen for political reasons."

6. The production of this recent successful piece of AV's — the realization of the ideas that over the years he had tried to put into practice at IRCAM —

contains some ironies. It was eventually made using high-quality commercial computer music technology that AV has at home, combined with the technology of IRCAM's rival and supposed technological inferior, the GRM—a machine called the Syter. AV recalled that an IRCAM director who was extremely enthusiastic about his piece was aghast and could not believe that he had made it using these technologies.

7. Just one record of IRCAM "examples" had been released by 1984, seven years after the institute's opening.

8. RIG, who arrived at IRCAM from the States for the first time in mid-1977, told me of his astonishment to find that IRCAM management was not recording the concerts. He immediately got hold of a high-quality portable tape recorder and taped as many as he could.

9. In 1984 IRCAM's recording studios, which had been equipped in 1976–77, were in urgent need of upgrading. Digital recording equipment had been around for some years, and for IRCAM not to be digitalized was an anathema. But the issue had caused conflict. Finance had not been forthcoming from the main budgets, and special bids were in process.

10. A very few individual young IRCAM musicians—those with previous electronic or pop music experience—were aware of studio production techniques and employed them. (See chapter 10).

11. We saw in chapter 5 one expression of this rebellion: the tutors' fight in '84 for new contracts that would allow them several months a year for their own musical work, which in turn implied their recognition as legitimate composers.

12. For a critical overview and discussion of the "neofuturist" discourse, in both its social-theoretical and popular manifestations, which portrays new technologies as harbingers of decentralization, democratization, and "community," see Carey (1989), esp. chaps. 5 and 7.

13. My own experience of patronage involved a staff composer who invited me after a few months to help him with basic programming for his piece. This man was thought to be secretive about his work, and the invitation was taken as a flattering sign that he was my patron. Jokes soon flew that I was his "amanuensis."

14. Thus a well-known American researcher was brought over for a year in 1992 specifically to crack IRCAM's continuing documentation problem. Having studied it, he felt that it was so deeply embedded in IRCAM's functioning that he would be powerless to change it.

CHAPTER 10

1. RIG recalled this exchange: "Boulez said to me, 'Well I see you've got hold of these Apples—good luck with them! But don't expect IRCAM to give you any support or money.' . . . It's because of that old thing, Pierre sees these things as for 'le grand public,' and so by definition not for IRCAM."

2. "The Fantastic Tale of Apple: Once upon a time there were two microcomputing fanatics who lived in Silicon Valley in Northern California. They imagined a small computer destined for enthusiasts. . . ."

3. NI offered to build me a modified Casio VL Tone for about fifty dollars.

4. Thus, the 1984 ICMC at IRCAM was mainly concerned with big-system research, and had just one section devoted to "affordable systems," which was treated condescendingly by many high-level researchers.

5. Examples of these views on the "information" or "postindustrial" society include, on the utopian side, the work of McLuhan, Masuda, and on the dystopian side, that of Baudrillard, and Bell.

6. The article on Braxton leads into IRCAM as follows: "Too subversive of jazz . . . to become a neo-Coltraneist hero; too interested in jazz to be a conservatoire cult figure; a compromised would-be European to some black Americans and a black man with no sense of rhythm to some whites, Braxton has fitted no niches. He recalls with some irony how Boulez welcomed Frank Zappa to perform a symphonic work at IRCAM, but that such an opportunity would still be denied to him." *The Guardian*, 24 June 1988, 32.

7. This can be exemplified by an interview in a mass-market music technology magazine with the group M/A/R/R/S, who had a major hit in the UK clubs and pop charts with their dance track "Pump Up The Volume," based on sampler technology, in the late 1980's. A member of the group ruminates, "When the stuff that's happening at IRCAM crosses over — basically, when the likes of me can afford it — then sound and rhythm will really begin to get interesting. . . . I'd like to get my hands on that [IRCAM] technology. Do you think we could get in there?" The interviewer remarks, as an aside: "I didn't like to say that musicians working in popular music have about as much chance of getting into IRCAM as Pierre Boulez has of writing a number one hit" (Trask 1987, 42).

8. The one exception, BYV — Boulez's unofficial American tutor, and 4X Software director — has become strongly identified with Europe, as shown by his taking out French citizenship.

CHAPTER 11

1. Miller Puckette, designer of the MAX software, and Eric Lindemann, director of the Musical Workstation project.

2. Like PL, WI inhabited a studio hidden away in the old building — "the furthest you can be from IRCAM and yet still be inside the place!" WI expressed his musical tastes to me when he mused about what music he might go to on a forthcoming visit to London. "Are there any good shows on in London now? *Starlight Express*? How's *Cats*? Have you seen it?"

3. Composers often mentioned as part of this rising cohort include: Philippe Manoury, Frédéric Durieux, Philippe Durville, Marc-André Dalbavie, Philippe Hurel, and Denis Cohen (French), Kaija Saariaho and Magnus Lindberg (Finnish), York Höller (German), Marco Stroppa (Italian), George Benjamin and Jonathan Harvey (British), and Ichiro Nodaira (Japanese). (See, for example, Bayle 1992, 21, 23).

4. It is true that in any detailed IRCAM publicity, tutors are cited as assistants to the composer. But overall, in most forms of discourse and exchange and in the public imagination, the composer is exclusively referred to and remains the dominant name associated with a piece. The publicity gesture does little to overturn this.

5. Roads (1980, 19–20) outlines several such projects: Snell's computer modeling of the musical structure of C. P. E. Bach's compositions, Haflich's project to devise a computer model of the (Chomskyan) "competence" at work in the musical structure of Mozart piano sonatas, or Levitt's attempt at a generative model of jazz composition. In relation to another AI music project, Roads qualifies, "While not purporting to be a cognitive theory of what human musicians do, it does bring into the open the different dimensions and levels of organization required for modeling even the more understood musical forms" (ibid., 19).

6. This range of applications of Formes was described in a paper given at a CGP conference in September 1985 (IRCAM, Rodet 1985c).

7. On this general tendency within cognitive science and its computer applications such as AI, see Poster (1990), chap. 5: "Whether in computerized databases . . . or as metanarratives of science, cognitive knowledge delimits being as it claims merely to know it" (1990, 153).

8. AV elucidated some of these qualities that continue to challenge computer analysis and simulation: for example, modeling the behavior of complex sounds over time or simulating the behavior of any complex sound as it interacts with other sound objects.

9. Teasing also in suggesting an analogy between Boulez and Stalin. The irony is, of course, that *perestroika* failed and gave way to the present unreserved enthusiasm for capitalism.

10. Boulez indicated an awareness of these issues at the very outset of IRCAM in his article "Donc on remet en question" in the IRCAM collection *La Musique en projet* (1975). See Jameux (1991), 171.

11. Boulez still holds a number of very powerful positions in cultural institutions such as the Bastille Opera, Radio France, the *Orchestre National*, and *La Sept*.

12. An informant told me that in 1992, in contrast with the previous decade, the Ministry of Culture was blocking grants and commissions to non-French composers, arguing that other countries should first show similar grants to the French.

13. However, there are signs that the EIC is becoming even more autonomous from IRCAM. It has its own new base in the City of Music at La Villette.

14. I have deliberately given this vision a provocative, dystopian tenor. However, for a more extensive discussion of the issues, see Barrière (1990), a paper by the current director of Pedagogy and a positive sign that some at IRCAM are themselves debating these issues.

General Bibliography

Adorno, Theodor (1978b), Culture and administration, *Telos* no. 37: 93–111.
———. (1984), *Aesthetic Theory* (London: Routledge and Kegan Paul).
Althusser, Louis (1971), Ideology and Ideological State Apparatuses, in *Essays on Ideology* (London: New Left Books).
Anderson, Perry (1984), Modernity and revolution, *New Left Review* no. 144: 96–113.
Apollonio, Umbro (1973) (ed.), *Futurist Manifestos* (London: Thames and Hudson).
Arato, Andrew, and Eike Gebhardt (1978) (eds.), *The Essential Frankfurt School Reader* (Oxford: Blackwell).
Armstrong, Timothy J. (1992) (ed.), *Michel Foucault, Philosopher* (London: Harvester Wheatsheaf).
Athanasiou, Tom (1985), Artificial Intelligence: Cleverly disguised politics, in T. Solomonides and L. Levidow (eds.), *Compulsive Technology*.
Avril, Pierre (1969), *Politics in France* (Harmondsworth: Penguin).
Barrett, Michele (1981), Materialist aesthetics, *New Left Review* no. 126: 86–93.
Barthes, Roland (1972a), Myth today, in Barthes (1972b).
———. (1972b), *Mythologies* (London: Cape).
———. (1977a), Rhetoric of the image, in Barthes (1977d).
———. (1977c), From work to text, in Barthes (1977d).
———. (1977d), *Image, Music, Text* (London: Fontana).
Baudrillard, Jean (1981), *For a Critique of the Political Economy of the Sign* (St. Louis, Mo.: Telos Press).
Becker, Howard (1974), Art as collective action, *American Sociological Review* 39, no. 6: 767–76.
———. (1978), Arts and crafts, *American Journal of Sociology* 83, no. 4: 862–89.
———. (1982), *Art Worlds* (Berkeley: University of California Press).

Belsey, Catherine (1980), *Critical Practice* (London: Methuen).

Benjamin, Walter (1978), The author as producer, in A. Arato and E. Gebhardt (eds.), *The Essential Frankfurt School Reader*.

——. (1979a), The work of art in the age of mechanical reproduction, in Benjamin (1979b).

——. (1979b), *Illuminations* (London: Fontana).

Bennett, Tony (1988), The exhibitionary complex, *New Formations* no. 4: 73–102.

——. (1990a), The political rationality of the museum, *Continuum* 3, no. 1: 35–55.

——. (1990b), *Outside Literature* (London: Routledge).

——. (1992), Putting policy into cultural studies, in Lawrence Grossberg, Cary Nelson, and Paula Treichler (eds.), *Cultural Studies* (London: Routledge).

Bennett, Tony, Graham Martin, Colin Mercer, and Janet Woollacott (1981) (eds.), *Culture, Ideology and Social Process* (Milton Keynes: Open University Press).

Berman, Marshall (1984), The signs in the street: A response to Perry Anderson, *New Left Review* no. 144: 114–23.

Bernstein, Richard J. (1985) (ed.), *Habermas and Modernity* (Cambridge: Polity).

Bion, Wilfred (1961), *Experience in Groups* (London: Tavistock).

——. (1977), Group dynamics: A re-view, in Melanie Klein, Paula Heimann, and Roger Money-Kyrle (eds.) *New Directions in Psychoanalysis* (London: Karnac).

Bloch, Ernst, Georg Lukács, Bertolt Brecht, Walter Benjamin, Theodor Adorno (1980), *Aesthetics and Politics* (London: Verso).

Bloch, Maurice (1991), Language, anthropology and cognitive science, *Man* n.s. 26, no. 2: 183–98.

Born, Georgina (1993), Against negation, for a politics of cultural production: Adorno, aesthetics, the social, *Screen* 34, no. 3: 223–42.

Bourdieu, Pierre (1968), Outline of a sociological theory of art perception, *International Social Science Journal* 20, no. 4: 589–612.

——. (1971a), Intellectual field and creative project, in Michael F. D. Young (ed.) *Knowledge and Control* (London: Collier Macmillan).

——. (1971b), Systems of education and systems of thought, in Michael F. D. Young (ed.), *Knowledge and Control*.

——. (1979), *La Distinction: Critique sociale du jugement* (Paris: Minuit).

——. (1981), The production of belief: Contribution to an economy of symbolic goods, *Media, Culture and Society* 2, no. 3: 261–94.

——. (1987), Legitimation and structured interests in Weber's sociology of religion, in Sam Whimster and Scott Lash (eds.), *Max Weber, Rationality and Modernity*.

——. (1988), *Homo Academicus* (Cambridge: Polity).

——. (1990), *In Other Words: Essays Towards a Reflexive Sociology* (Cambridge: Polity).

Bourdieu, Pierre, and Jean-Claude Passeron, (1977), *Reproduction in Education, Society and Culture* (London: Sage).

Bradbury, Malcolm, and James McFarlane (1976) (eds.), *Modernism 1890–1930* (Harmondsworth: Penguin).

Brookeman, Christopher (1984), *American Culture and Society since the 1930's* (London: Macmillan).

Buchloh, Benjamin, Serge Guilbaut, and David Solkin (1983) (eds), *Modernism and Modernity* (Halifax: Press of the Nova Scotia College of Art and Design).

Bundy, Alan (1991), Clear thinking on artificial intelligence, *The Guardian*, 5 December, 33.

Burchell, Graham, Colin Gordon, and Peter Miller (1991) (eds.), *The Foucault Effect: Studies in Governmentality* (London: Harvester Wheatsheaf).

Bürger, Peter (1984), *Theory of the Avant-Garde* (Manchester: Manchester University Press).

Burgin, Victor (1986), *The End of Art Theory: Criticism and Postmodernity.* (London: Macmillan).

Burke, Peter (1981), The "discovery" of popular culture, in Raphael Samuel (ed.), *People's History and Socialist Theory* (London: Routledge and Kegan Paul).

Calinescu, Matei (1987), *Five Faces of Modernity* (Durham, N.C.: Duke University Press).

Carey, James W. (1989), *Communication as Culture: Essays on Media and Society* (London: Unwin Hyman).

Caughie, John (1981) (ed.), *Theories of Authorship* (London: British Film Institute).

Clark, T. J. (1973a), *The Image of the People: Gustave Courbet and the 1848 Revolution* (London: Thames and Hudson).

——. (1973b), *The Absolute Bourgeois: Artists and Politics in France, 1848–51* (London: Thames and Hudson).

——. (1983), More on the differences between Comrade Greenberg and ourselves, in B. Buchloh et al. (eds.), *Modernism and Modernity.*

——. (1985a), Clement Greenberg's theory of art, in F. Frascina (ed.), *Pollock and After.*

——. (1985b), Arguments about modernism: A reply to Michael Fried, in F. Frascina (ed.), *Pollock and After.*

Clifford, James (1988), *The Predicament of Culture* (Cambridge, Mass.: Harvard University Press).

Clifford, James, and George Marcus (1986) (eds.), *Writing Culture: The Poetics and Politics of Ethnography* (Berkeley: University of California Press).

Clignet, Rémi (1985), *The Structure of Artistic Revolutions* (Philadelphia: University of Pennsylvania Press).

Cousins, Mark, and Athar Hussain (1984), *Michel Foucault* (London: Macmillan).

Coutts-Smith, Kenneth (1991), Some general observations on the problem of cultural colonialism, in S. Hiller (ed.), *The Myth of Primitivism.*

Crane, Diana (1987), *The Transformation of the Avant-Garde* (Chicago: University of Chicago Press).

Crow, Thomas (1983), Modernism and mass culture in the visual arts, in B. Buchloh et al. (eds.), *Modernism and Modernity.*

Cultural Critique (1986–87), *Modernity and Modernism, Postmodernity and Postmodernism* no. 5.

Czitrom, Daniel (1982), *Media and the American Mind: From Morse to McLuhan* (Chapel Hill: University of North Carolina Press).

Debord, Guy (1987), *Society of the Spectacle* (London: Rebel).

Dews, Peter (1985), The "New Philosophers" and the end of leftism, in Roy Edgley and Richard Osborne (eds.), *Radical Philosophy Reader* (London: Verso).

———. (1987), *Logics of Disintegration* (London: Verso).

Dimaggio, Paul (1986), Cultural entrepreneurship in nineteenth century Boston, in Richard Collins et al. (eds.), *Media, Culture and Society: A Critical Reader* (London: Sage).

———. (1987), Classification in art, *American Sociological Review* 52, no. 3: 440–55.

Dreyfus, Hubert L., and Paul Rabinow (1982), *Michel Foucault: Beyond Structuralism and Hermeneutics* (Brighton: Harvester).

Dufrenne, Mikel (1973), *The Phenomenology of Aesthetic Experience* (Evanston, Ill.: Northwestern University Press).

Eagleton, Terry (1976), *Marxism and Literary Criticism* (London: Methuen).

———. (1983), *Literary Theory: An Introduction* (Oxford: Blackwell).

———. (1986), *Against the Grain* (London: Verso).

———. (1990), *The Ideology of the Aesthetic* (Oxford: Blackwell).

Eco, Umberto (1976), *A Theory of Semiotics* (London: Macmillan).

Engelmore, Robert (1980–1985) (ed.), *Readings from the AI Magazine*, vols. 1–5 (Menlo Park, Calif.: American Association for Artificial Intelligence).

Enzensberger, Hans Magnus (1970), Constituents of a theory of the media, *New Left Review* no. 64: 13–36.

Eribon, Didier (1991), *Michel Foucault* (Cambridge, Mass.: Harvard University Press).

Fardon, Richard (1985) (ed.), *Power and Knowledge* (Edinburgh: Scottish Academic Press).

Forester, Tom (1985) (ed.), *The Information Technology Revolution* (Oxford: Blackwell).

Foster, Hal (1985a), Postmodernism: A preface, in Foster (ed.) (1985b).

———. (1985b) (ed.), *Postmodern Culture* (London: Pluto).

———. (1987), *Recodings* (Seattle, Wash: Bay).

Foster, Stephen (1980), *The Critics of Abstract Expressionism* (Ann Arbor, Mich.: UMI Research Press).

Foucault, Michel (1972), *The Archaeology of Knowledge* (London: Tavistock).

———. (1973), *The Birth of the Clinic* (London: Tavistock).

———. (1977), *Discipline and Punish* (London: Allen Lane).

———. (1980), *Power/Knowledge* (Brighton: Harvester).

———. (1981), *The History of Sexuality* vol. 1, *An Introduction* (Harmondsworth: Penguin).

———. (1982), Afterword: The subject and power, in H. Dreyfus and P. Rabinow (eds.), *Michel Foucault*.

———. (1984a), What is Enlightenment?, in P. Rabinow (ed.), *The Foucault Reader*.

——. (1984b), Nietzsche, genealogy, history, in P. Rabinow (ed.), *The Foucault Reader*.

——. (1984c), What is an author?, in P. Rabinow (ed.), *The Foucault Reader*.

——. (1989), Clarifications on the question of power, in *Foucault Live* (New York: Semiotext(e)).

——. (1991a), Politics and the study of discourse, in G. Burchell et al. (eds.), *The Foucault Effect*.

——. (1991b), Governmentality, in G. Burchell et al. (eds.), *The Foucault Effect*.

Frascina, Francis (1985) (ed.), *Pollock and After: The Critical Debate* (London: Harper and Row).

Frascina, Francis, and Charles Harrison (1982) (eds.), *Modern Art and Modernism* (London: Harper and Row).

Fry, Edward (1966), *Cubism* (London: Thames and Hudson).

Gadet, Françoise (1989), *Saussure and Contemporary Culture* (London: Hutchinson Radius).

Gay, Peter (1968), *Weimar Culture: The Outsider as Insider* (New York: Harper and Row).

Gilpin, Robert (1968), *France in the Age of the Scientific State* (Princeton: Princeton University Press).

Glasgow University Media Group (1976), *Bad News* (London: Routledge and Kegan Paul).

Goldwater, Robert (1967), *Primitivism in Modern Art* (New York: Random House).

Gombrich, Ernst (1966), *The Story of Art* (London: Phaidon).

Goody, Jack, and Ian Watt (1963), The consequences of literacy, *Comparative Studies in Society and History* 5: 304–45.

Gordon, Colin (1987), The soul of the citizen: Max Weber and Michel Foucault on rationality and government, in S. Whimster and S. Lash (eds.), *Max Weber, Rationality and Modernity*.

Greenberg, Clement (1983), To cope with decadence, in B. Buchloh et al. (eds.), *Modernism and Modernity*.

——. (1985a), Avant-garde and kitsch, in F. Frascina (ed.), *Pollock and After*.

——. (1985b), Towards a newer Laocoon, in F. Frascina (ed.), *Pollock and After*.

Guilbaut, Serge (1983), *How New York Stole the Idea of Modern Art: Abstract Expressionism, Freedom, and the Cold War* (Chicago: University of Chicago Press).

Habermas, Jurgen (1970a), Technology and science as "ideology", in Habermas, 1970b.

——. (1970b), *Toward a Rational Society* (New York: Beacon).

——. (1985), Modernity — an incomplete project, in H. Foster (1985b) (ed.), *Postmodern Culture*.

Hall, Stuart (1981), Cultural studies: Two paradigms, in T. Bennett et al. (eds.), *Culture, Ideology and Social Process*.

——. (1982), The rediscovery of "ideology", in Michael Gurevitch et al. (eds.), *Culture, Society and the Media* (London: Methuen).

Halliday, Michael A. K. (1978), *Language as Social Semiotic: The Social Interpretation of Language and Meaning* (London: Edward Arnold).

Hannerz, Ulf (1986), Theory in anthropology: Small is beautiful? The problem of complex cultures, *Comparative Studies in Society and History* 28: 362–67.

Harvey, David (1989), *The Condition of Postmodernity* (Oxford: Blackwell).

Haskell, Francis (1983), Enemies of modern art, *New York Review of Books*, 30 June, 19–25.

Hassan, Ihab (1971), *The Dismemberment of Orpheus: Toward a Postmodern Literature* (New York: Oxford University Press).

Hebdige, Dick (1979), *Subculture: The Meaning of Style* (London: Methuen).

———. (1988), *Hiding in the Light: On Images and Things* (London: Comedia/Routledge).

Herf, Jeffrey (1984), *Reactionary Modernism: Technology, Culture and Politics in Weimar and the Third Reich* (Cambridge: Cambridge University Press).

Hiller, Susan (1991) (ed.), *The Myth of Primitivism* (London: Routledge).

Hinshelwood, Robert (1987), *What Happens in Groups* (London: Free Association).

———. (1989), *A Dictionary of Kleinian Thought* (London: Free Association).

Hodge, Robert, and Gunther Kress (1988), *Social Semiotics* (Cambridge: Polity).

Hughes, Robert (1980), *The Shock of the New* (London: BBC).

———. (1983), There's no geist like the zeitgeist, *New York Review of Books*, 27 October, 63–68.

———. (1984), On art and money, *New York Review of Books*, 6 December, 20–27.

Hunt, Jennifer (1989), *Psychoanalytic Aspects of Fieldwork* (London: Sage).

Huxtable, Ada Louise (1983), After modern architecture, *New York Review of Books*, 8 December, 29–35.

Huyssen, Andreas (1984), Mapping the postmodern, *New German Critique* no. 33: 5–52.

———. (1986), *After the Great Divide: Modernism, Mass Culture, Postmodernism* (Bloomington: Indiana University Press).

Institute of Contemporary Arts (1986), *ICA Documents 4: Postmodernism* (London: Institute of Contemporary Arts).

Jameson, Fredric (1979), Reification and utopia in mass culture, *Social Text* 1, no. 1: 130–48.

———. (1984a), Postmodernism, or the cultural logic of late capitalism, *New Left Review* no. 146: 53–92.

———. (1984b), The politics of theory: Ideological positions in the postmodernism debate, *New German Critique* no. 33: 53–65.

———. (1985), Postmodernism and consumer society, in H. Foster (1985b) (ed.), *Postmodern Culture*.

Jay, Martin (1985), Habermas and modernism, in R. Bernstein (ed.), *Habermas and Modernity*.

Jencks, Charles (1977), *The Language of Postmodern Architecture* (New York: Rizzoli).

Johnstone, Diana (1984), How the French Left learned to love the bomb, *New Left Review* no. 146: 5–36.

Karp, Ivan, and Steven D. Lavine (1991) (eds.), *Exhibiting Cultures: The Poetics and Politics of Museum Display* (Washington, D.C.: Smithsonian Institution Press).

Karp, Ivan, Christine Mullen Kreamer, and Steven D. Lavine (1992) (eds.), *Museums and Communities: The Politics of Public Culture* (Washington, D.C.: Smithsonian Institution Press).

Kidder, Tracy (1981), *The Soul of a New Machine* (Harmondsworth: Penguin).

Klein, Melanie (1977a), Envy and gratitude, in Klein (1977b).

———. (1977b), *Envy and Gratitude and Other Works 1946–1963* (New York: Delta).

Kuhn, Thomas (1962), *The Structure of Scientific Revolutions* (Chicago: University of Chicago Press).

Laclau, Ernesto (1980), Populist rupture and discourse, *Screen Education* no. 34: 87–93.

Laing, Dave (1978), *The Marxist Theory of Art* (Brighton: Harvester).

Laplanche, Jean, and Jean-Bertrand Pontalis (1973), *The Language of Psychoanalysis* (London: Hogarth).

Larrain, Jorge (1979), *The Concept of Ideology* (London: Hutchinson).

Lash, Scott (1990), *Sociology of Postmodernism* (London: Routledge).

Latour, Bruno, and Steve Woolgar (1979), *Laboratory Life: The Construction of Scientific Facts* (Los Angeles: Sage).

Lévi-Strauss, Claude (1966), *The Savage Mind* (London: Weidenfeld and Nicolson).

———. (1977), *Structural Anthropology*, 2 vols. (Harmondsworth: Penguin).

———. (1986), *The Raw and the Cooked: Introduction to a Science of Mythology* (Harmondsworth: Penguin).

Lumley, Robert (1988) (ed.), *The Museum Time-Machine* (London: Comedia/Routledge).

Lyotard, Jean-François (1984), *The Postmodern Condition: A Report on Knowledge* (Manchester: Manchester University Press).

Macherey, Pierre (1978), *A Theory of Literary Production* (London: Routledge and Kegan Paul).

MacKenzie, Donald, and Judy Wajcman (1985) (eds.), *The Social Shaping of Technology* (Milton Keynes: Open University Press).

Mani, Lata, and Ruth Frankenberg (1985), The challenge of *Orientalism, Economy and Society* 14, no. 2: 174–92.

Manuel, Frank (1956), *The New World of Henri Saint-Simon* (Cambridge, Mass.: Harvard University Press).

Marbach, William D. et al. (1985), The race to build a supercomputer, in T. Forester (ed.), *The Information Technology Revolution*.

Marcus, George, and Michael Fischer (1986), *Anthropology as Cultural Critique* (Chicago: University of Chicago Press).

MacDonald, Sharon (1992), Making science: Knowledge construction in a museum exhibition, paper at Manchester University Social Anthropology seminar.

———. (1994), Authorising science: Public understanding of science in museums, in Brian Wynne and Alan Irwin (eds.), *Science, Technology and Everyday Life* (Cambridge: Cambridge University Press).

McDougall, Walter A. (1985), Space-age Europe: Gaullism, Euro-Gaullism, and the American dilemma, *Technology and Culture* 26, no. 2: 179–203.

Menzies Lyth, Isabel (1988a), *Containing Anxiety in Institutions* (London: Free Association).

——. (1988b), A psychoanalytic perspective on social institutions, in E. Bott Spillius (ed.), *Melanie Klein Today*, vol. 2.

Morley, David (1989), Changing paradigms in audience studies, in E. Seiter, H. Borchers, G. Kreutzner, and E.-M. Warth (eds.), *Remote Control: Television, Audiences, and Cultural Power* (London: Routledge).

Murdock, Graham, and Peter Golding (1977), Capitalism, communication and class relations, in James Curran et al.(eds.), *Mass Communication and Society* (London: Edward Arnold).

Myers, John B. (1983), The art biz, *New York Review of Books*, 13 October, 32–34.

New German Critique (1984), *Modernity and Postmodernity*, no. 33.

Norris, Christopher (1982), *Deconstruction: Theory and Practice* (London: Methuen).

October (1991), *High/Low: A Special Issue*, no. 56.

Owens, Craig (1985), The discourse of Others: feminists and postmodernism, in H. Foster (1985b) (ed.), *Postmodern Culture*.

Pavel, Thomas (1989), *The Feud of Language: A History of Structuralist Thought* (Oxford: Blackwell).

Peterson, Richard A. (1982), Five constraints on the production of culture: Law, technology, market, organisational structure and occupational careers, *Journal of Popular Culture*, Fall: 143–53.

Petras, James (1984), The rise and decline of Southern European socialism, *New Left Review* no. 146: 37–52.

Poggioli, Renato (1982), *The Theory of the Avant-Garde* (Cambridge, Mass.: Belknap/Harvard).

Poster, Mark (1990), *The Mode of Information: Poststructuralism and Social Context* (Cambridge: Polity).

Rabinow, Paul (1984) (ed.), *The Foucault Reader* (Harmondsworth: Penguin).

——. (1986), Representations are social facts: Modernity and postmodernity in anthropology, in J. Clifford and G. Marcus (eds.), *Writing Culture*.

——. (1989), *French Modern* (Cambridge, Mass.: MIT Press).

Reader, Keith (1987), *Intellectuals and the Left in France Since 1968* (London: Macmillan).

Richter, Hans (1965), *Dada: Art and Anti-Art* (London: Thames and Hudson).

Robbins, Derek (1991), *The Work of Pierre Bourdieu: Recognising Society* (Milton Keynes: Open University Press).

Rubin, William S. (1984) (ed.), *"Primitivism" in Twentieth Century Art: Affinity of the Tribal and the Modern* (New York: Museum of Modern Art).

Russell, Charles (1985), *Poets, Prophets and Revolutionaries: The Literary Avant-Garde from Rimbaud through Postmodernism* (Oxford: Oxford University Press).

Rycroft, Charles (1972), *A Critical Dictionary of Psychoanalysis* (Harmondsworth: Penguin).

Sahlins, Marshall (1976), *Culture and Practical Reason* (Chicago: University of Chicago Press).

——. (1981), *Historical Metaphors and Mythical Realities* (Ann Arbor: University of Michigan Press).

——. (1987), *Islands of History* (London: Tavistock).

Said, Edward (1978), *Orientalism* (New York: Pantheon).

——. (1984), *The World, the Text, and the Critic* (London: Faber).

——. (1985), Opponents, audiences, constituencies and community, in H. Foster (1985b) (ed.), *Postmodern Culture*.

Schlesinger, Phillip (1978), *Putting "Reality" Together* (London: Constable).

Schorske, Carl (1961), *Fin-de-Siècle Vienna: Politics and Culture* (New York: Vintage).

Segal, Hanna (1979), *Klein* (London: Fontana).

——. (1982), *Introduction to the Work of Melanie Klein* (London: Hogarth).

Shapiro, David, and Cecile Shapiro (1985), Abstract Expressionism: the politics of apolitical painting, in F. Frascina (ed.), *Pollock and After*.

Shapiro, Theda (1976), *Painters and Politics: The European Avant-Garde and Society 1900–1925* (Oxford: Elsevier).

Sherman, Barrie, and Phillip Judkins (1992), *Glimpses of Heaven, Visions of Hell: Virtual Reality and Its Implications* (London: Hodder and Stoughton).

Silverstone, Roger (1985), *Framing Science: The Making of a BBC Documentary* (London: British Film Institute).

Solomonides, Tony, and Les Levidow (1985) (eds.), *Compulsive Technology: Computers as Culture* (London: Free Association).

Sperber, Dan (1975), *Rethinking Symbolism* (Cambridge: Cambridge University Press).

——. (1985), *On Anthropological Knowledge* (Cambridge: Cambridge University Press).

Spillius, Elizabeth Bott (1988), *Melanie Klein Today: Developments in Theory and Practice*, 2 vols. (London: Routledge).

Suchman, Lucy (1987), *Plans and Situated Actions: The Problem of Human-Machine Communication* (Cambridge: Cambridge University Press).

Theory, Culture and Society (1988), *Postmodernism* 5, nos. 2–3.

Thompson, John B. (1990), *Ideology and Modern Culture* (Cambridge: Polity).

Timms, Edward, and Peter Collier (1988) (eds.), *Visions and Blueprints: Avant-Garde Culture and Radical Politics in Early Twentieth Century Europe* (Manchester: Manchester University Press).

Turkle, Sherry (1984), *The Second Self: Computers and the Human Spirit* (New York: Simon and Schuster).

Turner, Victor (1962), Three symbols of passage in Ndembu circumcision ritual: An interpretation, in Max Gluckman (ed.), *Essays on the Ritual of Social Relations* (Manchester: Manchester University Press).

Ulmer, Gregory (1985), The object of post-criticism, in H. Foster (1985b) (ed.), *Postmodern Culture*.

Varnedoe, Kirk, and Adam Gopnik (1990) (eds.), *High and Low: Modern Art and Popular Culture* (New York: Museum of Modern Art).

Vitz, Paul, and Arnold Glimcher, (1984), *Modern Art and Modern Science: The Parallel Analysis of Vision* (New York: Praegar).

Walker, John (1987), *Cross-overs: Art into Pop, Pop into Art* (London: Comedia/Methuen).

Weber, Eugen (1986), *France, Fin-de-Siècle* (Cambridge, Mass.: Harvard University Press).

Weber, Max, (ed.) Talcott Parsons (1964), *The Theory of Social and Economic Organization* (New York: The Free Press of Glencoe).

——, (eds.) Guenther Roth and Claus Wittich (1968), *Economy and Society* (New York: Bedminster).

Whimster, Sam, and Scott Lash (1987) (eds.), *Max Weber, Rationality and Modernity* (London: Allen and Unwin).

Whitford, Frank (1984), *Bauhaus* (London: Thames and Hudson).

Willett, John (1978), *The New Sobriety: Art and Politics in the Weimar Period 1917–33* (London: Thames and Hudson).

Williams, Raymond (1963), *Culture and Society 1780–1950* (Harmondsworth: Penguin).

——. (1977), *Marxism and Literature* (Oxford: Oxford University Press).

——. (1981), *Culture* (London: Fontana).

——. (1985), *Towards 2000* (London: Pelican).

——. (1988), Introduction: The politics of the avant-garde, in E. Timms and P. Collier (eds.), *Visions and Blueprints*.

——. (1989), *The Politics of Modernism* (London: Verso).

Wolfe, Tom (1981), *From Bauhaus to Our House* (New York: Farrar Straus Giroux).

Wolff, Janet (1981), *The Social Production of Art* (London: Macmillan).

——. (1983), *Aesthetics and the Sociology of Art* (London: Allen and Unwin).

Wollen, Peter (1987), Fashion/orientalism/the body, *New Formations* no. 1: 5–34.

——. (1989a), Cinema/Americanism/the robot, *New Formations* no. 8: 7–34.

——. (1989b), The Situationist International, *New Left Review* no. 174: 67–95.

Zeldin, Theodore (1983), *The French* (London: Collins).

Zolberg, Vera (1990), *Constructing a Sociology of the Arts* (Cambridge: Cambridge University Press).

Bibliography of Music-Related References

Adorno, Theodor (1973), *Philosophy of Modern Music* (New York: Seabury).
———. (1978a), On the fetish character in music and the regression of listening, in Andrew Arato and Eike Gebhardt (eds.), *The Essential Frankfurt School Reader* (Oxford: Blackwell).
———. (1990), On popular music, in S. Frith and A. Goodwin (eds.), *On Record*.
Allen, Warren Dwight (1962), *Philosophies of Music History: A Study of General Histories of Music* (New York: Dover).
Attali, Jaques (1985), *Noise: The Political Economy of Music* (Manchester: Manchester University Press).
Babbitt, Milton (1958), Who cares if you listen?, *High Fidelity* 8, no. 2, 38–40, 126–27. Reprinted as The composer as specialist, in P. Weiss and R. Taruskin (eds.) (1984), *Music in the Western World*.
Barrière, Jean-Baptiste (1990), Réflexions intempestives sur le statut social du compositeur, l'institution et l'industrie culturelle, *Inharmonique* no. 6: 149–59.
Barthes, Roland (1977b), Musica practica, in Barthes (1977d).
———. (1977d), *Image, Music, Text* (London: Fontana).
Bayle, Laurent (1990), Art et servitudes, *Inharmoniques* no. 6: 11–14.
———. (1992), Ne nous arrêtons donc pas en si bon chemin, in Bayle et al. (1992).
Bayle, Laurent, Andrew Gerszo, Jean-Pascal Jullien, Jean-Baptiste Barrière, Risto Nieminen, and Pierre Boulez, (1992), *Recherche et création: Vers de nouveaux territoires* (Paris: IRCAM/Centre Georges Pompidou).
Becker, Judith, and Alton Becker (1981), A musical icon: Power and meaning in Javanese Gamelan music, in W. Steiner (ed.), *The Sign in Music and Literature*.
Bennett, H. Stith (1980), *On Becoming a Rock Musician* (Amherst: University of Massachusetts Press).

Blacking, John (1973), *How Musical is Man?* (Seattle: University of Washington Press).

———. Transcultural communication and the biological foundations of music. Unpublished MS.

Bloch, Ernst (1985), On the mathematical and dialectical character in music, in *Essays on the Philosophy of Music* (Cambridge: Cambridge University Press).

Boretz, Benjamin (1987), Interface part II: Thoughts in reply to Boulez/Foucault "Contemporary music and the public," *Perspectives of New Music* 25, nos. 1 & 2: 608–11.

Born, Georgina (1987), On modern music culture: Shock, pop and synthesis, *New Formations* no. 2: 51–78.

———. (1991), Music, modernism and signification, in Andrew Benjamin and Peter Osborne (eds.), *Thinking Art: Beyond Traditional Aesthetics* (London: Institute of Contemporary Arts).

———. (1992), Women, music, politics, difference, *Women: A Cultural Review*, 3, no. 1: 79–86.

———. (1993a), Understanding music as culture: Contributions from popular music studies to a social semiotics of music, in Raffaele Pozzi (ed.) *Tendenze e Metodi nella Ricerca Musicologica* (Florence: Olschki).

———. (1993b), Afterword: Music policy, aesthetic and social difference, in Tony Bennett et al. (eds.), *Rock and Popular Music: Politics, Policies, Institutions* (London: Routledge).

Boulez, Pierre (1971), *Boulez on Music Today* (London: Faber).

———. (1976), *Pierre Boulez: Conversations with Célestin Deliège* (London: Eulenburg).

———. (1977), Technology and the composer, *Times Literary Supplement*, 6 May, 570–71. Reprinted in S. Emmerson (1986) (ed.), *The Language of Electroacoustic Music*.

———. (1984), On new music, *New York Review of Books*, 28 June, 14–15.

———. (ed.), Jean-Jacques Nattiez (1986), *Orientations: Collected Writings* (London: Faber).

———. (1990), From the Domaine Musical to IRCAM: Pierre Boulez in conversation with Pierre-Michel Menger, *Perspectives of New Music*, 28, no. 1: 6–19.

Boulez, Pierre, and Michel Foucault (1985), Contemporary music and the public, *Perspectives of New Music* 24, no. 1: 6–12. Translated and reprinted from *CNAC* magazine, no. 15, May–June (1983), 10–12 (Paris: Centre Georges Pompidou).

Bradby, Barbara, and Brian Torode (1984), Pity Peggy Sue, *Popular Music* no. 4: 183–205.

Bradley, Dick (1981), Music and social science: A survey, *Media, Culture and Society* 3, no. 3: 205–18.

Cage, John (1969), *Silence* (Cambridge, Mass.: MIT Press).

Chambers, Iain (1985), *Urban Rhythms* (London: Macmillan).

Chester, Andrew (1970), Second thoughts on a rock aesthetic: The Band, *New Left Review* no. 62: 75–82.

Cohen, Sara (1991), *Rock Culture in Liverpool: Popular Music in the Making* (Oxford: Oxford University Press).

Contemporary Music Review (1984), *Musical Thought at IRCAM*, 1, no. 1.

Cook, Nicholas (1990), *Music, Imagination, and Culture* (Oxford: Oxford University Press).

Cooke, Deryck (1959), *The Language of Music* (Oxford: Oxford University Press).

Cott, Jonathan (1974), *Stockhausen: Conversations with the Composer* (London: Pan).

Cutler, Chris (1984), Technology, politics and contemporary music, *Popular Music* no. 4: 279–300.

——. (1985), *File Under Popular* (London: November Books).

Dahlhaus, Carl (1983), *Foundations of Music History* (Cambridge: Cambridge University Press).

——. (1988), *Esthetics of Music* (Cambridge: Cambridge University Press).

——. (1989), *Nineteenth-Century Music* (Berkeley: University of California Press).

Dodge, Charles, and Thomas Jerse (1985), *Computer Music: Synthesis, Composition and Performance* (London: Schirmer).

Durant, Alan (1984), *Conditions of Music* (London: Macmillan).

Emmerson, Simon (1986) (ed.), *The Language of Electroacoustic Music* (London: Macmillan).

Etzkorn, K. Peter (1973), *Music and Society: The Later Writings of Paul Honigsheim* (New York: Wiley and Sons).

Faulkner, Robert (1971), *Hollywood Studio Musicians* (Chicago: University of Chicago Press).

——. (1973a), Orchestra interaction: Some features of communication and authority in an artistic organisation, *Sociological Quarterly* 14, no. 2: 147–57.

——. (1973b), Career concerns and mobility motivations of orchestral musicians, *Sociological Quarterly* 14, no. 3: 334–49.

Feld, Steven (1982), *Sound and Sentiment: Birds, Weeping, Poetics and Song in Kaluli Expression* (Philadelphia: University of Pennsylvania Press).

——. (1984a), Sound structure as social structure, *Ethnomusicology* 28, no. 3: 383–409.

——. (1984b), Communication, music, and speech about music, *1984 Yearbook for Traditional Music* 16: 1–18.

Finnegan, Ruth (1989), *The Hidden Musicians: Music-Making in an English Town* (Cambridge: Cambridge University Press).

Franklin, Peter (1985), *The Idea of Music: Schoenberg and Others* (London: Macmillan).

Frith, Simon (1978), *The Sociology of Rock* (London: Constable).

——. (1983), *Sound Effects* (London: Constable).

——. (1986), Art versus technology: The strange case of popular music, *Media, Culture and Society* 8, no. 3: 263–79.

——. (1987), Towards an aesthetics of popular music, in R. Leppert and S. McClary (eds.), *Music and Society*.

——. (1988), *Music for Pleasure* (Cambridge: Polity).

Frith, Simon, and Andrew Goodwin (1990) (eds.), *On Record: Rock, Pop and the Written Word* (London: Routledge).

Frith, Simon, and Howard Horne (1987), *Art into Pop* (London: Methuen).

Glock, William (1986) (ed.), *Pierre Boulez: A Symposium* (London: Eulenburg).

Goehr, Alexander (1988), *The Survival of the Symphony* (London: Faber).

Goehr, Lydia (1992), *The Imaginary Museum of Musical Works* (Oxford: Clarendon).

Goodwin, Andrew (1986), Editorial, *Media, Culture and Society* 8, no. 3: 259–62.

——. (1990), Sample and hold: Pop music in the digital age of reproduction, in S. Frith and A. Goodwin (eds.), *On Record*.

——. (1991), Popular music and postmodern theory, *Cultural Studies* 5, no. 2: 174–90.

Gorbman, Claudia (1991), Hanns Eisler in Hollywood, *Screen* 32, no. 3: 272–85.

Griffiths, Paul (1978), *Modern Music: A Concise History from Debussy to Boulez* (London: Thames and Hudson).

——. (1979), *A Guide to Electronic Music* (London: Thames and Hudson).

——. (1981), *Modern Music: The Avant-Garde since 1945* (London: Dent).

——. (1985), *New Sounds, New Personalities: British Composers of the 1980s* (London: Faber).

——. (1986), *Encyclopaedia of 20th Century Music* (London: Thames and Hudson).

Hamm, Charles (1983), *Music in the New World* (New York: Norton).

Hebdige, Dick (1987), *Cut 'n' Mix* (London: Methuen).

Hennion, Antoine (1981), *Les Professionels du disque: Une sociologie des variétés* (Paris: Métailié).

——. (1983), The production of success: An anti-musicology of the pop song, *Popular Music* no. 3, pp. 159–93.

——. (1988), *Comment la musique vient aux enfants: Une anthropologie de l'enseignement musical* (Paris: Anthropos).

——. (1991), La Médiation musicale. Thèse de nouveau régime, Ecole des Hautes Etudes en Sciences Sociales (Unpublished).

——. (1993), *La Passion musicale* (Paris: Métailié).

Hennion, Antoine, Jean-Pierre Vignolle, and Françoise Martinat (1983), *Les Conservatoires et leurs elèves* (Paris: La Documentation Française).

Heyworth, Peter (1973a), Profiles: Taking leave of predecessors, part 1, *The New Yorker*, 24 March, 45–70.

——. (1973b), Profiles: Taking leave of predecessors, part 2, *The New Yorker*, 31 March, 45–75.

——. (1986), The first fifty years, in W. Glock (ed.), *Pierre Boulez*.

Holoman, D. Kern, and Claude V. Palisca (1982) (eds.), *Musicology in the 1980s* (New York: Da Capo).

Hosokawa, Shuhei (1984), The walkman effect, *Popular Music* no. 4: 165–80.

——. (1987), Technique/technology of reproduction in music, in Thomas Sebeok and Jean Umiker-Sebeok (eds.), *The Semiotic Web '86: An International Yearbook* (Berlin: Mouton de Gruyter).

Inharmoniques (1990), *Musique et Institution*, no. 6. (Paris: Séguier/IRCAM/Centre Georges Pompidou).

Institut de Recherche et de Coordination Acoustique/Musique (IRCAM). The following is a selection of documents published or issued by IRCAM:

Bennett, Gerald (1978), *Research at IRCAM in 1977* (IRCAM Report 1).

——. (1979), *Research at IRCAM in 1978* (IRCAM Report 19).

Cointe, Pierre, and Xavier Rodet (1984), Formes: An Object and Time-Oriented System for Music Composition and Synthesis.

Di Giugno, Peppino, and Jean Kott (1981), *Presentation du système 4X* (IRCAM Report 32).

Ehresman, David, and David Wessel (1978), *Perception of Timbral Analogies* (IRCAM Report 13).

Gardner, John (1978), *Computer Facilities for Music at IRCAM, October 1977* (IRCAM Report 3).

Gerszo, Andrew (1985), Valorisation de la recherche, paper at the conference Actualité de la Recherche, Centre Georges Pompidou, September.

IRCAM (1975), *La Musique en projet.* (Paris: Editions Gallimard).

——. (1977), *Passage du vingtième siècle.* Concert series program books, 1 and 2.

——. (1985), *Seminaire sur le timbre.* Conference abstracts.

Koechlin, Olivier (1985), *La Station de travail musical 4X* (IRCAM Report 39).

Machover, Tod (1981) (ed.), *Le Compositeur et l'ordinateur.* Conference papers.

——. (1983) (ed.), *Le Concepte de recherche en musique.* Conference abstracts.

Mathews, Max, and Gerald Bennett (1978), *Real-Time Synthesizer Control* (IRCAM Report 5).

McAdams, Stephen (1985), *L'Image auditive* (IRCAM Report 37).

McAdams, Stephen, and Kaija Saariaho (1985), Qualities and functions of musical timbre, paper at ICMC.

Risset, Jean-Claude (1978), *Musical Acoustics* (IRCAM Report 8).

——. (1978), *The Development of Digital Techniques: A Turning Point for Electronic Music?* (IRCAM Report 9).

Rodet, Xavier et al. (1980), *Manuel Chant.*

——. (1985a), *Chant: De la synthèse de la voix chantée à la synthèse en générale* (IRCAM Report 35).

——. (1985b), *Formes: Composition et ordonnancement de processus* (IRCAM Report 36).

——. (1985c), Chant/Formes, paper at the conference Actualité de la Recherche, Centre Georges Pompidou, September.

Wessel, David (1978), *Low Dimension Control of Musical Timbre* (IRCAM Report 12).

International Computer Music Conference (1982), (1984), (1986), Conference Programs.

Jameux, Dominique (1991), *Pierre Boulez* (London: Faber).

Jay, Martin (1984), *Adorno* (London: Fontana).

Kealy, Ed (1974), The Real Rock Revolution: Sound Mixers, Social Inequality and the Aesthetics of Popular Music Production. Ph.D. thesis, Northwestern University.

———. (1979), From craft to art: The case of sound mixers and popular music, *Sociology of Work and Occupations* 6, no. 1: 3–29.

Keil, Charles (1966a), *Urban Blues* (Chicago: University of Chicago Press).

———. (1966b), Motion and feeling through music, *Journal of Aesthetics and Art Criticism*, 24, no. 3: 337–50.

Kenyon, Nicholas (1988) (ed.), *Authenticity and Early Music* (Oxford: Oxford University Press).

Kerman, Joseph (1985), *Musicology* (London: Fontana).

———. (1991), American musicology in the 1990's, *Journal of Musicology* 9, no. 2: 131–44.

Kingsbury, Henry (1988), *Music, Talent, and Performance: A Conservatory Cultural System* (Philadelphia: Temple University Press).

Kramer, Lawrence (1990), *Music as Cultural Practice, 1800–1900* (Berkeley: University of California Press).

Laing, Dave (1985), *One Chord Wonders: Power and Meaning in Punk Rock* (Milton Keynes: Open University Press).

Langer, Susanne (1953), *Feeling and Form* (London: Routledge and Kegan Paul).

Lebrecht, Norman (1985), Boulez and the well-tempered 4X, *The Sunday Times Magazine*, 17 February, 42–48.

Lehrman, Paul D. (1985), Multitalented ASP, *Studio Sound*, February, 66–68.

Leppert, Richard, and Susan McClary (1987) (eds.), *Music and Society: The Politics of Composition, Performance and Reception* (Cambridge: Cambridge University Press).

Lerdahl, Fred (1988), Cognitive constraints on compositional systems, in John A. Sloboda (ed.), *Generative Processes in Music* (Oxford: Clarendon).

Lerdahl, Fred, and Ray Jackendoff (1983), *A Generative Theory of Tonal Music* (Cambridge, Mass.: MIT Press).

Levi, Erik (1990), Music and National Socialism: The politicisation of criticism, composition and performance, in Brandon Taylor and Wilfried van der Will (eds.), *The Nazification of Art* (Winchester: Winchester Press).

Levy, J. (1987), Covert and casual values in recent writings about music, *Journal of Musicology* 5, no. 1: 3–27.

Lomax, Alan (1962), Song structure and social structure, *Ethnology* 1, no. 4: 425–51.

Manning, Peter (1985), *Electronic and Computer Music* (Oxford: Oxford University Press).

Mathews, Max (1969), *The Technology of Computer Music* (Cambridge, Mass.: MIT Press).

McClary, Susan (1985), Afterword: The politics of silence and sound, in J. Attali, *Noise*.

———. (1987), The blasphemy of talking politics during Bach Year, in R. Leppert and S. McClary (eds.), *Music and Society*.

———. (1989), Terminal prestige: The case of avant-garde music composition, *Cultural Critique* no. 12: 57–81.

———. (1991), *Feminine Endings* (Minneapolis: University of Minnesota Press).

McClary, Susan, and Robert Walser (1990), Start making sense! Musicology wrestles with rock, in S. Frith and A. Goodwin (eds.), *On Record*.

Menger, Pierre-Michel (1980), *Le Marché de la musique contemporaine sérieuse, la condition des compositeurs et les aides à la création en Europe* (Paris: Ministère de la Culture et de la Communication/SACEM/Conseil de l'Europe).

———. (1983), *Le Paradoxe du musicien: Le Compositeur, le mélomane et l'etat dans la société contemporaine* (Paris: Harmoniques/Flammarion).

Merriam, Alan (1964), *The Anthropology of Music* (Evanston, Ill.: Northwestern University Press).

Mertens, Wim (1983), *American Minimal Music* (London: Kahn and Averill).

Meyer, Leonard (1956), *Emotion and Meaning in Music* (Chicago: University of Chicago Press).

Middleton, Richard (1978), *The Rise of Modernism in Music 1890–1935: Documents* (Milton Keynes: Open University Press).

———. (1983), "Play it again, Sam": Some notes on the productivity of repetition in popular music, *Popular Music* no. 3: 235–270.

———. (1990), *Studying Popular Music* (Milton Keynes: Open University Press).

Minsky, Marvin (1981), Music, mind and meaning, *Computer Music Journal* 5, no. 3: 28–44.

Montgomery, David (1992), The myth of organicism: From bad science to great art, *Musical Quarterly* 76, no. 1: 17–66.

Mowitt, John (1987), The sound of music in the era of its electronic reproducibility, in R. Leppert and S. McClary (eds.), *Music and Society.*

Nattiez, Jean-Jacques (1986), On reading Boulez, in P. Boulez, *Orientations.*

Neighbour, Oliver, Paul Griffiths, and George Perle (1983), *Second Viennese School* (London: Papermac).

New Grove Dictionary of Music (1980) (London: Macmillan).

Nicholls, David (1990), *American Experimental Music, 1890–1940* (Cambridge: Cambridge University Press).

Norman, Michael, and Ben Dickey (1984), *The Complete Synthesiser Handbook* (London: Zomba).

Norris, Christopher (1988), Utopian deconstruction: Ernst Bloch, Paul de Man and the politics of music, in C. Norris (ed.), *Deconstruction and the Interests of Theory* (London: Pinter).

———. (1989) (ed.), *Music and the Politics of Culture* (London: Lawrence and Wishart).

Nyman, Michael (1974), *Experimental Music: Cage and Beyond* (New York: Schirmer).

Orlov, Henry (1981), Toward a semiotics of music, in W. Steiner (ed.), *The Sign in Music and Literature.*

Osborne, Nigel (1984), Editorial, *Contemporary Music Review* 1, no. 1: i–ii.

Pasler, Jann (1986) (ed.), *Confronting Stravinsky* (Berkeley: University of California Press).

Pennycook, Bruce (1986), Language and resources: A new paradox, in S. Emmerson (ed.), *The Language of Electroacoustic Music.*

Peterson, Richard A., and David Berger (1975), Cycles in symbol production: The case of popular music, *American Sociological Review* 40, no. 2: 158–73.

Peyser, Joan (1976), *Boulez: Composer, Conductor, Enigma* (London: Cassell).

Pleasants, Henry (1955), *The Agony of Modern Music* (New York: Simon and Schuster).

Post, Nora (1985), Survivor from Darmstadt, *Musical America*, February, 32–35.

Risset, Jean-Claude (1965), Computer study of trumpet tones, *Journal of the Acoustical Society of America*, 38, no. 5: 912.

Roads, Curtis (1980), Artificial intelligence and music, *Computer Music Journal* 4, no. 2: 13–25.

———. (1985) (ed.), *Composers and the Computer* (Los Altos, Calif.: Kaufmann).

———. (1990), La recherche musicale: Mythe et réalité, *Inharmonique* no. 6, pp. 229–39.

Roads, Curtis, and John Strawn (1987) (eds.), *Foundations of Computer Music* (Cambridge, Mass: MIT Press).

Rochberg, George (1984), Music: Science vs. humanism, in P. Weiss and R. Taruskin (eds.), *Music in the Western World*. Originally published in (1983) *The Aesthetics of Survival: A Composer's View of Twentieth Century Music* (Ann Arbor: University of Michigan Press).

Rockwell, John (1984), *All American Music: Composition in the Late Twentieth Century* (New York: Vintage).

Roseman, Marina (1984), The social structuring of sound: The Temiar of Peninsula Malaysia, *Ethnomusicology* 28, no. 3: 411–45.

———. (1991), *Healing Sounds from the Malaysian Rainforest: Temiar Music and Medicine* (Berkeley: University of California Press).

Rosen, Charles (1976), *Schoenberg* (London: Fontana).

Said, Edward (1991), *Musical Elaborations* (London: Chatto and Windus).

Sanders, Ronald (1980), *The Days Grow Short: The Life and Music of Kurt Weill* (New York: Holt, Rinehart and Winston).

Schoenberg, Arnold (1950), *Style and Idea* (Ann Arbor: University of Michigan Press).

———. (1970), *Fundamentals of Musical Composition* (London: Faber).

Schutz, Alfred (1964), Making music together: A study in social relationship, in *Collected Papers Volume 2* (The Hague: Nijhoff).

Scott, Derek B. (1990), Music and sociology for the 1990's: A changing critical perspective, *Musical Quarterly* 74, no. 3: 385–410.

Seeger, Charles (1977), *Studies in Musicology 1935–1975* (Berkeley: University of California Press).

Shepherd, John (1982), A theoretical model for the socio-musicological analysis of popular musics, *Popular Music* no. 2: 145–77.

———. (1991), *Music as Social Text* (Cambridge: Polity).

Shepherd, John, Phil Virden, Graham Vulliamy, and Trevor Wishart (1977), *Whose Music? A Sociology of Musical Languages* (London: Transaction).

Silbermann, Alphons (1963), *The Sociology of Music* (London: Routledge and Kegan Paul).

Simmel, Georg (1968), Psychological and ethnological studies on music, in *The Conflict in Modern Culture and Other Essays* (New York: Teachers College Press).

Smith Brindle, Reginald (1987), *The New Music: The Avant-Garde Since 1945* (Oxford: Oxford University Press).

Steiner, Wendy (1981) (ed.), *The Sign in Music and Literature* (Austin: University of Texas Press).

Stockhausen, Karlheinz (1985), To the International Music Council, *Perspectives of New Music* 24, no. 1: 38–44.

Stuckenschmidt, Hans H. (1977), *Arnold Schoenberg: His Life, World, and Work* (New York: Schirmer).

Subotnik, Rose Rosengard (1982), Musicology and criticism, in D. Holoman and C. Palisca (eds.), *Musicology in the 1980s.*

——. (1983), The role of ideology in the study of western music, *Journal of Musicology* 2, no. 1: 1–12.

Tagg, Philip (1979), *Kojak — 50 Seconds of Television Music: Toward the Analysis of Affect in Popular Music*, Studies from Gothenburg University, Department of Musicology, no. 2 (Gothenburg: Gothenburg University Press).

——. (1982), Analysing popular music: Theory, method and practice, *Popular Music* no. 2: 37–67.

Taruskin, Richard (1988), The pastness of the present and the presence of the past, in N. Kenyon (ed.), *Authenticity and Early Music.*

Théberge, Paul (1989), The "sound" of music: Technological rationalisation and the production of popular music, *New Formations* no. 8: 99–111.

——. (1991), Musicians' magazines in the 1980's: The creation of a community and a consumer market, *Cultural Studies* 5, no. 3: 270–93.

Tomlinson, Gary (1984), The web of culture: A context for musicology, *Nineteenth Century Music* 7, no. 3: 350–62.

Trask, Simon (1987), M/A/R/R/S, *Music Technology* 2, no. 1, November, 39–42.

Treitler, Leo (1989), *Music and the Historical Imagination* (Cambridge, Mass.: Harvard University Press).

Vignolle, Jean-Pierre (1980), Mixing genres and reaching the public: The production of popular music, *Social Science Information* 19, no. 1: 79–105.

Weber, Max (1958), *The Rational and Social Foundations of Music* (Carbondale, Ill.: Southern Illinois University Press).

Weber, William (1975), *Music and the Middle Class: The Social Structure of Concert Life in London, Paris and Vienna* (London: Croom Helm).

Weiss, Piero, and Richard Taruskin (1984), *Music in the Western World: A History in Documents* (New York: Schirmer).

Whittall, Arnold (1988), *Music Since the First World War* (London: Dent).

Wicke, Peter (1990), *Rock Music: Culture, Aesthetics and Sociology* (Cambridge: Cambridge University Press).

Wolff, Janet (1987), The ideology of autonomous art, in R. Leppert and S. McClary (eds.), *Music and Society.*

Index